Omaha Public Library

Omaha, Nebraska

DO NOT REMOVE CARDS
FROM POCKET

Please return this book on or before the
date due, so that others may enjoy it.

Books cannot be renewed.

THE FATHERS
OF THE CHURCH

A NEW TRANSLATION

VOLUME 69

THE FATHERS
OF THE CHURCH

A NEW TRANSLATION

EDITORIAL BOARD

MARIUS VICTORINUS

THEOLOGICAL TREATISES
ON THE TRINITY

Translated by

MARY T. CLARK, R.S.C.J.

Manhattanville College

Purchase, N.Y.

THE CATHOLIC UNIVERSITY OF AMERICA PRESS
Washington, D.C.

Nihil Obstat:

REVEREND HERMIGILD DRESSLER, O.F.M.
Censor Librorum

Imprimatur:

✠ WILLIAM CARDINAL BAUM, S.T.D.
Archbishop of Washington

January 18, 1978

Library of Congress Cataloging in Publication Data

Victorinus, C. Marius.
    Theological treatises on the Trinity.
    (The Fathers of the Church, a new translation; 69)
    Translation of Opera theologica.
    Bibliography: p. ix–xi
    Includes index.
    1. Theology–Collected works–Early church, ca. 30-600.
    2. Trinity–Collected works.   3. Arianism–Collected works.
I. Clark, Mary T., 1913–   II. Title.   III. Series
BR65.V532E5   1979   231   79-15587
ISBN 0-8132-0069-5

CONTENTS

PREFACE

I wish to express gratitude to Professor Paul Henry, S.J., who spent many years establishing the text of the theological writings of Marius Victorinus for the *Sources chrétiennes* in Paris. This text, free of the corruptions present in Migne's Latin Patrology, has been the basis for this English translation, which was made at the urging of Professor Henry. I have examined the critical edition prepared for the *Corpus scriptorum ecclesiasticorum latinorum* by Professors Henry and Hadot and I have followed any significant change made therein.

It is clear from the notes how very much I owe to the scholarship of Pierre Hadot, who is almost alone in researching the sources and the historical situation as well as the influence of Marius Victorinus. His two recent major works published by *Etudes Augustiennes* have been a great contribution to those of us who are working in patristics. I am also grateful to the administration of *Sources chrétiennes* for generously permitting the use of M. Hadot's outline-analysis, here represented by the headings and subheadings found within the text.

For his assistance with my translation at its early stage, I express sincere appreciation to Professor Harold Cannon, formerly of Manhattanville's Classics Department, now Director of Research at the National Endowment for the Humanities.

But, above all, I wish to express sincere appreciation for the careful guidance of the late Professor Bernard Peebles, Professor Emeritus of the Department of Greek and Latin, The Catholic University of America, without whose zealous interest this translation would not have continued. The early stages of this work were accomplished under his direction, the direction of a careful scholar.

Finally, my gratitude goes to Reverend Hermigild Dressler, O.F.M., the Editorial Director of the Fathers of the Church, who undertook the enormous task of examining this text and giving the needed criticism and advice for the completion of this translation, out of the abundance of his own years of scholarship and with a generous expenditure of time and energy. I also wish to thank the Editorial Board of the Fathers of the Church, especially Reverend Robert Russell, O.S.A. for his encouragement of this translation, and the helpful staff of the Catholic University of America Press, especially Richard Talaska.

SELECT BIBLIOGRAPHY

Texts of Marius Victorinus's Theological Works:
Galland, A. (ed.), *Bibliotheca veterum patrum* vol. 8 (Venice 1772).
Henry, P. and Hadot, P. (eds.), *Marius Victorinus, Traités théologiques sur la Trinité. Sources chrétiennes* vols. 68, 69 (Paris 1960).
_____, *Marii Victorini Opera, Pars prior: Opera theologica. Corpus scriptorum ecclesiasticorum latinorum* 83.1 (Vienna 1971).
Migne, J.P. (ed.), *Patrologiae Cursus Completus: Series Latina* 8 (Paris 1844)

Other Works:
Altaner, B., *Patrology.* English translation by H.C. Graef (New York 1960).
Benz, E., *Marius Victorinus und die Entwicklung der abendländischen Willensmetaphysik* (Stuttgart 1932).
Boulgakov, S., *Le Paraclet.* English translation by C. Andronikof (Paris 1946).
Bréhier, E., *La théorie des incorporels dans l'ancien stoicisme* 3d ed. (Paris 1962).
Clark, M., "The Neoplatonism of Marius Victorinus" *Studia Patristica* 11 *Texte und Untersuchungen* 108 (1972) 13-19.
_____, "The Earliest Philosophy of the Living God: Marius Victorinus" *Proceedings of the American Catholic Philosophical Association* 41 (1967) 87-93.
Courcelle, P., *Les lettres grecques en occident de Macrobe à Cassiodore* 2d ed. (Paris 1948).
Dodds, E., "New Light on the Chaldaean Oracles" *The Harvard Theological Review* 54 (1961) 263-73.
_____, "The *Parmenides* of Plato and the Origin of the Neoplatonic 'One'" *Classical Quarterly* 22 (1928) 129-43.
Fitzgerald, A., *The Essays and Hymns of Synesius* 2 vols. (London 1930).
Gore, C., "Victorinus" *A Dictionary of Christian Biography* Vol. 4 (London 1887) 1129-38.
Hadot, P., "Fragments d'un commentaire de Porphyre sur le *Parmenide*" *Revue des études grecques* 74 (1961) 410-68.
_____, "L'image de la Trinité dans l'âme chez Victorinus et chez saint Augustin" *Studia Patristica* 6 *Texte und Untersuchungen* 81 (1962) 409-42.
_____, "Marius Victorinus et Alcuin" *Archives d'histoire doctrinale et littéraire du moyen âge* 29 (1954) 5-19.
_____, *Marius Victorinus: Recherches sur sa vie et ses oeuvres* (Paris 1971).
_____, *Porphyre et Victorinus* 2 vols. (Paris 1968).
_____, "Un vocabulaire raisonné de Marius Victorinus Afer" *Studia Patristica* 1 *Texte und Untersuchungen* 63 (1957) 199-208.
Hadot, P. and Brenke, U. (eds.), *Christlicher Platonismus: Die theologischen Schriften des Marius Victorinus* (Zürich 1967).
Hardt, Fondation, *Les sources de Plotin* (Vandoeuvres-Genève 1960).
_____, *Porphyre* (Vandoeuvres-Genève 1966).
Henry, P., *Plotin et l'occident* (Louvain 1934).

————, "The *Adversus Arium* of Marius Victorinus, the First Systematic Exposition of the Trinity" *Journal of Theological Studies* n.s. 1 (1950) 42-55.

Henry, P. and Schwyzer, H.-R. (eds.), *Plotini Opera* 3 vols. (Paris 1951-73).

Kannengiesser, C. and Madec, G., "A propos de la thèse de Pierre Hadot sur Porphyre et Victorinus" *Revue des études Augustiniennes* 16 (1970) 159-78.

Koffmane, G., *De Mario Victorino philosopho christiano* (Breslau 1880).

Kroll, W., "Ein neuplatonischer Parmenidescommentar in einem Turiner Palimpsest" *Rheinisches Museum* 47 (1892) 599-627.

Leusse, H. de, "Le problème de la pré-existence des âmes chez Marius Victorinus" *Recherches de science religieuse* 29 (1939) 197-239.

Lewy, H., "A Latin Hymn to the Creator Ascribed to Plato" *The Harvard Theological Review* 39 (1946) 243-58.

————, *Chaldaean Oracles and Theurgy, Mysticism, Magic and Platonism in the Later Roman Empire*. Publications de l'institute français d'archéologie orientale, Recherches d'archéologie, de philologie et d'histoire 13 (Cairo 1956).

Marrou, H., "Synesius of Cyrene and Alexandrian Neoplatonism." In *Paganism and Christianity in the Fourth Century*, edited by A. Momigliano (Oxford 1963) pp. 126-50.

Metzger, M., "Marius Victorinus and the Substantive Infinitive" *Eranos* 72 (1974) 65-70.

Nautin, P., "Candidus l'Arien" *L'homme devant Dieu: Mélanges offerts au P.H. deLubac* 1 (Paris 1964) 309-20.

Plotinus, *The Enneads* ed. A. Armstrong (Cambridge, Mass. 1970-).

Porphyry, *Opuscula* ed. A. Nauck (Leipzig 1886).
    See also the edition of G. Wolff.

Prestige, G., *God in Patristic Thought* (London 1952).

Proclus, *In Platonis Parmenidem commentarius* ed. V. Cousin (Paris 1864).

————, *The Elements of Theology* ed. E. Dodds (Oxford 1933).

Rist, J., "Mysticism and Transcendence in Later Neoplatonism" *Hermes* 92 (1964) 213-25.

Rutten, C., "La doctrine des deux actes dans la philosophie de Plotin" *Revue philosophique de la France et d'Etranger* 146 (1956) 100-06.

Schmid, R., *Marius Victorinus Rhetor und seine Beziehungen zu Augustin* (Kiel 1895).

Séjourné, P., "Victorinus Afer" *Dictionnaire de théologie catholique* 15 2887-2954.

Solignac, A., "Réminiscences plotiniennes et porphyriennes dans le début du *De ordine* de saint Augustin" *Archives de philosophie* 20 (1957) 446-65.

Synesius, *Hymni et opuscula* ed. N. Terzaghi (Rome 1939-44).

Theiler, W., *Porphyrios und Augustin* (Halle 1933).

————, *Die chaldäischen Orakel und die Hymnen des Synesios* (Halle 1942).

Vagany, L., "Porphyre" *Dictionaire de théologie catholique* 12 2555-90.

Van Winden, J., *Calcidius on Matter* (Leiden 1965).

Wöhrer, J., *Studien zu Marius Victorinus* (Wilhering 1905).

Wolff, G. (ed.), *Porphyrii de philosophia ex oraculis haurienda* (Berlin 1856).

Ziegenaus, A., *Die trinitarische Ausprägung der göttlichen Seinsfülle nach Marius Victorinus* (Munich 1972).

MARIUS VICTORINUS

ABBREVIATIONS

CSEL	*Corpus Scriptorum ecclesiasticorum latinorum* (Vienna 1866–).
DCB	*A Dictionary of Christian Biography* (London 1877–87).
DTC	*Dictionnaire de théologie catholique* (Paris 1903–50).
FC	*The Fathers of the Church: A New Translation* (New York [afterwards Washington, D.C.] 1947–).
MV	P. Hadot, *Marius Victorinus: Recherches sur sa vie et ses oeuvres* (Paris 1971).
ODCC²	*Oxford Dictionary of the Christian Church* 2d ed. (London 1974).
PG	*Patrologiae Cursus Completus: Series Graeca* (Paris 1857–1866).
PL	*Patrologiae Cursus Completus: Series Latina* (Paris 1844–1864).
PV	P. Hadot, *Porphyre et Victorinus* (Paris 1968).
SC	*Sources chrétiennes* (Paris 1941–).
TTT	P. Hadot and P. Henry, *Marius Victorinus: Traités théologiques sur la Trinité* (Paris 1960).

To facilitate the use of the present work in conjunction with the scholarly edition of Henry and Hadot, to which it frequently refers, Victorinus's theological writings are herein cited in the form used by these two scholars. Thus, the reader will find, for example, *adv. Ar.* I 8, 30–32 or III 4, 6–5, 31 instead of *Adv. Ar.* 1.8.30–32 or 3.4.6–5.31.

The same procedure is followed in references to the *Hymns*.

WORKS OF MARIUS VICTORINUS

Theological Works

Cand. I	*Candidi Arriani ad Marium Victorinum rhetorem de generatione divina.*
ad Cand.	*Marii Victorini rhetoris urbis Romae ad Candidum Arrianum.*
Cand. II	*Candidi Arriani epistola ad Marium Victorinum rhetorem.*
	Adversus Arium . . .
adv. Ar. I	*IA . . . liber primus (pars prior).*
	IB . . . liber primus (pars posterior).
adv. Ar. II	*. . . liber secundus.*
III	*. . . liber tertius.*
IV	*. . . liber quartus.*
de hom. rec.	*De homoousio recipiendo.*
hymn. I	*Hymnus primus.*
II	*Hymnus secundus.*
III	*Hymnus tertius.*

*Exegetical Works**

in Eph.	*In epistolam Pauli ad Ephesios libri duo.*
in Galat.	*In epistolam Pauli ad Galatas libri duo.*
in Phil.	*In epistolam Pauli ad Philippenses liber unicus.*

Secular Works

Ars grammatica.
Explanationes in Ciceronis Rhetoricam.
In Ciceronis Topica commenta (lost).
De syllogismis hypotheticis (lost).

*All footnote references to these exegetical works are to column numbers in PL 8.

MARIUS VICTORINUS

INTRODUCTION

The name of Marius Victorinus[1] is not a familiar one[2] in the history of ideas or of education. He was, nevertheless, an outstanding educator of the late Roman Empire and an important link in intellectual history with the periods that would follow. He formed a new philosophical language which was of great help to the logicians and the metaphysicians of the Middle Ages. Indeed, it has been said that he should have a place among those whom E. K. Rand has called the Founders of the Middle Ages.[3] Long passages from Victorinus were copied by Alcuin in his *De fide*[4] and a citation from Victorinus appears in Hincmar, while, earlier, Boethius borrowed heavily from Victorinus. Not only is he important in the history of Latin and Greek Neoplatonism by reason of his translation of the "Platonic books" significantly mentioned by Augustine[5]—books now believed to be treatises of Plotinus and Porphyry—but Victorinus also made use of traditional themes from the entire philosophical and religious tradition in new ways. Philosopher and theologian, he affirmed the Neoplatonic distinction between, on the one hand, "To

---

1 From C. Gore, "Victorinus," DCB 4.1129, we learn that he was called Caius Marius as well as Marius Fabius; he is known as Afer from the region of his birth.

2 From Latin grammarians Victorinus deserves special consideration for his pioneering exploitation of the substantive infinitive, a syntactical device especially important for the expression of philosophical and theological ideas. For more than eighty years, however, this distinction was denied him, and through an unfortunate confusion, granted instead to the Fifth-Century rhetor and poet Claudius Marius Victor(ius). See M. Metzger, "Marius Victorinus and the Substantive Infinitive," *Eranos* 72 (1974) 65-70.

3 P. Hadot, "Un vocabulaire raisoné de Marius Victorinus Afer," *Studia Patristica* 1 (*Texte und Untersuchungen* 63) 194-208.

4 *Ibid.* 200; see below, sect. 107.

5 Augustine, *Confessions* 7.9.13 (trans. V. Bourke, FC 21.177); cf. below, n. 11.

Be," pure Act transcending every form, and, on the other, being, a
subject receiving a determined form of "to be." In asserting the
direct derivation of the "to be"[6] of beings from the first "To Be,"
he transmitted through Boethius one of the great insights of medieval metaphysics.[7] The importance Victorinus gave to existence and
his effort to understand existence put him in touch with the Twenti-
eth Century.[8]

(2) Born and married in Africa, Victorinus later moved to Italy.
The date of his birth has been placed between A.D. 281 and 291. He
is first heard of around 350, in Rome, where his statue in the Forum
of Trajan is a tribute to his eloquence and to the gratitude of the
senators he taught. He was steeped in Neoplatonism and was initi-
ated into the mysteries of Osiris.[9] His exaggerated spiritual philosophy made him hostile to the body and therefore to the "Word made
flesh," and to the Christian obligation of external worship. In reading the Christian Scriptures, however, Victorinus discovered a deep
harmony with his own philosophical ideas on the first principles.
Apparently this reading of Scripture opened the mind and heart of
Victorinus to receive the gift of faith in Christ as the Divine Son of
God. The year 356 has been declared the most likely date for this
conversion, so sympathetically described by St. Augustine of Hippo
in Book VIII of his *Confessions,* for it seems to be the case that
Victorinus's *Letter to Candidus* was written around 359. Victorinus
lived under three Emperors: Constantine, Constantius and Julian,
disciple of the Neoplatonic philosopher, Iamblichus. We know that
Victorinus had to abandon his teaching in 362, when the Emperor
Julian forbade Christians to teach. Victorinus chose, as Augustine
said, "to give up his wordy school rather than God's Word."[10]
Although as a teacher Victorinus had found time to write grammati-
cal and logical treatises, commentaries and translations of philosophical treatises, he had begun, since his conversion, to write

---

6 "To be" is used in the same sense as "l'être" is used by Scipion Du Pleix
as cited by E. Gilson, in *L'être et l'essence* (Paris 1948) 15. See also below,
sect. 110.

7 Cf. J. Pieper, *Guide to Thomas Aquinas* (New York 1964) 122–25.

8 Cf. J. Mihalich, *Existentialism and Thomism* (New York 1960) 73–75.

9 P. Séjourné, "Victorinus Afer," DTC 15.2887.

10 Augustine, *Confessions* 8.5.10 (trans. Bourke, FC 21.206).

theological and exegetical treatises; his increased leisure was devoted to theological writings.

(3) By translating the "books of the Platonists,"[11] which came into Augustine's hands around 386, Victorinus helped Augustine to understand, to some extent, spiritual reality and the nature of evil, thereby removing an intellectual block to his believing what the God of Scripture was teaching. Victorinus also translated and wrote a commentary on Porphyry's *Isagogē* ("Introduction") to Aristotle's logic, which Boethius used when writing his own commentary. It is probable that his commentaries on Cicero's dialogues, although lost to us, were known to Alcuin.

(4) It can be suggested that through Augustine, Boethius, Cassiodorus, Bede, Alcuin, Isidore of Seville, Europe became a new forum for Victorinus. We do not know that the theological treatises of Victorinus were directly studied at the medieval University of Paris; still, if the scholastic method means the harmonizing of reason and faith for their common benefit, Victorinus is an early example of this method. As the first Latin writer to compose a systematic metaphysical treatise on the Trinity, he is the precursor of the medieval theologians; he is also the first Latin commentator on the Epistles of St. Paul.

(5) To understand Victorinus we must be aware of the traditions from which he emerged. He stood at the crossroads of three different paths: the traditions of classical Rome—Cicero, Virgil; the new trends in philosophic thought—Plotinus, Porphyry; the new positions of Christianity, with the crisis in conscience these brought for the Roman citizen. The foundation of Constantinople, the new Christian Rome, reduced the rank of ancient Rome; in 357 the Senate of Constantinople became the equal of the Roman Senate. Because these three paths met in Victorinus, he became the leader

---

11 See above, sect. 1. There is no general agreement yet on the authors of the books read. They may have included some of the *Enneads* of Plotinus (1.6; 1.8; 5.1); extracts from the *Enneads* with commentaries by Porphyry, [see Porphyry, *Sententiae ad intelligibilia ducentes* ed. B. Mommert (Leipzig 1907)]; texts of other Neoplatonists, including Porphyry; perhaps the *De regressu animae* of Porphyry. Cf. P. Henry, *Plotin et l'Occident* (Louvain 1924) 128; P. Courcelle, *Recherches sur les Confessions de saint Augustin* (Paris 1968) 167, and *Les lettres grecques en occident de Macrobe à Cassiodore* (Paris 1948) 164 ff.

of the spiritual movement of Platonic Christianity which gained its
full strength between 380 and 415. The whole Fourth Century was
a century of conflict between pagan and Christian culture: the
renaissance of pagan culture, the birth of Christian culture. In the
pagan renaissance there was a joining of forces with the magical
element in eastern Neoplatonism. Porphyry was among the first to
oppose these pagan religious practices of magic, dismissing them as
good only for people incapable of philosophizing and as able to
purify only the lower parts of the soul.[12] Porphyry had studied
at Athens under Longinus, a Middle Platonist favorable to
Numenius,[13] and was a student of Plotinus, though for only six
years. Between the doctrines of Numenius and that body of Middle
Platonic teaching that has been handed down as the "Chaldaean
Oracles,"[14] there is a close relationship. As we read in Porphyry's
life of Plotinus, he was once accused of plagiarizing Numenius.
Plotinus, however, had explicitly rejected certain Middle Platonic
positions present in the so-called Chaldaean Oracles on behalf of a
First God absolutely simple, so that the One gave *Nous* what the
One did not have, namely, existence. Plotinus took the position,
moreover, that contemplation rather than rituals achieved man's
union with the One. Porphyry supported this Plotinian point of view
over the urging of the Chaldaean injunctions, namely, the view that
the way of philosophy is the way to transcendent union with God.
And in Victorinus we find a man who remained faithful to philosophy but not to pagan religion. In fact, Victorinus as a philosopher

---

12 Augustine, *City of God* 10.28–29 (trans. G. Walsh and G. Monahan,
   FC 14).
13 Numenius of Apamea (c. 150–200), "a Neo-Pythagorean for whom Plato
   was Moses writing Attic Greek" (ODCC[2] 960).
14 The "Chaldaean Oracles" were revelations claimed by the seer and theurgist Julian, a contemporary of Marcus Aurelius; he presented his doctrine,
   which was saturated with Middle Platonism, as the Chaldaean world view.
   There is a problem as to whether Numenius was influenced by the
   "Chaldaean Oracles" or the reverse. These Oracles also teach the identity
   of intelligence with intelligibles and a distinction between a First and
   Second Intelligence. A. Armstrong (ed.), *The Cambridge History of Later
   Greek and Early Medieval Philosophy* (Cambridge 1967) 104, n. 6. Cf. H.
   Lewy, *Chaldaean Oracles and Theurgy, Mysticism, Magic and Platonism
   in the Later Roman Empire* (Cairo 1956).

was distressed that the theology of Basil of Ancyra[15] was vitiated by bad philosophy, and he set to work to show that scriptural statements about the equality and the distinction of Father, Son and Holy Spirit can be reconciled if one does not make philosophical mistakes. It is apparent that Victorinus used Neoplatonic principles and phrases and passages in his theological works, but until recently many historians, especially Paul Henry[16] and P. Séjourné,[17] saw Plotinus as the main influence upon the thought of Victorinus. But it was pointed out some time ago by W. Theiler that non-Plotinian philosophical influences were at work in the texts of Victorinus. Most of the Greek words Victorinus uses without translating them in his text are foreign to Plotinus and some are even foreign to the Porphyrian writings that we have on hand. Theiler,[18] in his work on the "Chaldaean Oracles" and the *Hymns* of Synesius, discovered the similarities between the Oracles and certain expressions of Victorinus. And he thought that the intermediary between the Oracles and Victorinus was a commentary on the Oracles by Porphyry.

(6) In the last few years Pierre Hadot has not only reconstituted the historical unity of all the writings of Marius Victorinus[19] but has devoted two volumes to the influence of Porphyry upon Victorinus.[20] Fundamentally different from that of Plotinus, Porphyry's philosophy is the key, Hadot claims, without which the reader cannot fully unlock the meaning or appreciate the digressions within the theological treatises of Victorinus. Hadot shows in great detail all that Victorinus owes to Porphyrian philosophy, assembling

---

15 Fourth-Century Bishop of Ancyra who took part in the Arianizing Synods of Sirmium (351), Ancyra (358), and Seleucia (359).

16 Henry, *Plotin et l'Occident*, 72.

17 Séjourné, DTC 15.2890. Cf. n. 9 above.

18 W. Theiler, *Die chaldäischen Orakel und die Hymnen des Synesios* (Halle 1942) 13, n. 2; 14, n. 4; 18, n. 2; 19, n. 5; 29 n. 1.

19 P. Hadot, *Marius Victorinus: Recherches sur sa vie et ses oeuvres* (Paris 1971). A problem in chronology is presented by *ad Cand.* 31, where Victorinus says that he has treated extensively of the Holy Spirit "in other books." In writing these words is he referring to books that then existed but were subsequently lost? Or was this reference added by Victorinus after he had composed *adv. Arium* I–IV? Or, finally, have we here a "citation programmatique" (see Hadot, MV 260)?

20 Hadot, *Porphyre et Victorinus* (Paris 1968). Hereafter cited as PV.

from all of Victorinus's theological treatises, in the second volume of his *Porphyre et Victorinus,* whole passages or texts of, he believes, Porphyrian origin, as well as reediting the existing fragments of an anonymous commentary on the *Parmenides*[21] that he holds to be Porphyry's reconciliation of the "Chaldaean Oracles" with the *Enneads* of Plotinus. Hadot considers this anonymous commentary to be the source of Victorinus's philosophical passages and basic metaphysical principles, that is, his conceptual structures. Whereas Hadot has made available indisputable evidence, namely, common vocabulary and common positions, that Victorinus knew the anonymous commentary on the *Parmenides,* it has not been conclusively proven that Porphyry was the author of this commentary. Research on this problem continues. Moreover, Victorinus could have had access to the "Chaldaean Oracles" themselves and to the writings of Numenius without depending upon commentaries by Porphyry. Nevertheless, whatever Porphyry did write would have been of great interest to the pagan Neoplatonic grammarian, Victorinus. Certain principles like the implication of life and thought in "to be" are present in the anonymous commentary. Hadot also thinks that since scholars admit that the *Hymns* of Synesius[22] had Porphyry as principal source, and since these *Hymns* share the conceptual structures of Victorinus, it can be concluded that Porphyrian Neoplatonism was used by Victorinus. These conceptual structures, which will be discussed in detail later (sects. 90-96) seem to have been formed by a transposition and transformation of Stoic physics into a metaphysics of intelligible reality. This reversal of Stoicism begun with Antiochus of Ascalon[23] penetrated all Neoplatonism down to Damascius.[24]

(7) Hadot's research has already gone far toward dissipating the

21 W. Kroll, "Ein neuplatonischer Parmenidescommentar in einem Turiner Palimpsest," *Rheinisches Museum* 47 (1897). The Greek text with French translation is now available in Hadot, PV 2.64-112.

22 H. Marrou, "Synesius of Cyrene and Alexandrian Neoplatonism," in *Paganism and Christianity in the Fourth Century,* ed. A. Momigliano (Oxford 1963) 126-50. Cf. A. Fitzgerald, *The Essays and Hymns of Synesius,* 2 vols. (London 1930).

23 See Cicero, *Academica* 1.12.43.

24 Born 480 and head of the Platonic Academy when Justinian closed it in 529.

obscurity in Victorinus's writings which St. Jerome[25] has not been the only one to signal. Charles Gore could scarcely have been more sweeping in his statement: "Indeed from every point of view, and in every stage of his life, the author presents almost insuperable difficulties to his commentators."[26] Despite the difficulty in reading Victorinus, those who understand him are gratified. Centuries before this recent research, Louis Thomassin spoke of Victorinus as a man "inferior to none in the profundity of his insight into the most inmost mysteries of the Divine Being and the relations of the Persons of the Trinity to one another."[27]

(8) There is no doubt, however, that an awareness of an author's sources can heighten one's understanding of him. The recent scholarly monographs not only emphasize Porphyry's role in the formation of Victorinus's theology but bring to mind the other intellectual influences upon him. In addition to the obvious influences from Aristotle, Cicero, Plotinus, Porphyry, St. John's Gospel, St. Paul's Epistles, we are made aware of the extent to which Victorinus is indebted to Basil of Ancyra,[28] and of the influence of Marcellus of Ancyra,[29] of Athanasius,[30] of Phoebadius[31] and of Gregory[32] of

---

25 In his *De viris illustribus* 101, Jerome wrote: "Victorinus, in the manner of the dialecticians, wrote some extremely obscure books *Against Arius,* understood only by the learned."

26 Gore, DCB 4.1129.

27 L. Thomassin as quoted in translation by Gore, DCB 4.1131; Thomassin's Latin may be read in his *De incarnatione verbi Dei* 2.1.6, *Dogmata Theologica,* Nova editio 3 (Paris 1866) 162–63.

28 Hadot, MV 263–75.

29 A deposed bishop of Ancyra (d. 374) who taught that in the unity of the Godhead the Son and the Spirit only emerged as independent entities for the purposes of creation and redemption (ODCC[2] 869), cf. Hadot, MV 271–73; also Victorinus, *adv. Ar.* I 5,1–9.

30 Bishop of Alexandria (328–73); attacked Arianism at Nicaea, 325; when the Arianizing party became powerful he was deposed several times but was eventually reinstated. The Council of Alexandria, 362, was led by him.

31 A friend of Hilary of Poitiers (d. ca. 395), he was a strong opponent of Arianism and attacked the formula of 357 in his *Liber contra Arianos;* he signed the formula of Ariminum but denounced it later (ODCC[2] 1087).

32 Bishop of Elvira near Granada (d. after 392); an opponent of Arianism, he refused to pardon those who Arianized at the Council of Ariminum (359). Cf. *adv Ar.* II.

Elvira, as well as of that of Origen's exegesis as found in Hilary of Poitiers[33] and Ambrose.[34]

OVERVIEW OF THE WRITINGS

(9) At Nicaea (A.D. 325) the Council Fathers had expressed in the language of reason what Scripture said of the Son's equality with the Father, his status as true Son really begotten by the Father in the way in which spirits beget. That the Son is consubstantial with the Father was declared at the Council of Nicaea. It does not follow that this statement was clearly understood. There was no ready-made philosophy to clarify it. The word *homoousion*[35] appears in the *Enneads*[36] of Plotinus, but there it refers to the Intelligible Triad, not to the One. Victorinus translated the Greek word *homoousion* used at Nicaea into the Latin word *consubstantialitas*. The word *homoousion* was used to express the relations of the Father and the Son within the Godhead in order to exclude the Arian heresy which denied the divinity of the Son. Arius,[37] a

---

33 "The Athanasius of the West" (ca. 315–67); a convert from Neoplatonism, he opposed Arianism and defended the cause of orthodoxy at the Council of Seleucia. He wrote *De trinitate* (trans. S. McKenna, FC 25), *De synodis, Opus historicum* (ODCC[2] 649).

34 Bishop of Milan (ca. 339–97), a lawyer and governor, he was educated in Christianity by Simplicianus and opposed paganism and Arianism. He wrote, in addition to other works, *De officiis ministrorum*, a treatise on Christian ethics based on Cicero; he was responsible for bringing eastern theology into the west (ODCC[2] 42-3).

35 Three Greek roots underlie the terminology, ancient and modern, concerned with the Son's relationship with the Father. (1) *homo,* same; (2) *homoi-* (or *homeo-*), similar; (3) *ousia,* being (as a noun) or substance. The first root plus the third yields *homoousios-homoousion,* signifying identity in substance. The second root plus the third yields *homoiousios-homoiousion* or *homoeousios-homoeousion,* signifying similarity in substance. These terms apply either to the Son himself or to a doctrinal position concerning him in relation to the Father. The theologians and their followers who espouse these terms with their theological implications are called Homoousians, those holding identity in substance, or Homoiousians (Homoeousians), those holding similarity in substance. Futhermore, the *ousia* element can be left out, yielding Homoeans (Homoians). Those who hold total dissimilarity in substance are called Anomoeans, a word formed by combining a negative prefix with *homo.*

36 Plotinus, *Enn.* 4.4.28; and 4.7.10.

37 Arius (ca. 250–336), in teaching that the Son was created by the Father, sought the support of Eusebius of Nicomedia but was excommunicated at

Libyan by birth and ordained at Alexandria, championed a sub-ordinationist teaching which was condemned, first at Alexandria, then at Nicaea. Arianism held that the Son of God was not eternal but created by the Father from nothing as an instrument for the creation of the world; although a changeable creature, the Son was dignified with the title of Son because of his righteousness. The Arians divided into three groups: the Anomoeans (dissimilar) spoke of the Son as unlike the Father; the Homoeans (similar) spoke of the Son as like the Father in all things according to the Scriptures; the semi-Arians or Homoiousians (of similar substance [with the Father]) thought that similarity rather than consubstantiality left more room for distinctions in the Godhead.

(10) And so the alternatives were: (1) to accept the consubstantiality of the Son with the Father by faith, believing that this expresses what is said in Scripture, transferring one's faith in Scripture to the dogma as declared in 325; (2) to deny the Son's identity with the Father because no known philosophical extrapolation allowed two individuals to be identical in substance, and then to produce scriptural verses against identity; (3) to return to Scripture for suggestions as to the source of identity within the Trinity as well as the source of otherness or distinction, and then to replace the traditional philosophical categories with mutually inclusive transcendentals, thus freely creating new language as required by the realities discussed. In choosing the third alternative, Victorinus was challenged to use a new vocabulary as well as to forge neologisms in an attempt to translate technical philosophical Greek phrases without sacrificing clarity to rhetoric. But he would seek first those philosophical principles which were closest to a triune reality.

(11) While the first alternative would appeal to all who appreciated the inestimable worth of faith, was there not a well-nigh obligatory challenge to a Christian to take up the third alternative, namely, to show reason why the second alternative chosen by Arians not only contradicts Scripture but is an inadequate philosophical analysis of the things as they are?

---

a Synod of Alexandria held by Alexander of Alexandria; Constantine offered reconciliation but his mission of peace failed. An Ecumenical Council was convened at Nicaea in 325, where, under the leadership of Athanasius, Arius was condemned (ODCC[2] 87).

(12) Victorinus began with the dogma of divine consubstantiality as a human expression of the Divine Reality revealed in Scripture and proceeded to show that what the theologians declared in technical language is so guided by biblical experience that any philosopher intending to elucidate their statement must return to the Scriptures to learn the truth about trinitarian existence (but see below, sect. 73). Then, what Victorinus read in Ex 3.13, Jn 1.1, and Jn 16.15 convinced him that he had in the Neoplatonic triad of *esse* (to be), *vivere* (to live), *intelligere* (to understand), a philosophic formulation that was homogeneous with the trinitarian God and could therefore offer a correction to the "similarity in substance" position adopted by the party of Basil of Ancyra at the Synod of Sirmium, 358.

(13) In general, Victorinus states his proposition that Father and Son and Holy Spirit are consubstantial. Then follow the names and functions of the Divine Persons as given in Scripture. From these facts, reason draws certain conclusions about the nature of the Divine *Esse* (To Be). These conclusions are then supported by philosophical reasoning so that the original Nicene dogma can now be repeated as not contradictory to reason. Such is the Christian philosophical analysis practised by Victorinus: beginning with God's words or dogma and then proceeding to their underlying meaning to discover what the Divine Reality is, as far as one can.

(14) Specifically, Victorinus finds in Scripture certain common names applied to all three Persons and he shows that philosophically these names signify consubstantiality: *Spiritus, Logos, Nous, Sapientia, Sanctus Spiritus.*[38]

(15) Likewise in Scripture he finds the various Persons referred to as Begetter, Savior, Sanctifier, and these he interprets as signifying distinction in identity. In the philosophical order such determinations correspond, so to speak, with the forms: substance, life, wisdom.

(16) Victorinus's sensitivity to the possibilities in the Neoplatonic triad grew out of his faith in salvation history. Although it

---

38 That is, "Spirit, *Logos, Nous,* Wisdom, Holy Spirit." The two middle terms (Greek) mean, respectively, "the Word," and "Mind" or "Intellect"; in the accompanying translation the two words are frequently left as (transliterated) Greek.

takes faith to recognize certain historical events as salvation history, this recognition provides the Christian with new possibilities for knowing God. But it is above all in his discussion of substance that we find Victorinus most forceful and resourceful. He declares that as substance the Father is the "potentiality-power of being," omnipotence of being, whose act or action is the Son or *Logos*. His deeply biblical view of the Father as the living God enabled him to oppose Candidus's static *esse* (to be) with *agere* (to act) as the reality within *esse*. Candidus also refused to call the Father "substance" because the word was not used in Scripture, he said, and he feared the suggestion of composition of nature and qualities; on the other hand, Victorinus considered substance in the Neoplatonic sense of concrete reality with spiritual reality the prototype of substance. He declared that in divine substance the substantial quality or form would be identified with the substance. In fact, Victorinus's main philosophical argument against the Son's being a similar substance to the Father is precisely this: that substances are said to be alike by their qualities except when we are dealing with the naturally simple divine reality; then, similarity of quality would be reducible to identity of substance.

(17) For the internal and external motion of the substantial quality or form of God, Victorinus turned to some current Neoplatonism which had been influenced by Numenius's doctrine of the two states of intelligence, one in repose and one in motion. The scriptural God is alive, actively and eternally begetting; the movement of divine *Esse* in which *vivere* and *intelligere* preexist is mysteriously immanent and transitive. Procession in God introduces no change into one who is trinitarian process. Two Neoplatonic clarifications assist Victorinus in answering Candidus, who argued against consubstantiality for fear of bringing change into God. The divine begetting does not contradict God's immutability and impassibility, for divine action does not introduce change when *agere* is implicit in the divine *Esse*; and the Son as begotten is not passible, because it is really God who is begotten, one therefore who is the cause of his own begetting. In Victorinus's doctrine, act is not added to a potency; Neoplatonic potentiality-power is closer to biblical omnipotence than to Aristotelian potency, which expresses a lack or privation. Even Plotinus considered motion within the

perspective of the Stoic pneuma exercising a "tonic" movement—
outwards and inwards: procession and conversion. Hence the importance of the only text from Plotinus literally quoted by Victorinus:
God as " 'one that is all and not one; for he is principle of all things,'
therefore not one that is all, but all in a transcendent mode."[39]

(18) Action is not to be denied God but, strictly speaking, he
is above both potentiality and act as we know them. In one way
Esse is a force turned within, almost like vision which sees not, voice
which speaks not, when *Agere* is considered as nonmanifested; but
the Father's self-revelation is Life and Wisdom. Thus, the Father is a
unique movement with two distinct terms, Son and Holy Spirit,
being respectively the outgoing action of life and the returning
action of wisdom. As eternal silence the Father is inaudible, unknowable, but he is knowable through his Form and Word, the Son
whose voice reaches men's hearts through the Holy Spirit's utterance. Thus the Father as silence, repose, essence or nature is manifested in salvation history by Christ the giver of life through the
Holy Spirit as giver of truth. The Father dialogues with the Holy
Spirit through the Word and dialogues with our world through the
Holy Spirit.

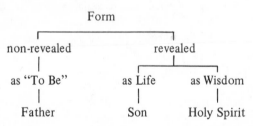

The Father and Son are one Dyad; the Son and Spirit are one Dyad.
From this double dyad a triad results by applying two Neoplatonic
principles in the tradition of Numenius:

(a) the principle of implication: every form implies *esse*, and so
     the Divine Persons are consubstantial.
(b) the principle of predominance: the predominant form dis-
     tinguishes the reality. Thus, the Father is distinguished by

39 Plotinus, *Enn.* 5.2.1; Victorinus, *adv. Ar.* IV 22,8–9.

Esse, the Son by *Vivere,* the Holy Spirit by *Intelligere;*
corresponding to this are the various divine "economic" or
salvific operations which distinguish only three Divine
Persons.

(19) And so as a result of his trinitarian thinking Victorinus takes
up several important positions:

(a) Procession implies origin without priority and without
superiority so that there can be equality. Yet what proceeds
without inferiority is both related to its origin and identical
with it. This relationship is called a substantial—more accurately, a subsistent—relation. The Son's relation to the
Father is subsistent because it makes the Son God and likewise Son. The mystery is not removed but magnified when
Victorinus asserts that this relationship not only accounts
for the Son's divinity but, insofar as the Son really is a Divine
Son, it makes the Son the cause of his own begetting, of his
own Being, so to speak.

(b) The economy of salvation has been used as a scriptural model
for understanding the order within the Trinity. The distinction of persons is grounded upon salvific functions, appropriate operations, rather than upon mutual personal relations
within the Trinity.

(c) The Son, insofar as he is consubstantial with the Father, is
also origin of the Holy Spirit's procession, but the Holy
Spirit proceeds from them as from a single principle which
Victorinus expresses thus: from the Father, through the Son.

(d) Victorinus's view of action not as an accidental but as a substantial category allows for further insight into the nature of
personality when action is seen as self-affirmation, self-
development, with no dichotomy between the substantial
and the dynamic order.

(20) Although Victorinus's systematic exposition (treated in
sects. 28–89 below) was made possible by Neoplatonic principles,
the whole of this teaching on the Trinity emerges as the heart of a
religion centered on Christ. Victorinus keeps the functions of the
Incarnate Word in the closest possible relation to the cosmic function of the pre-Incarnate Word within the dynamically related

Trinity. Therefore the Son is distinct from the Father as known but one with the Father as the Father's own essence. In knowing the Son the Father knows himself. In the fourth book against Arius, as we shall see, knowledge becomes the model used to illuminate "otherness in identity." Thus the generation of the Son is the revelation of the Father; substance is known by its action. The eternal utterance of the Divine Will is actual. The Son is that Act, always existing. The Father eternally begets the Son and eternally knows himself in the Son. The infinite God limits himself in knowing himself in his Son. Knowledge is that limitation or form, a relationship of knower and known.

(21) Yet the Spirit proceeds in the same movement in which the Son proceeds. It is a dyad of life and intelligence. Hence the Spirit seems more one with the Son than the Son is one with the Father. Christ is "hidden Spirit" and the Holy Spirit is the "hidden Christ."

(22) All things are potentially in the Father, actually in the Son. The Father is "To Be," the Son is "To Act," and Perfect Being requires Perfect Act. Hence the Son is essential to the Father. The Holy Spirit as Spirit precedes (in order) the Son as that in which the Father begets the Son, and yet the Spirit is from the Father through Christ. The Spirit brings forth from God and returns all to God. All things preexist in God as eternal life, potentially in the Father, actually in the Son. Therefore the *Logos* is Archetypal Reality. It is the Son's essence to act, as it is the Father's to repose. The Son acts like a river of life proceeding throughout the universe, bringing life to all and culminating in the Incarnation.

(23) The model for creation is Neoplatonic emanation, with the soul as mediator between spirit and matter, and with the return or conversion of all things to God through *Nous*. But matter has the possibility of corrupting the soul unless Christ enters into the corruption of material life to redeem fallen souls and restore them to a better state than they ever had—fellowship with God in trinitarian life. This revitalization of man is done by Christ through the sacraments. The Christian is right to seek understanding, but St. Paul is right in teaching that man is justified by faith.

(24) The most remarkable result of his work may well be the mood of mystery Victorinus is able to sustain in the midst of close-knit reasoning. Although he has, like his correspondent Candidus,

spoken syllogistically, he nonetheless leaves us with the sense of God as a mystery rather than as a problem. We are certain that Victorinus sees meaning in the world, but he does not supply the reader with clear and distinct ideas to express this meaning. For Victorinus as for St. Paul, the meaning of the world is to be found in the "unity which the One Spirit gives in the bond of peace." For St. Paul this required the end of all divisions between Jew and Gentile, while for Victorinus it would entail the harmony of pagans and Christians, of philosophical and scriptural truth; every century will face its own temptations to division. For Victorinus only a "consubstantial" Trinity can assure the ultimate meaning of the world's mystery and adequately account for the mystery of its meaning: the unity of all in God, under One Lord, Christ, in One Spirit, the bond of peace. Central to any understanding of this mystery is some appreciation of the plenitude of the *Logos*—Spirit-soul-body—the Pauline doctrine of "all in all" (Col 2.19; 1.20; 1 Cor 15). The world's meaning, which somehow entails the creative and redemptive mystery, is polarized in the *Logos,* not unconnected with the Platonic problem of the presence of the incorporeal in the world, the association of passion with particularization, and salvation with universalization. Christianity has somehow brought these together in an incarnate God, a *mundus verus.* For if the world is given meaning through the *Logos,* this meaning is understood insofar as Christ is the principle of intelligibility in history. That Victorinus's trinitarian theology brings with it an exigency for a Christian philosophy of history is traceable to the freedom with which he interpreted the Neoplatonic triad under the influence of St. Paul's experience of Christ alive in man by the Spirit's indwelling. And if the Holy Spirit is to be the "mean" between the world and Christ, the Church must dialogue with the world. In a sense Victorinus did just this when he took seriously all that the philosophers taught, and, in his first work as a Christian theologian, made Neoplatonic principles the basis of his theological synthesis.

(25) The trinitarian doctrine of the Christians was neither an outright adoption of the philosophic triads popular among the Middle and Neoplatonists, nor was it any mere adaptation of triadic thought. At the moment of the Nicene formulation the acceptance of the Christian dogma of the Trinity meant a rejection of the philo-

sophic triads as they were understood. Arius did not rise to this rejection. The statements he offered were reasonable but were contrary to the mystery revealed in Scripture. Victorinus found nothing ready at hand within his philosophical milieu that did not require some good, hard, creative interpretation on his part. When he tried to interpret, he turned to the tradition of Neoplatonism, where many of the best insights in Platonism, Aristotelianism and Stoicism had come together. In some Neoplatonic source he found a reconciliation of Plotinus and Numenius, and it was Numenius who had influenced the "Chaldaean Oracles."

(26) To get the most out of Victorinus's treatises on the Trinity, one should be familiar with all of Neoplatonism as well as with the commentaries on the *Categories* of Aristotle, and the commentary tradition concerned with the *Sophist,* the *Parmenides,* the *Timaeus* of Plato, with the "Chaldaean Oracles" and especially with the anonymous commentary on the *Parmenides,* apparently a common source for Victorinus and Synesius. The notes for each treatise will try to recall for the reader what is relevant from this literature.

(27) And finally, when Victorinus's explanation of trinitarian life expands into a doctrine of the Son as Image, the foundation is present for a theophany doctrine like that of John Scotus Erigena, as well as for the vocation to a life of "wisdom." The soul, in making matter "live," is the image of Life, the Son; as intelligent, it is the image of the Holy Spirit. Thus the human soul images the twofold action of the Word of God by manifesting him in life and by returning to its source in contemplation.

THE THEOLOGICAL TREATISES
IN HISTORICAL PERSPECTIVE

(28) Victorinus wrote his theological works during a most difficult moment in Church history. Since the death of Constantine, and with the eastern Emperor Constantius an Arian, certain anti-Nicene forces united to depose Athanasius, who was condemned in 351 and 355. Although Pope Liberius refused to sign the condemnation, Athanasius had to take flight and Liberius was exiled. Felix, deacon of the Roman Church, was then consecrated bishop by three bishops,

including the Arian Acacius of Caesarea. The Emperor was easily influenced by Ursacius[40] and Valens,[41] who saw to it that the Emperor approved the formula, formed in the summer of 357 at Sirmium, known as the "Blasphemy of Sirmium," which reinstituted Arianism and rejected the words *homoousios* and *homoiousios.* They also declared that no one was capable of expressing the generation of the Son. Thus, the end of the year 357 and the beginning of 358 saw a return of Arianism under the form represented by the dialectic of Aetius[42] and Eunomius.[43]

Letter of Candidus[44] *to Victorinus*

(Cand. I)

(29) As an Arian who was convinced that the "Unbegotten" was the essential definition of the Divine Being, Candidus writes to Victorinus to establish the thesis that God as unbegotten must be unbegetting; the Son would not be God if indeed he were begotten. Moreover, any begetting by God would be incompatible with the changlessness of God. Hence, the Son must be made or created, not begotten. Therefore the Son comes from nothing, not from the being of the Father, and the Son is the product of the Divine Will. Because Candidus makes important use of the substantive infinitive "to be," it was once thought that he simply shared with Victorinus a

---

40 Bishop of Singidunum (now Belgrade) (ca. 335–71), a pupil of Arius and a leader with Valens of the western Arians.

41 Bishop of Mursa in the Fourth Century; along with Ursacius he opposed Athanasius and at Sirmium (357) maintained the extreme Arian (Anomoean) position.

42 A Christian sophist (d. ca. 370) who pushed Arianism to extreme positions. He and his followers were known as Anomoeans, asserting the total unlikeness of the Son to the Father (ODCC[2] 21).

43 Arian Bishop of Cyzicus (d. 394); a pupil of Aetius, he was deposed by Constantine on account of charges brought by Basil of Ancyra. His doctrine was Anomoean. The Cappadocian Fathers formed their doctrine of God and of the human knowledge of God in critique of Eunomius (ODCC[2] 480).

44 P. Nautin, "Candidus l'Arien" *L'homme devant Dieu: Mélanges offerts au P.H. de Lubac* 1 (Paris 1966) 309-20. P. Henry and P. Hadot, *Marius Victorinus: Traités théologiques sur la Trinité*, (Paris 1960) 23-27 hereavter cited as TTT).

common philosophical source, but it is now thought that Candidus is a fictitious correspondent who presents the arguments of Neo-Arianism for Victorinus to demolish.

(30) Candidus's triad (3,16-21) does not specify three distinct principles derived by begetting but defends the fullness of divine "To Be" as meaning God is, lives and knows (cf. Plato, *Sophist* 248e). He remains faithful to God as the One, and methodically considers every type of imagery in the theological tradition to describe the begetting of the Son by the Father, only to reject each one. Candidus does not deny that there is immanent motion in God but he refuses to admit that it begets a distinct hypostasis. He teaches that the Son is produced as effect by the Father's will (8,11) but not begotten as act consubstantial to the will. Moreover, he denies the existence of all substance prior to the creative act. Jesus Christ is the first effect of God (10,5), the first substance (11,12). This first substance, the Son, will also create by drawing things from nothingness. The Son has not only a cosmic and creative role but a redemptive one (11,19-22). Candidus uses in his discussion the same classification of existents into intelligibles, intellects, sensible things and matter (11,14-17) which Victorinus uses in *ad Cand.* 7-11 and *adv. Ar.* I 61.

Letter of Victorinus to Candidus

(ad Cand.)

(31) After a prologue on the difficulty of speaking of God without a careful study of the names given him in Scripture (1,4-16), Victorinus examines the teaching of Scripture that Jesus Christ is the Son of God (1,17-2,9). Candidus had begun with reasoning and only ended his letter with scriptural citations. Victorinus calls on the prophets, St. Paul, and Jesus himself to witness that he is the Son of God.

(32) Jesus is called Existent (Ex 3,13) and *Logos* (Jn 1.1). And so Victorinus argues that, if Christ is the Existent and the *Logos,* he cannot come from nothing, as Candidus asserts. To show that the Existent can come only from the Nonexistent superior to the Existent, namely God, Victorinus has to give a long exposition on the kinds of existents and nonexistents (3,1-14,5), a list commonplace

in the schools of philosophy. To show that not only does the Son not come from nothing but from the Transcendent Nonexistent, the plenitude of being, and yet his generation brings about no change in God, Victorinus proves that the Transcendent Nonexistent is already the Existent in potentiality so that the begetting of the Existent is manifestation and actuation.

(33) He likewise proves that God is already *Logos,* that is, that the divine *Esse* is already *Agere* (life and knowledge). "To Act" manifests "To Be." In its state of repose, "To Act" is identical with "To Be"; in its state of motion, "To Act," that is, the *Logos,* springs forth to make beings appear.

(34) It is notable that Victorinus examines some of the same names of Jesus listed at the end of Candidus's letter. They both agree that the Son is the First Existent who is Act, *Logos,* Life and universal Substance. But Victorinus's reasoning about these names leads him to conclude that the Son is begotten by the Father, whereas Candidus said that the Son was created as an effect of the Father. One of Victorinus's main arguments is that the perfection of the Son implied by the names given by Candidus would be impossible in a being arising from nothingness (2,10-16). For, the principle of an existent must possess the qualities of that existent to an eminent degree. In calling God the Preexistent, that is, above existents, Victorinus means to say that God is both nonexistent and existent. He is not actually Existent because he is the potentiality-power (14,5-25) of existence, life, knowledge (2,22) and therefore begets the Existent, who is actually these things (chs. 3-16). Potentiality for Victorinus is a state of nonexpansion or hiddenness. The Existent is a self-manifestation, self-actuation; it is self-begotten (14,5; 16,24). This assures consubstantiality: the Father is the Son in potentiality; the Son is the Father in act. The theology of a God who is the Nonexistent beyond the Existent will be largely negative theology (13,1-14,5).

(35) An important point in the development is the identification of Existent with the Son, Son with *Logos,* and *Logos* with Jesus Christ (2,30-35). Instead of discussing Candidus's long list of the kinds of possible begetting, Victorinus simply shows that the Existent preexisted in the Preexistent.

(36) Finally, he unites the scriptural study of the names of Jesus

with the philosophical description of the begotten, concluding that the Existent, begotten by the Nonexistent, is the Son, Jesus, whose scriptural names are derived from that of the Existent (14,25-16,17). Jesus is the only begotten, the Image, the Existent, the *Logos*. John the Baptist and the demons witness that Christ is the Son of God.

(37) In the last section, Victorinus substitutes the *Esse-Agere* (To Be-To Act) opposition for the Preexistent-Existent opposition. Here *Esse* represents transcendent indetermined potentiality whereas *Agere* represents the movement of actuation and externalization. The Existent is activity; the Preexistent is pure *Esse* (17,1-23,10). As *Agere,* the *Logos* is the creative power of God, the actuation of all that preexists in God; God himself is unbegotten *Logos,* for the *Logos* is in God (Jn 1.1); in act the *Logos* is Life and Knowledge. Consubstantiality (23,3) is assured by the relationship between *Esse* and *Agere.* And finally there is a detailed refutation of the Arian objections to the divine sonship (24,1-30,26). The treatise ends with a summary of the modes of begetting (30,27-31,3); an insistence that the Holy Spirit is to the Son what the Son is to the Father, one as to being, different as to act, existence (31,3-13); and a final prayer for faith (31,1-10), a more excellent knowledge than negative theology or any other kind.

Second Letter of Candidus to Victorinus

(Cand. II)

(38) Candidus presents two letters in support of the Son being made, not born. One letter is from Arius and one from Eusebius of Nicomedia. The Arian view is strongly presented in these letters.

Synods of Sirmium
Liberius's Return to Rome

(39) At Easter in 358, when Basil was dedicating a church in his episcopal city of Ancyra, he forcefully criticized by a series of anathemas the profession of faith drawn up at Sirmium (summer 357) by Bishops Ursacius, Valens and Germinius.[45] Although he was

---

45 Bishop of Cyzicus, an Arian and joint composer with Valens of the third

right to condemn the heretical profession of faith, he himself was rejecting the *homoousion* in the Nicene formulation. After this rejection of the *homoousion,* Basil sent to all bishops a letter anathematizing those who did not confess the Son's similar substance to the Father, that is, the consubstantialists as well as those who misinterpreted the statements of Jesus to mean that he was "unlike" the Father, that is, the Anomoeans or extreme Arians. The Homoiousians, to whom Basil belonged, aimed at avoiding dogmatic precison by affirming that the Son is similar in substance to the Father according to the Scriptures. A third group, the Homoeans, wished merely to say that the Son was similar to the Father (but would not use the word *substance*).

(40) Then in the summer of 358, a synod at Sirmium tried to assemble a doctrinal dossier to harmonize the existing disagreements over consubstantiality. This dossier brought together the anathemas of Basil of Ancyra with the Antioch creed (341), with the creed of Sirmium (351) and the anathemas against Photinus (a Fourth-Century heretic who denied the preexistence of Christ), and, finally, with the letter of Basil of Ancyra, *De homoousio et homoiousio.* Pope Liberius signed this dossier, which Hilary of Poitiers considered to be orthodox. Hilary[46] tells us that Basil's letter defended the notion of *homoiousios* (similarity in substance) and set forth three principal objections to the notion of *homoousios* (consubstantiality). These were: (1) the notion of consubstantiality presupposes a substance prior to the Father and Son; (2) the Fathers who condemned Paul of Samosata at the Council of Antioch in 268 also rejected the word *homoousios* because in using this word Paul was implying that the Father was alone and was his own Son; (3) the Fathers of Nicaea had been forced to use the word *homoousios* against those who affirmed that the Son was a creature; but this word should be rejected because it cannot be found in Scripture.

(41) The delegates to the Sirmium synod of 358 saw their dossier as reversing the blasphemous formula of 357 and successfully oppos-

Sirmium creed, called the "Dated Creed," because its heading bears the consuls for the year (359) and the day of the month, May 22. At the Council of Ariminum this creed was rejected by the Nicene party and Germinius was deposed.

46 Hilary, *De synodis* 81 (PL 10.534); cf. Hadot, MV 266.

ing Ursacius and Valens, who had insisted that all mention of the word *substance* and its compounds be forbidden and that the Son be subordinated to the Father. The new Homoiousian doctrine, apparently satisfactory to Hilary and Athanasius, had been defined and signed by the Emperor Constantius; and Pope Liberius, the legitimate Bishop of Rome, recently in exile (above, sect. 28), was to return to his see. However, the Emperor decided that Felix the usurper would also remain in Rome. Felix was turned back by the populace at the gates of Rome, but Liberius was welcomed along with the Sirmium dossier, which he was to explain to the Roman priests.

(42) Victorinus cites six passages from Basil's letter (*adv. Ar.* I 28,12; I 28,32; I 29,1-10; I 29, 35; I 30,4-5; I 32,1-3) and it is clear that Basil of Ancyra is Victorinus's chief adversary in his first book against Arius. Victorinus believed that Basil, with duplicity, led Pope Liberius to betray the Nicene formula. Yet Victorinus learned from the dossier of Basil new ideas, a new theological method and exegesis to help him answer the problem set forth under the name of Candidus, the problem of the generation of the Son. The name of "Life" and "Image" given to the Son in Scripture will help Victorinus to maintain that the Son is indeed begotten, not made.

Against Arius, Book IA (A.D. 359)

(adv. Ar. IA)[47]

(43) This book continues the reply to Candidus (4-9; 27,23-29; 43,34-43); refutes the arguments of the letters of Arius and Eusebius (15,24; 23,3-6; 27,7; 28,36; 45,3-4); opposes the errors which Victorinus recently learned of in the Homoiousian document brought to Rome by Pope Liberius. There is a response to Marcellus (10,9; 21,33; 22,21; 23,1; 27,6; 28,33-38; 45,7), to Photinus (21,28-39; 22,21; 31,18-19; 39,20-25; 45,7-23); to the Homoiousians themselves (15,9; 20,66; 23,7; 25,4; 28,8-32,15; 41,1-20;

---

47 The division of *adv. Ar.* I into a First Part (IA: chapters 1-47) and a second (IB: chapters 48-63) does not entail separate systems of chapter enumeration; there is one simple enumeration for the two together. The remaining three books show no such division.

43,5-33; 45,23-48), and to the Patripassians[48] (17,35; 22,44-55; 24,16; 32,57-78; 40,19-32; 44,1-50; 47,18-26).

(44) Victorinus (2,1-5) states his intention of examining the scriptural testimony that the Son is really begotten, not made; of reflecting upon the names of Christ: *Logos,* Image, Virtue, Wisdom, Life, as found in the professions of faith; and of showing that these names can only be understood if the Son is substantially Son. Although it is impossible to know about God from reason alone, we can know God if the Son is substantially Son, because the true sources of our knowledge of God are the Son and the Holy Spirit, Scripture and inspiration (2,6-42).

(45) In a prolonged meditation on St. John's Gospel, Victorinus stresses the identity between *Logos* and the Son and Christ (3,1-15,12). From this he concludes to the consubstantiality of the Father, Son and Holy Spirit.

(46) Reflecting on St. Paul's names for the *Logos*—Son, Image and Form—Victorinus shows that these names define the Son's relation to the Father (32,16-43,4). These concepts of Image (cf. Plotinus, *Enn.* 4.5.17; 5.1.6) and Form provoke long philosophical digressions (19,1-20,67; chs. 21 and 22).

(47) His study of St. John enables Victorinus to distinguish between the *Logos* interior to God and the *Logos* related to the world by creation and salvation. He proves against the Arians and Photinians that the *Logos* within God was begotten of the substance of God and became incarnate to save the world (3,1-15,12). Once again he uses the concepts repose and action, namely "To Be" and "To Act," respectively; the Son, "To Act," is the expression or declaration of the Father, who is "To Be" (4,1-25). "He hath declared him" (Jn 1.18). Therefore, "To Be" is not only "To Be" but it is also "To Act." However, it is called "To Be" inasmuch as repose is proper to it. This is Victorinus's first use of the principle of predominance (4,5-11). "To Act" is also "To Be" but it is properly "To Act" as externalization, manifestation of Being.

(48) Mindful of the Homoiousian documents, Victorinus is care-

---

48 Patripassianism was the erroneous doctrine that the Father himself underwent the passion on the cross; this was linked to Sabellianism, a confusion of the Divine Persons.

ful to point out that only unity of substance (not similarity) (20,37-67; 21,39-22,10) can make sense of the scriptural statements about the Son (7,18-24). And with the discovery in Scripture of the identity between the Son and the Holy Spirit, the consubstantial appears (8,1-15,12), a total community of substance between Father, Son and Holy Spirit. Jn 14.9-10 is the important text here. Victorinus sees the gospel of St. John as coinciding with his own doctrine that the divine life reveals itself as *Esse, Vivere, Intelligere.*[49] And since life and light (knowledge) are substantial, the gospel teaches consubstantiality (15,1-9).

(49) But the synoptic gospels also testify to consubstantiality (15,13-17,8), teaching that the *Logos* is the Son of God, and that Christ is the Son of God. It is in St. Paul's Epistles that Victorinus finds that the three hypostases are Spirit, therefore consubstantial, but each with a proper act which assures the distinction of the hypostases (17,9-26,54). With St. Paul's use of Image and Form (Phil 2.6; Col 1.15-20), there is begun a long argument that the names given to Jesus in Scripture imply his consubstantiality to the Father (17,9-26,54; 32,16-43,4). Indeed Victorinus has used the whole of Scripture to answer the Arians.

(50) There follow some direct answers to the Homoiousian objections (28,8-32,15) with special attention to the self-movement of the *Logos* as implied in Jn 5.26, a text much favored by the Homoiousians. This is followed by a study of many of the names of the Son found in Scripture and in the creeds, a study which concludes that consubstantiality is implied in them all (32,16-43,4).

(51) Speaking to the Homoiousians, Victorinus concludes that since it has been shown that similarity in substance implies two different substances, the Homoiousians are really Anomoeans (43,5-14).

(52) And finally, speaking again to the problematic of Candidus, he repeats that the self-begetting movement of the Son (27,25-29; 32,3-6; 32,44-46) does not violate the divine immutability and impassibility (43,34-43). The book ends with a consubstantialist profession of faith (46,16-47,48).

---

49 For the terms, see above, sects. 12 and 18.

Against Arius, Book IB (A.D. 359)

(adv. Ar. IB)

(53) This book is a prolonged reflection upon the divine names: *Spiritus,* Jn 4.24; *Logos,* Jn 1.1; *Nous,* Rom 11.34; *Sapientia,* Rom 1.16 and 1 Cor 1.24.[50] As for *substantia* (48.1), Victorinus had tried to show in I 30 that it was scriptural. These words are also found in the creeds, especially in the creed of Antioch (341). For the Homoiousians, the common names of Father, Son and Spirit, such as the names God, Spirit, Light, do not imply identity, but similarity of substance, whereas for Victorinus the common names imply identity of substance. Nevertheless, these common names are proper to each of them insofar as there is a predominance of one aspect rather than another in each of them (*adv. Ar.* I 20,13-16; 54,9-12; 55,1-56,35). Victorinus proves that these names are not only equivalent to substance but identical to one another. Using an identity-otherness rhythm throughout his discussion of each name, he is able to show their original unity in substance, their distinction and otherness in action, with return to identity in self-knowledge (48,1-23). He also brings in a masculinity-femininity opposition: a male Christ in a female Virgin supposes a phase of feminine existence for Jesus, witnessing to a feminine phase in the movement of the *Logos* within the eternal begetting of the male Son of God. He continues the theme of the triad "to be," "to live," "to understand" (49,8-58,35).

(54) In chapters 54 and 55 there is a masterly demonstration that the common names that denote substance are simultaneously predominant names, denoting action and characterizing the hypostasis of each one. Thus, otherness among the Divine Names appears only in action.

(55) The Father is purely One; the second One, the *Logos,* is a dyad: Wisdom and Spirit in act. The movement of the *Logos* is twofold: procession-conversion; life-wisdom; feminine-masculine. Life, turning itself toward wisdom, passes from vivification to contemplation of the paternal existence (51,21-43). The resurrection and ascension of Christ represent his masculine stage when spirit trans-

---

50 For the terms, see above, sect. 14.

forms soul and flesh; our resurrection will also be a passage from femininity to masculinity (51,28-43). This androgyny of the *Logos* assures its self-begetting (64,25-27). The *esse-vita* (to be-life) relationship of the Father-Son becomes a *vita-motus* (life-movement) relationship with life as self-movement (52,1-53,31). The movement of life is within the depths of being. To distinguish the state of identity and the state of otherness in the five divine names is also to distinguish their state of masculinity and of femininity (54,1-58,36). Because of this reciprocal interiority of Father and Son it is concluded that they are consubstantial (56,24-35). Finally, the Holy Spirit is the mother of Christ in the two births, eternal and temporal (56,36-58,36; cf. Lk 1.35). And Victorinus ends this book with a contemplation of the image of the Trinity in man, with bisexuality as the image of the masculinity-femininity status of the *Logos* (60,1-64,30).

The Triumph of Homoeanism; Dated Creed (May 22, A.D. 359)

The Synods of Ariminum and of Seleucia

(56) In preparation for the Western and Eastern synods which were called to arrive at a common understanding of the Trinity, the bishops met with the Emperor Constantius to draw up an acceptable profession of faith. The Anomoeans wished to exclude from the new formulation the word *substance (ousia),* from which the compounds *homoousios* and *homoiousios* were derived.[51] They feared that the philosophical overtones of the word might indicate Greek influence on the Christian faith. Finally, the Emperor proposed a compromise with the phrase *similar in all things.* This compromise really, by its imprecision, favored the Anomoeans. This new formula was presented to the Western and Eastern councils. However, the majority of the Western council, held at Ariminum (July-November 359) settled on an orthodox formula, but the Arian minority, led by the skilled diplomats, Valens and Ursacius, succeeded in modifying the anti-Arian decision when it reached the Emperor. Therefore, all the bishops including the orthodox ones had to subscribe to an Arian creed drawn up at Nice in Thrace.[52] The Eastern bishops later met

51 See above, n. 33.
52 The Nicaea of the Council of 325 is in Asia Minor, in Bithynia.

at Seleucia (September-December 359). Present at the council were the Western diplomats, Valens and Ursacius. Under the leadership of the Anomoeans, Acacius and Eudoxius,[53] the creed of Nice was accepted, a profession of the Son's similarity to the Father, which became known as the Nice-Ariminum formulation, proclaimed at Constantinople in early January of 360. Arianism had at last taken the form of Homoeanism. Basil of Ancyra, Eleusius of Cyzicus, Eustathius of Sebaste (three Arian bishops), the Sirmium delegates of 358, were exiled and deposed; Aetius, the author of the Anomoean heresy, was likewise deposed, but Eudoxius, his friend, was made Patriarch of Constantinople. The true victors were Valens and Ursacius in the West, Acacius of Caesarea in the East.

Against Arius, Book II (A.D. 360)

(adv. Ar. II)

(57) This second book is a discussion with the Homoeans, those who said that the Son was simply similar to the Father and who denied that the word *substance* could be applied to God.

(58) Therefore, Victorinus proceeds to show that God is a substance (1,21-27). He uses the orthodox profession of faith to refute the heresies against consubstantiality (1,38-52). For the most part, these heretics hold that there is no essential difference between the making of the Son and the making of all creatures (above, sects. 16-18). They thereby assign to the Son a beginning (2,1-15) and ignore the scriptural statement that the Son is "in the father." That is why the Arians, who assign to Christ a beginning of being, are linked with Marcellus and Photinus (2,15-19).

(59) Once again Victorinus gives full attention to the arguments between the Homoiousians, who assert the Son's similarity in substance to the Father, and the Homoeans, who mean only to say that the Son is similar to the Father (above, sect. 9). This discussion was stimulated by the "dated Creed," approved in May of 359 at the Synods of Ariminum and of Seleucia.

---

53 Anomoean leader (300-70) of Germanicia who took part in Fourth-Century Arian Councils. He became Bishop of Antioch in 358 and of Constantinople in 360.

(60) Victorinus speaks first to the Homoiousians. He argues that the passage from Is 43.10 excludes any notion of a "similar" God, that there are no like substances, only like qualities (2,29-35) and that consubstantiality does not imply preexisting substance (2,35-40).

(61) Victorinus then addresses the Homoeans, the adversaries who triumphed at Ariminum (above, sect. 28)—Ursacius, Valens, Germinius, Gaius—in their attack against the words *substance* and *consubstantial* (2,40-49). Ursacius and Valens at Sirmium in 357 and 359 begged for the suppression of these words (above, sect. 39-41). Victorinus shows that the Latin word for substance stands for the Greek word for existence. If God is real, one can apply the word substance to him (3,6-27).

(62) Although we find previous arguments for substance in I 30,36-59 and I 59,17-28, in this book Victorinus has before him the conciliar decisions of Ariminum and now he argues that if the spirit of the law is greater than the letter of the law, then human reason is justified in going beyond the letter of Scripture and using the word substance for an existing reality (3,50-52). Moreover, the Homoeans, who refuse to use the word substance of God, have a merely physical notion of substance as a subject with accidents.

(63) After showing that being and existence and substance and subsistence are synonyms, Victorinus concludes that since the word *substance* designates "to be" purely and simply, therefore, by the principle of predominance, God should be called substance (4,1-6,19). He then reserves the word subsistence to designate the determination of the divine substance, namely, Father, Son. Where-ever the word *substance* is used it refers to the "To Be" of God.

(64) In this long discussion against the Homoeans, Victorinus goes to Scripture for the reality: the Father in the Son and the Son in the Father, Jn 14.11; *adv. Ar.* II 6,19-12,19). The word *consubstantiality*, therefore, is found in Scripture, but implicitly, just as "God from God, Light from Light" are not to be found in Scripture explicitly but result from theological reasoning. Moreover, expressions synonymous with consubstantiality are used by the adversaries in the eucharistic liturgy. Hadot claims that the word *consubstantialis* was unknown in the Latin controversies before Candidus the Arian and Victorinus (TTT II, *adv. Ar.* II 10,1; cf.

Cand. I 7,1; *ad Cand.* I 8,28).

(65) In his own explanation of *homoousios* Victorinus distinguishes between the substantial common names and the qualitative common names of God: God, Light and Spirit are names which designate the substance, whereas Father, Omnipotent, Good designate quality. Yet whether we hear the word *Father* or *God* or *Omnipotent,* we think of the pure "To Be" of God (10,4-20). Victorinus is arguing that anyone who distinguishes qualities proper to the Son and to the Father is already saying that there is something common to them, namely, substance, and thereby admitting the unity of substance, the consubstantial (10,17-18). It would be better, indeed, to say *deum in deo, lumen in lumine* ("God in God," "Light in Light"), to be true to Scripture, where we are told that the Son is in the Father (11,9-12,19).

The Emperor Julian (A.D. 360-63)

(66) While Constantius was busy resisting the attacks of the Persians, his pagan cousin Julian in the Western Empire revolted and assumed power. This suspended the effects of the Council of Ariminum. In fact, in 360, the Synod of Paris under Hilary's influence repudiated the Nice-Ariminum formulation (above, sect. 56), excommunicated Ursacius, Valens, Auxentius, Gaius, Megasius and Justin, and professed an orthodox interpretation of *homoousion.* On November 3, 361, Constantius, still in Asia Minor, died, and in the next month (December 11), Julian entered Constantinople.

(67) In the spring of 362, Julian reinstated the orthodox bishops exiled by Constantius; in the same year a council was called in Alexandria by Athanasius. The council admitted as legitimate the use of the word *homoousion* to designate the unity of substance or the use of "Three Hypostases" to designate the trinity of persons. It condemned those who taught the Holy Spirit to be a creature separated from the substance of Christ. And it affirmed, against a growing Apollinarianism,[54] that the Savior did have body and soul, feeling and reason, all that a true man would have.

---

54 The heresy that denied Christ's humanity by attributing only a human body and soul to Christ, but no spirit, the spirit being replaced by the divine *Logos.*

(68) This document, sent to Antioch, was apparently known by Victorinus. When, in June of 362, an edict of Julian forbade Christians to teach, Victorinus resigned his position as rhetor in Rome and was able to give full time to his theological writings (see above, sect. 2).

Against Arius, Book III (A.D. 361)

(adv. Ar. III)

(69) After a summary of the preceding books (1,4-2,11), this book discusses not merely the Father-Son dyad which has been central to the previous books but the Father-Son-Holy Spirit triad. This is due to a new heresy about the Holy Spirit. Victorinus strongly asserts that the Trinity is always included when one speaks of the Father and Son. The Trinity is a double dyad: Father-Son, Son-Spirit (7,5-8; 18,18-25). This entire treatise concentrates on the identity and difference between the Son and the Holy Spirit. Victorinus utilizes the philosophical triad *esse-vivere-intelligere* to explain that life and knowledge are the movement of being (chs. 4 and 5). He looks for this same triadic pattern in the scriptural texts referring to the Holy Spirit (chs. 10-16). Moreover, it is because the soul is *esse-vivere-intelligere* that the soul is indeed the image of God (1,4-13). Yet the true image of God is found only among divine realities because a true image is consubstantial with its model. The intelligible world has no parts, only consubstantial images. The *Logos,* light of light, is the consubstantial revelation of the Father (1,30-2,11). Our knowledge of God is therefore through the *Logos.* Insofar as men are identified with the conversion of the *Logos* to the Father, with the divine return, they can know God and be saved. This conversion, like that of Christ, will involve death (Rom 6.10).

(70) The Father and Son are shown to be consubstantial as substance or "To Be" and movement (2,12-4,5). The movement is vivifying, saving movement. Turned within, this movement is Father; externalized, it is Son (2,12-54). This leads to the theme of self-knowledge (4,30; 8,19), the final fruit of the externalization of movement or life which communicates itself to particulars so that it may draw them to universal life (3,1-4,5).

(71) In trying to convince the Homoiousians Victorinus uses the

two texts from St. John which direct his own reflection upon the Trinity: Jn 16.15, denoting consubstantiality, Jn 5.26, denoting the autonomy of Father and Son as two movements (3,6-17). After treating the cosmic role of the *Logos* (4,1-5), he devotes chapters 4 and 5 to the relationship between Father, Son and Holy Spirit by progressing from the substance-movement opposition to the division of movement into Life and Wisdom (4,6-17,9). There follows his longest philosophical development of the reciprocal implication of "to be," "to live," "to know" (4,6-5,31). He points out that this metaphysical triad clearly shows that the Three are in each one and he illustrates this point from Scripture (9,9-11,21). A digression in the form of a polemic against Apollinarianism argues that the full *Logos* is soul and body (11,22-12,46), and finally Victorinus appeals to Scripture to support his favorite formula: Father and Son are two Ones, Son and Holy Spirit are two in One (13,1-17,9).

(72) In speaking of knowing God at the moment of conversion, Victorinus proceeds naturally to the soul's contemplation of God, enumerating all the means of knowing God (6,1-23), and he says that the true knowledge of God is linked to faith in the consubstantiality of Son and Holy Spirit with the Father. The main theological exposition of the Son and Spirit as life and knowledge in one sole movement is found here (6,23-9,8), with the Victorine theology of the Holy Spirit summarized in 7,7-8.

(73) Scripture is called to witness for the position that each One of the Trinity is the Three (9,9-17,9). Whereas in Book IA Victorinus had proceeded from faith or divine authority to reason, in this third book he has proceeded from reason to divine authority (Rom 8 and 9; Jn 5.26-17.19; Eph 1.9). In Jn 16.8-10, Victorinus sees the best statement on the Holy Spirit, his main concern in this third book. In his proper action of testifying to Christ, the Spirit acts upon the Apostles to make of them witnesses to Christ; he convicts the world of sin, of justice, of judgement, and sanctifies the baptized by communicating knowledge of Christ's salvific action. The Holy Spirit is our knowledge of Christ: the Son saves, the Spirit reveals. True salvation is found only in consciousness of salvation.

(74) Victorinus concludes by appealing to Scripture for his understanding of the Trinity as two dyads (17,10-18,10) and adds a final word on the Holy Spirit's role in the life of Christ (18,18-28).

Against Arius, Book IV (A.D. 362)

(adv. Ar. IV)

(75) In this book Victorinus discusses the Father and Son no longer as *Esse* and *Motus* but as *Actus* and *Forma.* The *esse-vivere-intelligere* triad defines the content of the Act of "To Be," which the Father is, and of the Form, which the Son is. The Form which is the Son results from the Father as self-acting and therefore results in a Form that is self-acting.

(76) This book is therefore a treatise on the consubstantial Form of God based upon Jn 5.26 and 6.57 as well as Phil 2.5-7. Since the Father is called "To Live," the Son is therefore Life (1,4-7,33) and, of course, these two are identified (8,1-15,32). A summary of Life as the Form produced by the act which is "To Live" is followed by a synthesis of the doctrine on the Holy Spirit developed in the third book (16,1-18,44).

(77) Returning to his main position that the *Esse* which is the Father conceived as Act is best expressed by "To Live" (See above, sects. 33-34), and that the Form of the latter is Life, Victorinus argues here for consubstantiality by reemphasizing the fact that among the intelligibles and intellects there is no difference between substance and quality, "To Be" and its Action (2,1-3,38). However, there is a predominance of the "To Live" or a predominance of Life. The Father is then the Living God of whom the Scripture speaks (4,1-5,4) and the Son is his begotten Life spoken of in Scripture (6,18-7,33), and this is the case because God is Spirit.

(78) In the next part of the treatise (8,1-18,44) Victorinus brings in the concept of Form and argues that the Son is consubstantial Form of the Father as Life is the form of "To Live."

(79) In the last part of the treatise the form issuing from "To Act" is placed within the relationship of "To Know" and Knowledge (18,45-29,38). Victorinus's main problematic is to show the consubstantiality of *actus-forma* (act-form) (13,15-14,35). He now has to account for the Holy Spirit in this new perspective (16,1-18,44). In the unity of one movement, Christ and the Holy Spirit are distinguished by their "economic" or salvific functions (17,19-18,13).

(80) Finally, he devotes himself to describing the emergence ,or begetting of Form, now considered as Knowledge (21,19-29,23).

Knowledge is said to be interior Form and self-knowledge; it is natural for the scriptural source here to be Phil 2.5. It is then shown that this Life or Wisdom of the Father becomes the Son as Life and Wisdom without change or passion. Here the resources of philosophy are used (21,18-29,38) to elucidate the generation of the *Logos*, thought of thought. The movement of the Form is Knowledge, thanks to which it is established both as Form of God and as Form, both knowledge of "To Be" and Knowledge. Its act of self-begetting consists in being simultaneously "To Be" and Form, God and itself. This doctrine corresponds to the logical distinction introduced by Numenius between knowledge which knows and knowledge which knows itself, a distinction denied by Plotinus in 2.9.1 and affirmed in 3.9.1. It is in this section (22.8-9) that there is found the only literal citation of Plotinus, *Enn.* 5.2.1 (see above, sect. 17). And in *Enn.* 5.2.1 we learn that the soul moves itself to beget.

(81) In any case, this treatise repeats in a new way, more philosophically, that God is three powers which are distinguished by predominance; therefore, each is three and they are the point of departure for the existence, the life, the knowledge of particular existents (21,26-22,6). But God himself is conceived as Act and Form identified in Unity, a motionless center of all things (24,21-39). God himself is knowable only because he is already Knowledge (23,31-24,39). He is knowledge in the first state without object, whereas in the second state there is knowledge of itself as knowledge, a distinction noted in *Enn.* 2.9.1.

(82) In studying the relationship between the two knowings, interior and exterior, Victorinus is able to show that they are consubstantial (27,1-29,23). At last there is the identification of the Form with the Son (29,39-31,9), the Son with the *Logos* (31,9-32,13) and the *Logos* with Jesus (32,14-33,25). The Form, identified with God, begets himself so that he is Son, and in this externalizing movement he unfolds life and knowledge into the world as Jesus and Holy Spirit. The present argument for consubstantiality is based upon the community of names (29,24-33,25). *Esse, Vivere, Intelligere,* which are the Form, are hidden in the Father, manifested in the Son. It is this *Logos* and preexisting Son who became incarnate (32,14-22). This is confirmed by the prophets, the evangelists and by St. Paul, especially in Phil 2.5-7.

The Holy Spirit is hidden in Jesus as Jesus is in the Father (33,26-45). Hence Christ is the "mean" in the processive movement, whereas the Holy Spirit is the "mean" in the returning movement. This book concludes with a precise analysis of what *homoousion* accurately means.

Orthodoxy reinstated at Rome (A.D. 362-63)

(83) The Arian Emperor Constantius having died and the Emperor Julian remaining aloof from Christian affairs, certain bishops led by Pope Liberius experienced freedom from the constraints of political power and annulled the decisions of Ariminum and returned to the Nicene formulation of the faith. It was decided that there would be condemnation of those heretics who were culpable but amnesty for those who had been led astray.

The Necessity of Accepting the Homoousion (A.D. 363)

(de hom. rec.)

(84) In this work, Victorinus distinguishes the Christian God from the God of the pagans and Jews (1,7-16) and asserts that the *homoousion* is the best expression of Christian dogma (1,16-22). Speaking to those who have been unduly influenced by Valens and Ursacius, those who fear any dividing of God or any undue investigating of how the Son was begotten (3,1-4,14), Victorinus asserts that he is not trying to know the mode of begetting but to show that the *homoousion* is worthy of belief (4,8-14), and that belief in the Nicene formulation requires an understanding of substance. It is in this spirit that he has translated the Greek word *homoousion* with the new Latin word *consubstantialitas*. To safeguard the understanding of consubstantiality he proposed adding to the Creed the phrases: *deum in deo, lumen in lumine,* which for him perfectly express consubstantiality and could be a bridge with the moderate Arians (4,14-38).

(85) Although this treatise has been devoted to the mode of begetting, there is ample discussion about consubstantiality itself in Book IA, where Victorinus argued against the Homoiousians (cf. I 28,8-32,15), and he mentions here (4,21-22) for the only time, the Anomoeans, who are condemned by all.

Hymns

(86) The hymns, although placed in the present volume at the end, to accord with the Henry-Hadot editions, are of uncertain date. It has been suggested that they were in fact written before the prose treatises on the Trinity.

(87) *First Hymn.* A brief introduction refers to the three Ones (7-16). Closely resembling the third book of the *adv. Ar.,* this hymn celebrates a divine triad constituted of two dyads: Father-Son, *Logos*-Spirit (17-73), with Father and Son opposed and mutually implied as "To Be" and "Movement," the movement identified with the *Logos*-Life (17-38 and 39-49). This hymn, however, is more Christocentric than is the third book (63-73). It closes (74-78), as it opened (2-6), on the theme of the divine substance.

(88) *Second Hymn.* Comparable in many ways to the fourth book because it deals with the "To Live-Life" opposition, this hymn is a witness to Victorinus's view that salvation is well conceived as universalization and spiritualization. In becoming the *Logos* of souls and bodies, the universal *Logos* rejoins concrete beings with their eternal forms, leading them out of dispersion to their original and essential unity (7-10). Thus, the hymn becomes a prayer that the soul, as image and likeness of eternal life which the Father and Son are, will at last become itself, that is, life eternal (27-34). Described here are the metaphysical state of the soul (35-46) and its moral state of weakness, desire, hope (47-62), as well as its need of grace for the strengthening of the wings for the return to God. The Holy Spirit opens the gates of Heaven but Christ gives the key to Heaven.

(89) *Third Hymn.* Like *Hymn* I, this hymn insists on the Holy Spirit as bond of the Trinity (242-46). At the outset there is an enumeration of the names and the "economic" or salvific functions of the Father, Son and Holy Spirit (1-108). The relationships between the three are illuminated by the use of the substance, form, notion triad (140-251). Victorinus states that every notion affirmed of any member of the Trinity is at once proper and common, designating both One of the Three and each of the Three. After a proclamation of the redemptive role of Christ (252-69), there follows a final prayer.

NEOPLATONIC CONCEPTUAL STRUCTURES[55]

(90) The dependence of Victorinus upon Prophyry was noted in some of the earlier scholarly literature,[56] but there was no strong agreement as to which work of Porphyry influenced Victorinus. Hadot has, however, now published the Greek Neoplatonic texts present in the anonymous commentary on the *Parmenides* (see above, sects. 6 and 26). Hadot makes the double claim that Victorinus's thinking on the Trinity was guided by these texts and that Porphyry was their author. These texts are said to be the source not only of the metaphysical principles used in Victorinus's theological synthesis but the source as well of those literary and conceptual structures which seem to have been imported as groups into this synthesis. Thus the obscurity of Victorinus's Christian writings would have been found in those who were ignorant of the Greek sources used. It was once thought that Victorinus depended primarily upon the *Enneads* of Plotinus, which he had translated, and that the equality of the three Principles, which is non-Plotinian, was original with Victorinus, who reached this doctrine of consubstantiality in the light of scriptural statements on the unity and trinity of God. But Hadot claims that in certain sections of the *adversus Arium* we find Greek vocabulary never used by Plotinus,[57] and many of the words in the "philosophic fragments" (the name given by Hadot to the groups of conceptual structures transferred from philosophical treatises to Victorinus's theological treatises) appear rarely, in some cases only once in the entire text. He also claims that Victorinus's fundamental principles are Porphyrian. He admits, however, that Porphyry does not raise *esse-vivere-intelligere* to the status of hypostases (concrete substances), as Victorinus does.

(91) Here we are not directly concerned with the Neoplatonic principles successfully integrated by Victorinus into his theological synthesis. We are concerned with those imported "philosophic fragments" which have their own movement, which were originally

---

55 Hadot, PV I 45–146.
56 See W. Theiler, *Porphyrios und Augustin* (Halle 1933), and his already-cited *Die chaldäischen Orakel und die Hymnen des Synesios;* F. Kohnke "Plato's Conception of *ouk ontōs ouk on,*" *Phronesis* 2 (1957) 32–40; Séjourné, DTC 15.2896.
57 Hadot, PV II 157.

directed to another problematic and therefore seem to function as abrupt interruptions of the main flow of the Victorine synthesis. These interruptions or digressions seem to be paraphrases, extracts or translations; they stand out because their conceptual structure is inseparable from the literary substrate in which it is expressed; they therefore remain somewhat autonomous within the whole.

(92) There seem to be four literary groups of philosophic materials which have been detected by Hadot through certain doctrinal and stylistic peculiarities proper to their own problematic rather than to the demonstration of consubstantiality in the light of Scripture.

(93) These fragments have been the source of the principles taken over from philosophical literature by Victorinus to work out his theological synthesis, such principles as he considered compatible with the Christian teaching on consubstantiality. Among the four groups into which Hadot has assembled these philosophic fragments, groups I, II and III derive from the Neoplatonic Commentary on Plato's *Parmenides* attributed by Hadot to Porphyry (above, sects. 6, 26 and 90); group IV derives from commentaries on Aristotle's *Categories* (above, sect. 26).

(94) In his work *Porphyre et Victorinus,*[58] Hadot analyzes the fragments of this anonymous commentary on the *Parmenides* to show that there is found in them the same attitude toward and use of the "Chaldaean Oracles" which can be found in other works of Porphyry, and he analyzes each fragment to show that the doctrines in this commentary are identical with those present in the Neoplatonic philosophic fragments (Groups I, II and III) imported into the theological synthesis of Victorinus. Hadot does not insist that Victorinus read this commentary on the *Parmenides,* but holds that, if he did not, he was influenced by some writings of Porphyry in which these same ideas were repeated. It is even suggested that such writings may have been among the "books of the Platonists" translated by Victorinus and read by Augustine.[59] For example, the conceptual structure found in Group II, especially self-begetting, is applied by later Neoplatonists, but it can be found in other works

---

58 *Ibid.,* I 102–46.
59 See above, sect. 1.

of Porphyry. Or it may have come from the Neo-Pythagorean tradition,[60] the generation of number from the monad or from a metaphysical transposition of Stoicism, perhaps under the influence of
Plotinus's interpretation of the five genera of Plato's *Sophist* as
ontological entities.

(95) In any case, the anonymous commentary on the *Parmenides*
is attributed to Porphyry by Hadot because it is typically Porphyrian
as a synthesis of traditional Platonism, Plotinianism and Chaldaean-
ism. The author must be an independent disciple of Plotinus because
there is fidelity to a Middle Platonic interpreter of Plato, probably to
Numenius (above, sects. 5 and 6), who taught that there were two
states of Intelligence, one in repose within the One, and one in
action within *Nous,* a doctrine which would enable Porphyry to
reconcile the Plotinian doctrine of the transcendence of the One with
the Chaldaean doctrine of the preexistence of potentiality-life and
of knowledge in the Father.

(96) Although the overall main arguments of Victorinus's synthesis are consistent with the Christian theology of the equality of
Persons in God, he does not seem to need these imported Hellen-
isms for the argument. It is helpful for the reader to recognize these
fragments as they appear in Victorinus's text. In the notes the reader
will be referred to them in this manner, e.g., Philosophic Fragments:
Group I or II or III or IV. Apparently, these Neoplatonic Greek
texts or others like them, along with commentaries on Aristotle's
Categories, were close at hand when Victorinus was engaged in
polemic with Basil of Ancyra and the Homoiousians.

VOCABULARY

(97) Hadot has already made a study of the philosophical
vocabulary of Marius Victorinus.[61] No exhaustive study, however,
has yet appeared.

(98) We can, however, at least list some of the outstanding

---

60 Hadot, PV I 311; Cf. Porphyry,*Philosophica Historia* 18,*Porphyrii Opuscula,*
    ed. A. Nauck (Leipzig 1886) 14.21.
61 See above, n. 3. For a recently recognized feature of Victorinus's syntax,
    see above, n. 2.

characteristics in the vocabulary of Victorinus as frequently noted by students of his works. There is, first of all, the presence of many neologisms such as: *alteritas, cirumformare, ens, essentialitas, essentitas, existentialitas, existentialiter, inparticipatus, praeexsistens, praexsistentia, praexsistentialis, praeintelligentia, praeviventia.* These were first noted by Cardinal Mai in his work on Victorinus's commentaries on the Epistles of St. Paul.[62] Such abstract compounds are present in Fourth-Century Greek and in Hermeticism, Gnosticism, and later Neoplatonism. These neologisms can serve as clues in the discovery of the philosophic sources of Victorinus, or they may represent the need that Latin writers felt to create new terminology for describing in abstract terms the concrete realities found in human experience and in literature.

(99) In addition to neologisms there are words with extended meanings, born of a comparison of a Latin word in Cicero, for example, with a parallel Greek word. Thus, some words go through a certain evolution and assume new meanings in the new context of a theological treatise.

(100) Victorinus is also very conscious, perhaps because of the challenges of the Arians, of the philosophic words used in Scripture, and he has filled these philosophic words with their scriptural connotations as a sacred inheritance from the history of ideas.

(101) The use to which Victorinus put the word *substantia* as referring primarily to the pure "To Be" of God necessitated his use of a new word *existentia* to refer to *esse* that is determined by a form. Of course, *substantia* is not understood by him in the Aristotelian sense of what is opposed to accidents and qualities. Substance for him means a concrete being, and this seems to be one of his Plotinian reminiscences (*Enn.* 6.1.3; 12.8; cf. *adv. Ar.* I 30). This may be the individual substance later used by Boethius to define person. For Victorinus, however, this *substantia* was pure *esse* (cf. Adv. Ar. II 4,23), and therefore designated the commonness of the Three Persons. It is thus used to designate *Esse* improperly, but the word *Esse* is used as the proper name of the Father.

(102) In view of the above, Victorinus found it necessary to

---

62 A. Mai (ed.), *Scriptorum veterum nova collectio* 3 (Rome 1828), pars ii, 1–146 (*Editoris monitum* 147).

make use of *existentia* to indicate what stands outside the common-ness. Hence, *existentia* means "to be" with form or determination and is used to distinguish each of the Three: one substance and three existences. And so when he is speaking strictly of his own trinitarian doctrine, Victorinus has bypassed *hypostasis* and *persona* (used freely by Hilary of Poitiers), perhaps to keep his doctrine distinguished from the Plotinian triad and perhaps because the Sabellians conceived God as *triprosōpos* (of three persons). It is not quite certain that Victorinus is the first to use *subsistentia.* He generally uses "subsistence" to denote the individual indicated by *existentia;* thus, *subsistentia* is properly used of the Son because it designates *Esse cum forma* ("To Be" with Form).

(103) Thus, what the Greeks call nature, Victorinus calls substance, and what the Greeks call hypostasis, Victorinus calls existence. Apparently a substance has individuality by the character of its action, and so action is self-revelatory. The term *consubstantial* is used by Victorinus to safeguard the divine equality. But even *substantia,* although the common name for Father, Son and Spirit, may be used as a synonym for *existentia,* for in Victorinus the common names are also the predominant names of each of the Three. Indeed, he tries to show that each divine Person is the Three, rather than following the more usual way of arguing that all Three are one or even that one God is in three Persons.

(104) Negative theology (cf. above, sects. 31-37) is featured in Victorinus's long digression (*ad Cand.* 3,1-14,5) on the "Non existent" as above the Existent. He describes this Nonexistent as the Existent in potentiality–power. And from this we gather the nuances present in Victorinus's use of the word *potentiality,* which apparently signifies for him a state of nonexpansion and hiddenness. Rather than Aristotelian possibility or capacity, Victorine potentiality entails superabundance or omnipotence; it is a principle of plenitude.

HISTORY OF THE TEXT

(105) The first complete edition of the theological writings of Victorinus is that of A. Galland; this is found in Vol. VIII of his *Bibliotheca veterum patrum* (Venice 1772). The edition in the

Patrologia latina of J.-P. Migne (VIII, cols. 1013-1146; Paris 1844) reproduces that of Galland. After P. Henry's first construction of the text in *Sources chrétiennes* 68 (Paris 1960), we now have the critical text of P. Henry and P. Hadot, *Corpus scriptorum ecclesiasticorum latinorum,* vol. 83 (Vienna 1971).

(106) No manuscript contains all the theological works of Victorinus. The direct sources of the text, whether printed or in manuscript, from the earliest (Ninth Century) up to the Galland edition, show a division of the corpus into two parts:

  (A) *Cand. I* and *ad Cand.*—Six manuscripts[63] showing this pair of works have been used; the first printing is that of J. Ziegler (Basel 1540).
  (B) The remaining works, viz. *Cand II,* the four books of *adv. Ar.,* the *de hom. rec.,*[64] and the *Hymns*—Only one manuscript is known to contain these writings, a Tenth-Century codex (*Berolinensis Phillips* 1684). This larger portion of Victorinus's theological output was first edited by J. Sicard (Basel 1528).

The two groups were first brought together by Galland in 1772.

(107) In his *De fide* of c. 802, Alcuin of Tours made use of works found in both parts of the divided tradition, drawing both from the *ad. Cand.* and from the *adv. Ar.* (through I 47) and the *Hymns.* He thus witnesses to a tradition of the corpus that preceded its division into two.[65]

TRANSLATION

(108) The Latin text of Marius Victorinus's writings on the Trinity gives the beginnings of the transition from the classical Latin to the fully developed scholastic Latin of several centuries later. The use of Greek terms shows that Latin had not yet been molded to the needs of Christian philosophy or theology. In the interest of clarity

---

63 Hadot, MV 254.
64 Of this work there is a separate MS of the Tenth Century, Parisinus Lat. 13371, BN fols. 16v-.
65 Hadot, "Marius Victorinus et Alcuin," *Archives d'histoire doctrinale et littéraire du moyen âge* 21 (1954) 5-19.

and precision Victorinus frequently uses expressions in Greek—syllables, single words, phrases, or (rarely) an entire verse from the Greek Bible or some other ancient source. In this English translation care has been taken to reflect his practice, and therefore transliteration has been used with the English equivalents placed within parentheses. No English equivalents for *Logos* and *Nous* and *hypostasis* have been given.

(109) Some translations succeed in excluding foreign idioms to such an extent that they read like originals. Such attempts are desirable when translating a modern author whose style is not of considerable importance. In the case of an ancient classic, the translation ought to reproduce the peculiar turns of expression which reveal the author's mode of thought and chain of reasoning. That is why I have remained as faithful as possible to Victorinus's own form of expression.

(110) To avoid all the philosophical confusion surrounding the words "being" and "existing," I have in appropriate contexts translated *esse* as the substantive "to be," which seems to me, at any rate, equivalent to the later medieval *actus essendi.* The Greek *on* has been translated as the "existent," which seems equivalent to the later *quod est.*

THEOLOGICAL TREATISES
ON THE TRINITY

LETTER OF CANDIDUS THE ARIAN
TO MARIUS VICTORINUS THE RHETOR
ON THE DIVINE BEGETTING

I. GENERAL THESIS:
GOD IS UNBEGOTTEN AND NONBEGETTING

Y DEAR OLD VICTORINUS, every kind of begetting is some sort of change. But whatever is divine, namely God, is unchangeable. Yet God, who is father, is the first cause of all things and in all things.

If therefore God is unchanging and unchangeable, but whatever is unchanging and unchangeable is neither begotten nor begetting; if then this is so, God is unbegotten. For begetting is begetting through alteration and through change.

II. GOD IS UNBEGOTTEN

1. Nothing Can Beget God

Of course, neither substance nor substantiality,[1] neither an existent being nor essentiality, neither existence nor existentiality nor potentiality have preceded the "to be" of God. For who is more powerful than God? It would not be potentiality, would it, nor existence, nor substance, nor *on* (an existent)? Either he himself is all of these or they are subsequent to him. For he himself produced them all.

But suppose those things preceded him. And how could they beget God if they wished to do so? For they were neither perfect nor self-subsistent; therefore they were imperfect. Since they were

---

1 One of the philosophical fragments (Group II) possibly derived from Porphyry, assembled by Hadot from the writings of Victorinus; see above, Introd., sects. 92 and 93 and Hadot, PV II 27–28.

imperfect, how by their very own power could they have begotten or made the perfect God? If God, however, is also imperfect, there is no reason to beget what already existed. The reasoning is the same if they were perfect and begot the perfect. To beget God was either without reason or superfluous or impossible.

First of all, potentiality is certainly prior, they say, to that which exists. But without act and operation, potentiality by itself cannot come to be something, since it is potentiality, not action; and potentiality without having been empowered cannot beget anything, least of all God. For potentiality remains in that which is potentially "to be," without action. Whence therefore was God born? Therefore, God is unbegotten.

(2) Let us see, therefore, whether by some chance substance or substantiality, existence or existentiality preceded God.

But substance,[2] since it is rather a subject of another, is subject of that which is in it, and is different from that which is in it. But no difference is received in God. For when it is God there is nothing in another as other. For God is not anything other than "to be God." For God is something simple. He is not, therefore, from a pre-existent substance. God is therefore unbegotten.

For it is God who produces substance rather than that substance exists before God. For substance is subject, subject of another thing from which it differs and of which it becomes the receptacle, so that that of which it is the receptacle, being superior to it, is therefore naturally later.

In the same way we must understand existence and existentiality.[3] Existence differs, however, from existentiality, since existence is already in the state that "to be" belongs to it, but existentiality is the potentiality, so that while it is able "to be," it is not yet itself "to be." Much more, however, does existence differ from substance, since existence is "to be" itself, "to be" which is neither in another nor subject of another but solely "to be" itself, whereas substance has not only "to be" but also has a "to be" something qualified. For it is subject to the qualities within it and on that account is called

---

2 In denying substance to God Candidus uses Aristotle's notion of substance as subject (composed); Aristotle, *Metaphysics* 7.3 (1028b33).

3 Another set of philosophical fragments (Group II); see note 1 and Hadot, PV II 21.

subject. How therefore was God born of preexisting existence or of existentiality whether these be the power of existence or existence itself if for these existents there is only "to be" and no action or strength and power of acting?

(3) Since such is the case, neither the *on* (existent) nor the *ontotēs* (entity) was prior to God. For they are multiple and composed of substance and quality. If therefore neither potentiality nor existence nor existentiality, all of which have an appearance of simplicity, was prior to God, with greater reason neither *ontotēs* (entity) nor the *on*[4] (existent) nor substantiality nor substance was prior to God. For they are begotten after existentiality and existence. If all these realities are begotten afterwards, then they were begotten. Unbegotten therefore is that from which all these come, from which all things come. And what is that from which all things come? It is God. God is therefore unbegotten if God is indeed the cause of all these things.

2. God Is Cause of His "To Be"

What indeed? "To be" God—what kind of cause or what is its cause? This: the very "to be" God. Truly the first cause is cause of itself[5] also, not so that it is cause as something other than itself, but the selfsame God is cause that he is. He is for himself his own dwelling and his own tenant without any appearance of duality. He himself is the single one. For he is solely "to be."

And indeed "to be" itself is precisely to live and to understand.[6]

---

4 There is only a difference of accent between the notion of substance and that of existent. Substance is subject as subject; the existent is the subject taken with its qualities (as opposed to Plotinus, *Enneads* 6.1.1). However, the distinction between *existentia* and *substantia* appeared in Plotinus's treatise *On the Kinds of Being.*

5 The tradition of God as self-caused goes back to *Metaphysics* 7.6 (1031a15), where Aristotle raises the question whether, with regard to some beings, the intelligible constitution and the being are not necessarily the same. Plotinus speaks of the One as self-caused when he discusses the unity of intelligible constitution or essence and being in intelligible beings, as in *Enn.* 6.8.14; cf. 6.8.21.

6 God exists, lives and understands (cf. Plato, *Sophist* 248e) without this triad implying begetting or multiplicity. For texts in Victorinus which directly oppose Candidus, cf. *ad Cand.* 30,1-20; *adv. Ar.* I 43,34-43; IV 21,19-25. Cf. above, Introd., sect. 29. For comparisons between this letter and Arian fragments see M. Meslin, *Les Ariens d'Occident* (Paris 1968).

For insofar as it is, it lives and understands, and insofar as it lives, it is and understands, and insofar as it understands, it is and lives; and insofar as it is one, it is all three, and insofar as it is all three, it is one, and insofar as it is three times the three, it is one simple unity and unified simplicity.

The simple is, moreover, the principle of composites. But the principle is without principle. For it precedes, having no prior principle; that is why it is principle. But this is God. God therefore is without origin and is unbegotten. God is therefore unbegotten.

III. GOD IS UNBEGETTING

1. Every Begetting Implies Change

But that which is unbegotten is without beginning, that which is without beginning is without end. For there is an end only to what begins. But if God is without beginning and end, he is infinite. If he is infinite, he is incomprehensible, unknowable, invisible, unchanging, unalterable. For beginning and ending are change and alteration: the beginning of one thing is the end of another. But God is none of these things. God is therefore unchangeable and unalterable.

But if God is such, neither does God beget.[7] For to beget or to be begotten is a certain change and alteration. Moreover, to beget is to give something to the one begotten: either all or part. Whoever begets something either perishes, if he gives all, or is diminished, if he gives a part. But then God remains always the same. Therefore he does not beget.

2. All Kinds of Begetting Imply Change

(4) This same conclusion will hold even if someone says that begetting by God occurs in these ways: by reflection, by ray pro-

7 In a development which extends through to ch. 9, the author treats of God's unfruitfulness. Athanasius, *Contra Arianos* 2.2 (PG 26.149E); Hilary, *De trinitate* 8.3 (PL 10.239B; FC 25.276–77); *Contra Constantium* 12 (PL 10.591). The Arians had a sterile God, as did the Anomoeans. Arians denied the true divinity of Jesus Christ because they thought that the Son of God was not eternal but was created by the Father as an instrument for the creation of the world. The Anomoeans were the extreme Arians of the Fourth Century, so called from their doctrine that the Son is

jection, by a line from a point, by projection, by image, by impression, by progression, by superabundance, by motion, by act, by will, finally by so-called "type" or by any other method. For none of these occurs without change. First of all, reflection is both movement implying time and a certain withdrawal into its own substance. If this reflection lasts forever, it is a part separable from the whole. If it does not last forever, then a begetting from that which is eternal into that which is transitory is meaningless. What next? Is not reflection a change? Certainly a reflection is a brilliance escaping or given off from a luminous substance: it is substantial but not substance, and if it is substance, certainly not the same substance. So therefore that which is later is a change of the prior.

(5) Let us therefore consider begetting according to ray projection. Certainly it is a connected ray and connected with that from which it proceeds. A change, however, is nonetheless accomplished if there is begetting, or there is no begetting if the ray remains always within the thing itself.

But begetting there is a flowing from a point.[8] And how is that? For the point is motionless and the limit of a line because it neither has a part nor is it the part of another. If therefore this is so, the point does not proceed from itself. For if it proceeds it is no longer a point but already a line. It is therefore changed. But then God is unchangeable. Therefore God is not that which is a point. If, however, the point remains a point, there is no line from it. For a point is immobile. But a line is either in motion or from motion and according to this method there is no begetting by God.

What next? Is there begetting by God according to some kind of projection? Certainly if he projects something from himself, first of all he is diminished in his substance or in his divinity or in his act, or in some other aspect, and then what is projected is either of identical power with him or it is not. If what is projected is equally powerful, how can there be two equal Gods? And what is the point of two, if they are equal? Whatever one can do, the other also can do. It is useless to multiply a plenitude which is a single perfection. If, how-

---

"totally unlike" the Father. Their leaders were Aetius and Eunomius; see ODCC[2] 83. Eunomius, *Apology* 15 (PG 30.849D) rejected a physical or natural, substantial begetting but admitted a begetting by will or creation.

8 The notion criticized here is found in Victorinus, *adv. Ar.* I 60,3–7.

ever, that which proceeds is not of identical power, God is both changed and suffers in his wholeness by the loss of a part, which is inconsistent with the nature of God. Therefore there is also no begetting by God according to this method.

(6) Moreover, it is likewise also according to the image. For the image differs much from what is imaged. The latter is substance, the former a shadowy representation only in the order of quality. For the image has substance only in another and does not subsist in itself, either as in itself or as in that other. That which is begotten by God is therefore not image. For the image is only an accompaniment of that whose image it is.

The same reasoning also holds if the begetting is according to impression. For an impression is an exterior sign of a substance: by itself it is nothing and it is in another which is impressed. Nothing like this, therefore, is begotten by God.

But consider begetting by God according to procession and according to movement.[9] Procession, however, differs from movement in that every procession certainly comes from movement and is made in movement but not all movement is also procession. For interior movement is not procession but only movement. Procession is indeed movement proceeding outward. What then? Shall we say that there is begetting by God according to procession once, often, or always? Once? What would be the use? And if that which proceeds is good, why is God sterile in procession? If it is often or always, why has he begotten anew? And the first procession was necessarily imperfect if there was a need for others to complete it.

(7) Whence it appears that begetting by God is neither consubstantial nor without change. But if change is unsuitable for God, there is no begetting by God. It appears to us more unsuitable, however, if the begetting is according to movement. For movement is either interior or progressive. If it is interior, there is no begetting; if progressive, there is no identity, and there is therefore change. And if the movement is progressive, it is not consubstantial. Then if it is progressive it proceeds into its own substance or is an efficient

---

9 Candidus distinguishes procession from movement, but Victorinus will attribute to God a movement that proceeds; *intus motus,* immanent movement begets substance; transitive movement, *foras spectans,* begets action. Cf. *adv. Ar.* III 2,28–30.

cause of another. First of all God having moved himself into motion has suffered and that is change. Next, if he proceeded into his own substance, he had no substance. If he proceeded into the substance of another, it was other than God because this other was made and is more an effect of God than a begetting by God. There is no consubstantial therefore, and that which is later is a change from the former. Therefore there is no begetting by God.

But some say there is a begetting by God according to superabundance. They speak of the superabundant as an impetuous spring, brimming over, so full that it overflows, remaining always full. In like manner God like an overfull spring overflows, and this is begetting by God. This reasoning again runs into the same difficulty. For if the overfull is begetting and the spring is always full, there is ceaseless begetting by God. The spring is certainly not emptied because although it is poured forth, it increases. Does that which is added remain within? No. That which is superabundant is therefore poured forth since it is unsuitable that that which superabounds should not be poured forth. But the spring pours forth and always pours, for it always overflows. Therefore both new angels and new worlds! For it is inconsistent that that which always flows should be poured into nothingness. But once full always full. There is therefore a twofold alteration and change in God. Thus this also is unsuitable. There is also no begetting by God according to superabundance. Moreover, that which flows over is no longer consubstantial with God himself. For God is superabundant. However, that which flows over is itself only an overflow, and not superabundant.

(8) Some say: there is begetting according to will and according to action. But it is possible to consider these two, the will and the action, as one same thing, especially in God. For to will and to act are simultaneous for God. Nevertheless, there is also a difference, although for God the act is also in the will. And indeed the will as will is the cause of action, but action is the effect of will. Will is therefore different from action. And where there is a before and after, it is impossible then for both to be the same. God therefore first has will, afterwards action; I say this not according to time but as to the fact of one being the cause of the "to be" of another. The will is therefore clearly neither substance nor action. Then the effect is something different from will and from action. For the effect is

effect of the agent, but the effect is not the agent itself. The effect is therefore not consubstantial with the agent and there is no begetting, but because it was made, it was begotten. Since therefore that which is produced by God as an effect, not by begetting, this effect is neither sonship, nor son, nor only begotten, nor consubstantial, especially since until God wills to beget something there is not yet a substance.

For every substance[10] is an effect of God. God therefore is not substance. For through God there is substance. How, then, if substance is after him, do we say that God is substance? For if we say that God is substance, reason forces us also to this: to profess that substance is prior to God. But in fact substance in the true sense is a sort of subject. But whatever is a subject is not simple. For on hearing the word subject the intellect at the same time grasps something else found in this subject. But then God is simple. Therefore God is without substance. But if God is without substance, nothing is consubstantial with God even if it either manifests or is born of God.

(9) Some say that begetting by God is according to what is called "type."[11] For God is spirit. But spirit sometimes extends its own nature outside and sometimes recollects itself within. A motion of this kind is called "type." But what happens next? From such a motion there suddenly comes forth a certain filiation, and such is the begetting by God. But what is this like? Is it like a flux, a projection, a reflection, or something other? Again, what else? Is it like a part of a whole or like a whole? And whether it be one or the other,

10 Candidus reserves the word "substance" for effects of the divine will. Eunomius denies substantiality of the divine will as a defense against the eternity of the world. The same argument will be used by the Homoiousians against the word "consubstantial" (cf. *adv. Ar.* I 29,9) and by the Homoeans against the word "substance"; cf. Gregory of Elvira, *De fide orthodoxa* 4 (PL 20.39). Cf. J. Kelly, *Early Christian Doctrines* (London 1960) 223–71.

11 This is a motion of tension and release, an ontological motion of the Stoic *pneuma*. The mind self-stretches and self-returns: output and intake. This teaching was attributed to Photinus (a Fourth-Century heretic, see ODCC[2] 1087) by the Sirmium formula of 351 (see above, Introd., sect. 40); cf. Hilary, *De synodis* 38 (PL 10.510B); Athanasius, *De synodis* 27 (PG 26.737A). Cf. Hadot, "Typus, Stoicisme et Monarchianisme au quatrième siècle d'après Candidus l'Arien et Marius Victorinus," *Recherches de théologie ancienne et médiévale* 18 (1951) 177–87.

either indeed God is imperfect if he pours out a part of himself and
is thereby diminished, the Son being a part of the Father; or indeed
this begetting is meaningless, if the whole has come forth from the
whole. For the begetting of the same thing from the same thing is
useless. And if it were necessary that both be begotten, it would
mean that both were imperfect, and the first would undergo change.
But then the spirit arising within itself only appears to be something
else without any reflection. It is therefore evident that what comes
forth as second proceeds from nonexistents and is therefore made,
not born, and on that account not consubstantial. Therefore there is
no begetting by God.

IV. JESUS IS THE EFFECT OF GOD

(10) What conclusions are we obliged to allow from all this, my
dear Victorinus? That the Son[12] of God, who is the "*Logos* with
God," Jesus Christ, "through whom all things were made and without whom nothing was made,"[13] is, not by God's begetting but by
God's operation, the first and original effect of God. "But God gave
him a name above all names,"[14] calling him Son and only begotten,
because he has made him alone by his own activity. He has made
him from nothing, because the power of God leads the nonexistent
to be. This also Jesus does, he "through whom all things were
made;"[15] that is, he has made things from nonbeing.

But there is this difference: that God has made Jesus absolutely
perfect whereas Jesus has made other things not in the same way
although he made them perfect. Therefore insofar as Jesus is creator
of things from nothing "He is in the Father and the Father is in

---

12 Note that according to Candidus the name of Son was *given* to Jesus by
God; cf. *Fragmenta Arianorum* (PL 13.597B, 602A–B, 603A, 618C).
Cf. also Athanasius, *Contra Arianos* 3.42 (PG 26.412A–B); Augustine,
Contra Maximinum 2.12.3 (PL 42.768). Jesus Christ is the first substance,
according to Candidus, the first effect of God; God is the principle; that is
all one can say; for the implications of this principle see above, Introd.,
sect. 30. All else is negative theology, that is, a statement of what God is
not rather than an attempt to describe or define God.

13 Jn 1.1.

14 Phil 2.9.

15 Cf. Jn 1.3.

Him,"[16] and "both are one,"[17] according to act. But insofar as he cannot do the same thing, he can be considered as different. And indeed he has not the power to make another absolutely perfect. But neither does he act by his own act nor by his own will, but he wills the same things as the Father, and he himself, although he has a will, nevertheless says: "But not as I will but as you will."[18] And he was unaware of much in the Father's will, such as the day of judgment. And he can suffer, but the Father cannot suffer; the latter sends him, he is sent; and there are other differences of the same kind which are based upon the fact that he became incarnate, that he died, that he rose from the dead, all these being things that befell the Son: what would be unsuitable for the Father is not unsuitable for his effect, because this effect is of the order of substance, which is receptive to opposed and even to contrary qualities.

(11) But that God made Jesus Christ, this the Holy Scripture says in the Acts of the Apostles: "But let the whole house of Israel know most certainly that God made for us the Lord Jesus Christ whom you have crucified."[19] Likewise in Solomon: "You have made of me the head of all your ways."[20] This is also what is signified in the Gospel according to John: "And what was made in him was life."[21] If something was made in him, he also was made, above all if it is he who is life.

Let no one then consider it difficult to accept that Jesus is the absolutely perfect effect of God by the power of God, Spirit above all spirits, only begotten by action, Son by power, made a substance and not from substance.

Truly Jesus is the universal and first substance, the universal act, the universal *Logos,* the beginning and end; for of all that has been made, he is the beginning and end; of all the existents,[22] corporeal or incorporeal, intelligible or intellectual, thinking or thought, sensible or sensing, he is the preprinciple or the precause, the first

16 Cf. Jn 14.10.
17 Cf. Jn 10.30.
18 Mt 26.39.
19 Acts 2.36.
20 Prv 8.22.
21 Jn 1.3-4.
22 Candidus's classification of existents is like that of Victorinus, *ad Cand.* 7-11; *adv. Ar.* I 61.

fruits and the maker,[23] the receptacle and the plenitude, "he through whom all was made and without whom nothing was made,"[24] our Savior, reformation of all things, as a slave[25] to save us but a Lord to punish sinners and the disobedient, truly the glory and crown of the just and holy.

---

23 Candidus begins this paragraph by speaking of the universality of Jesus but before the paragraph is concluded he has referred to the cosmic, creative and redemptive role of the Son.

24 Jn 1.3.

25 Phil 2.7. Jesus takes only the *form* of the slave. Phil 2.7 is of paramount importance in Victorinus's theology of the Trinity and spirituality.

LETTER OF MARIUS VICTORINUS,
RHETOR OF THE CITY OF ROME,
TO CANDIDUS THE ARIAN

I. PROLOGUE: THE IMPOSSIBILITY OF SPEAKING OF GOD

 OUR GREAT INTELLIGENCE, O NOBLE CANDIDUS,[1] who has bewitched it? To discourse on God[2] is an audacity too great for man. Yet because the *nous patrikos* (paternal nous) is innate to our soul and the spirit sent from heaven arouses analogies of ideas which have been engraved within our soul from all eternity, our soul by a kind of spiritual elevation wishes to see ineffable things and the inscrutable mysteries of the will or works of God. And yet, dwelling in this

---

1 In his commentary on this letter *ad Cand.*, Hadot (TTT 689) asserts that it has not the dialectical rigor of Candidus's letter; Candidus was forceful, precise and demonstrative, while Victorinus affirms more than he demonstrates. Since that statement, there has appeared an article suggesting that Candidus is a fictitious name, even a pseudonym for Victorinus himself as skeptical believer (cf. Introd., n. 44). In his more recent work (PV I 40 n. 3), Hadot admits that *ad Cand.* was written by Victorinus, but, unlike Nautin, he thinks that Victorinus simply used Candidus to reconstruct around this name the objections which any Neo-Arian would make; the philosophical principles are shared by Victorinus and Candidus, but Victorinus shows that philosophers starting from the same premises can arrive at opposed conclusions. Both admit that God is a unique act of being, of living and of thinking, but Candidus concludes that God is not only unbegotten but unbegetting. Gore (DCB 4.1131-35) thinks that Candidus was indeed an actual correspondent who feared that the generation of the Son would introduce "change" into God.

It was F. Kohnke (see Introd., n. 56) who first recognized in this letter of Victorinus the influence of Porphyry's *Commentary on the Sophist.* Hadot (TTT 689) states that he and Kohnke worked independently of each other but have converged on important points.

2 The difficulty of naming God has a long tradition from Plato through Albinus and Neoplatonists, and after Victorinus through Proclus and the Pseudo-Dionysius. Cf. A. Festugière, *La Révélation d'Hermès Trismégiste,* vol. 4, *Le Dieu inconnu et la gnose* (Paris 1954) 216. Cf. also H. Wolfson,

body, it is difficult for the soul to understand these things, but impossible to express them.

For the blessed Paul says: "O the depth of the riches, of the wisdom, and of the knowledge of God! How incomprehensible are the judgments of God and how unsearchable his ways."[3] And Isaiah also says: "Who then has known the mind of the Lord or who has been his counselor?"[4] You see therefore a saint's knowledge of God.

II. TEACHING OF SCRIPTURE:
JESUS CHRIST IS THE SON OF GOD

Do you judge these Scriptures to be untrustworthy? But since you are Christian in name, you must necessarily accept and venerate the Scriptures[5] which proclaim the Lord Jesus Christ. If this is necessary for you it is also necessary to believe what is affirmed there of Christ and precisely as affirmed.

For they affirm that Jesus Christ is the only begotten Son of God, as David the prophet says: "Thou art my Son, this day I have begotten thee."[6] The blessed Paul also says: "He who has not spared even his own Son."[7] Again: "Blessed be the Father of our Lord Jesus Christ."[8] What is more, Jesus himself frequently said: "The Father and I are one."[9] And "whoever has seen me has also seen the

---

"The Knowability and Describability of God in Plato and Aristotle," *Harvard Studies in Classical Philology* 56–57 (1947) 233–49; and "Albinus and Plotinus on Divine Attributes," *The Harvard Theological Review* 45 (1942) 115–30. In these two paragraphs Victorinus chides Candidus for his overconfidence in reason and leads him to Christian faith in the scriptural revelation of God. Candidus ended his letter with Scripture whereas Victorinus begins with it. Within these paragraphs Victorinus also speaks of the soul awakened by the Holy Spirit because the soul has innate notions or symbols relating it to the intelligible world. This doctrine issues from the "Chaldaean Oracles"; cf. Hadot, TTT 690.

3 Rom 11.33.

4 Is 40.13.

5 Hilary argues in this same way in his *De trinitate* 6.22 (PL 10.173C; FC 25.189–90). Alexander of Alexandria's letter addressed to all the bishops in 324 used these same texts: Ps 2.7; Rom 8.32; Jn 10.30; 14.9–11.

6 Ps 2.7.

7 Rom 8.32.

8 Eph 1.3.

9 Jn 10.30.

Father,"[10] and "I am in the Father and the Father is in me."[11] In saying this, if he was God, he did not lie; therefore Christ is the Son of God. And if he did lie, he is not even the effect of God. Often and in a thousand ways such things are said. Is it not evident to you that Scripture speaks thus everywhere?

(2) Listen to another argument concerning ourselves. Do we not say that God is a father to us? Yes, and very rightly. Why and how? Because God in his love "has predestined us to adoption through Christ."[12] But does God also have Christ as son by adoption? No one has dared to say this, probably not even you. See what blasphemy would arise from such a statement. We say that we are heirs of God the Father and through Christ are we heirs, being sons through adoption. And do we affirm that Christ is not Son, he through whom it is achieved that we are sons and become coheirs in Christ?

III. TEACHING OF REASON: THE EXISTENT AND THE *LOGOS* COME FROM DIVINE NONBEING

A. THE EXISTENT IS BORN OF THE NONEXISTENT, WHICH IS ABOVE THE EXISTENT

1. General Exposition

You have said many things of Christ; they are all true and really so: that he is power of God, and omnipotent power, and universal *Logos,* and all action, all life, and many others. Therefore, can such good effects come from the nonexistent? And blessed is the nonexistent from which there is the existent! An atheistic opinion and sacrilegious and full of blasphemy! The Lord who is above all things, all existents[13] and all nonexistents, would make the existent from nonexistents, not from existents!

Indeed, what do we think God is? Even if we think that God is

---

10 Jn 14.9.

11 Jn 14.10.

12 Eph 1.5.

13 This is the beginning of a long exposition on the kinds of existents and nonexistents in order to show that Christ whom Scripture calls both Being (Ex 3.13) and *Logos* (Jn 1.1) cannot come from another as Candidus

above everything, both existents and nonexistents, nevertheless we
believe that God is existent and not nonexistent.[14] He produces
therefore the existent, and does so by an ineffable begetting; he produces existence, the *nous* and life,[15] not as one who is these things
but as above all things. If, therefore, God is not the nonexistent, he
is, however, what is above that which exists, which is truly *on*
(existent), the potentiality[16] of the *on* (existent) itself, potentiality
which, when the begetting act is awakened in it, will beget in an
ineffable motion the fully perfect *On* (existent), an *On* (existent)
proceeding in its totality from the totality of potentiality; it follows
that God is the total *Proon*[17] (preexistent), and Jesus is the total
On (existent), but the absolutely existent and already totally[18] perfect in existence, in life, in knowledge.

This is the Son, the universal *Logos,* the *Logos* "with God" and

---

asserts. See above, Introd., sect. 32, on the role these categories play in
Victorinus's argument.

14 Extending from here into sect. 15 we have one of the longest sets of
philosophical fragments (Group I) cited by Hadot, PV II 13–20. In PV I
147–212 Hadot notes the Porphyrian themes: the modes of existents and
nonexistents, the soul's noetic levels, the begetting of the First Existent by
the Nonexistent above Existence, or, as we would say today Transcendent
Being.

15 The *esse-vivere-intelligere* triad met in *Cand.* I 3,16 appears here in
Victorinus for the first time, not in infinitive form and with *Nous (intelligere)* before life. According to Hadot and others, this doctrine is rooted in
the tradition of the commentaries on Plato's *Sophist* 248E. In his own
commentary on the *Sophist,* Plotinus (*Enn.* 2.6.6) asserts that the One
provides being, life and knowledge to others; cf. *Enn.* 5.5.10; 1.6.7; 5.1.7
P. Séjourné (DTC 15.2918) thinks that Victorinus felt authorized by Scripture to correct Plotinus by placing soul or life prior to *nous* or knowledge.
Séjourné adds that Victorinus found in Porphyry's *De regressu animae* the
triad *substantia-vita-intelligentia* as a prototype for his trinitarian doctrine.
Hadot thinks that Victornus's triad follows that of the anonymous
commentary on Plato's *Parmenides* which he attributes to Porphyry.

16 Potentiality as used by Victorinus is a plenitude, not a possibility as with
Aristotle. As a plenitude it is active and can actualize itself; the opposition
here to *Cand.* I 1 is sharp. Cf. *adv. Ar.* I 50,27–32; I 51,10; *Sophist* 248E;
Enn. 6.6.6; 3.6.6. It is best translated at times by power, and this has been
done.

17 The word "preexistent" is used to point out that God is not nonexistent
by privation but by perfection or transcendence.

18 Emphasis on "totality" refers to the formula of the Council of Antioch
(341); cf. ODCC[2] 65.

"in God," this is Jesus Christ;[19] "before all things," existents and truly existents,[20] the first and universal existence, the first and universal knowledge, the first and totally perfect *On* (existent), the *On* (existent) itself, the "first name above all names";[21] for from him come all names, as will be shown.[22]

2. God's Place among the Existents and the Nonexistents

a) God, cause of existents and of nonexistents

(3) But I wish to know, my very dear Candidus, what you consider the nonexistent to be.

For if God is the cause of everything, God is the cause of being *(esse)* and of nonbeing *(non esse)*. But if he is cause, he is not nonexistent. For a cause is, as it were, an *on* (existent), but an *on* (existent) such that "to be" is still future. But by this very fact, since he is cause, he is above the truly *on* (existent). Therefore that which is not yet an *on* (existent) is a nonexistent. Therefore, because it is not yet an *on* (existent), it is nonexistent. But because it is cause of the *on* (existent), it is truly called *Proon* (preexistent). And for this reason God is cause both of existents and of nonexistents.

b) The nonexistents: their four modes[23]

(4) Therefore the nonexistent must be defined. This is indeed conceived and named according to four modes: according to negation, so that absolutely and in all ways there is privation of exist-

---

19 The opening sentence identifies the Son with the *Logos* and with Christ, remaining close to the Scriptural names of Christ, which are not unlike Neoplatonic names. The description of the Existent or the One Who Is relates to the second hypothesis of the *Parmenides;* cf. *ad Cand.* 12,6. Victorinus uses "existence" here as Candidus used "substance," *Cand.* I 11. These arguments may also be against Marcellus of Ancyra (Fourth-Century bishop, cf. ODCC[2] 869) and Photinus.

20 Cf. Jn 1.1; Col 1.17.

21 Cf. Phil 2.9.

22 Cf. *ad Cand.* 16,4.

23 In this sect. and the following appear another group of philosophical fragments (cf. above, n. 14 and Hadot, PV II 14) on the four kinds of nonexistent beings; this whole tradition is an effort to reconcile Plato and Aristotle. Only the transcendent Nonexistent can beget the Existent; these four modes also correspond to different directions of the soul's attention.

ence; according to difference from another nature; according to "to be" which is not yet but which can be and will be; according to "to be" which is above all existents.

What therefore do we say that God is, *on* (existent) or *to mē on* (the nonexistent)? We shall certainly call him *on* (existent) because he is the father of existents. But the father of existents is not *to on* (the existent). For the things of which he is the father do not yet exist; and it is not permitted to say and it is impious to think and to call the cause of existents *on* (existent). For the cause is prior to what it causes. Therefore, God is above *on* (existent), and insofar as he is above, God is called *mē on* (nonexistent), not through privation of all that is his, but as another *on* (existent), the very one which is *mē on* (nonexistent). In relation to what is yet to come, he is *to mē on* (the nonexistent); insofar as he is the cause for the begetting of those things which are, he is *to on* (the existent).

(5) It is therefore true to say that God is father only insofar as he is cause both of existents and nonexistents. By the will of God therefore both existents and nonexistents come to be begotten. And do not consider these nonexistents as nonexistents through privation of existents. For from such nonexistents nothing is known nor exists. For if the world and all things on high subsist and exist, there is no *mē on* (nonexistent) according to privation; but it is a kind of fiction to imagine, starting from existents, the privation of them, and this fiction has neither the subsistence nor the existence of things which do exist.

There are, therefore, some nonexistents which exist in a certain way, such as those which after their birth have "to be" and name, but which before their birth, were either within their own potentiality or within another whence they have been begotten. These are the nonexistents according to these modes: according to difference from another nature and according to "to be" which is not yet, which will be and can be.

c) The existents: their four modes[24]

(6) In the first place, then, God is above existents and nonexistents as one who is, insofar as he is cause, their begetter and their

---

24 In sects. 6 through 11 Victorinus deals with the four kinds of existents

father. Secondly, by God's begetting or making, existents have appeared. But *mē onta* (nonexistents) have also appeared. Of the existents, however, there are some which truly exist, others which exist, others which are not truly nonexistents, others which are nonexistents.[25] But those which are truly nonexistent, the plenitude[26] of God does not allow to be. For plenitude is plenitude according to "to be" or to some mode of "to be"; of the truly non-existents there exists only an illusory image in thought; our thought at a lower level, beginning with those things which if they are not truly existent, are at least in some way existents, sketches a shadowy image in respect to the truly nonexistent.

(7) Listen to what I say. Among those which exist there are certain existents which are evident by nature: thus the truly exist-ents, and all the supercelestial existents, like spirit, *nous,* soul, knowledge, science, virtues, *logoi,* opinions, perfection, existence, life, understanding, and still higher, existentiality, vitality, the power of understanding, and above all that, *on* (existent) alone, the very one who is the one and only *on* (existent).

If our *nous*[27] is rightly introduced to these concepts, it under-stands them and is formed from them and our knowledge is firm, no longer remaining in the confusion of questioning. But since such understanding is of another, by a certain comprehension and defini-tion it is shown that other *onta* (existents) are merely *onta* (exist-ents), since in that which is knowledge of another, the intellect

---

with the Son at the summit. Hadot remarks (TTT 706) that the commenta-tors who introduced a class of being to correspond with each Platonic dialectical distinction in the *Sophist* doubtless felt that this was justified by the ultrarealism of the Platonic forms. The root of philosophic idealism is here, inasmuch as what is intellectually known is real whereas what is not intellectually known is unreal. Hence, consciousness is not merely mental but ontological.

25 *ad Cand.* 8,20 and 11,2.

26 Creation is from abundance; Victorinus does not specify any creation *ex nihilo.*

27 In this paragraph and the next we are introduced to the intellectuals which, as distinct from their objects, are souls. The soul's intellect is not a separated intellect, and inquiry into reality (philosophy) begins in the soul. Cf. *ad Cand.* 8,3. The soul's consciousness of "otherness" through knowledge lets it know itself as an intellectual rather than as an intelligible, and witnesses to its lack of self-identity. The intellectuals are potential and passive; the intelligibles are actual.

is as[28] another with respect to the intelligible. Therefore the intelligibles are the truly existents, the intellects are the merely existents. But all these latter are in the nature of intellectual souls, not yet having knowledge but disposed for knowledge. For when the *nous* has been aroused in the soul, it illuminates the intellectual potentiality of the soul, enlightens it, giving it face and form, and there is born to the soul knowledge and perfection. And that is why the soul is also called substance, since every substance is a subject. But every subject underlies something else. But the soul underlies the *nous* and spirit. Therefore the soul is substance.

(8) Therefore all those things which are souls are merely *onta* (existents) and nothing more, not truly existents. Our soul therefore comprehends the truly existents since if the *nous* enters into the intellectual soul, it comprehends likewise also the *onta* (existents) that is, the intellectuals themselves—for the soul knows since it is soul—and thus by means of the existents knowledge is brought about of the existents, that is, of the truly existents.

As for the other two modes, the not truly nonexistents and the nonexistents, a notion of these is obtained through a conversion[29] of the notion of *tou ontos* (the existent). For one does not know *to mē on* (the nonexistent) through *to mē on* (the nonexistent), but through *to on* (the existent) *to mē on* (the nonexistent) is grasped. Therefore *to mē on* (the nonexistent) is, as it were, a removal of *tou ontos* (the existent). Such a removal is a certain formlessness, but nevertheless it is, yet not as *on* (existent) is. For every *to on* (the existent) both in existence and in quality has form and appearance. Therefore *to mē on* (the nonexistent) is unformed. But that which is unformed is something. Therefore *to mē on* (the nonexistent) is something. Therefore the *mē onta* (nonexistents) are and for this reason are the not truly nonexistents. And these not truly nonexistents have more potentiality for "to be" than *mē onta* (nonexistents). For this reason we have this natural order of *tōn ontōn* (the existents): *ontōs onta* (truly existents), *onta* (existents), *mē*

---

28 The "as" derives from an *ut* added in the CSEL edition.
29 Conversion here indicates deception. Soul can be distracted from the knowledge of reality by imagination portraying the nonexistent (the sensible) as existent. Frightened by the indefinite, the formless, the nonexistent, the soul imagines what is unreal to be real. Cf. *Enn.* 2.4.10.

ontōs mē onta (not truly nonexistents), *mē onta* (nonexistents).

(9) But we have said what the truly existents and the existents are. Now, however, we shall say what the not truly nonexistents and the nonexistents are.

Since the power of God is both intelligible and intellectual, through intelligence existents appeared. But intelligence operates in two ways:[30] by its own intellectual power and according to an imitation of understanding, even by sense. But in return, sense, since it is an image of what is understood and an imitation of intellectual knowing, becomes if it receives perfectly the act of intelligence which strengthens it in its own action, a close neighbor of pure intelligence. Such is the intelligence which comprehends heavenly realities and those realities which are in the aether, those which are in nature and which are born and reborn in *hulē* (matter), all things of this kind are within the power of sense intelligence; and "to be" is for them in some way "to be" and "not to be." For the heavens and all in them and the entire world are a mixture consisting of *hulē* matter) and form; therefore it is not simple. Therefore the parts of the world which participate in intellectual soul constitute the potentiality and the nature of those which are not truly nonexistent. For these use intelligence but intelligence according to sense and according to sense they are changeable and alterable, but according to intelligence, unchangeable and unalterable. But how so? Because sense understands nothing else but qualities, whereas it does not perceive nor comprehend the subject, that is, substance. For qualities are changeable but substance is unchangeable. But although the soul is a substance, it is also said to be changeable. How so? Consider the following:

(10) When the soul considers and knows existents in the world, if these are animals and animated things that it is knowing, these insofar as they have a soul are not truly nonexistents.[31] For in some way they are *onta* (existents) insofar as they have a soul, and in

---

30 In sects. 9 and 10 there is treatment of *Logos* as creative intelligence (cf. *Sophist* 265C), whose double aspect, noetic and sensible, is noted by Hadot (TTT 709) as a Chaldaean doctrine. This second *Nous* is a dyad. In matter as in soul, quality defines the substance; materiality constitutes the substance of matter; intellectuality constitutes the substance of soul.

31 Cf. *ad Cand.* 8,20 and 9,20.

some way they are *mē onta* (nonexistents) insofar as they have a changeable *hulēn* (matter) and changeable qualities. And these are those which we have called *mē ontōs mē onta* (not truly nonexistents).

But when we imagine inanimate *hulē* (matter) alone—but I call inanimate whatever is without intellectual soul—the sense bewildered through qualities, the soul comprehends, as it were, *mē onta* (nonexistents). For qualities are changeable and in that respect are *mē onta* (nonexistents). Indeed that very subject which is called *hulē* (matter) is indetermined, and that is why it is said to be without quality. But if it is determined, it is called quality and not qualified *hulē* (matter). And the first qualities are fire, air, water, earth. *Hulē* (matter) according to itself is without mixture of anything else. If therefore that which is qualities is that which is *hulē* (matter), therefore qualities are *hulē* (matter). For quality does not come to *hulē* (matter) as an accident, but quality is *hulē* (matter). For it cannot be quality through itself, but by that which it is, by that it is *hulē* (matter) and since it is always *hulica* (material), it is nothing other than *hulē* (matter). And just as the soul, because it is intellectual, is soul, and because it is always moving and self-moving—the soul is these things not as an addition or accident, but because it is these qualities the soul is substance—so also the very quality *hulē* (matter) is the very substance *hulē* (matter). But the soul differs from *hulē* (matter). For some do say that the soul is *hulē* (matter), because subject and quality are one same identical substance both for soul and *hulē* (matter). But there is a difference, as I said, because the soul, since it is intellectual, knows itself through itself. But in fact *hulē* (matter), since it is absolutely and totally unknowing, has neither knowledge nor feeling in sensation. And that is why the soul when it is alone and pure is the existents; mixed with *hulē* (matter), it is the not truly nonexistents, but the *hulē* (matter) alone is the nonexistents. The soul is the nourisher of all things and *hulē* (matter) is nourisher of all things. But the soul by its own power is the nourisher of all things and the begetter of life. *Hulē* (matter), however, without soul, rarified and condensed, always awaits animation, having soul from soul. These are therefore and are called *mē onta* (nonexistents). Let us now consider these nonexistents.

(11) You have, therefore, four modes: the truly existents, the existents, the not truly nonexistents, the nonexistents. Through the turning round and intertwining of these terms one can imagine two more modes: the not truly existents and the truly nonexistents. But the not truly existents signify the same thing as the mere existents. For they are simply the not truly existents. But in fact, the truly nonexistents have no place so that they may exist. For since all is full of God, it is sacrilegious and impossible that the truly nonexistents both be named and have being, those which by the intelligence alone, as we have declared,[32] are born in the soul not from nonexistents but from existents according to privation, these truly nonexistents being neither in their substance nor in thought.

d) God's place among existents and nonexistents

(12) Let us therefore come to see what God is and among which existents he is.[33] The truly existents are the first and the most honored. Is God among these? But for them also he is cause, for them he is giver and father. And it is not possible to say that he is, himself, the things to which he has given being. For since he is the one and only, although he willed that there be many things, he did not will that he himself be one of them, but willed that which is the One-Being, and in this way he willed the many to be.

Perhaps now you say, Candidus: I recognize there my own words, and for this reason I say that it is from nonexistents that is born the son of God according to creation, not according to begetting. But the *mē onta* (nonexistents), what have we said that they are? The absolutely nonexistent—we have not said this, have we? But already it is evident that this is not so. It is also evident that the nonexistents are described according to four modes, of which two are: the absolutely nothing and the absolutely transcendent, and the others, according to difference in nature and according to that which is not yet, because it is potential being, not yet actual being.

---

32 Cf. *ad Cand.* 5,8.
33 In sects. 12–14 we find the heart of Victorinus's answer to Candidus. God the One transcends this list of existents but he does so as the abundance or plenitude of existence. Hence his mediation with multiplicity is achieved through the One–Being, the Son or Creative Intelligence possessing the multiplicity of existents; in this sense there is no creation *ex nihilo.*

(13) What therefore in fact is God if he is certainly not one of
these: neither the truly existents, nor the existents, nor the not truly
nonexistents, nor the nonexistents?[34] For God produced these so
that he is cause of them all. It is sacrilegious, however, to suggest
that God is among the truly nonexistents. Necessarily we say
that through superiority and preeminence over *tōn ontōn* (the existents) God is above all existence, above all life, above all knowledge,
above every *on* (existent) and the *ontōs onta* (truly existents);
indeed he is unknowable, infinite, invisible, without idea, insub-
stantial, inconceivable, and because transcendent, he is nothing of
existents, and because he is above existents, he has nothing from
existents. God is therefore *mē on* (nonexistent).

(14) What, however, is this *to mē on* (the nonexistent) above
to on (the existent)? He is that which is known neither as *on* (existent) nor as *mē on* (nonexistent), but as knowable in ignorance since
he is simultaneously *on* (existent) and not *on* (existent), who by his
own power has produced and led *to on* (the existent) into manifestation. But this process is *logos*.

3. The Begetting of the Son As Existent

What is the fact? Has God who is above the *on* (existent) produced from himself just as he is or from another or from nothing?

---

34 In sect. 13 and the greater part of 14 we are told what God is not. It is
thus the first lengthy treatment of negative theology which stresses that
God the Nonexistent transcends the Existent. Cf. *adv. Ar.* I 49–50; IV 19,
also *Cand.* I 1,26–31 and 8,27. In sect. 13 note the doctrine of "participation." This is an important section for understanding what Christian
thought, unlike pagan thought, means by preexistence. All things preexist
in the Son; the Son preexists in the Father. The Nonexistent (God the
Father) transcending the Existent is the Existent in potentiality or a state
of nonexpansion or hiddenness. The manifestation of the Existent is a self-
manifestation, a self-actuation. Thus, consubstantiality is safeguarded; the
Father is the Son in potentiality, the Son is the Father in act. To exist is to
manifest. The emphasis here is on the Son's preexistence; there was no
need for the Son to be created since he always preexisted, that is, was in
the bosom of the Father. According to Hadot (TTT 715) this notion of
begetting as manifestation developed in Neoplatonism under the influence
of the "Chaldaean Oracles" written by Julian the Chaldaean, a contemporary of Trajan (see above, Introd. n. 14); cf. W. Kroll, *De oraculis
Chaldaicis* 16 (*Breslauer philosophische Abhandlungen* 7.1 [Breslau
1894]), and C. Ruelle (ed.), Damascius: *Dubitationes et solutiones* 96

From another? But from what other? For there was nothing before God. Nor was there an equal so that God was from another God. Therefore, from nothing? And how? For if he produced *to on* (the existent), it is true to say that he who is above *to on* (the existent) has begotten *to on* (the existent) rather from himself than from nothing.

For that which is above the *on* (existent) is the hidden *on* (existent). Indeed the manifestation of the hidden is begetting, if indeed the *on* (existent) in potentiality begets the *on* (existent) in action. For nothing is begotten without cause. And if God is the cause of all, he is cause also of the begetting of *tou ontos* (the existent) since he is certainly above *to on* (the existent) although he is in contact with *tō onti,* (the existent) both as his father and begetter. Indeed, the one who is pregnant has hidden within what will be begotten. For the embryo is not nonexistent before birth but it is in hiding and by birth there comes into manifestation the *on* (existent) in action which was *on* (existent) in potentiality; and so that, to tell the truth, *tou ontos* (the existent) comes to manifestation by the action of *on* (existent). Indeed the action begets outside. But what begets it? That which was within. What therefore was within—in God? Nothing other than *to on* (the existent) the truly *on* (existent), but rather the *proon* (preexistent), which is above the universal *on* (existent) genus that is above the *ontōs onta* (truly existents), the *on* (existent) by potentiality having now become act.

4. *The Begotten Existent Is the Son Jesus*

This is Jesus Christ. For he himself said: "If it will be asked: who sent you? Say *"ho ōn"* (He who is). For only that *on* (existent) who is always *on* (existent) is *ho ōn* (He who is)."[35]

(15) Therefore Jesus Christ is Son and only begotten Son, since that *proon* (preexistent) has begotten nothing other than the *on* (existent) before all things and the absolutely perfect *on* (existent)

(Paris 1889) 1.244.15. This leads to the explanation of the begetting as self actuation, without any passivity. Act is manifestation; potentiality is hiddenness. Cf. *adv. Ar.* IV 18,62.

35 Victorinus as theologian inquiring how the Scriptural names for Jesus correspond with the characteristics of the Existent as described by the philosopher. Cf. Ex 33.13; Jn 1.18; Col 1.15–18; Phil 2.9.

which can coexist with no other, because that which is absolutely perfect has no need of another. For the one and only *on* (existent) is the universal *on* (existent) and above the supreme genus *on* (existent) is the one and only *on* (existent).

Since truly this *on* (existent) is not that *on* (existent) which has perfect potentiality, this *on* (existent) is born of potentiality, "before all things."[36] before the truly existents and the existents, first *on* (existent) from whom are all things which exist, and "through whom" and "in whom." Thanks to this the *on* (existent) in act is the image of *tou ontos* (the existent) which is more powerful insofar as he remains always in himself with no progression.

(16) What then? We say that Jesus is the first *on* (existent), the *on* (existent) before all things,[37] through whom are all existents. For this is the "name above every name."[38] For *to on* (the existent) is the principle of names and principle of substances, as I have frequently and in many places declared.[39]

On the other hand, indeed, have we not said that Jesus is the *Logos* "with God"?[40] Even more. We say also that he is the *Logos* "in the principle," and we say that this *Logos* is "God."[41] This reality proclaims itself through the herald John. Even demons profess that this is so. But it was said that "in the principle was the *Logos*."[42] And, as you yourself say,[43] that is not a principle, that which precedes another principle. For "without principle" is the "principle" if it is true both that it is and is called principle. Therefore the one who was "in the principle" is from all eternity either in God or "with God." For the *Logos* was "with God" and was "in the principle." Therefore he always was. If he always was, it is necessary that he is not from nonexistents, nor is he made. John says: "No one has ever seen God. The only Son who is in the bosom of the Father, he himself has declared him."[44]

---

36 Cf. Col 1.16–17.
37 Cf. Col 1.15–18.
38 Phil 2.9.
39 Cf. *ad Cand.* 2,34–35.
40 Jn 1.1.
41 Cf. *ad Cand.* 2,30–31.
42 Jn 1.1.
43 Cf. *Cand.* I 3,22–24.
44 Jn 1.18.

5. The Scriptural Names of Jesus Witness That He Is the Son of God

We have therefore these simultaneous names, that Jesus is the *on* (existent), that he is *Logos,* that he was "in the principle," that he was "with God," that he was "in the bosom of God."[45] Does not all this signify with evidence and clarity that he is Son, to whom are attributed these predicates: he is the *on* (existent), and the *on* (existent) before all things? If the Father is God before there is the *on* (existent), "to be" is conceived as potentiality of that which is the *on* (existent). Because truly *to on* (the existent) has sprung forth by his own power, that he has in his Father, *to on* (the existent) himself, which had been hidden, beginning its manifestation. And this is the divine and ineffable begetting.

Therefore the dogma that Jesus is from nonexistents must be destroyed.

B. THE *LOGOS* WAS BORN OF GOD AS THE ACT OF "TO BE"

1. Definition of the Logos

(17) Let us consider something else if Jesus is the Logos.[46] What is the *Logos*? I say that it is a certain active paternal power which so

---

45 Cf. Jn 1.1; 1.18.

46 In sects. 17–23 there is a sustained contrast of *esse–agere,* corresponding to Father and Son. *Agere* is the procession of the *Logos.* God the Father is the hidden *Logos;* the Son is the revealed *Logos,* the Creative Intelligence through whom things come to exist. Cf. Jn 1.1; *adv. Ar.* I 6,1–9; *Sophist* 263E. The analogy is with the human *logos* by which the soul knows. Note both the ontological priority of being over action as well as the identity of action and being. The Existent acts as *Logos* in function of the creative will of God. Cf. *Enn.* 5.1.6; 6.7.13. The Son's self-begetting is fundamental to Victorinus's trinitarian theology; cf. *adv. Ar.* IV 13,5; III 17,15; and Introd., sect. 19,a. Hadot (TTT 726) underscores the indebtedness to Porphyry for this; cf. Porphyry, *Philosophica Historia* 18.14–15: "For the procession of the *Nous* did not take place thanks to God's motion as moved to beget the *Nous,* but the latter with his own motion advanced from God." The *Logos* is *agere* hypostasized. The exegesis of the "Chaldaean Oracles" influences this development; for example, Synesius (ca. 370–414, Neoplatonic philosopher and bishop of Ptolemais) *Hymn* 4.6; Hadot, PV I 467.

We find here the first appearance of the word "consubstantial" in Victorinus's treatise; consubstantiality is indicated by the identity of *esse* and *agere.*

moves itself and disposes itself that it is in act, not in potentiality. If it is thus, why was the *Logos* with God? Necessarily on account of this: so that through this *Logos* there might be produced "all things" and "without" him "nothing." Therefore God acts through the *Logos* and always acts. The *Logos* is therefore the active power which puts itself in motion so that what was potentiality might be actuality.

2. *God Himself Is the Unbegotten* Logos

Therefore we call him Logos when he was "in the principle." But does not to be "in the principle" signify to be unbegotten? Truly so. That is why the *Logos* is also God because he was "with God" and "in the principle,"[47] just as God also is the unbegotten *Logos* since God himself is *Logos,* but *Logos* silent and in repose. So you see the necessity of knowing that the *Logos* is unbegotten rather than made from nonexistents.

(18) What next? How is our knowledge induced, how is it put in movement? According to *Logos.* Not so that it sees the *Logos* as such, for the *Logos* is *Logos* of another or for the sake of another. According to what it is, it is for this: to establish that another exists. And it is absolutely not otherwise.

The *Logos* is therefore father and producer of all things, he "through whom all things have been made and without whom nothing has been made."[48] But power of this kind which belongs to the *Logos,* power of establishing and making another should not be understood in the same way as power in the cause of all things, God. For God is the one who also establishes the *Logos* himself. For if God is first cause, he is not only the cause of all things, but he is also cause for himself. Therefore God is through himself both *Logos* and God.

3. *"To Be" and "To Act," that is, God and* Logos, *Are Father and Son*

(19) But since "to be" itself, which is to move itself and to know, that is, to act, is first through power, first, I say, through

---

47 Cf. Jn 1.1.
48 Jn 1.3.

creative power, therefore by necessity "to be" itself precedes. Therefore, to move oneself and to know and to act are from that which is "to be." But that which is "to be" in act is second: this is to be Son. The Son and the Father are therefore the same, all the more so because this "to be" itself, which is the Father, by the very fact that it is "to be" is to act and to work. For up there "to be" does not differ from "to act." For that "to be" is one and simple and always one and alone. In the Father is therefore the Son, and in the Son the Father.

4. How Are God and Logos Father and Son?

(20) How therefore is it achieved, how are they Father and Son, if they are together or rather not two together but one both alone and simple? If it is necessary to inquire—for it suffices only to believe—let us explain insofar as it is allowed.

First, it is clear that the *Logos* "with God" is neither other than God nor from another than God. For the Gospel says: "in the principle was the *Logos* and the *Logos* was with God." Again it says: "the only begotten Son, who is in the bosom of the Father." How do you understand or interpret these expressions? The Romans translate *pros ton theon* by *apud Deum* (with God),[49] as if it were completely interior, that is, within God's existence. And this is true. For in "to be" there is also inherent "to act." For in God is the *Logos* and thus in the Father is the Son. For "to be" itself is the cause of action. For it is necessary that "to be" be first, for "to act" is within it. And these are two; according to power I say two, but according to our knowledge of their simplicity, one and only. If therefore the cause of action is "to be" itself, "to act" is begotten from "to be." But "to be" is the Father; therefore "to act" is the Son.

(21) What therefore is begetting or appearance of action?

First—if one must use this term, and so that one does not imagine the least appearance of time, I say first according to our knowledge—first, then, "to be" itself turned towards itself, both to move itself and to know interiorly preserves an absolutely perfect happiness, established in repose. But it belongs also to the very happiness and

---

49 Jn 1.18.

greatness of God both to move himself and to act both within and without.[50] How it is possible that God is existing both within and without both in all things and in the totality, must be said later.

(22) But now consider the cause for imagining the appearance of time, according to before and after when all is accomplished absolutely outside of time. For all this is from all eternity.

Therefore God, absolutely perfect and perfect above all kinds, he who has created and who is cause of all, has not been and has not willed to be the unique one which is one and only, but he has been and willed to be also those Many and that Totality which "to be" is by power. Indeed without action how was it possible for all the others to be? Action therefore sprang forth from the will of God. But the action itself was the will itself. For there all is simple. Therefore the *Logos* who is "in God" is *God himself* and also will, knowledge, and action and life has proceeded by a self-begetting movement from "to be" towards his own "to be," that is, into "to act" and there appeared "to act" itself which truly made all things. Indeed he himself was born from "to be" into "to act," having in "to act" also "to be." Just as that "to be" has both "to act" and "to be," so this "to act" has also "to be." But this "to act" itself is "to be" just as that "to be" is that which is "to act." Therefore these two are one and simple.

5. Conclusion: Jesus, the "To Act" of "To Be" Does Not Come from Nothing and Is Consubstantial with God

(23) If this is so, Jesus does not come from nothing, because from "to be" action has appeared, since action itself was already in "to be," nor was Jesus not *homoousios* (consubstantial) because "to be" which is substantial is unique for both, and action is unique, since indeed "to be" itself is also "to act" itself, and "to act" is also "to be."

This is the Son, this one who is from the Father, the one who is "with God," the one who is "in the bosom of the Father," the one who is within and the one who is without. For in act he is without, in "to be" he is within and in the Father, so that "in God he is God"

---

50 We are confronted with another set of the philosophical fragments (Group II) dealt with in sects. 91–95 of the Introd.; cf. Hadot, PV II 28.

but in action he is Son, so that wherever he is, he is both "to be" and action; and in this way the Father is and the Son is both God and *Logos*.

IV. REFUTATION OF ARIAN OBJECTIONS

1. Jesus Comes from Nothingness

(24) Where therefore is that impious and blasphemous opinion?[51] Where is there room for the opinion that Jesus Christ, the Son, is something other, is from another, and, what is more, is from nothing? Where is that very thing which is nothing? That which truly is nothing does not occur in God nor in God's knowledge. For the true thinking of God is of true things. But that which truly is not is false. Therefore God does not think that which truly is not. But we are mistaken when we believe that the power of God is greater if it makes existents from truly nonexistents. But in the measure that the power of God can do all things, in that same measure, according to its power, it produces nothing other than that of which it is the power for their existence. But of the truly nonexistents, there is absolutely no power at all.

(25) But how therefore has there been made the action of existents when there is no existing power of nonexistents? Certainly if it is by the power of God that "to be" comes from nonexistents, then

---

51 In sects. 24–30 we find a refutation of Arian objections. If God made all by his *Logos,* then God could not have made the *Logos;* since the *Logos* is no other than the Son, the Son is *not made* like all things. Note that for Victorinus substance indicates *esse* or *to be,* not a composition of subject and accidents. Cf. *adv. Ar.* I 30,26–30. As Hadot indicates (TTT 729), Candidus, like any Arian, misinterprets Scripture, failing to note that *factus,* whenever used of Christ, is used with a complement and not used absolutely. In these instances Scripture speaks of salvation, of the Son's action, not his substance. Athanasius, in his *Orations against the Arians* (PG 26.120 ff.), knew this Arian use of *factus* and his refutation is the same; all the texts cited by Arians actually relate to the economy of salvation (PG 26.141B, 145B, 256A). It is amazing that the Arians denied the begetting of the Son lest change be implied in the Father and yet seem strangely certain that creation introduces no change in the Father. Cf. *adv. Ar.* I 43,38. Yet in their own souls they had a model for spiritual begetting: *Nous* begets *Logos* rather than creates it. The word creature can be applied neither to Son nor Spirit. Cf. *adv. Ar.* IV 33,26–42; III 17,17–24, I 16,29.

those *mē onta* (nonexistents) are already *onta* (existents) as potential "to be," and that is why we said that those things did not exist, which, dwelling in hiddenness and in power had not yet appeared in action.[52] For all things were in God. For the *Logos* is the seed of all existents, but the *Logos* is in God. By action, that is, by the force of God, which is the Son, all things have been made and have appeared.

2. *"The* Logos *Is Outside of God"*

(26) But some sacrilegious people say: if the *Logos* was "with God" and if the Son is reposing in the "bosom" of God, not within, in the bosom, he is understood to be outside, not within.

What indeed? Did not God breathe out from within himself the soul of man? Did he not send out from within himself the creator of all things, the liberator and sanctifier of this very soul and the savior of this whole man and the one who raises him to angelic dignity? But what in truth?

From the earth God has formed man as well as the other animals, the quadrupeds and all others; from water he formed the living soul of the birds and of other creatures living in water; that is, he has made things by using one to make the other, and that is what is signified by "from nonexistents." In truth, whence do you say that Jesus is? For the Son is before all things. He wouldn't come from the void or in any way from nothing, would he?

Furthermore, did God animate the Son's body by soul or by spirit? He had no body before he entered the world. But he had soul. Therefore, was it already breathed upon him? No, not upon him. For how would he have breathed upon him? For he had no body. But if God did breathe something, it was the Son himself. If this is so, the Son is from God.

Likewise also he breathed the Spirit. For the Spirit is not from nothing. For God says: "all spirits I have sent forth by breathing."[53] If God himself breathed, the Son is from God and the Son is born; God has not made him. Therefore likewise neither "with God" nor upon the "bosom" of God is outside, but each one signifies within.

---

52 Cf. *ad Cand.* 4,4 and 5,11–16.
53 Cf. Is 57.16.

David also testifies to this where God says: "My heart has uttered a good word."[54]

3. Jesus Is Made by the Word of God

But is it that the Son has not been made like all things: "God spoke and it was made?"[55] Before there was a Son, neither was there a Word of God.

(27) What then do we say? Is it not necessary to profess that if the Word of God has made all things, the Word is first, the Word is the procreation of God, the Universal Word, the absolutely perfect Word that we and the prophets, the evangelists, and the apostles also call the *Logos* and Son?

Moses says it thus: "In the principle God made heaven and earth."[56] According to Aquila, this same text reads thus: *in capitulo:* "in the head, God has made . . . " And the Hebrews have this understanding. Whether "in capitulo" or "in principio," God has created in Christ. For Christ is principle and head, and this was frequently said.[57] He created all things in Christ; for Christ, as the seed of all things, is the *Logos.* Therefore Christ is first; for, "before every creature, he was."[58]

Whence therefore is Christ? If he is the Word, he is from God; if he is the will, he is from God, if, moreover, he is motion or action, he is from God. And if "to act" itself is also "to be," insofar as he is "to be," he is the Father, but as action he is Son. And since "to be" itself is action and "to act" is "to be," therefore Father and Son are also *homoousion* (consubstantial).

---

54 Ps 44(45).1.

55 Cf. Ps 32(33).9.

56 Victorinus refers to "Moses" the text (at Gn 1.1) of the Septuagint, but renders that Greek translation into Latin. He then repeats, again in Latin, a much later Greek rendering of the Hebrew, that of Aquila (about A.D. 140, see ODCC[2] 79). The two versions differed in a single word, that following "In the . . . "; the Septuagint gives "beginning" (Latin *principium*), Aquila "head" (*capitulum*).

57 Cf. *ad Cand.* 16,3; 2,34–35.

58 Cf. Col 1.15–16.

4. There Cannot Be a Consubstantial
Before the Substance Exists

(28) But how can there be a *homoousion* (consubstantial) when there is not yet an existing substance?

Names are discovered and drawn from those things which are later, from those which are after God. And since it is not possible to find a name worthy of God, from those things which we know we name God, bearing in mind that we are not speaking of him properly. In such a manner we say: God lives, God knows, God foresees: from our actions we describe the actions of God, that one existing above all things, not existing but as if existing, not being an *on* (existent), but as if an *on* (existent). It is in this way also that we attribute to God substance and existence and that we call his "to be" *ousian* (substance), although he possesses his "to be" otherwise.

5. "Christ Has Been Made"

(29) Likewise also when it is said that Christ has been made, this is not to say that he truly was made, but that although one, he is also in all and all is in him; for this reason we say he was made all in all, not that he was made to be but that he was made to be in such a way. For it is not said: the Son has been made, but: "he was made Lord for us."[59] So also Solomon says: "You have made me above your ways."[60] For, concerning spiritual generation, he immediately adds: "He has begotten me before all things."[61] John also says: "And what was made in him, is life."[62]

What further? Did not God make the creature and among creatures, first "heaven and earth?"[63] Therefore He did not make Christ. Christ is therefore born, not made.

Whenever, therefore, it is said that he has been made, it is after that first begetting that it is said: he has been made. In this way it is also said: "He was made of woman."[64] And in the Acts of the Apostles: "therefore let the house of Israel know most certainly

59 Acts 2.36.
60 Prv 8.22.
61 Prv 8.25; Jn 1.3–4.
62 Jn 1.3–4.
63 Cf. Gn 1.1.
64 Cf. Gal 4.4.

that God made this Christ, whom you have raised upon the cross."[65] All that is after the begetting that is unique, holy and ineffable. All these things are said not in respect to his existence, but in respect to his action and the ministry of his power and force.

Concerning begetting it is therefore evident that he is Son of God and they are *homoousion* (consubstantial), his substance being understood in its noble sense according to an improper signification, being a substance according to "to be." And so it has been shown how they are *homoousios* (consubstantial).

6. Last Appeal of Candidus: "Every Movement Is Change"

(30) Now, my dear Candidus, you offer the only remaining argument: if Jesus is Son, he is Son by begetting. But if begetting is movement and movement is change, yet it is impossible to conceive change in God and impious to speak of it, it is necessary that nothing is producible from God by begetting. Jesus is therefore not Son by begetting from God.

You have deployed your forces well, but against whom, friend Candidus? Perchance yourself? But especially yourself.

For you say that "God made Jesus."[66] What then? Is not making a movement? No less than acting. There is, therefore, change also in making, if there is motion in acting. But to act is to make, and to make is to act. If both imply movement, there necessarily occurs change which is unsuitable to God, as already asserted.

It must therefore be proclaimed either that making is not a movement or that not every movement is change. But making is a movement, and God, for whom it is absolutely impossible to change in any way, makes by movement. It remains therefore that not every movement is a change.

If not every movement is a change, what is it better to choose to say in respect to Jesus, that he is through begetting or through creating? That he is by begetting, according to divine knowledge. For although as soon as God speaks, God makes what he makes, yet speaking is a movement in relation to preexistent silence. Speaking would therefore be a change for the one who was in silence. But if

65 Acts 2.36.
66 Cf. *Cand* I 10,11.

through the Word God has made, there was the Word before any making. If the Word was prior, it was so by begetting. For the *Nous* begets the Word. Therefore, by begetting Jesus is, since Jesus is *Logos.*

V. CONCLUSION

1. The Modes of Filiation

Those who are learned speak of three ways to be son: by truth, by nature, by convention. To be son according to truth is to be son by his very substance, and on that account, to be both of the same substance; according to this mode are Father and Son, God and *Logos.* But son by nature is the mode in the generation of animals. Son by convention is, as it were, by adoption. There are also other ways: as by customs, age, teaching and as Paul says: "I have begotten you."[67] Therefore the mode of filiation according to truth is different from other modes and more divine than all others.

But the mode of filiation by this begetting, whether he is follow-ing the modes indicated or other modes, I confess to God—for it is by his power that it has been done—(31) has been sufficiently described by us in other books.[68] I have declared with the help of the Holy Spirit the whole procession, descent and return and I have declared the triple unity and the one trinity.

2. Doctrine of the Holy Spirit

For I do not admit your blasphemous teaching concerning the Holy Spirit: you pretend that he is sent for sanctification and that he has only a teaching function, and that he himself was also made just as all things in creation.

Indeed the Holy Spirit by his own action[69] differs from the Son, although he is himself Son, just as the Son by action is different

---

67 1 Cor 4.15.

68 On the interpretation of this clause (along with the words that close the sect.), see above, Introd., note 19.

69 This word "action" is important; Father, Son and Holy Spirit share a common substance but are distinguished according to act or movement. See above, Introd., sects. 18 and 19.

from the Father, he who is Father in respect to "to be." And thus of these three existing as one and the same, one is the divinity and undivided the majesty, and there is neither *antithea* (opposition to God) nor *atheia* (privation of God), but the three are one, the one is three, the three are three times three, and the same and only one. But concerning these three I have another treatise.

3. Final Prayer

(32) Now, save us, O father, pardon us our sins. And indeed it is a sin to say of God what he is and how he is and with a human voice to will to express divine realities instead of adoring them. But since you have given us the Spirit, O holy all-powerful Father, we both have and express a partial knowledge of you. But when we have a total ignorance of you we have knowledge of you. And again through faith[70] we have a perfect knowledge of you when in every word and always we proclaim you to be God the Father, and the Son Jesus Christ our Lord, and the Holy Spirit.

---

70 Faith is a more excellent knowledge than both negative theology and positive or analogical knowledge of God. By analogical knowledge of God we mean a knowledge of him derived from a knowledge of things that are like him, but denying in him any imperfection present in things.

LETTER OF CANDIDUS THE ARIAN TO
MARIUS VICTORINUS THE RHETOR

PREFACE OF CANDIDUS TO VICTORINUS[1]

LTHOUGH, MY DEAR FRIEND, VICTORINUS, you mar-
shal many arguments and illustrations by which you
try to prove that Christ was born, not made, yet Arius,
a man of keen intelligence, as well as his disciples,
and Eusebius excelling the most eminent of these, have expressed in
ther letters[2] opinions concerning this matter. We now subjoin those
letters.

Letter of Arius to Eusebius

To you, most loving master, man of God, faithful, right-thinking,
Arius, who is unjustly suffering persecution from Bishop Alexander
on account of the all-conquering truth for which you also struggle,
sends greetings in the Lord.

At the moment my father Ammonius was journeying to Nicomedia, it seemed quite fitting to send you through him greetings and
at the same time to remind you of the innate love and affection
which you have toward the brethren, for the sake of God and his

---

1 For the most part, this treatise is made up of Arius's Letter to Eusebius of
Nicomedia (d. 341/42) and Eusebius's Letter to Bishop Paulinus of Tyre
(d. 358); for the two letters see J. Quasten, *Patrology,* 3 vols. (Utrecht/
Antwerp 1950-60) 3.10 and 191 respectively. Paulinus strongly opposed
Arianism and died in Phrygia, where he was exiled after the Synod of Arles
in 353. Although Eusebius signed the Nicene Creed in 325, he was the
leader of the Arian party in the first half of the fourth century. He was a
fellow student with Arius in Lucian's theological school at Antioch. Lucian
had succeeded Paul of Samosata, whose Adoptianism denied the divinity of
Christ, a position which survived in the teaching of Arius. Quasten makes
the point that Arianism therefore arose at Antioch and not at Alexandria,
where it was first taught; cf. Quasten, *Patrology,* 2.143.
2 Both reason and authority must enter into theological thinking.

Christ. For this bishop is haughtily banishing and persecuting us and working all kinds of evil against us, in order to chase us from the city as though we were atheists, because we do not agree with him publicly affirming: "the unbegotten-begotten is always God, always Son; together Father, together Son; uncreated, the Son is consubstantial with the Father; he is always begotten; he is the unbegotten-begotten; neither for thought nor for one sole instant does God precede the Son. Always is God; always is Son; the Son is from God himself."

And since Eusebius, your brother, who is at Caesarea, as well as Theodotus, Paulinus, Athanasius, Gregory, Aetius and all who are from the East say that God, without principle, preexists the Son, they were made anathema except for Philogonius and Hellanicus and Macarius, about whom the anathema was silent—heretical men who call the Son, some an exhalation, others a projection, others a co-unbegotten.

And we cannot listen to these sacrileges even if the heretics threaten us with ten thousand deaths!

But as for us, what do we say, what do we think, what has been, and what is our teaching?

The Son is neither unbegotten nor part of the unbegotten in any way at all, nor drawn from a subject, but he subsists by will and thought, before time and the eons, fully God, only begotten and unchangeable. And before he was "begotten" or "created" or defined or "established," he was not. For he was not unbegotten. We are persecuted because we have said: the Son has a beginning, but God is without beginning. On account of that we are persecuted and also because we said that he is from nonexistents. But we said this to signify that he is not a part of God nor does he come from any subject.[3] That is why we are persecuted, you now know.

I pray that you may be strengthened in the Lord whenever you recall our tribulations, co-Lucianist, rightly named Eusebius.

(2) That is what Arius says. And concerning these matters Eusebius writes thus to Paulinus as follows:

---

3 Cf. *adv. Ar.* I 1,34–35.

⟨ *Letter of Eusebius to Paulinus* ⟩

. . . For since we have not heard of two unbegotten, and we have not been taught or believed in one divided into two nor in a corporeal something which suffers, lord, but in one truly unbegotten and one truly from him, and not made from his substance. This latter does not participate in his universal nature which is unbegotten, nor is the *on* (existent) from his substance but made absolutely other by nature and by power to the perfect likeness of both the disposition and the power of the one who made him. His origin is not only inexpressible by word, but even incomprehensible to thought, not only of men, but also of those who are above men; we believe it to be incomprehensible to all.

And these things are not established for us by *logismous* (syllogisms), but from Holy Scripture we have learned them. We say that he is created and established and made in substance, and we have learned that he is of unchangeable and ineffable nature, and that he has that likeness which is had to a maker, as the Lord himself says: "God has established me the beginning of his ways and before the eon he founded me and before all the hills he has begotten me."[4] But if he were from God, that is, if he were from him as his part or from the emanation of substance, it would not be said truly in Scripture that he is created or established, nor are you indeed ignorant of this, lord. For that which is existing from the unbegotten would not have been, in addition, created or established by another or by himself, because it would have been unbegotten from the beginning.

But if to say that he was born is to accord a certain subsistence[5] as if he were from the paternal substance itself and had from it identity of nature, we know that it was not of him alone that Scripture spoke of being born, but it has said it also of beings totally dissimilar to him in nature. And indeed it also says of men: "I have begotten sons, and I have exalted them, but they have rejected me."[6] And: "The God who has begotten you, you have

---

4 Prv 8.22–23; 8.25
5 Subsistence: the use of this word here is one of the reasons for Hadot's opinion that this word is not Victorinus's creation.
6 Is 1.2.

abandoned."[7] And elsewhere: "who," he says, "is the one who has begotten the dewdrops?"[8] He is not expressing that their nature is drawn from his nature, but that the nature of each one of these things which have been begotten is a production of his will. For nothing is from his substance, but all has been made by his will, each thing being as it has been made. And he indeed is God, but certain things are destined to be similar through him to the *Logos,* but certain are made according to the participation of substance, but all are made by God through the *Logos,* and all is from God.

On receiving these thoughts and affirming them according to the grace which by divine mercy is within you, take care to write to my lord Alexander. For I have come to believe that if you write to him you will make him ashamed. A greeting to all who are in the Lord. May the divine grace keep you safe and praying for us, lord.

---

7 Dt 32.18.
8 Jb 38.28.

AGAINST ARIUS

FIRST BOOK, PART A[1]

I. PROLOGUE

1. *Address to Candidus*

 Y DEAR CANDIDUS: In the first discourse of this work,[2] you proffered and developed many arguments, and some of them are stronger than the arguments of these men, i.e., Arius[3] and Eusebius. However, although their arguments have been aptly demolished, we were desirous of hearing them from their own letters, so that, while we are exposing their falsity by a complete refutation, we may also disprove your arguments by a refutation of theirs.

---

1 This so-called first part of a new work can be considered the last of the treatises against Candidus; cf. I 4–9; 23–29; 43,34–43. It refutes the letters of Arius and Eusebius communicated by Candidus; it also refutes the errors of Marcellus of Ancyra (d. ca. 374, see ODCC2 869) and of Photinus (*Cand.* I, n. 11) as presented in the Homoiousian document (which teaches that the Son is similar, not identical, to the Father). Apparently this document from the Synod of Sirmium (summer 358) was received by Victorinus as this book was being composed. This document forbade all mention of the term "substance" and its compounds, including *homoousion* and affirmed the Son's subordination to the Father. Séjourné (DTC 15.2892) points out that Victorinus rallied to the cause of consubstantiality at the precise moment that Pope Liberius signed the formula of Sirmium. Séjourné adds that this circumstance may well explain Victorinus's silence upon the subject of episcopal teaching and papal authority; his arguments are from Scripture and philosophy.

There are three divisions of Part A: 1) scriptural evidence for the begetting of the Son of God; 2) discussion of the letter of the Homoiousians; 3) a theological study of the names of Jesus, names which make sense if and only if the Son is substantially God, drawn from the divine substance. Cf. Augustine, *De trinitate* 1.2.4 (FC 45.7).

2 Victorinus evidently regarded his treatises *adv. Ar.* I–IV as a unity.

3 Arius (c. 250–c. 336) was probably a Libyan by birth and a pupil of Lucian of Antioch; after ordination he was charged with the church of

2. *Arian and Orthodox Positions*

First of all, the opinions of Arius and Eusebius must be definitively established in order to see on what points they are in agreement with us, on what points they disagree, and on what points they seem to be in mutual opposition.

Arius said: "That the Son is not unbegotten."[4] Likewise Eusebius said what amounts to the same thing: there are not two "unbegotten."[5] This is likewise our opinion. Arius said: the Son is not "a part of the Unbegotten," "nor is he from any subject."[6] Eusebius also affirms these two points. And he added: "nor is the one divided into two," but this is to say that the Son is not a part of the Unbegotten.[7] But Eusebius said: "he is neither a part nor an emanation."[8] That we deny [but] not in the same way. For the Son is not a part of the Father nor an emanation which by emanating would diminish that whence it had emanated. Finally in truth we cannot tolerate that he should be from no subject, not that we should say that he is from any other subject, but that he is from the Father as Son.

Arius said: "By the will of God the Son subsists before time and eons."[9] Eusebius also agrees. We say that he is before all eons and all time, but begotten, not made nor created nor established. Arius says that the Son was made, to wit, the "complete God, the only begotten, the unchangeable, who before he was created was not because he is not unbegotten."[10] Eusebius says the same, adding that the Son is similar in everything to his maker. We say the

---

Baucalis at Alexandria and was reputed an ascetic. When under Bishop Alexander of Alexandria he began preaching the subordination of Christ to the Father, he sought support from Eusebius of Nicomedia but he was excommunicated by Alexander. The Council of Nicaea in 325 condemned Arius. Although exiled, Arius, through the court influence of Eusebius, returned to Alexandria where Athanasius refused to receive him.

4 *Cand.* II 1,35.
5 *Cand.* II 2,3.
6 *Cand.* II 1,36.
7 *Cand.* II 2,4.
8 *Cand.* II 2,20-21.
9 *Cand.* II 1,37.
10 *Cand.* II, 1,38-40.

contrary. For we say that he is not similar but the same, because he is from the same substance.[11]

Furthermore, Eusebius adds that the "principle" of the Son cannot be known by man nor by any higher power or by "thought."[12] And he dares, nevertheless, to say that the Son is a creation, that he subsists not from any existent but by the Father's will and wisdom. Is not this to speak of the Son's origin? For if he says this: "he is not from existents, neither is he a part or emanation from the Father,"[13] then he knows not only the principles but the *logous* (definitions) of the principles. But if he does not know them, what boldness to say: God is this, Christ is that, the Father is this, the Son is that! But as for us, we speak of the Father as Father, the Son as Son.

3. The Plan of the Book

(2) And first of all, as with five brief passages Eusebius believed that he had proven that it could be taught that the Son is made, not born, so we shall teach that the Son is born, first of all by the use of all of Scripture. Then we shall prove this selfsame thing, that the Son is substantially Son,[14] if the Spirit of God permits and according to our power.

4. Introduction

And so, first of all, an introduction is undertaken. Paul to the Ephesians: "By favor of this reality I bend my knees to the Father of our Lord Jesus Christ, from whom all paternity in heaven and earth is named, that he may grant us, according to the riches of his

---

11 *Cand.* II 2,17.
12 *Cand.* II 2,11–12.
13 Cf. *Cand.* II 1,42 and II 2,20-21.
14 Ch. 2 responds against Eusebius that knowledge of God is possible if we attend to Scripture: Eph 3.14-21; Jn 1.18; 8.19; Rom 1.20; Jn 14.26. Through the Son who is substantially Son we can know the Father, and through the Spirit sent by the Father we can know him. Cf. *adv. Ar.* I 18,30; *ad Cand.* 20,3; 30,35. Cf. P. Séjourné, art. *Victorinus* (DTC 15.2900), who sees Victorinus teaching that the two sources of theological knowledge are the Son and the Holy Spirit or Scripture and inspiration. See above, Introd., sects. 10–12 for Victorinus's theological methodology.

glory, to be strengthened through his Spirit with might in the interior man. That Christ may dwell by faith in your hearts; that being rooted and founded in charity, you may be able to comprehend, with all the saints, what is the breadth and length and height and depth, to know also the charity of Christ, which surpasseth all knowledge, that you may be filled unto all the fulness of God. Now to him who is able to do all things more abundantly than we ask or understand, according to the power that worketh in us; to him be glory in Christ Jesus and in the Church unto all generations of time."[15]

What does this show? That it is possible to know God and the Son of God, and how one is the Father and the other the Son.

But there is also this in the Gospel according to John: "No man has seen God at any time except the only begotten Son who is in the bosom of the Father, he hath declared him."[16] It is therefore possible to speak of God and consequently of the Son also. For who has declared the Father? "The Son." Who is he? "He who is in the bosom." Therefore not only did he come forth, but the Son is always in the bosom, as the capable teacher about the Father. What did he tell? That there is a God? But Jews and pagans had previously said this. What therefore did he say? That God is Father, but that he is Son, and that he is of the same substance and that he has come forth from the Father. For he says: "Neither me do you know, nor my Father; for if you had known me, you would have known my Father also."[17] This he would never have said if he were not the Son and the Son substantially: "If you had known me, you would have known my Father." For if he were a creation, the Father would not be known through him, but the power of God and the Divinity, as Paul said: "For the invisible things of him from the creation of the world, are clearly seen, being understood by the things that are made; his eternal power also, and divinity."[18]

And the Holy Spirit has also declared Christ, as the Savior says in the Gospel according to John: "For the Holy Spirit whom the

---

15 Eph 3.14–21.
16 Jn 1.18.
17 Jn 8.19.
18 Rom 1.20.

Father will send in my name, he will teach you all things."[19]

If, then, such is the case, we have learned to know both the Father and the Son from Holy Scripture and from that Spirit whom by faith a holy man has as teacher.

II. SACRED READING

1. Saint John

A. THE *LOGOS* IS SON

(3) Let us therefore speak of the Scriptures and first, according to John.[20]

For he also says that the *Logos* was both "in the principle" and "was with God" and that the *Logos* was "God." Does he call any other, *Logos*? Only the Son.[21] What then? If the *Logos* is from no subject, how does the *Logos* have power so that all things are created through him, he who is from no subject? For it is impossible that that which is made from nothing be the seed of all existents. Next, if "he was in the principle," since the principle as principle is without beginning, he who "was in the principle," always was. What boldness then, what blasphemy to say that "once he was not,"[22] when John so often repeats: "The *Logos* was in the principle; he was with God; the *Logos* was God himself; he was in the principle with God. for

---

19 Jn 14.26.

20 Cf. *Cand.* II 1,36.

21 To the five verses of Eusebius (*Cand.* II 2) Victorinus, in the many pages that follow (into ch. 45), exposes the whole of Scripture but especially those verses employed most frequently by Arians, namely, Phil 2.5–7; Col 1.15–20. The adversaries are Arius and Eusebius (ch. 15,24; 23,3–6; 27,7; 28,36; 45,3–4); neo–Arians who say that the Son is made by the Existent (15,25; 45,4–5); Marcellus and Photinus (10,9; 21,33; 22,21; 23,1; 27,6; 28,33–38; 45,7); the Homoiousians themselves (15,9; 20,66; 22,2; 23,7; 25,4; 28,8–32,15; 41,1–20; 43,5–33; 45,23–48) the Patripassians, that is, those teaching that the Father suffered just as Christ suffered and underwent other human experiences (45,1–2). In all of this, St. John and St. Paul are mainly cited with emphasis upon *Logos* and *Imago* or *Forma,* leading to a philosophical elaboration from chapters 19–22.

22 Cf. *adv. Ar.* I 23,5–6. This is the doctrinal affirmation attributed to Arius by the conciliar anathemas since Nicaea.

granted that "was" often has the meaning of past time without excluding the idea of beginning, but here it must be understood as without beginning, since he said: "He was in the principle." This is what you yourselves signify when you say: "Before time, before eons."[23]

"All things,"[24] he says, "have been made through him and without him nothing has been made."[25] Indeed, without the *Logos* what is there to receive being? For only the *Logos* insofar as he is *Logos* both for himself and others gives "to be" to all existents. And on account of that he is truly equal to the Father—for the principal cause is cause both for himself and for others, being cause both by power and by substance—but the Father is precause. Whence it follows that the Son will differentiate himself this way, that he moves himself and acts for the sake of manifestation, whereas the Father, because of his transcendent divinity, acts in a way unknowable to us. For the Father is beyond beatitude, and for that reason he is "to repose"[26] itself. For to act, even to act towards perfection, is a troublesome motion. Such beatitude is achieved according to what is done.

(4) Therefore listen also to another thing! "To be" is the Father, "to act" is the Son. And "to be" is first, "to act" is second. Certainly "to be" itself has innate action within; for without motion, that is, without action what is life or what is understanding? Therefore there is not only "to be," but the first "to be" is "to be" itself, alone, insofar as repose is proper to it. In this way too that which is "to act," which is second, is called "to act" because it acts not internally but externally. For with the appearance of action, it both is and is called action, and it both is and is regarded as self-begetting. Thus therefore, that itself which is "to act" has also "to be" itself; but, rather, it does not have it; for "to act" is itself "to be"—for

---

23 *Cand.* II 1,37–38.

24 For this second part of ch. 3 and the whole of ch. 4, cf. *ad Cand.* 17,5–6; 18,5-12; 19, 1ff; *adv. Ar.* IV 19,26–29; I 13,9–16; Plato, *Sophist* 248E-249A. In explaining that "to be" is also "to act" but predominantly "to be," while "to act" is also "to be" but predominantly "to act," Victorinus makes his first use of that notion of predominance which was current in the Platonic tradition, cf. I 20,15.

25 Jn 1.3.

26 There is a brief appearance here of those philosophical fragments (Group II) cited by Hadot in PV II 28.

they are simultaneous and simple—and as to the "to be" and "to act" of those things above, it is generation which defines and divides them according to repose into "to be" and substance, and according to movement into action, operation.

And that is why "he was the light, which is the true light, which illumines every man coming into the world." The *Logos* is therefore light, that which is the true. And that is why "that which has been made in him is life and the life was the light of men." And the *Logos* himself, the true light, "was in the world and the world has been made through him," he who is the Son of God, of whom it says: "No one has ever seen God; the only begotten Son who is in the bosom of the Father, he has declared him."[27]

(5) All the above he said of the *Logos*[28] and linked it to the Son, declaring that there is no other Son than the *Logos*. Therefore the Son "was with God" and "was in the principle," and he was "God" himself and "through him all things have been made," and he himself is the "only begotten, and coming forth somehow, as it were, from the Father, he was "with" the Father in regard to that which is "to act" but in regard to that which is "to be," existing "in the bosom of the Father: he has spoken of the Father, having become the manifestation of the Father as "to act," which in the highest degree is *Logos,* the son, the Light, the Life.

B. THE *LOGOS* IS SON AND THE SON IS CHRIST

That the Son is God, John says in this way: "And the *Logos* was God." And again: "No one ascends into heaven except him who descends from heaven."[29]

That the Son is life: "So that whoever believes in him, shall not

---

27 Jn 1.18.

28 The passage, chs. 5–6, can be taken as the completion of the analogy of the revelation of God: as the Son reveals the Father, so the Holy Spirit reveals the Son. Or, Hadot may be right in suggesting (TTT 742) that the listing of the names of Christ implicitly refutes Marcellus of Ancyra who claimed that before the Incarnation the *Logos* had no other name than *Logos*. I 5,2–9 renders Victorinus's original conviction upon reading St. John's Prologue that the second hypostasis was originally confused with the first but, as self-knowledge, it distinguished itself from the first, merely making explicit the hidden knowledge of God, his self-identity.

29 Jn 3.13.

perish;"[30] and again: "But let him have hope, eternal life."[31]

That he is Son: "Wherefore he hath delivered up his only begotten Son."[32] He calls him Son, his Son, his only begotten Son. What else could be added to show that he is true Son?

That he is life: "So that whoever believes in him shall not perish, but may have eternal life."[33]

That Christ is the Son himself: "For God has not sent his Son to judge the world, but to save the world"[34]

That he is the light, he says of himself: "Since the light has come into the world."[35] John was not the true light, and that is why he says: "I am not the Christ but I have been sent."[36] John therefore was sent. But Christ is Son: "The one who comes from above is above all."[37] And again: "The one who comes from heaven."[38] Certainly it is also said that he was sent by God, for example, "For God sent his Son."[39] But these two words, both "coming" and "sent," signify that the Son is in the Father and that the Father is in the Son.

That Christ is life, he says to the Samaritan woman: "You should have asked him and he would give you living water."[40] And again: "Whoever will drink of this water will thirst again; but he who will drink of the water that I shall give him will not thirst forever, but the water that I shall give will rise in him like a spring of gushing water unto eternal life."[41]

That Christ is savior: "And we know that this one is the Savior of the world."[42]

That he is Son of God: "My Father worketh unto now."[43] Who

---

30 Jn 3.15.
31 Jn 3.15.
32 Jn 3.16.
33 Jn 3.16–17.
34 Jn 3.16–17.
35 Jn 3.19.
36 Jn 3.28.
37 Jn 3.31.
38 *Ibid.*
39 Jn 3.34.
40 Jn 4.10.
41 Jn 4.13–14.
42 Jn 4.42.
43 Jn 5.17.

says this? Christ. What blasphemy on his part to call Father someone who is not his Father! What wrath on the part of the Jews as they heard God called Father and were outraged against him who said that he was Son of God when he was not Son of God! If he were not, he would not have said it. But he did say so and he said so as a worshiper of God. He therefore spoke truthfully, and for that reason the unbelief of the Jews is punished.

(6) After that his whole response to the Jews makes evident that Christ is Son and the Father is God: "What the Father does, I also do."[44] "The Son does not act of himself unless he sees the Father acting."[45] For "the Father loves the Son."[46] "The Father raises from the dead, and the Son too raises."[47] "The Father has life in himself, and so has the Son."[48] And so on.

That the Son is *Logos* and that Christ is Son: "And you will not have his *Logos* dwelling in you, for you do not believe the one that the Father has sent."[49]

That he is Son: "My Father gives you true bread from heaven."[50]

That Christ is not man coming from a man:[51] "For this bread is from God who has descended from heaven."[52]

That he is life: "also giving life to the world."[53] And afterwards he says: "I am the bread of life."[54]

That he is from God: "No one has seen the Father except him who is from the Father."[55]

That the Father and Son are within each other: "as the living Father has sent me."[56] If the Son is life, the Father living, the Son is

---

44 Cf. Jn 5.19.
45 *Ibid.*
46 Cf. Jn 5.20.
47 Cf. Jn 5.21.
48 Cf. Jn 5.26.
49 Jn 5.38.
50 Jn 6.32–33.
51 Photinus's doctrine is rejected; cf. *hymn.* III; *adv. Ar.* I 21,34. Consubstantiality refers to identity of the subject and its quality in the order of simple "to be"; cf. *ad Cand.* 10, 19–24.
52 Jn 6.33.
53 *Ibid.*
54 Jn 6.35.
55 Jn 6.46.
56 Jn 6.57.

in the Father. For just as there is first something qualified, then the quality, so there is first the living God, and thus life. For he who is living has begotten life. Life lives through the living Father. For life is not prior to the living God, but first there is the living God and thus life and thus a living life. And that is why he next says: "And I live because of the Father."[57] Therefore the Father is also in him.

That he is both bread and life: "And whoever receives me will also live because of me. This is the bread coming down from heaven. Not as your fathers have eaten and are dead. He who eats this bread will live for all time."[58]

(7) Would a man who was only a man say this of himself? For if a man says this, he blasphemes and "God does not hear sinners."[59] But indeed Christ says that God hears him. He is therefore neither sinner nor mere man. It has also been said: "Vain is the hope in man."[60] And it is said: "As for us we hope in our God."[61]

Christ is therefore God, not coming from any other substance; "The Father is living and I live because of the Father,"[62] and: "I am the bread of life, the one who eats this will live for all time."[63] All these statements signify one substance. And that is why Jesus says that he is from above who says this: "If therefore you will see the Son of man ascending, where was he before?"[64]

That God is spirit, it is said: "God is spirit," and that the Son "is the vivifying spirit."[65]

That such is perfect faith in Christ, Peter says: "You have the word of eternal life. And we have believed in you, Lord, since you are Christ, the Son of God."[66] What is the word of eternal life? That if anyone hears you, "he will have eternal life."[67]

That he is from God: "I know him, because I am from him."[68]

---

57 *Ibid.*
58 Jn 6.57-58.
59 Jn 9.31.
60 Ps 59(60).12.
61 Ps 19(20).8.
62 Jn 6.57.
63 Jn 6.35; 6.58.
64 Jn 6.62.
65 Jn 4.24; 6.63.
66 Jn 6.68-69.
67 Jn 6.59.
68 Jn 7.29.

That Christ is the substance of the Father: "I in the Father and the Father in me."[69] And this is not through rank alone, but through substance.[70] If indeed it were through rank alone, how does he himself say: "My Father is greater than I,"[71] and how does one explain that the Father sends and the Son is sent? And, what is more, rank is given to the Son by the Father; according to this, therefore the Father is in the Son. Does the Son ever give rank to the Father, as to one not having it? By substance therefore both the Father is in the Son and the Son is in the Father. (8) But enough about that.

C. THE FATHER, THE SON, AND THE HOLY SPIRIT ARE CONSUBSTANTIAL

And again: that Christ himself who is the Son of the Father is also himself the Holy Spirit: "Jesus stood and cried out: if anyone thirsts, let him come and drink. Whoever believes in me as the Scripture has said, out of him flow streams of living water."[72] And this indeed was said of the one who receives the Spirit, who in receiving the Spirit is made a source pouring forth streams of living water. But Christ gives this Spirit, gives also living water as he himself says and the Scriptures: "This he said of the Spirit."[73] The source therefore is the one who receives the Spirit, and the source is the Spirit himself from whom flow streams of living water, as the Scripture says. "But he said this of the Spirit whom all those believing in him were to receive; for the Spirit had not yet been given, because Jesus had not yet been glorified."[74] But once again, the streams are the Spirit, but the source from which the streams flow is Jesus; for Jesus is the Spirit. Now therefore Jesus is the source whence flow the streams of the Spirit. For just as the Son is from

---

69 Jn 14.10.
70 In the remainder of this chapter and in chs. 8 and 9 Victorinus makes the point against the Anomoeans of Sirmium (357) that voluntary inferiority can only occur in cases of natural equality.
71 Jn 14.28.
72 Jn 7.37-38.
73 Jn 7.39; cf. Ez 47.1-12.
74 Jn 7.39.

the bosom of the Father and "in the bosom"[75] of the Father, so the Spirit is from within the Son. The three are therefore *homoousioi* (consubstantial) and on that account in all there is one God.

That he is not of this world: "I am the light of the world."[76] For on account of him the world lives and will live as long as it obeys him.

That all three are Spirit he already said: "God is Spirit."[77] And now to those saying: "Where is your Father?" he said: "You know neither me nor my Father. If you knew me, you could also know my Father."[78] But the Holy Spirit is clearly Spirit. But all these are both the Father and from the Father. Therefore *homoousioi* (consubstantial). For they are not spirits like other spirits; for they are made by God not from God. Therefore these three are *homoousia* (consubstantial).

That he is true Son: "For I came forth from God," as from the "bosom" of the Father, "and I come into the world."[79]

That before he was in the flesh Christ was: "Abraham your father rejoiced that he was to see my day; he both saw and was glad."[80] And again: "before Abraham was, I am."[81]

That he was not mere man: "As long as I am in the world I am the light of the world."[82] Who, moreover, gave sight to the blind? A mere man? Impossible!

That he is the Son of God: "Do you believe in the Son of God? He replied: "Who is he Lord so that I may believe in him? Jesus said to him: "You have both seen him and he who speaks with you is he."[83]

That they are from the same substance and power: "I and the Father are one."[84] (9) And again: "The Father is in me and I in

---

75 Cf. Jn 1.18.
76 Jn 8.12.
77 Jn 4.24.
78 Jn 8.19.
79 Jn 8.42; 1.18.
80 Jn 8.56.
81 Jn 8.58.
82 Jn 9.5.
83 Jn 9.35-37.
84 Jn 10.30.

Him."[85] Whence it is said in Paul: "Who being in the form of God did not consider it robbery to be equal to God."[86] These texts therefore signify both that they are one substance and one power. For how is it said: "I and the Father are one," and "The Father in me and I in the Father," if he did not have from the Father substance and power, wholly begotten from the All.[87] And how explain: "He did not consider it robbery to be equal to the Father." For he did not say: he did not think that he was equal, but: "he did not think it robbery." Therefore he willed to be inferior, not wishing his equality to be considered robbery. For among those who are equal, to be equal is considered or is not considered robbery. But we think that equality according to power is spoken of here.

First, such is not the opinion of Arius, namely, that the Father is greater in honor, power, glory, divinity, action; for Paul did say: "equal." And if they are equal in all these things, this is impossible without their being also of the same substance. For in God there is complete identity between power, substance, divinity, and act. For in him all is unity and simple unity. In addition: if the Son was from another substance and especially if he was from nothing, what must that substance be that is capable of receiving such divine powers? For equal is joined to equal and like to like. Therefore Father and Son are equal and on account of that also the Son is in the Father and the Father in the Son, and both are one.

(10) But enough of this for the moment.

Let us look at other texts of John. The Savior himself says: "I am the Resurrection"[88] because he is life itself.

But who is this one? Martha says: "Whereas thou art Christ, the Son of God, who has come into the world."[89]

That he is not a son such as we are: for we are sons by adoption, he by nature; and truly, Christ is also son by a certain kind of adoption, but according to the flesh: "This day have I begotten thee."[90] For if this is so, God has for son only a man. But in saying: "Before

---

85 Jn 14.10.
86 Phil 2.6.
87 Formula of Antioch (341).
88 Jn 11.25.
89 Jn 11.27.
90 Ps 2.7.

Abraham[91] was, I am,"[92] Christ has declared that he was first of all Son by nature. Therefore the opinion of Photinus is not true.[93] Then we are "not only nations" but also "sons who have been scattered."[94] Christ is therefore Son of God, we also are sons; but we are through adoption, we are through Jesus Christ, we are as scattered sons. But Christ is not a son in this way, is he? Therefore Jesus is Son by nature, we are sons by adoption.

That he is Son by nature, he himself also often says: "Father, I give you thanks that you have heard me."[95] And: "Father, save me from this hour;"[96] and again: "I have come forth from the mouth of the Father."[97] These words are not addressed to God the Father as we speak to him. For in calling himself Son and in calling God his Father, God is neither a liar nor impious, as he would be if this were not fully so. But through the body he endured the passion so that all might be accomplished in the mystery.

That before being in the body, Christ already was: "and I have glorified and again I glorify."[98] For in the mystery in the flesh "he humbled himself."[99] Therefore, before and after that, Jesus was glorified.

That on account of the mystery he is led into fearing and praying something like this: "Not for me did this voice come but for you."[100] This amounts to: I do this not for myself but for you.

(11) That Christ the son of man is the Son of God, light in the world: "We have heard from the law that Christ abides forever. And how do you say that the Son of man must be raised? Who is the Son of man? Jesus said to them: 'Yet a little while the light is among

---

91 In the CSEL text *Adam* has been substituted for *Abraham*, the reading of the SC edition. It is true that *Adam* is found in the Berlin Phillips 1684 MS and in the edition of J. Sicard, 1528. But *Abraham* appears in the text of Galland and I have retained *Abraham*.
92 Jn 8.58.
93 Doctrines attributed to Photinus correspond to anathemas of Sirmium (351).
94 Cf. Jn 11.52.
95 Jn 11.41.
96 Jn 12.27.
97 Sir 24.3(5).
98 Jn 12.28.
99 Phil 2.8.
100 Jn 12.30.

you.' " And next: "While you have the light, believe in the light, that you may become sons of the light."[101]

That he is *homoousios* (consubstantial) with God: "I am the way, the truth, and the life. No one comes to the Father but through me. If you have known me, you will also know my Father. And henceforth you do know him, and you have seen him."[102] And again to Philip: "He who sees me sees also the Father. Do you not believe that I am in the Father and the Father is in me?"[103] And again he repeats these texts and similar ones in which it is evident that the Father is what he is, the Son is what he is, and therefore there are two.[104] But since the Father is also in the Son and the Son in the Father, they are *homoousioi* (consubstantial).

That he does and will do all things: since I am from the Father,[105] "whatever you ask in my name, that I will do, so that the Father may be glorified in me."[106]

That Christ is also the Paraclete: "If you will have loved me and have kept my commandments, I will ask the Father and he will give you another Paraclete to dwell with you forever."[107] But who is the other Paraclete? "The Spirit of truth whom the world cannot see because it does not see him."[108] But the other Paraclete, that is, Christ, they have seen because[109] he was in the flesh and they have not believed in him.

That the Paraclete is the power of Christ: "But you know him because he dwells with you."[110] Therefore Christ has given him to them, for he said: "He dwells in you and is in you."[111]

(12) What does this mean? If God is Spirit and Jesus is Spirit

---

101 Jn 12.34–36.
102 Jn 14.7.
103 Jn 14.9–10.
104 Cf. Jn 14.9–10.
105 Cf. Jn 14.12.
106 Jn 14.13.
107 Jn 14.15–16.
108 Jn 14.17. Victorinus's text shows "see" in both clauses; in the Greek the first "see" is "receive" (or "accept").
109 The CSEL has added *quod* after *viderunt;* I have accepted this as strengthening the distinction between the visible and invisible Paraclete.
110 Jn 14.17.
111 *Ibid.*

and the Holy Spirit is Spirit, the three are from one substance. Therefore the three are *homoousion* (consubstantial).

That the Holy Spirit is from Christ as Christ is from God, and consequently the three are one: "I will not leave you orphans, I will come to you."[112] And again he says: "In that day you will know that I am in my Father, and you in me, and I in you."[113] This is known through the Spirit.

That the Paraclete is from the Son: "But the Paraclete, the Holy Spirit, whom the Father will send in my name, he will teach you all which I shall have said."[114] From this it is clear that God is in Christ and Christ is in the Holy Spirit; first, Christ is Paraclete and the Holy Spirit is Paraclete; then, God has sent Christ. What Christ has said, the Holy Spirit himself says.[115] But Christ spoke in parables and performed miracles; therefore he did all in a hidden way because he was in the flesh; just as he himself was within, so also the true was within parables and miracles. But the Holy Spirit teaches all things; indeed the Holy Spirit speaks to the spirit of men; he says whatever is so, and whatever is so he says without any figure of speech. And because of that: "He will teach you."[116] And what does he say? "Whatever I shall have said,"[117] said Christ. "I shall have said" is in the future. What future? Not the immediate future, but the one that comes after his ascent to the Father. And if this is so, the Paraclete coming from God in the name of Christ teaches what Jesus says. Is it therefore Jesus himself, or is he another Jesus, or is Jesus present in this other Paraclete, that is, the Holy Spirit, as God is present in him? Although existing as three in a series, these

---

112 Jn 14.18.
113 Jn 14.20.
114 Jn 14.26.
115 While Father and Son are one sole substance, Son and Holy Spirit are one sole movement or act with a twofold aspect: as vivifying, this is Christ; as illuminating intelligence, this is the Holy Spirit. Jesus is the Spirit manifested; the Holy Spirit is Jesus hidden in souls. The truth is hidden in Christ's teaching and action under external forms which simultaneously signify it and hide it; but the Holy Spirit speaks immediately to the soul. When Christ's action is being exercised in the sensible order, its intelligible aspect is hidden and attainable only by the interior action of the Holy Spirit.
116 Jn 14.26.
117 *Ibid.*

three are also one and the three are *homoousion* (consubstantial).
For Christ certainly says: "I go away and I am coming to you,"[118]
and "You will be given by God another Paraclete"[119] who has from
me all that he has; and all that the Father has he has given to me.
Indeed the whole mystery is this: the Father, unacting act, the Son,
acting act in respect to creating, but the Holy Spirit, acting act in
respect to recreating. But these things have also been said in other
books.[120]

(13) That the *Logos,* that is, Jesus or Christ, is both equal[121]
and inferior to the Father: "I go to the Father because the Father is
greater than I."[122] Likewise, Paul said: "He did not consider it
robbery to be equal to God,"[123] and that which has been said:
"I and the Father are one,"[124] because both Father and Son are
also act, and because he would not say: "The Father is greater than
I"[125] unless he had been equal to him. There is also added: if he is
the whole from the whole as light from light, if the Father has given
to the Son all that he has—but all includes substance and power and
dignity—the Son is equal to the Father. But the Father is greater
because he gave all to the Son and is cause of the Son's being and
mode of being. But he is also greater because he is inactive
action;[126] such act has more happiness because it is without effort;
it is unsuffering, the source of all existents, dwelling in repose, self-
sufficient and with no need. But the Son receives being and advancing by action toward act, comes into perfection by achieving
fullness by movement, having made all things which exist. But since

---

118 Jn 14.28.

119 Cf. Jn 14.16.

120 Cf. *hymn.* III 105-107.

121 The Son is not only equal to God as the synodal letter of Ancyra put it,
      but equal to the Father. Directed against Anomoeans, Homoeans, and
      Homoiousians, and argued from their own profession of faith at Antioch
      (341) and Sirmium (351).

122 Jn 14.28.

123 Phil 2.6.

124 Jn 10.30.

125 Jn 14.28.

126 Another appearance of those philosophical fragments assembled by
      Hadot from the writings of Victorinus and said to be "importations"
      from Prophyry; cf. Hadot, PV II 29.

"in him, for him, through him are created all things,"[127] he is always the fullness and always the receptacle; for this reason he is both impassible and passible. Therefore he is both equal and unequal. Hence the Father is greater.

That the Paraclete is from God and from Christ: "When the Paraclete will come, whom I shall send you from the Father, the Spirit of truth who will proceed from the Father."[128]

That there is a twofold power of the *Logos* with God, one visible, Christ in the flesh, the other in hiding, the Holy Spirit—therefore while the *Logos* was in presence, that is, Christ, the *Logos* in hiding, that is, the Holy Spirit, could not come: "Indeed, if I do not go, the Paraclete will not come to you."[129] Therefore these are also two, one coming from the other, the Holy Spirit from the Son just as the Son comes from God and, as a logical consequence, the Holy Spirit also comes from the Father.

That all three are one: the Father not an empty silence, but a silent voice, the Son already a voice, the Paraclete, utterance of the voice: "When he, the Spirit of truth, will come, he will go before you in all truth. But he will not speak the truth from himself," for Christ is truth, "but whatever he will hear he will speak, and what is to come he will tell you. He will honor me, since he will receive from me and he will announce it to you."[130] Then he adds: "All things that the Father has are mine."[131] Therefore he says: "he receives from me,"[132] because Christ and the Holy Spirit are one sole movement, that is, act which acts. And first there is "to live"[133] and from "to live" there is also "to understand." Indeed Christ is "to live" and the Spirit is "to understand." Therefore the Spirit has received from Christ, Christ himself from the Father, and for that reason the Spirit has also received from the Father. (14) Therefore all are one, but from the Father.

---

127 Cf. Col 1.16–17.
128 Jn 15.26.
129 Jn 16.7.
130 Jn 16.13–14.
131 Jn 16.15.
132 Jn 16.14.
133 First appearance in this treatise of the triad "to be," "to live," "to understand," fundamental to Victorinus's trinitarian theology. The great lines of his theological synthesis are latent in these metaphysical concepts and their reciprocal relatedness.

That Christ also has proceeded from the Father,[134] that is, that God sent him, and that is: he proceeded from God; for he says: "Since I proceeded from God, I proceeded from the Father."[135] It should be known that he also said: "And I have gone forth."[136] But because this is "from God" he previously said: "I proceeded from God" which signifies that God sent him. Believe therefore this first statement: "Since I have come forth from God." But from what God and as what? From that God who is my Father: I have come forth from the Father and have come into the world." The natural order of this discourse is this: I have proceeded from the Father, I have come forth from God, I came into the world. But the order of speaking is rendered from the standpoint of men: "Since you have loved me and have believed that I have come forth from God." For this is the first step toward faith. Next, however, "I have proceeded from the Father," explaining further he said from whom he was. Whence they also say: "We believe that you have come forth from the Father."[137] But what? Has he left on high God and Father? No. For he says: "I am not alone, for the Father is with me."[138] And this is not to understand that the Father has suffered. Nor did he himself suffer, but his human nature did.

That he came for the resurrection of the flesh: "Glorify the Son, that the Son may glorify you, even as you have given him power over all flesh, so that to all you have given him he may give everlasting life."[139] Therefore Christ is not only man but God in man.

That to have life is to believe in God and in his Son: "But this is eternal life: to know[142] you, the only true God and him whom you have sent, Jesus Christ."[141]

That he existed before the world: "And now glorify me, Father,

---

134 In this paragraph we see the Incarnation as occasioning not only the acknowledgment that Christ came forth into the world from the Father but that he is eternally generated from the Father.
135 Jn 16.27-28.
136 Cf. Jn 16.27-28.
137 Jn 16.30.
138 Jn 16.32.
139 Jn 17.1.
140 I have accepted the CSEL text change from *cognoscant* to *cognoscat*, to indicate that Christ had eternal life.
141 Jn 17.3.

with yourself, with the glory that I had before the world existed."[142]

That men come from God but not out of God: "I have manifested your name to the men whom you have given me"—from this it is clear that it is not all men—"they were yours, and you have given them to me and they have kept your word. Now I have known that all that you have given me is from you."[143] And what is so astonishing, if men came from God, if flesh also, because he himself has formed it? What then? Is it the same way with Christ? God forbid! This whole passage establishes this: that men came forth from God, but not all; also this again: that Christ existed before the foundation of the world.

That the Father has given all things to the Son, if he also gave his name; for he says: "I have kept them in your name, that which[144] you have given me."[145]

(15) We hold therefore that Christ has the name of the Father and that he is life[146] and has the power to give "to live." That he himself is life and the Father is life, it was said: "The living Father sent me."[147] And this is the substance of God and of Christ. They are therefore *homoousioi* (consubstantial). Next it was said that Christ is light[148] and God true light; for these terms refer to knowledge. And is the Holy Spirit anything different? Not at all. Well, then, is not light substance? It is. Therefore they are *homoousia* (consubstantial). And whatever God has, the Son has. Therefore they are *homoousia* (consubstantial). They are not therefore *homoiousion* (similar in substance) by any means. But of that we shall speak later.[149]

---

142 Jn 17.5.

143 Jn 17.5-6.

144 A new conjecture in CSEL, namely *quod* instead of *quos* would seem to be more consistent with the succeeding sentence. Instead of people whom God had given to Christ, it is the Father's name that has been given.

145 Jn 17.12.

146 Victorinus identifies John's doctrine of Father and Son as Life and Light as twofold aspect of *Nous* or *Logos* with his own triad: "to be," "to live," "to understand." Since life and light are substantial, the Gospel teaches consubstantiality. This is an allusion to the letter of Basil of Ancyra (4th century representative of the moderate party of the Arians).

147 Jn 6.57.

148 Cf. Jn 1.9; 3.19; 8.12; 9.5; 12.46.

149 Cf. *adv. Ar.* I 28,8 ff.

That he was born:[150] "For this was I born and for this I came into the world,"[151] to rule.

That the Holy Spirit is from Christ: Christ "breathed on them and said: receive the Holy Spirit.' "[152] All that is according to the Gospel of John.

2. The Synoptics

Let us even look also at some texts according to Matthew, for I pass over similar ones.

That Satan[153] also testifies that Christ is the Son of God; for he says: "If you are the Son of God;"[154] and he says that three times. But a second time testifying to the Son of God, he tried to discover if the Son of God was this Christ; for he says: "If you are the Son of God, cast yourself down. For it is written: that he will put his angels in charge of you."[155] He testifies, who says: "of you," he testifies that there is a Son of God and testifies that this is the Son of God. Next, the demons in their turn testify to him: "The demons also came forth from many, crying out and saying: "You are the Son of God."[156]

Listen Arius, listen Eusebius, and all you Arians, listen, especially you who say that Christ is from "to be," but according to the serpent's understanding: saying that since the Father, who made Christ, is the *on* (existent), the Son is also from "to be." Listen therefore. Satan calls Son of God the one to whom he promised the kingdom of the world; and he knows all that which is on high; for he is from there. What then? After the third temptation because the devil withdrew, he testified that Christ is the Son of God.

That the demons also have said that he is Son of God: "What have we to do with you, Son of God? You have come . . . "[157]

---

150 Same interpretation of Jn 18.37 in Ambrose, *De Isaac et anima* 5.46 (trans. M. McHugh, FC 65.37).
151 Jn 18.37.
152 Jn 20.22.
153 This argument is found in Hilary, *De trinitate* 6.49 (PL 10.196B; trans. S. McKenna, FC 25.218–19).
154 Mt 4.3.
155 Mt 4.6.
156 Lk 4.41.
157 Mt 8.29.

That we should not doubt Christ: "Blessed is he who is not scandalized in me."[158]

That the Son has everything the Father has: "All things have been given to me by the Father; and no one knows the Son except the Father; nor does anyone know the Father except the Son, and him to whom the Son chooses to reveal him."[159] What is the reason that only the Son knows the Father and only the Father knows the Son except that no one has his substance? For all who know the Father in his glory and his divinity, in his power, in his very act, also adore him. But since to know this is to know the very "to be" of God himself, that is, his substance, for that reason no one knows God except the Son having the same substance and having it from God. For no one can see in any other way God's "to be," as it is said: "The only begotten Son who is in the bosom of the Father, he has declared"[160] what is God's "to be." For he is in the bosom and in the *mētra* (matrix) of substance. Each one of the two is *homoousios oun* (consubstantial therefore), each one being, both by substance and by divinity, in the other, and each one knowing each other.

(16) Why then, Valentine, do you too say: "The first eon came forth and was not able to see the Father although wishing to"? John says that the Son is "in the bosom of the Father" and that he is always there; not only therefore does he see the Father, but he is always in the Father.

That it is a great sin to speak against the Holy Spirit: "Every blasphemy and sin shall be forgiven men. And whoever speaks a word against the Son of man, it shall be forgiven him. But whoever speaks against the Holy Spirit, it will not be forgiven him, either in this time or in the future."[161] First it should be clearly recognized that the Holy Spirit is the Spirit of God.[162] For he said: "In the

---

158 Mt 11.6.
159 Mt 11.27.
160 Jn 1.18.
161 Mt. 12.31–32.
162 In defining the Spirit as *Spiritus dei*, Victorinus faces the problem of the Holy Spirit's place in the Trinity. According to Mt 12.28 the Holy Spirit issues immediately from the Father; according to Jn 16.15 the Holy Spirit is after the Son, from whom the Spirit receives all. But then Son and Holy Spirit are one *Logos*, the unity of the Father's movement. The

Spirit of God I cast out demons."[163] Next we must see, with regard
to blasphemy and sin, what was the sin against the Holy Spirit which
the Jews committed, as he said. First, that no one will be forgiven
blasphemy and sin against the Holy Spirit. It is a sin to speak volun-
tarily in a blasphemous manner. But that does not suffice. He said
afterwards: even if someone says, involuntarily, such a word—which
is not a sin—it will never be forgiven him. If therefore the Holy Spirit
is the Spirit of God and the Holy Spirit has everything from the Son
of God, from the substance of the Father there is one substance for
the three. Therefore the three are *homoousia* (consubstantial), that
is *ousia* (substance) together. For if the substance of the Father is
Spirit, and if the Son is Spirit, but the Holy Spirit is the Spirit of the
Father, in what rank is the Holy Spirit placed? For he both precedes,
if he is the Spirit of the Father, and follows, if he has his being from
the Son. And again, if the Son as Spirit is one with the Father also,
and the Father is in the Son and all are existing in the others, they
are therefore *homoousioi* (consubstantial), having one and the same
substance and always together *homoousioi* (consubstantial), while
having their own subsistence according to action in respect to divine
relation.

(17) But enough about this. And, once more, what was said in
the Gospels suffices for us. For there are some texts of the same
kind in the others, as in the Gospel according to Luke: that Christ is
the Son of God, the Savior himself says: "How do they say that
Christ is the Son of David? And David himself says in the Book of
Psalms: 'The Lord said to my Lord, sit at my right hand.' David
therefore calls him Lord; how then is he his son?"[164] In this text he
himself proves this: that Christ both existed before he was in the
flesh and that he is the Spirit of God and is God.

Divinity is diversified according to action. Victorinus uses *subsistence*
here without comment; cf. Epiphanius, *Panarion* 73.11.6, which defines
the notion of hypostasis. Subsistence was already used in *adv. Ar.* I 2,25.
Séjourné (DTC 15.2914) states that the word "subsistence" is a creation
of Victorinus; Hadot does not think so (TTT 733).
163 Mt 12.28.
164 Lk 20.41–44.

3. Saint Paul

A. EPISTLE TO THE ROMANS

The three are Spirit, therefore consubstantial

Let us examine therefore also the Apostle.[165] For he says this of Christ to the Romans: that Christ is God: ". . . on the day of wrath and of the revelation of the just judgment of God."[166] Without doubt this is said of Christ. For he himself will judge.

That for God *to mē on* (the nonexistent) is nothing, Paul introduces a quotation from Genesis: "Because I have made you the father of many nations in the sight of God whom you believed, who gives life to the dead and calls things that are not as though they were."[167]

That the Spirit of God is the Spirit of Christ and at the same time the Holy Spirit: "You, in truth, are not in the flesh but in the Spirit, if indeed the Spirit of God dwells in you. But whoever does not have the Spirit of Christ, he is not his. But if Christ is in you, the body, it is true, is dead by reason of sin, but the spirit is life by reason of justice. But if the Spirit of him who raised Jesus from the dead dwells in you, then he who raised Christ from the dead will also bring to life your mortal bodies through that Spirit who dwells in you."[168] The whole force of the mystery is in Baptism, his power

---

165 In the extended presentation of St. Paul's evidence ending with ch. 26 Victorinus argues against the Homoiousians that image is opposed to likeness as substance is opposed to quality. This is the first mention of Victorinus's central critique of the Homoiousians, namely, that the notion of "similar substance" is self-contradictory, since similarity refers to a quality shared by at least two different substances. The image requires its model; cf. *Enn.* 6.49.9. The triad is within God's plenitude of power; it is actuated in the *Logos* and distributed among all existents. This creation is a revelation of the plenitude. The word "creation" will be used to signify "revelation" in this same manner by John Scotus Erigena, *De divisione naturae.* Note that the appropriation of the common substance (God, Spirit) is called existence *(existentia)* by Victorinus in 18,39–57, or simply "his substance" *(substantia sua).* Hadot thinks that Victorinus knows the semantic distinctions between these terms but does not always abide by them (TTT 760).

166 Rom 2.5.

167 Rom 4.17; cf. Gn 17.5.

168 Rom 8.9–11.

in the receiving of the Spirit, that is, the Holy Spirit. Since this is so, it was said: "You are in the Spirit," that is, that whom the Holy Spirit gave you. Who is this Spirit? He added: "If nevertheless the Spirit of God dwells in you." Who is this? "But whoever has not the Spirit of Christ." Therefore the Spirit of God and the Spirit of Christ are the same. In this text it also should be clearly recognized that the Spirit of Christ is the same thing as Christ himself. For there follows: "But if Christ is in you." Whence also the Spirit of God is God. Therefore there is only one substance because there is the same Spirit, but the same in three; therefore, they are *homoousion* (consubstantial). Whence the substance is not similar, because it is the same Spirit. Yet because there is one Spirit, it does not follow that the same passions are also in the Father. For only in two of them are there, as it were, passions, because they are Spirits who have already proceeded. (18) But this will be treated more fully later.[169]

"Since from him and through him and in him are all things."[170] "From him," is said as of the Father; "through him," as of Christ; "in him," as of the Holy Spirit. Elsewhere, however, he says this: "in him, through him, for him."[171]

That Christ is God: "from whom came Christ according to the flesh, who is over all things, blessed God forever and ever."[172]

B. FIRST EPISTLE TO THE CORINTHIANS

a) *The mystery of the Son's mode of begetting*

First epistle to the Corinthians: "For if they had known, they would never have crucified the Lord of Majesty."[173]

That Christ, like God, is incomprehensible, or is scarcely comprehensible: "But as it was also said: 'Eye has not seen nor ear heard, nor has it entered into the heart of man, what things God has prepared for those who love him.' "[174] Then he says that as the

---

169 Cf. *adv. Ar.* I 22,48 ff.; I 44,20.
170 Rom 11.36.
171 Col 1.16–17.
172 Rom 9.5.
173 1 Cor 2.8.
174 1 Cor 2.9.

spirit of man knows what is in man, so the Spirit of God knows the things of God. If he says that of Christ, it follows that it is not easy to know the begetting of the Son. For the *nous* neither perceives the Son of God nor can it know the mode of the begetting. But if that was said of Christ's presence, then the Son of God and the mode of begetting is also beyond the eye, beyond the ear, and beyond the *nous*. But if, as some think, he says this, of those things there "that God has prepared for those who love him," then if these things are so inconceivable, how yet more wonderful and more difficult to understand is the begetting, if these things are so incomprehensible.

How from this can one say that Christ is from nonexistents or that Christ is similar in substance? Such things are definite and comprehensible. But indeed to be *homoousion* (consubstantial) not only is incomprehensible but involves many contradictions! For if he is *homoousios* (consubstantial), is he also unbegotten? If he is *homoousios* (consubstantial), how is he different, how is the Father different, how is the Son different? If he is *homoousios* (consubstantial), how is it that one has suffered, the other has not? For from this arise the Patripassians. But since by God's will the Spirit who dwells in us discerns all, even the things of God, the mode of the divine begetting is discovered, by which both the *homoousios* (consubstantial) will be revealed and those heresies will be destroyed. "For we have received not the spirit of the world but the Spirit of God."[175]

b,¹ That the three are Spirit, therefore consubstantial

That God, Christ and the Holy Spirit are the same Spirit, and one and the same Spirit: "Wherefore I give you to understand that no one speaking in the Spirit says 'anathema' to Jesus, and no one can say 'Jesus is Lord' except in the Holy Spirit. Although there are varieties of graces, there is the same Spirit; and there are varieties of ministries but the same Lord; and there are varieties of workings, but the same God who works all in all."[176] If therefore "in the Spirit of God no one says 'anathema' to Jesus," then he himself is the Spirit of both God and the Holy Spirit of whom likewise he says this: "And no one can call Jesus Lord except in the Holy Spirit." In

175 1 Cor 2.12. For the sentence immediately preceding, cf. 1 Cor 2.11.
176 1 Cor 12.3-6.

addition he says this: that the varieties of graces are from the Spirit; the graces truly come from God, but the varieties from the Holy Spirit; for in action the Holy Spirit is another existence, in substance he is *homoousion* (consubstantial), since he is the Holy Spirit. And likewise the ministry of the Lord: truly he himself working in the action of life divides the "ministries," and he himself is in his own substance according to the action of life, but according to substance, he is *homoousios* (consubstantial). That the Spirit and actions are from God: but although there are many actions, the same God is in all. But God is different in that he himself makes the "varieties of workings," yet he himself works all in all. For "to be" itself, although it is the cause of action, makes the varieties of action, and God himself, since according to substance he is Spirit, is *homoousion* (consubstantial) with action. All three are therefore *homoousia* (consubstantial) with respect to action and *homoousia* (consubstantial) with respect to substance, because all three are Spirit; and because Spirit is from the Father, substance is from the Father.

C. SECOND EPISTLE TO THE CORINTHIANS

a) *The notion of image*

(19) That Christ is life and that he is Spirit has been said: "But the Spirit vivifies,"[177] and again he says there: "But the Lord is Spirit."[178]

That Christ is from God, not from nonexistents: "That they should not see the light of the gospel of the glory of Christ who is the image of God."[179] If Christ is the "image of God" Christ is from God. For an image is an image of what is manifested; but God is manifested; Christ is therefore the image. But an image is an image of what is manifested, and what is manifested is the original; but the image is second and different in substance from that which is manifested. But we do not conceive the image up there as it is in sensible things. For here we do not conceive the image to be a substance. For it is a sort of shadow in air or in water through a sort of corporeal

---

177 Jn 6.63.
178 2 Cor 3.17.
179 2 Cor 4.4.

light formed through the reflexion of a corporeal emanation. By itself it is nothing nor has it movement of its own—only what is manifested by it is a substance; and it has neither body, nor senses, nor understanding. And when that in which it is reflected is removed or disturbed, it is no longer anything nor anywhere. Therefore in a different way we say that Christ is the "image of God." We say that the image is, first, through itself and so that it is knowing, that it is both living and life-giving and the seed of all existents. For it is the *Logos* through whom are "all things" and without this, "nothing." But all these things are also attributed to God. Therefore God and the *Logos* are *homoousion* (consubstantial).

And why is the *Logos* the "image of God"? Because God is hidden, for he is in potentiality; but the *Logos* is manifest, for he is action. This action, having by life and knowledge all things which are in potentiality, produces according to movement, and thus all things are manifest. That is why action is the image of all that which is in potentiality, specifying each one of the things which are in potentiality and existing through itself; for no substance comes from nothing.[180] For every being has an inseparable species, or rather, the species itself is the substance itself, not that the species is prior to "to be," but because the species defines "to be." Indeed "to be" is the cause of the "to be" of the species, insofar as the "to be" of the species is "to be," and for this reason "to be" is the Father, the species is the Son. Again because that itself which is "to be" gives "to be" to species, the "to be" of the species is the image of that which is "to be" which as cause is the first "to be," therefore "to be" for both is *homoousion* (consubstantial); and the second "to be" is the image of the first "to be"; I speak of first and second without reference to time, the Father and Son differing from each other in respect to the cause of "to be" itself. But because causality is irreversible, for that reason the Father is Father, and the Son is Son. But in respect to "to be" they are both together and always together *homoousion* (consubstantial) according to "to be." But according to potentiality and action, the Father is potentiality, the Son is action. The Son is therefore born, having "to be" in action and potentially just as the one who is "to be" potentially has action

---

180 Much of the rest of the paragraph shows Stoic influence; cf. *Enn.* 5.1.6.

itself in that very self which is "to be" potentially. But the word "has" is a mental expression; for he does not have, but he is himself; indeed, up there all is simplicity; but I spoke according to the gospel: "All that the Father has, the Son likewise has."[181] For this reason both the Father is in the Son and the Son is in the Father and both are *homoousion* (consubstantial) and the Son is the image of the Father. For the "to be" itself of the two is *homoousion* (consubstantial). But because one is from the other, there is the image, and there is that which is represented. And again because one comes from the other, one is the Father, the other the Son. And again because one comes from the other, one is unbegotten, the other begotten. But this is to be taken without reference to time because this was in the beginning and from eternity to eternity. Therefore there is no room for those who say that Christ[182] is mere man or that he comes from nothing or that he began at a certain moment and similar ideas.

(20) Moreover, let us also consider this.[183] Moses says what was said by God: "Let us make man according to our image and likeness."[184] God says that. He says "Let us make" to a cooperator, necessarily to Christ. And he says: "according to the image." Therefore man is not the image of God, but he is "according to the image." For Jesus alone is image of God, but man is "according to the image," that is, image of the image. But he says: "according to our image." Therefore both Father and Son are one image. If the image of the Father is the Son and if the image itself is the Father, they are therefore *homoousioi* (consubstantial) in respect to image.

---

181 Jn 16.16.

182 A trace of the Profession of Faith of Sirmium (351); the doctrines attributed to Arius emerge from the anathemas of the dossier from Sirmium (358).

183 This chapter presents again the impossibility of "similar substance." According to Gn 1.26 the human soul (the heavenly man) images God as an intellectual substance; it is like God and the *Logos* by its quality. Cf. Augustine, *De diversis quaestionibus* 83, Q. 51.4 (PL) 40.33); *De trinitate* 7.6.12 (FC 45.228–29). This distinction between image and likeness is not in Plotinus (*Enn.* 5.3.8–9) but it is in the Greek patristic tradition, with image referring to nature, likeness to spiritual progress. Cf. H. de Lubac, *Surnaturel* (Paris 1946) 189. The fall of man was, for Victorinus, the loss of likeness, not the loss of the image; therefore, salvation is concerned with the order of quality, not of substance.

184 Gn 1.26.

For the image itself is substance. For both "to be" and "to act" are one and simple up there. But so also are substance and species. But since the image is substance, Father and Son are *homoousioi* (consubstantial), the Father existing as "to be" and also "to act," the Son existing as "to act" and also "to be," each of the two having individuality according to what he especially is,[185] with the "to be" preceding the "to act." The "to be," however, is Father, and above all the Father is that very "to be" in which action is potentially inherent. And again, as a later existent, the Son as "to act" is like a later "to be," the Son having "to act" from the first "to be." That is why there is one Father according to "to be," one Son according to "to act," each one of them simultaneously existing in the other, as has been proven.[186] They are therefore *homoousioi* (consubstantial).

Let us say therefore what is meant by "let us make man," and "according to the image" and what is meant by "according to our image"; finally, what is meant by "according to our likeness";[187] for such a statement signifies a difference between image and likeness. Since it is a great question as to what was intended by: "Let us make man according to our image," we must for the moment concede that it refers to the soul of man: for whether it refers to the composite or to the soul alone, it has not been understood to refer to anything else except the soul; for the soul alone is "according to the image" of God and "according to the likeness." We say that Christ is the "image of God," but he is the *Logos*. We say that the soul is therefore "according to the image" of God when we say that it is rational; for the soul is not the *Logos*, but it is rational. And because Christ is totally life, but the soul lives because it has life as substance, the soul is therefore "according to the image" of God. But Christ is the "image of God."

---

185 Definite use of the notion of predominance is referred to in 4,5-11. Basic and constant is the conceptual pair, "to be–to act," accounting for two substances by the predominance of "to be" or by the predominance of "to act." It also accounts for the triad, "to be," "to live," "to understand." Predominance is a sort of active appropriation by which each hypostasis is, according to its own mode, the other hypostases; cf. Porphyry, *Sententiae* 10; TTT 765.

186 Cf. *adv. Ar.* I 20,16-20.

187 Cf. Gn 1.26.

But how shall we understand this: "according to the likeness"? Just as the *Logos* is substance, as was declared, since also to be *Logos* is itself also "to be,"[188] yet *Logos* is "to act" and to be movement and, since all is simple up there, this "to act" and to be movement is "to be" which is substance up there. So also the soul as soul is "to be" and to be substance; but insofar as it is self-movement, it is the image of substance rather than substance itself, the substance specified. And for that reason, in the definition of soul, when we say what the soul is, we speak properly and substantially: that which is self-movement. From this it is also evident that self-movement is the substantial image, nay, more, the substance of the soul. But this is rational, rational "to be" according to the image of the *Logos*. Therefore it is one thing to be "according to the image," which indeed is substance, but another thing to be "according to the likeness" which is not a substance but the name of a quality manifest in substance. But just as we understand God to be substance, so also the image, that is, Christ. But we understand perfection as signifying something qualified. And if "like" signifies something qualified, necessarily, since we say that the soul is rational and perfectly rational, we say that the soul is perfect according to the likeness of the perfection of God. Therefore now and in the world it is "according to the image," but afterwards "according to the likeness" by faith in God and in Jesus Christ, such as it would have been if Adam had not sinned. Therefore insofar as it is rational, it is "according to the image" because of reason; insofar as it will be perfect, it is "according to the likeness." Therefore it is one thing to be "the image," and another to be "according to the image" and still another to be "according to the likeness." What blasphemy therefore to say that the Father and Son are *homoiousion*[189] (alike in substance) when the Son is image according to substance, not "according to the likeness."

(21) But so much for now. Let us indeed pass to other texts.

b) The three creations

That in Christ is the creation but not one creation. For there are

---

188 Cf. *adv. Ar.* I 19,22–55 and I 20,8–23.
189 Allusion to the letter of Basil of Ancyra.

three creations: one indeed when all things are created through Christ; the second creation is our own in Christ according to baptism, but in Christ; and there was another transformation in Christ; whence it was said: "If any man is in Christ he is a new creation."[190] That Christ existed before he was in the flesh: "He who did not know sin, he was made sin for us;"[191] because there was a time in which he did not know sin, before he was in the flesh.

D. THE EPISTLE TO THE EPHESIANS AND THE EPISTLE TO THE GALATIANS

The Preexistent Christ

To the Ephesians.[192] That Christ existed before he was in the flesh: "Blessed be the Father of our Lord Jesus Christ who has blessed us with every spiritual blessing in heavenly things in Christ Jesus insofar as he has chosen us before the foundation of the world."[193] That Christ existed before he was in the flesh: "Since you were at that time without Christ, alienated from the way of life of Israel."[194]

That Christ is God: "Having no hope and without God,"[195] that is, without Christ.

That it is the Spirit who unites all: "Wishing to keep the unity of the Spirit in the bond of peace; one body and one Spirit, one Lord, one faith, one baptism; one God and Father of all, who is in all and throughout all, and in all."[196]

To the Galatians: That Christ is God: "Paul, an apostle, not from men nor through a man, but through Jesus Christ and God the Father."[197] And again: "The gospel which was preached by me is

---

190 2 Cor 5.17.
191 2 Cor 5.21.
192 From the letters to the Ephesians and Galatians Victorinus cites texts opposed to the Photinians, for whom Christ did not exist before coming in the flesh.
193 Eph 1.3-4.
194 Eph 2.12.
195 *Ibid.*
196 Eph 4.3-6.
197 Gal 1.1.

not according to man. For I did not receive it from man, but through the revelation of Jesus Christ."[198]

E. EPISTLE TO THE PHILIPPIANS: CHRIST FORM OF GOD

a) "Form of God," against the Photinians

To the Philippians.[199] That he is Christ:[200] "And in the support of the Spirit of Jesus Christ."[201] That the Son is *homoousios* (consubstantial) and together with the Father, powerful: "For, feel that in you which was also in Christ who, existing in the form of God, did not consider it robbery to be equal to God, but emptied himself taking the form of a slave, made in the likeness of man and found with the shape of a man."[202]

First of all the Photinians and those after Photinus and before him who say that Jesus is mere man and also made from man recognize the blasphemy as impious. "In Christ who existing in the form of God."[203] "Existing" when? Before he came into the body. For he said that he had emptied himself and taken the form of a slave. Therefore he also existed before he became man. And what was he? The *Logos* of God, the "form of God."

b) "Equal," against the Homoeousians

What is this: "existing equal to God?" That he is of the same power and substance of God. For he said: "being equal." Indeed

---

198 Gal 1.11–12.
199 Victorinus's handling of Phil 2.5–7 runs through ch. 23. With the help of this text, Victorinus uses the new name for Christ, Form of God, to show consubstantiality against the Photinians, the Anomoeans and the Homoiousians who cherished this text; cf. M. Victorinus, *in Phil.* 2.5–7, probably later than *adv. Ar. I*. Hadot (TTT 769) points out that the long tradition of commentaries on Aristotle's *Categories* was available to dissipate the confusion between "equal" and "like" found with the Homoiousians. Equal refers to quantity, like to quality; quantity has most in common with substance. Hence St. Paul in calling Christ equal to God refers to a concrete identity with substance. Athanasius may have been an important source for Victorinus's thought; cf. *De synodis* 53 (PG 26.788B–C).
200 I read "Christ" rejecting the CSEL conjecture *Spiritus*.
201 Phil 1.19.
202 Phil 2.5–7.
203 Cf. Phil 2.5–7.

"equal" signifies size and quantity.[204] But size is size by the mass of substance. For quality does not have size nor does it have its being from substance. Only quantity is quantity by the size of substance. And that is why blessed Paul, describing the substance of God, speaks of all the quantities: "So that you may know the height, the length, the breadth, and the depth of God."[205] (22) According to these statements then, Christ exists as an "equal to God." He did not say: like to God, which does not signify substance[206] but something in substance, as an accident, in a relationship of likeness, just as man is related to God "according to likeness," whereas the substance of man is one thing, the substance of God another; wherefore it is blasphemous to say that man is equal to God.

If therefore Christ is the "form of God" but the form is substance—for form and image are identical—but the form and image of God is the *Logos* and the *Logos* is always "with God," the *Logos* is *homoousion* (consubstantial) with God, "with" whom both "in the principle" and always he is *Logos*.

But that the image is both substance and together with the substance which is called *homoousion* (consubstantial), is clear from this: for the Apostle said: "He emptied himself, taking the form of a servant." Did he take only the form[207] of man but not the substance of man? For he has also put on flesh and was in the flesh and suffered in the flesh, and this is the mystery, and this is what saves us.

c) "He emptied himself," against Marcellus and Photinus

If therefore "he emptied himself," and this is Christ who "emptied himself" before he was in the flesh, then Christ existed before he was in the flesh. And if he existed before that, since "he emptied himself," he himself put on flesh. For why "he emptied

---

204 The philosophical fragments found here are from Group IV of those assembled by Hadot, PV II 57. They are derived from Aristotle and his commentators.

205 Eph 3.18.

206 The philosophical fragments specified in note 204 are also present here.

207 In the Platonic tradition the word "form" is equivalent to substance. Athanasius had already linked form with image; cf. *Contra Arianos* 2.6–6 (PG 26.332B).

himself" if, as you say, Marcellus[208] or Photinus, "he assumed man" as if that were a fourth thing. For it was necessary for the *Logos* to remain who he was, to assume man and in some way to breathe the Spirit for the sake of actions. But Paul said: "He emptied himself." Rightly so, he who had to put on man. What therefore is the meaning of: "he emptied himself?"[209] The universal *Logos* is not universal insofar as he is the *Logos* of the flesh and was made flesh. Therefore he did not assume but he became man.

d) Concerning "consubstantial," against the Photinians, the Arians, and the Homoeousians

Substance and form

Therefore the form is substance along with the substance in which it is form. The substance of the form is therefore *homoousios* (consubstantial) with the principal substance and prior in power because the latter gives to the form "to be," to be substance, to be in substance, to be always together with substance; for without one, the other is not. Therefore insofar as the form being form of the substance is substance by substance, this is the Son of God, insofar as the form is substance. But because the substance is always with a form, the Father is always Father, the Son always Son and the Son is always with the Father, that is, the *Logos* "with God," and this always. But since this form is substance which is that image and *Logos* that we call the Son of God, insofar as it is the *Logos*, is the *Logos* of all existents. For the Son of God is the universal *Logos* by whose power all things come forth and proceed unto birth and subsist. Therefore proceeding by his own power[210] and existing together with the Father, he makes all and produces all things. And

---

208 Victorinus sees the misunderstanding of "form of slave" (Phil 2.6) to be that of Marcellus of Ancyra as well as that of Photinus.

209 Cf. P. Henry, "Kénose," *Dictionnaire de la Bible, Supplement* 5 (Paris 1951) 115. Cf. Plotinus, *Enn.* 6.4.16; Porphyry, *Sententiae* 37; W. Theiler, 18, n.2. Cf. *adv. Ar.* IV 15,22; *hymn.* III. The Incarnation is a particularisation whereby Christ became the Exemplar of man, Universal Life sending into the world the Holy Spirit enabling men to think and so to live spiritually that they may return to their original nature as spirits. Cf. *in Eph.* 1.4 (PL 8.1238C–42C); 1.21–23 (PL 8.1250C); *adv. Ar.* I 2,21–23; I 5,6; I 61,11; III 3,27; III 1,39; IV 11,7–20; IV 8,37.

210 Power is used here as quality, not as opposed to "act."

this very power, insofar as it is proper to it to progress, which indeed is called action, if it suffers at all, it suffers according to the materials and substances to which it gives what is proper to their being, while the universal *Logos* who is always "with the Father" and *homoousios* (consubstantial) remains immutable and impassible. And that is why it is said of the Son that he is both impassible and passible, but this suffering occurs only in his progression and, above all, in his extreme progression, that is, when he was in the flesh. For these things are not called passions: begetting by the Father, first movement and being the creator of all things, for these things, since they are substantial, are more of the order of substance; for the *logoi* of existents, according to power, are the substances of these things; they are not therefore passions.[211] (23) But so much for that, and let us return.

Against the notion of homoiousios (likeness)[212]

What therefore do the Photinians say? If the Son is *homoousios* (consubstantial) with the Father, how did God have a Son who was a man born from Mary? But what do the Arians also say? If he is *homoousios* (consubstantial) and *Logos,* the Son is together with the Father a substance. For it is sacrilegious to say this: "There was a time when he was not,"[213] and sacrilegious to say this: "He is from nonexistents." Again they are also impious who say that the Son is *homoiousion* (like in substance) to the Father. For substance, as substance, is not different from another, so that it can be like another. For it is the same substance in both and it is not similar substance, but the very same substance. But when there is a different substance, it is not in respect to substance that it is called

---

211 Passions are in things receiving existence. In the creation of the world the Universal *Logos* becomes particularized. This is for the *Logos* a progressive *kenosis*, reaching its extremity in the Incarnation. Thus, salvation comes through a greater and greater universalization. Cf. *adv. Ar.* III 3,47–50.

212 In this chapter allusion is made to the letter from Basil of Ancyra who had objected that consubstantiality presupposes a prior substance. Victorinus's reaction is that of a philosopher who knows that two things are similar in quality but not in substance.

213 H. Opitz, *Athanasius Werke* 3.1, *Urkunden zur Geschichte des arianischen Streites* 24 (Berlin 1934).

similar, but in respect to a certain quality. Therefore it is both impossible and absurd that something be *homoiousion* (like in substance). Besides, this similarity, which is found in otherness, is either in the same substance, divided into two parts, or in another substance. But substance as substance does not admit of being similar or dissimilar. It is said to be similar or dissimilar insofar as it is receptive of quality, but substance itself remains the same or different in its power or existence. What then? This substance of God or of the *Logos,* is it that it is receptive of dissimilarity that it is said to be similar? But if this is impossible, neither is it therefore similar. It is therefore not *homoiousion* (similar in substance).

Let us also then consider this. If there is similarity in substance, it is either in the same genus of substance, such as man or animal: for man is similar to man and animal to animal, or the similarity is in another genus of substance, such as a stone similar to a man or a statue to a horse. How then do they say that these two are *homoiousia* (similar in substance). If they are in the same genus of substance, as in the genus of animal, all the more must there be a preexisting substance. But if the similarity is within the same substance, this must be divided into two or begotten from a higher different substance. But each of the two is either dependent on the other or a different subject. But if the substance is divided, whether in equal or unequal parts, neither one is perfect. But there are two perfects, and a perfect from a perfect. Therefore there is no similarity, especially with respect to similarity within the same substance. If this is so, it is necessary that similarity take place in a different genus. Whence comes this different genus or is it a different subject? From nothing therefore, or there are two principles. But not one of these is the case since there is both one principle and the Father is the cause of all existents through the *Logos* who was "in the principle" and consequently always was. Therefore the *Logos* was not from nothing. If this is also true, neither is there similarity in that which is of a different genus.

e) Robbery

But in what sense does Scripture say not that: Jesus thought that he was himself equal to God, but that: "he did not consider being

equal . . . to be robbery."[214] For those things which are not equal
by nature nor by their own divinity, but which are made equal as
though by fortune, are equal by a sort of robbery. Not to consider being equal to God a robbery shows great confidence toward
being equal and a truly natural divinity. (24) But enough of this,
and again we proceed.

F. EPISTLE TO THE COLOSSIANS AND
THE FIRST EPISTLE TO TIMOTHY

1) Epistle to the Colossians: The First Begetting of the Son and
the Creation of the Intelligible World

a) Col. 1.15–20: the whole mystery

What does he say to the Colossians?[215] That Jesus is the first
"before all things." For his begetting is twofold, one indeed into
divinity and into filiation, hidden, divine and known by faith, but
another is the coming into the flesh and taking the flesh. Indeed
only this begetting by God, the manifestation of power, is a begetting; the other, however, is a taking of flesh, not a begetting. If
therefore the begetting by God is prior, the Savior is also not from
man. If there is begetting, there is not a creature. But if there is
begetting from God, it is not from nothing. If Jesus is the image of
God, he is *homoousios* (consubstantial).

---

214 Phil 2.6.
215 In studying (chs. 24–26) the Epistle to the Colossians and the First
Epistle to Timothy, Victorinus comes face to face with the mystery, the
creative and redemptive role of the *Logos,* and the "passions" introduced
by the external radiation of the *Logos.* Hadot (TTT 776) describes it in
this way: "The act of the self-begetting of the *Logos* is accompanied
immediately by the creation of the intelligible world; this latter is like the
halo of the *Logos.* But the exterior act of the *Logos* does not stop; it
extends even to matter and is terminated at the Incarnation. This is why
in order to expose the mystery Victorinus describes the two generations
of the *Logos:* in the Epistle to the Colossians, Victorinus recognizes a
description of the creative aspect of the first begetting, in the First to
Timothy a description of the second begetting, the Incarnation. He
finally argues against the Homoiousians that only "consubstantiality" can
assure the ultimate meaning of the "mystery" which is the unity of all
in God (25,2–13)."

For the image is substance with the substance from which and in which it is image. And because the image is substance begotten by the substance of which it is image, in which it is or subsists, to reveal the power within, hence the Father is within, the Son is exterior. Again, because the Son is *Logos,* a substance hastening into action, for the *Logos* is life and understanding, the *Logos* advances to give substance to existents both intelligible and material. And consequently the action of the *Logos* itself, on account of the weakness of the recipients, both suffers and is passible or rather is called passible.

Therefore of Christ blessed Paul says: "Who is the image of the invisible God, the first-born before any creature, since in him were created all things in the heavens and on the earth, visible and invisible, whether Thrones, or Dominations, or Principalities, or Powers. All things have been created through him and unto him, and he is before all creatures, and in him all things hold together. He is the head of the body, of the Church, he who is the principle, the first-born from the dead, that in all things he may have the primacy. For it has pleased God that in him all fullness should dwell, and

---

Eternal creation, the creation of the intelligible world, is linked to the eternal begetting of the *Logos* according to the third verse of St. John's prologue. Hadot believes (TTT 777) that this may be directed to Marcellus of Ancyra who considered the second begetting to be the only true generation. For Victorinus the second begetting is the addition of something alien. In the first begetting the Son is Plenitude, the preexistence of all things in the *Logos,* the Intelligible World; cf. Porphyry, *Sententiae* 11 (Mommert, 3.6); Plotinus, *Enn.* 5.9.10; 5.8.7. For Victorinus, this *unum omne* is the whole mystery. Return to unity is return to plenitude of life. Cf. Col 1.20; I Cor. 15.28. The body of the world is nourished by its head, Christ. The Pleroma of all things is one and is in the One; it is the unfolding in time and space of the universal order concentrated in the *Logos.* Victorinus understood the 5th verse of St. John's prologue to apply to the generation of the sensible world with a certain opposition to the intelligible world. Cf. *adv. Ar.* I 26,36–40.

We note here that Victorinus's insistence on consubstantiality was not merely in the service of his philosophical and theological interest. He was deeply conscious that unless Christ is consubstantial with the Father, there is no salvation. The Incarnation is the great mystery because and only because Christ is consubstantial with God. He descended to give life to man whose soul was fascinated and seduced by the very forms found in the sensible world which had been created through the *Logos* himself. Cf. Synesius *Hymn* 1; Plotinus, *Enn.* 4.4.40.44; 1.8.14.

through him to reconcile to himself all things, whether on the earth or in the heavens, making peace through the blood of his cross."[216]

The whole mystery is expressed in this exposition. That he is *homoousios* (consubstantial) he says according to this: "He is the image of the invisible God." That he is the Son: "the first-born." That he is not created: "before all creatures," he said. For if he himself had been created, he would not have said "before all creatures." And he properly said: "First-born," which is said of a son. Let us therefore put together the meaning: "The first-born before all creatures." Therefore this one is begotten as a Son, the creation as that which is created. Not that there was begotten another after him, but because he was "the first-born before all creatures." Moreover, it says "all creatures, both of heaven and earth, visible and invisible." Without a creation therefore, the Son is. Therefore by nature and by begetting, he is Son.

That Christ is *Logos* and that the *Logos* is cause of the being of all existents is said by this: "Because all things are established in him," both established "through him" and established "in him." For the *Logos* is both the cause of the being of existents and the receptacle of the existents which are in him. But because all things are "in him," the receptacle itself is filled by all existents, and it is itself also fullness, and that is why all things are "through" him, all things are "for him," all things are "in him."

(25) If therefore the Son was from nothing, how is this so? Without faith it is also impossible that these things are so. And again, if they are not *homoousion* (consubstantial), how are both the Father and the Son fullness? For fullness is all things together. Is *homoiousion* (likeness in substance) fullness, like souls and other created things? Absolutely impossible. Indeed, *homoiousion* (likeness in substance), as it was said,[217] is located in otherness. For a substance cannot be called like another, unless it is not the same substance. But if a substance is different from its power, and by this substance all things have their own being, it is impossible that all be one. Now indeed, if God the Father and the Son, the *Logos,* are *homoousioi* (consubstantial), since through the *Logos* all are called

---

216 Col 1.15–20.
217 Cf. *adv. Ar.* I 23,7–12.

into oneness, both all things are from God and God is "all in all," the Father existing without suffering, as was proven.[218] But because Jesus who is *Logos* of all existents is "vivifying Spirit" and source of eternal life, coming, according to the mystery, in the flesh and into the death of sins, conquered death and raised the dead into eternal life. But because God is the power of the source itself of eternal life and because the Son is *Logos,* the source of eternal life by the Father's power, he is the "first-born from the dead", and therefore "all things" turned "towards him" will become one, that is, become spiritual. Therefore, the Son of God is *homoousios* (consubstantial) because he is the source of eternal life, just as the Father is his power, and because "through him," the Son, all things become one, since "all things are through him."

b) Col. 2.9: Jesus is the act of all things

That Jesus, that is, the *Logos* is both the seed and, as it were, the element of all existents, but especially now in the energy and the manifestation of existents: "Because in him dwells all the fulness of the Godhead bodily,"[219] that is, substantially in action. For all things dwell potentially in the Father, and for that reason Jesus the *Logos* is the image of God the Father; for that very thing which is to be power is already that which is to be action. For anything which goes out into action is image also of that which is potentially, and that which is in action is Son of that which is potentially. From this, the Son and the Father are that which is *homoousion* (consubstantial).

c) Col. 2.19: All things come from Jesus, therefore from God

That all things come from Jesus and therefore all things come from God, all things, I say, which exist: "Not uniting to the head of Christ from whom the whole body, by contact and by connection, draws its nurture and its development to realize the growth from God." For all existents, although they are different, are one. For the body of the whole universe is not like a mass formed by merely contiguous particles, but it is a body insofar as it is held together like

218 Cf. *adv. Ar.* I 13,12 and I 17,35.
219 Col 2.9.

a chain by the mutual overlapping of its parts. For the chain is God, Jesus, the Spirit, *Nous,* the soul, the angels, and finally all corporeal things. The fullness therefore has an economy, namely, a development. (26) If therefore all is one, namely, in substance, much more are God and the Son not only in substance but of the same substance. For all *onta* (existents) are in substance in Jesus, that is, in the *Logos,* as it was said: "All things are established in him."[220] But these existents are not *homoousia* (consubstantial). For this first "to be" which is God is not a quasi-*ousia* (substance), no more than the image which is the Son is a quasi-substance, but only that which for both of these is the "to be" of divinity, is in the function of cause, the "to be" of existents. Only therefore God and the *Logos* are *homoousia* (consubstantial).

2) First Epistle to Timothy: The Second Birth of the Son and His Sensible Appearance in the Mystery

First epistle to Timothy: "And obviously great is the mystery of godliness: which was manifested in the flesh, was justified in the Spirit, appeared to the angels, was preached to the Gentiles, believed in the world, taken up in glory."[221] This is not said of the first birth but of the second. For this is a "great mystery": that God "emptied himself, when he was in the form of God,"[222] then that he suffered, first by being in the flesh and sharing the lot of human birth and being raised upon the cross. These things, however, would not be marvelous, if he had come from man alone, or from nothing, or from God by creation. For what would "he emptied himself" mean if he was not before he was in the flesh? And what was he? He said: "equal to God." But if he were a creature from nothing, how is he equal? That is why it is "a great mystery which was manifested in the flesh." He existed therefore before he existed in the flesh. But he said: "manifested in the flesh." For he existed intelligibly and intellectually; but he was then manifested sensibly and in the flesh. For the power of the *Logos* according to its own substance is always the substance of life, insofar as it is life, and it vivifies and revivifies, and

---

220 Col 1.16.
221 1 Tim 3.16.
222 Cf. 1 Tim 3.16; Phil 2.6–7.

it does not allow that which it vivifies to be in death. Therefore in the first movement it has led forth all things into life, and this is the descent of the *Logos* because, going forth from the Father he has given to existents which are in the heavens, to the angels, to the thrones, to the glories, to other existents of this kind, his own life by the fatherly power: for he is the *Logos* of all things, "through whom all has been created." And again, because there was nothing to vivify, unless there was matter available to the vivifying power, matter was made to be, a dead nature, and brought to life by the divine vivification it produced its own vices and corrupted man. But the *Logos,* perfect life, fulfilled the mystery and appeared in matter, that is, in flesh and in darkness. For how was it possible that he should have appeared, except in the flesh, that is, appeared to the senses? The *Logos* has therefore made all and is in all; he has produced all and saved all; and he has ruled, being eternal life.

Therefore "in the Spirit he was justified"; "he appeared to the angels"; coming therefore; "he was preached to the nations"; therefore he existed before he came; "he was believed in the world." For thus also Isaiah proclaims, prophesying: "The Egyptian has worked for you, and the merchants of the Ethiopians and Sabaeans; the tallest men will walk to you and will be your servants and bound by handcuffs they will follow behind you and will venerate you and invoke you because God is in you and there is no God outside of you. For you are God and we knew it not. God of Israel."[223] Therefore, "he was believed in[224] the world, he was received in glory." All divinity is from the beginning and in the beginning and after and always from eternity and forever and ever. Amen.

4. Conclusion (Inspired by Isaiah 45.14) about the Consubstantial and against the Heresies

(27) But consider this also in relation to the *homoousion*[225] (consubstantial), how the Spirit says to Isaiah: "God is in you and

---

223 Is 45.14–15.
224 CSEL gives "believed in" *(creditus)*, replacing *praedicatus*.
225 In this chapter and the opening paragraph of the next appears the final development of the conception of consubstantiality, namely, the unity of the divine substance with the Father and Son distinguished as repose and

there is no God outside of you."[226] That he says this to the Son, our Lord, is clear: "God is in you," this is what was said: "The Father is in me." But the other: "And there is no God outside of you." In this word he predicts all the heresies. Included are all the Jews and those who say that Jesus is only a man, and those who say that he has "come from nothing" or that "there was a time when he was not."[227] For God was and always was one God. For if Jesus is the *Logos,* and if the *Logos* is always "with God" and if the *Logos* is "God," there is only one God and there is no other. Therefore God and the *Logos* are *homoousion* (consubstantial). Again, if God is "to be" but if Jesus, that is, the *Logos,* is "the power and the wisdom" of this God and of this "to be" there is only one God and there is not another. *Logos* and God are therefore unity, and "to be" itself and "to be *Logos*" are simultaneously within subsistent "to be" and for that reason they are *homoousion* (consubstantial). But that which the *Logos* is, that is, to be life and *Nous*—for these things are the "power and wisdom of God" which the Savior Jesus is—that which is the *Logos* then is the action of advancing and begetting and procession into the substance of filiation and into action by a luminous manifestation and the reflection of the light. But this does not mean "there was a moment when he was not," but he always was. Always, therefore, Father, always Son. And the Father is only Father and the Son only Son, but relative to the Father, since the "to be" which is God and Father, is cause of the "to be" of the *Logos,* but that is not reciprocal. And the property of the first "to be" is to remain tranquil; but the property of the *Logos* is to move and to act, and not to move locally nor by change in place, but moving itself by a movement which is that of the soul, yet more excellent and more divine, by which self-movement it both gives life and begets thoughts, by a movement subsisting in itself, and not cut off from its own power when it goes into action. (28) But enough for now; and return later.

For there are also other things in Holy Scripture: that Jesus is

---

motion. The *Logos,* like the soul whose model it is, is a self-mover; it is substantial motion having its own hypostatic reality: *subsistens in se ipsa.*
226 Is 45.14–15.
227 Cf. *adv. Ar.* I 23,5–6.

God, that he is before eons, that he is Son, Son by nature and Son in
the flesh, and that it is especially in the flesh that he is called Son
because he then saved all *onta* (existents) and conquered the enemies
of divinity and also all death which he himself suffered, he who is
in movement, but not the Father, who is in repose.

III. AGAINST A LETTER EMANATING FROM THE HOMOEOUSIAN PARTY

1. *The* Homoiousios *(likeness in substance) Is Not as Traditional as This Letter Pretends*

If these things are so, there is lacking only this: how to conceive
the Son; is he *homoousion* (consubstantial) or *homoiousion* (like in
substance) to the Father?[228] For this doctrine is a current opinion
and was for a long time rumored, that it is not obligatory to say
homoousion (consubstantial) but rather *homoiousion* (like in substance). Now this doctrine has been invented. But they also dare to
say this that for some time—I do not say when; for it suffices for me
to know that it is neither since the origin of the world, nor since the
appearance of Jesus, but for some time the word *homoiousion* (like
in substance) was permitted. I grant that it may have been permitted
a hundred years ago or more.

But then, forty years ago, where was it hidden, where was it
dormant when, in the city of Nicaea, the formula of faith which
excommunicated the Arian faction was approved by more than three
hundred bishops? In this synod of illustrious men there were present

---

228 The vocabulary and solutions found in a long development beginning
here and ending with the first paragraph of ch. 32 presuppose the
Sirmium (358) dossier. Cf. Hadot, MV 226. How shall we reconcile
Hadot's two statements, one in TTT 768 that Victorinus's commentary
on the Philippians was "probably posterior to our *adv. Ar.* I," and his
statement in TTT 784 that "this whole argumentation against Homoi-
ousianism was already previously developed in commentaries on St.
Paul"? Perhaps he is referring in the latter statement to the lost commentaries. In any case Hadot thinks that *homoiousios* was first mentioned when the Emperor came to Rome in April–May 357. Four African
bishops had signed, along with Liberius (pope from 352–66) the homoiousian formula of Sirmium (summer 358). Cf. above, Introd., sects. 40–
41. The remark, therefore, about Nicaea as forty years prior is to be

all the luminaries of the Church and of the entire world. Where then had this ancient doctrine fled? But if it did not exist, it was not condemned, and then it must be a recent doctrine! If it already existed, either it escaped discussion or it was put to flight by right thinking and true opinion.

And perchance then you, the defender of this doctrine, were not only alive but already a bishop!

You kept silence, you as well as your colleagues, disciples and fellowteachers!

And during the whole time that followed, as long as the Emperor was in Rome, you heard said in your presence many things contrary to this doctrine, living in communion with those men whom now you anathematize. Furious either that without you they wrote their confession of faith, or constrained by imperial agents you have come as a legate to defend treachery. But what difference whether there are thirty or seventy participants, or more; what difference whether it is more or less often! The same faith has been established for the annihilation of all *haireseōn* (heresies), one because it both originates from the One and has been effective until now. You, however, you write and say this: that Paul of Samosata and Marcellus and

---

taken as an approximate statement. Victorinus warns against the dangers of philosophical errors and imprecisions committed by those who are philosophically naive but whose terms have ontological implications. For example, the use of the word "similar," a reciprocal term, would indicate that the Father is also like the Son. Cf. Aristotle, *Metaphysics* 5.15 (1021A9); *Categories* 7 (6B29). Note that Victorinus defines the substance of God as Light and Spirit whereas the Image of God is defined as Will. Hadot speculates (TTT 792) that the source of Victorinus's distinction between existence and substance is some commentary on Aristotle's *Categories,* a distinction found also in *Cand* I 2,25. As we said, however, this distinction is also present in Plotinus. Here existence is pure "to be" which is a potential substance. The Son is a voluntary self-definition of the divine substance. As the Will of the Father, the Son is born of the Father and of Self-Will inasmuch as every will is autonomous. Cf. *ad Cand.* 22,8 for the will's important role. The scholar who has done most to highlight the will in Victorinus's metaphysics is E. Benz, *Marius Victorinus und die Entwicklung der abendländischen Willensmetaphysik* (Stuttgart 1932). Will is no longer function, but substance. The *Logos,* Image, Form and Will relate the Father to himself, to his absolutely simple act of being. The autonomous life of the Father is the source of the Son's self-begetting. The Father gives the Son to have "life in himself." The Son does all things because the Father is power of all things, all-powerful.

Photinus,[229] and now Valens and Ursacius[230] and others of this kind who were found impious in heresy have been refuted. Were they not saying *homoousion* (consubstantial)? No. But then how were they blasphemous? Like Arius Paul of Samosata held: "The Son comes from nothing; there was a time when he was not; the Son is a creature; he is in every way totally unlike the Father."[231] What did Marcellus and Photinus hold? That Jesus is merely a man from a man and Jesus is outside the Trinity. And now, Valens and Ursacius, the dregs of Arius. Therefore each had his own blasphemy for which he was excommunicated. But you, for this reason have you conquered them, because you say *homoiousion* (like in substance)? Indeed they have not said *homoousion* (consubstantial) and thus they have been conquered!

(29) Let us consider also, therefore, what you say and how you say: thus do both all the Africans and all the Easterners think. Why therefore do you write to them to rid the holy Church of *homoousion* (consubstantial)? Do they teach the *homoiousion* (like in substance)? Then it was not necessary to write to them. And if it is necessary to write to them, you should persuade them not by an imperial command alone but by reasonings and by the Holy Scriptures. Indeed you ought not only to refute the *homoousion* (consubstantial) but also to prove the *homoiousion* (like in substance).

2. *The Objection:* Homoousion *(consubstantial) Supposes a* Preexistent Substance, as Opposed to Homoiousion *(like in substance)*

Now, however, previously and lately, to falsify the *homoousion* (consubstantial), you say nothing but that in affirming this it is necessary to confess a preexisting substance, and thus from it are the Father and the Son.

---

229 Cf. *adv. Ar.* I 1,33.
230 Ursacius (c. 335–71) was bishop of Singidunum (now Belgrade), and leader with Valens, a Fourth-Century bishop of Mursa, of the Arians in the west. They were bitter enemies of St. Athanasius and at Sirmium (357) held the extreme Arian (Anomoean) position.
231 Concern with Sirmium (358) dossier; Photinian doctrines in anathemas, Sirmium (351).

In the first place this is not necessary. Indeed, God himself is both substance and cause of substance, and he preexists all things, both all existentiality and all essentiality. For from him are all things, both existents and names. From this God therefore who is the principle of substance and likewise must be substance, comes a *homoousios* (consubstantial) Son, in him and with him, certainly his "form" which must be both "image" and "character," without which neither is God known nor does intelligence ascend. Nevertheless, this does not deny that God is simple, for these things are not in him as something alien, or as accidents; but they are the very "to be God." And to be thus is *homoousion* (consubstantial) with "to be." The Father is "to be," the Son, "to be thus." For God is "to be"; but "to be thus" is the *Logos*. And this always signifies what is said: "I and the Father are one," and: "The Father is in me and I am in the Father,"[232] and: "Whoever sees me, sees the Father."[233] For they are *homoousia* (consubstantial). What therefore does he affirm in saying: a substance preexists if *homoousion* (consubstantial) is held? Truly what? If *homoiousion* (like substance) is held, is it not necessary to think that there preexists a substance by which these two substances are made alike? And according to your reasoning you also run into the very same difficulty which you fear with regard to *homoousion* (consubstantial). Or are you alone allowed so to understand *homoiousion* (like in substance) as the Father giving substance to the Son? But is not this our conception, that they are *homoousion* (consubstantial), that is, the Father existing as cause, [to give] substance[234] to the Son?

3. *Critique of the Notion of* Homoiousion *(like in substance)*

You, you also confess that God is substance; for you say that Father and Son are *homoiousion* (like in substance). Who is like to whom? According to dignity and the dignity of names, is not the Son like the Father? But nevertheless the Father is also like the Son: for so it is with relatives.

---

232 Jn 10.30; 14.10.
233 Jn 14.9.
234 The CSEL textual change which adds the word substance *(substantia/m)* and changes *filius* to *filio* strengthens Victorinus's argument that the Father gives his substance to the Son.

If it is likeness and we say *homoiousion* (like in substance), we are saying that the Son is like the Father. And how do we understand the word of Isaiah? For he says: "Before me there was no other God, and after me there will not be a like one."[235] (30) What therefore? Is the *Logos* before God, or after God, or with God? If before God, God is not unbegotten, nor is God Father, nor the principle of principles. But if after God, he is *oukh homoios* (not like) him. But a like God is "another God." But if this is the case, it is a sacrilege. You say alike, not only in power, in dignity, in divinity, but also in substance. What is it to be alike in substance? According to substance itself, insofar as it is substance itself, it is the same, not alike. For a resemblance is achieved by means of quality.[236] Such a resemblance is a resemblance in respect to color, state, disposition, power, form. But Jesus, that is, the *Logos,* is the "image of God," not the likeness. He is called "image of God"; for God is not image, but God as image and God as substance are not as two things: for there is one substance and one image, whence there is one God and one *Logos* and one Father, one Son and they are one. For the One and this One are not two, and that is why the other One is also consubstantial, and that is why it is not another One, but rather also the Only One. But enough of this; let us continue.

b) *The substance of God: it is light and spirit.*
To be a substance is to be something

What do we say that substance is?[237] As the sages and ancients defined it: "That which is subject, that which is something, that which is not to be in another." And they differentiate between existence and substance; indeed they define existence and existentiality as preexisting subsistence without accidents because they subsist purely and only in that which is only "to be"; but they define substance as a subject with all its accidents inseparably existing within it.[238]

---

235 Is 43.10.
236 One of the philosophical fragments assembled by Hadot and derived from Aristotle (Group IV); cf. Hadot, PV II 57; cf. Aristotle, *Categories* (9B 10–12) (8B27–28) (9A16) (10A12).
237 See following note.
238 The sentences referred to in the preceding note, along with those

But taking existence and substance in ordinary usage we use these
terms everywhere in the same way when signifying that something
exists. So it must be, whether we speak of eternal or mundane
things; for one is allowed to say either existence, or substance, or
"to be." True substance[239] on high is movement and not only
movement but first movement, which is a kind of movement which
is also a state of repose, and for that reason is substance itself. But
this refers to both a longer and far different question. But for the
moment let us admit that there exists there substance which has as
its proper signification, this: to be a certain *on* (existent).

God has a substance: against the adversaries of the word "substance"

Against those who say that the term "substance" is not found in
Holy Scripture: perhaps in fact the term substance is not found
there, but derivatives from substance are there.[240] For whence is
derived *epiousion* (supersubstantial) if not from the word "substance";[241] "Give us this day the *epiousion* (supersubstantial) bread."
Since Jesus is life and his body is life—body, however, as bread, as it
was said: "I shall give you bread from heaven,"[242] therefore
epiousion (supersubstantial) signifies "from that or in that substance
itself," that is, the bread of life. Likewise Paul, in the epistle to

---

indicated here, form one of those philosophical fragments (Group II)
assembled by Hadot and probably derived from Porphyry; cf. Hadot, PV
II 21. This refers to the One and the Intelligible Triad of Being, Life and
Thought. See above, Introd. sects. 101–03 on Victorinus's notion of
substance.

239 An inconsistency since here substance is made equivalent to qualified "to
be" whereas normally unqualified "to be" is equated with substance;
cf. *adv. Ar.* III 9,4; *hymn.* I, 35.

240 Mt 6.11.

241 In searching the Scriptures for derivatives of "substance," Victorinus
adduces the Greek word from Mt 6.11, "supersubstantial," and explains
later (II 8,9–20) that it means "bread from the same substance." He confirms moreover the usage of *cotidianum* in the *Vetus Latina* edition of
both the Matthaean and Lucan versions when he explains this translation
as the result of ignorance or the inability of the Latin language to express
the idea. Jerome [*Commentarii in evangelium Matthaei* 1.6 (PL 26.43)]
gives the textual reasons for introducing *supersubstantialis* into the
Vulgate as the more accurate translation of *epiousion*. See J. Hennig,
"Our Daily Bread," *Theological Studies* 4 (1943) 445–47.

242 Cf. Jn 6.51.

Titus, spoke of "the people *periousion,*"[243] (close to the substance), that is, close to the life constituting a people, as it is said in the oblation prayer: "Purify for yourself this people, standing fast in life, zealous for good works, assembling around your substance." And it seems to me that the same thing is signified in Jeremiah the prophet, where he says: "Who is he who stands in the substance of the Lord, who has lent his ear and heard?"[244] And after awhile he says: "And if they had stood in my substance."[245] But for "in substance" they write "subsistence," not "in substance." But if someone understands the meaning exactly, he finds nothing other than this: if someone stood in that which is the "to be" of God, that is "in substance," immediately he sees his *Logos* because the Son is *homoousios* (consubstantial) with him. For it is necessary that we make subsist in the interior something which is not interior, *ton Noun* (the Intellect) in the subsistence of God, that is, "in the substance," and immediately we understand both God and *Logos.* For they are *homoousion* (consubstantial), and both together are one. (31) But you will see this.

The substance of God is to be light and spirit

Let us say hypothetically that the substance of God is "to be" and the "to be" *tou Iēsou* (of Jesus). Both piety and the profession of Christian faith affirm that God is. What therefore is the substance of God if the word substance is used of earthly things? Is it necessary to say that God is substance among eternal things as animal, as man is substance? But you will see.

The substance of God is God himself according to "to be" which we call either light or Spirit or "to be" itself or power of "to be" or universal knowledge or power of universal knowledge or of universal life or of action or power of other things of this kind insofar as it is proper to him to be the source of the truly existents or the existents. But the Scriptures say that God is "light," God is "Spirit." But these terms designate substance. For "to be" is not an accident. For to what primarily does "to be" come, if it is an accident? But to

---

243 Cf. Ti 2.14.
244 Jer 23.18.
245 Jer 23.22.

nothing. For it is impossible that there should be something beyond, above "to be." Then light and Spirit, according to "to be," are substance. But because things there are simple and without composition, light and Spirit are the same thing.

c) The image of God: it is the Logos will of the Father.

But there is one image of light and of Spirit, not by the necessity of nature but by the will[246] of the Father's greatness. For he himself has circumscribed himself. And that is why it is said: you, you know yourself. But he is also knowable through the Son. The image, the form, the *Logos,* the will of the Father are therefore Son in the Father. Different from the Father as will of the Father; Son of the Father as will of the Father. For every will is a birth. As the universal will of the Father, he is the only begotten. For it is only once that the *Logos* of all plenitude has leapt forth from the power of God. This power existing as *Logos* has begotten the *Logos,* that is, has led him into manifestation and operation. So therefore by the will of the Father, there has appeared as will the *Logos* himself, the Son. He is therefore will of God, this *Logos* who is always with him and "with" him; this will itself is filiation. The one who has the will is therefore Father; the will itself, Son; and the *Logos* is will. Therefore the *Logos* is Son.

For the *Logos* is not a certain speech but the power of creating something, defining, for all those who will come to be according to the power of *ontotētos* (essentiality), to each one its proper substance. And the *Logos* himself is the form which is the knowledge of God. For only through the *Logos* is knowledge achieved. That is why it was said that the *Logos* is "with God." And the *Logos,* the

---

246   The remainder of this chapter and the first paragraph of ch. 32 show how the Father's substance is identical with his will. Therefore the Father's generation of the Son is not merely a natural generation but a willed generation. What is generated is the same, a Son who is the image of the Father, not merely his likeness. There is nothing in the Father that is not communicated to the Son, and therefore the Son also begets himself; since every will is autonomous, the Son is hypostatically distinct from the Father but substantially identical. In this way Victorinus responds to Basil of Ancyra's point that there is a creative as well as a generating activity when the Father begets the Son. Victorinus presents this Arian position as establishing a conflict in the divine substance.

Word, is light from light, Spirit from Spirit, and substance from substance, not first and second according to time, but insofar as one is cause of the other, so that by power they are always together. For the shining of the light is not separated but is always in the light; and the *Logos* being itself light is all-acting, moving himself by himself, and always in movement, having as resource that all-powerful "to be" which belongs to the Father.

(32) Therefore where here is the resemblance, where the sudden movement so that there might be created and generated, as you say, what is needed for the generation of the Son? The Father moving himself by himself, the Son begetting himself by himself,[247] but by the power of the Father the Son begetting himself by himself: for the Son is will. For, consider: if the will itself is not self-begotten, it is not will. But since this is the will of God, truly that which is begetting, it is begotten in God, and therefore God is Father, the will, Son: and both are one, but rather they are both one and solely one, not by union but by simplicity; the will indeed has developed into an active power, but in that movement which is at once proper and common, it is not separated from the substance. For on high these three are one: substance, movement, will. The Father is substance, and as substance, movement and will. Again, the Son is movement and will and as that, he is also substance. And this is *homoousion* (consubstantial).

IV. THE CONSUBSTANTIAL SHOWN BY THE NAMES OF THE SON

1. *The Consubstantial in the Soul*

We have the light of an example, this which I now recount.[248] For it is necessary to say—although some say that the body is in the

---

247 On self-generation. The passage confirms the writer's concern with the Sirmium dossier which eliminated the use of the word "substance" and taught the subordination of the Son to the Father; the Son as will wills himself and is life because life is desire to live. From "For look!" through "movement, will" we find once again those philosophical fragments (Group II) assembled by Hadot in PV II 31.

248 The remainder of ch. 32 is composed of two groups of philosophical fragments: Group II where the soul is identified with its definition, namely,

soul, but the usual thing to say is that the soul is in the body—that the soul is in the human body. In that it is soul, it is substance, just as matter or body is substance. For in this world these two are substances. And just as matter has a form, that is, a species, whether it is body or something else,—it is *hulikōs* (materially) a certain unity, condensed into a mass; for it is necessary that something be a certain quantity; and therefore that which is material is also quantified; for matter is thus limited by quantity so that it may subsist and become a substance, now something existing—in this way also the soul, which is an incorporeal substance, has a definition and image: its living and knowing power. For it is doubly powerful and of double light. Indeed, it both vivifies, giving life to animals, and it also has the *Nous,* which is innate and *homoousion* (consubstantial) and therefore all things in it are *homoousia* (consubstantial).

For the soul is simultaneously substance and movement; insofar as it is subject the soul is identical with that which lives and vivifies and with that which knows and is understanding, with one motion which is its species, since it itself is also one. For the soul is defined by movement and exists as one *on* (existent), with a double power existing in one movement of life and understanding. And it itself is without passion; but in action they are two in one movement, it is that which is begotten, the only begotten son of the soul, existing as life itself, *nous* itself.

And the first power accompanying the soul's "to be" is life. Through its very "to be" the soul is life. For this very "to be" which is proper to it, which is its substance, is at once life and above life. For it does not vivify something other, not even itself. For it does not receive life from another as something other than it. For that which is the "to be" of the soul is for it both to move itself and to be movement, and that which is movement, that is life, and that which is life, that is understanding. For these things are substantial, I say: movements, life, understanding, but I am not referring to sensible motion nor locomotion. Therefore, these two, life and

---

life and thought; cf. Hadot PV, II 22–23 and from the section beginning "for what is something . . . " Group IV; cf. Hadot, PV II 57; Porphyry *In Aristotelis categorias commentarium* 100.14. However, in his book *Plotin et l'Occident,* Henry speaks of this last section as an anonymous reference to *Enn.* 5.5.9.

understanding, are *homoousia* (consubstantial) with "to be," that is, the "to be" of the soul. These two are one movement. And the first power is life. For form by its "to be" is life. For the first power of movement defines that which is infinite "to be." But the second power is the notion[249] itself since that which is defined is also grasped by understanding, not born by life, being itself a substance insofar as it is subsistent knowledge, having drawn itself forth through itself from the substance of life. These two are one, also one in movement, which is the only begotten son of the soul which as soul undergoes no passion. But the soul[250] is either mother or father of the only begotten son, while it is the movement proceeding into a double power which alone suffers. For movement is passion, and passion is by movement. For in movement are both movement and repose. But to be in repose from movement is passion, and to be in movement from repose is passion also; therefore also movement. Hence all passion is from movement. But this passion is double, according to life and according to understanding. Indeed there is passion according to life because life always has need of the other which it wishes to vivify, and for that reason, according to that which is a participant in it, it also undergoes other passions even unto death. But there is passion according to understanding since this also is in need of the intelligible to subsist as understanding; it incurs greater passions and infirmities as it becomes both involved in sensible things and is driven through imagination into false reality. With these two powers going out and undergoing passions, the soul[251] remains as substance preserving in the principle of movement the power of life and of understanding, and because this power is permanent, life and understanding are enkindled as light, but the soul uplifts them when, herself awakened, she arises to the original life, that is, to Christ and to the original understanding, that is, to the Holy Spirit.

---

249 I read the CSEL conjecture, *notio* (idea, notion or image).
250 The structure and destiny of the soul illuminates not only trinitarian relationships but to some extent the mystery of the Incarnation. Cf. Augustine, *De trinitate* 9.4.5 (FC 45.274-75); Plotinus, *Enn.* 1.1.2.
251 The body participates in the life of the soul; the body suffers, not the soul. On the soul's fall, cf. I 61,10ff. The soul falls when, forsaking its natural object—the soul itself and the intelligibles—it vivifies the sensible

2. The Logos, Act, Image, Reflection of God
Is Consubstantial Son to the Father

a) God, interior Logos and act[252]

(33) But this is, so to speak, by way of resemblance. For now that it is a matter of God and of the *Logos,* that is, of the Son Jesus Christ and the Holy Spirit, using an understanding more capable of examining divine things, let us defend their *homoousion* (consubstantial) unity. First is to be questioned[253] whether God and for God "to be" are the same thing or something different? If the same, already both "to be" is also "to act." But if for God "to be" is different, different from "to be God," then for God "to be" is preexistent, certainly existing in potentiality to "to be" because it is more truly "to be." For it is, in potentiality, the preexistence of all things, it is the preprinciple and prior to the truly *on* (existent). But this One the saints[254] believe to be in repose, absolutely and in all respects, and in movement only as cause of all those which exist in any movement whatsoever. And they say that he is conceived by preknowledge which through itself is nothing, but is formed from the conception that he preexists. But Scripture and common knowledge affirm both that this God is and there is nothing before him, him who is at once "to be" and "to act." We confess and adore

---

world and is misled by sensible knowledge. Inward return is conversion to the source of the soul's life and knowledge—Christ and the Holy Spirit of whom the soul is the image; cf. I 20,38–55; I 58, 18–24; I 63–64.

252 In chs. 33 and 34 there is an appeal to Plato's *Parmenides* and to Scripture. Can Victorinus reconcile the biblical living, creative God and the Neoplatonic One? Victorinus rejects the tradition of a first immobile God and a second creative God. Cf. Plotinus, *Enn.* 1.1.2. Aristotle, *Metaphysics* 8.3 (1043b1); Victorinus, *in Eph.* 3.9 (1266AB); *ad Cand.* 2,16–30; *adv. Ar.* I 30,20–26; 29,11–14; 29,39–30,5; *hymn.* II 14; *ad Cand.* 17,1–23,10. The Formula of Antioch (341) intended to replace strict Nicene theology provides a list of the Son's names which directs the whole movement of thought at the end of this first book.

253 In ch. 33 beginning with the words "First is to be questioned . . . " there is present a new group of philosophical fragments (Group III) where "to be" is discussed as indetermination and "being" as intelligible determination. Cf. Hadot, PV II 46.

254 I accept the CSEL conjecture; SC's *beati* (the saints or sages) would be subject of the verb, "consider," which, when the conjecture is used, remains without an expressed subject (hence they). In either case we do not know who are being referred to.

this God as the principle of existents; for by act are those things which are; for before action they do not yet exist. For we believe in a God who acts, as for example: "In the beginning God made heaven and earth,"[255] and he made the angels, man, and all things in the heavens and on earth. Therefore he is the true God and the only God, because he is God both in potentiality and in action, but internal action, whereas Christ is both in potentiality and in action, but now external and manifest. God the Father is therefore first act and first existence and substance, and original *To On* (The Existent), who by his own action begets himself, existing always without origin, existing from himself, infinite, perfect in all ways, omnipotent, unchanging, always existing thus and in the same way; existing in himself as substantial *Logos* so that all things might be, he is not that *Logos* as something different or other than himself, but coexisting together in simplicity and union, he is one. For that which is the *Logos* is itself "to be" and by that by which he is "to be," he is *Logos;* for the *Logos* himself is God; they are therefore one and *homoousion* (consubstantial). For God is not without action, but God acts within, as was said.[256]

b) The Logos, *image and son of God*

(34) But action is the image of the substance of God and is the Son and through this image God is known as it was declared: "Whoever sees me, sees the Father."[257] And this image is itself substance having "to be" also from itself. But since that of which it is image is its cause, the image itself is therefore the Son of that of which it is image, by an ineffable begetting, and especially by an "unbegotten begetting" or better, "by a begetting always begetting", which Alexander also said. Also it is said: "always Father, always Son, existing together." Therefore also insofar as the Son is always consubstantial, coexistent, existing as one, the Son is in the Father. But when he acts, he proceeds; when he proceeds, the Father is in the Son. But how this can be, we shall say.

---

255 Gn 1.1.
256 Cf. *adv. Ar.* I 33,22; I 4,3.
257 Jn 14.9.

c) *The image of God: it is the* Logos, *will of the Father.*

God and the *Logos* are one and united and therefore *homoousion* (consubstantial). But God, as God, is cause both of potential "to be" and of all existents with respect to their "to be." The *Logos,* as *Logos,* is the paternal power to give subsistence to "to be"; he is himself the original "to be," both origin and completion. For from the universal "to be" and the superuniversal, all universal "to be," whether genera, species or individuals, receive the "to be" proper to each of them. If therefore the *Logos* has "to be"—for the *Logos* is that very thing which is its own "to be"—therefore the *Logos,* too, is "to be" from the superuniversal "to be." But the universal "to be" is the *Logos.* But God is the superuniversal "to be." But the Son is the universal "to be." Therefore the Father is the superuniversal "to be." They are therefore both *homoousion* (consubstantial) insofar as "to be" is to "to be" as the superuniversal is to the universal. But this is also a progression: from the superuniversal proceeds the universal, and, understood more exactly, it both goes forth and remains; for the universal is not left to itself. Therefore the universal both subsists through itself and is within the superuniversal; therefore, they are united and inseparable. This is what is called the reflection of the light, having everything from the light, but not as receiving it from without; nor has it come from the outside but is connatural, and therefore always existing *homoousios* (consubstantial) with the light. Therefore not by locomotion nor by a change is it a reflection. For the Father is unchangeable, the Son is unchangeable, and the Father is always, the Son is always, even if the Son is considered in the Father as image and form of "to be," as was said,[258] or if the Son has proceeded as reflection of the light. When these are thus existing, and, more so, when they are existing as one—for the reflection is the splendor of light—and he has in himself the light from the Father and he is both in the light and outside—therefore, the Son is also in the Father. And because the splendor surrounds the light, it is said rather that the splendor is with the light, not in the light, and yet if it shines from the light, it is in the light. And this signifies: "In the principle was the *Logos*

---

258 Cf. *adv. Ar.* I 31,21.35; I 22,28 ff.

and the *Logos* was with God."[259] Therefore both Son and Father are *homoousion* (consubstantial), and they are always such, both from eternity and for eternity.

3. The Logos is Consubstantial Son Because in Him, through Him, for Him Are All Things

a) The image of God is the son of Mary, is the son of God and is the Logos

(35) We shall also speak of other names. Is the *Logos* "with God"?[260] Evidently he is. What is the *Logos*? The one "through" whom are all things, and "in" whom are all things, and "for" whom are all things.[261] It is evident that this *Logos* is also Jesus because the *Logos* is the Son of God but the Son is Jesus of whom St. Paul says: "He has rescued us from the power of darkness and transferred us into the kingdom of his beloved Son."[262] Who therefore is this Son? The one, he says, "in whom we have redemption through his blood, remission of our sins."[263] Who is this one? He who was born of Mary. What then? Is that all? No. What is he saying above all? That in the Son who was from Mary was also the Son who was before[264] he came from Mary. But what does this lead to? "He who is image of God." Is this the name only of the Son of Mary? No. For the "image of God" is image from eternity. If then we have hope in

---

259 Jn 1.1.

260 Chs. 35–39 form a unit. The Anomoeans considered the propositions used by Scripture (by whom, for whom, in whom, through whom, from whom) as an expression of different substances. Cf. Basil, *De Spiritu Sancto* 2.4 (PG 32.69B) for proximate source of this prepositional theology, and its remote source can be found in the philosophical classification of causes. But, argues Victorinus, Scripture uses the same prepositions for the Father as for the Son because there is community of action between Father and Son, denoting community of substance—a great mystery: cf. *hymn.* I 68-9. In comparing Pauline texts to establish identity between *Logos,* Son of God and Son of Mary, Victorinus seems to be imitating the exegetical method of Basil of Ancyra.

261 Cf. Col 1.17.

262 Col 1.13.

263 Col 1.14.

264 Victorinus distinguishes the preexisting Christ *(Logos)* from the carnal Christ, but he himself confuses at least here the carnal Christ with the humanity of Christ or his animated body.

the Son, and he has redeemed us "through blood," but he himself is the "image of God," therefore the Son is the image of God. Is it I who assert this? Not only I, but also Paul. How indeed does he express it? "Firstborn of all creation."[265] Who is this "firstborn"? A Son. What Son? The Son of Mary. What Son of Mary? "Firstborn of the whole creation." Who is the "firstborn of the whole creation"? He who is "image of God." For it is necessary that the "firstborn" before "all" creation be the "image of God."[266] But who is the "image"? The *Logos*. Who is the *Logos?* He who "was in the principle." For without an "image" how would God be? And who is the *Logos*? He who "was with God" and "through" whom "all things were made," and "without" whom "nothing was made." How the *Logos* is image and how the Son is *Logos,* the Son who is Son of Mary, but especially the Son who is in the Son of Mary, this is clear from these texts. If the Son of God has redeemed us "through his blood," he who is the Son of Mary, and if he himself is the "image of God," he is the Son of God. For if he is the "firstborn of the whole creation," necessarily he is Son. Is there another? Far from it! For the Son of God is the only begotten one. It is necessary therefore that this be the same one: the Son, and the image, and he who is from Mary. For how would the Son be the "image of God" if he were not the "firstborn of the whole creation"? And how would he be the "image of God," he who was the Son of Mary, if he were born after all things were created? Therefore it is evident that he himself is the "firstborn." What then? Is the one born of Mary not a creature? But if the Son of God, the "image of God," was born before every creature, he was also born before that one who was born of Mary. Therefore, he who was born before all creation, he is in the one who was born of Mary. Therefore, it is evident that he is the only begotten Son.

(36) After that, we must be attentive to how this same one, both image and Son, is the *Logos*. It is evident that the Son is image. For Paul said: The "Son" of God is the "image of God." I say therefore that he is the *Logos,* of whom it was said: "In the principle was the *Logos,*"[267] For Paul says how the Son is the "firstborn of the

---

265 Cf. Col 1.13–16.
266 Col 1.15.
267 Jn 1.1.

whole creation, because in him all things have been created, those which are in the heavens and which are on earth, which are visible and invisible, whether Thrones or Dominations or Principalities or Powers; all things have been created through him and in him, and he himself is before all, and in him all things hold together."[268] You see what he said of the Son: that because "all things have been created in him and through him and for him,"[269] on that account, he is the "firstborn."

He says, therefore, three things. Among them is this one: "All through him"—to whom has this always been attributed? As it is in the confession of faith: to the *Logos*. If then Paul attributes "through him" to the Son, but the him which is "through him" John attributes to the *Logos*, the first Apostle and the preeminent Evangelist agree in what they have said. One must not doubt that the *Logos* is Son.

What then? As for the other two things, which he attributed to the Son, to whom are they more properly attributed? Necessarily, to the *Logos*.[270] For his power is the subsistence of all existents. But if this is also the case, in him are all things, as it was said: "Because in him all things have been created." And for that reason "all things are for him," since all things will be spiritualized. Paul also signifies this at the end of the world: "For when all things will have been made subject to him, then he himself will be subject to him who subjected all things to him, that God may be all in all."[271] What this is and how it will be, we shall see later.[272] Now, let us admit that it is because all things will be spiritual.

It is therefore true that the Son of Mary is the Son of God, and that he is Image, and that he is *Logos*, and that he is before time and all creation, and that every creature has been "created through

---

268 Col 1.16–17.

269 This formula emerged from the Council of Antioch (341), attended by ninety-seven bishops as well as the Emperor Constantius himself. According to ODCC[2] 65 "no less than four creeds were put forward, all of them defective from the standpoint of orthodoxy since they were intended not to supplement, but to replace, that of Nicaea."

270 A philosophical notion of *Logos* supports the argument; passions are localized in the activity of the *Logos*, not in the substantiality.

271 1 Cor 15.28.

272 Cf. *adv. Ar.* I 37,42–39,34.

him" and "in him," and "for him," and what was said afterwards. (37) Who then will be as foolish, as sacrilegious as Arius, who so godless that he does not see who Jesus is, and whence comes the only begotten Son?

b) God and the Logos are consubstantial, because all things are through them and for them

But that both God and the *Logos* are *homoousion* (consubstantial) that is, Father and Son, is evident from the preceding. Whatever Paul attributed to the Son, he attributed the same things also to the Father, with those three prepositions, although in one of them he referred to paternal dignity so that there would be evident both one divinity and the substance and power proper to the Father. To the Colossians he said the former statements of the Son. But to the Romans he said the same of the Father: "For who has known the mind of the Lord or who has been his counselor, or who has first given to him and been recompensed, since from him and through him and for him are all things?"[273] You see how he has attributed both to the Father and the Son the same things, but not precisely the same, for the sake of *homoousion* (the consubstantial). First, there were three prepositions for one, and three for the other. Then the same prepositions were used for both Father and Son.

But this: "Through whom are all things" is attributed to both the Father and the Son since the Son who is the *Logos* of all existents is the actual power in existents, and because the Father is in the Son, the Father also exists in him as actual power. For at the same time the Son is in the Father, and the Father in the Son. Therefore, there is one power, that is, one substance; for there, power is substance; for power is nothing else, other than substance. Therefore, this is the same for Father and for Son.

But this expression: "From whom are all things" he attributed to the Father. For all things are from the Father, the Son himself also. This is therefore attributed to the Father as something proper to him.

But this is attributed as proper to the Son: "In whom are all things," because the *Logos* is also place. Indeed he is the receptacle

---

273 Rom 11.34–36.

of creatures and of the effects made through him. But when all things are existing there, he becomes plenitude. Indeed, Jesus also is the Father of all effects, of those which are made through him. The Father and the Son are therefore one. But because the effects are not introduced from outside, whence do they come? For there is nothing outside; he has therefore created all things in himself. Therefore, "all things are in him." Hence he is both receptacle and inhabitant. And since the Father is in the Son, the Father also is inhabitant. Therefore, this is proper to the Son: "In whom are all things."

Therefore this remaining preposition: "And for him," I say that this is common to both. For at the end of the world all things will be one. And that is why Paul says to the Corinthians: "There is one God, the Father from whom are all things and for whom we are, and one Lord Jesus through whom are all things and through whom we are."[274] Or as others say: "for whom," since in other passages there is used of the Father: "From whom are all things, through whom are all things, for whom[275] are all things." Therefore Paul has attributed both to Father and to Son totally equal functions. Rightly so, because the Father and Son are *homoousios* (consubstantial).

And on that account it was said: "Then he will be made subject to him who subjected all things to him, that God may be all in all."[276] (38) Notice the force of the expression; for it leads to the *homoousion* (consubstantial); the Son "subjects all things" to the Father, by his own power, so it seems, but really by the paternal power. For he says: "to the one subjecting all things to him." To

---

274 1 Cor 8.6.

275 From here to almost the end of sect. 39, Victorinus argues according to his reading of 1 Cor 8.6: *in ipsum* instead of *per ipsum* as read by the Anomoeans (those who taught that the Father was totally unlike the Son). Victorinus applied *in ipsum* to Father and Son as final cause of the universe, assuring it unity by their own unity; helpful also was that interpretation of 1 Cor 15.24–28 which implies the unity of the activity of Father and Son. Action linked to creation and incarnation is directed to the return of all things to God, that consummatory contemplation when all existents shall be spiritualized. The end of the mystery is the unity of the entire universe and of souls in the divine unity. Cf. Victorinus, *in Phil.* 3.21 (1226B). The contemplative act achieves the return to God and transfiguration. This links up with Victorinus's original inspiration from St. John's Prologue: the *Logos* as Life and Light effects the return to the Father.

276 1 Cor 15.28.

whom will he be subjected? To God. Who "will be subjected"? The Son, to whom God "has subjected all things." Both Father and Son are therefore action. Where then is the substance? There where action itself is; rather, that is action which is substance; therefore, *homoousion* (consubstantial). Paul also says this: "When he will have delivered the kingdom to God the Father."[277] Therefore he now reigns also according to his own action—for Christ is action—he "subjects all things" and destroys hostile forces and death itself. Therefore he himself "subjects," just as Paul says: "Since he does away with all sovereignty, authority, and power."[278] He speaks thus because the Son does that by his own power. He also adds this: "For he must reign."[279] Certainly God is king of all things. But since the Son is also *homoousios* (consubstantial), and above all, *Logos,* that is the "power and wisdom of God,"[280] it is necessary that there should first reign wisdom, through whom all things will be "subjected." For through the *Logos* all things subsist and will be subjected, as will be affirmed and has been affirmed.[281] Because the *Logos,* that is, the Son, "subjects all things to the Father," Paul has for that reason also added: "Until he has placed all his enemies under his feet."[282] Who places these enemies? Whose enemies? Evidently, because the Son acts, the enemies are the Father's. But since the Father is in the Son, for that reason the Father "subjects all things" to the Son, and consequently, it is above all the Son who has enemies, not the Father; and since both have them, there is a fortunate ambiguity of meaning, and consequently they are *homoousioi* (consubstantial). "The last enemy will be destroyed, death."[283] For if Jesus is life, and eternal life, "death will be destroyed" by life. Therefore Jesus, that is, the Son "subjects all things" to the Father. But since he is *homoousios* (consubstantial) with the Father, both by very substance and by very power, and since to be first is to be Father and simply "to be" whereas to be second is to act, to live, to know, and since that which

---

277 1 Cor 15.24.
278 1 Cor 15.24.
279 1 Cor 15.25.
280 Cf. 1 Cor 1.24.
281 Cf. *adv. Ar.* I 37,23–32; 39 15–25.
282 1 Cor 15.25.
283 1 Cor 15.26.

is first is the cause of the two, it is necessary to say that the Father subjects all things to the Son. Paul therefore says: "When he delivers the kingdom to God the Father," necessarily the Son does this; and "Since he does away with all sovereignty and power," necessarily the Son does this. Again he says: "But when all things have been subjected, evidently he is excepted who subjects all things to him";[284] this is no small conception. (39) But let us drop it for the moment.

What does he wish us to understand? That God who is cause, both very powerful and the preprinciple of power, that he himself accomplishes all things when the Son accomplishes them,[285] and if the Father is in the Son and the Son in the Father, he himself accomplishes in the Son whatever the Son accomplishes, and "What the Father does, the Son does."[286] Therefore all things are attributed indifferently either to the Father or to the Son, whether actions or things. For each one of the two is in the other and that which is other in each one is not really other; but the Father is by his own subsistence, the Son is by his own subsistence, from the one substance which is from the Father. But the Son, that is, the *Logos,* is active power, both that which creates and that which vivifies, and is power of understanding. All these things the Son both generates and creates through life and regenerates them through the understanding of the truth and of God that Jesus gives to all, since he is *Logos* of all things, both of the living and of those having understanding and of all those which exist in any way whatsoever. If therefore he generates and regenerates all things, he "will subject all things," not only men but also, as Paul says: "Every principality and every power."[287] Does he do that as man or as *Logos?* Indeed, this "subjecting" not only occurs at the moment in which he became Son of Mary, but it occurred both before and after. For if there was a deluge, if Sodom and Gomorrha were destroyed by fire, if these

---

284 1 Cor 15.24, 25, 27.
285 A trace of the profession of faith of Sirmium (351) which was directed against Photinus who wished to attribute to the Father acts which were proper to the Son.
286 Cf. Jn 5.19.
287 For the Scripture adduced here and in the next few sentences, cf. 1 Cor 15.24-28.

events and many others occurred, if, in the first coming, he "triumphed" in himself over his enemies, if, in the second coming "the last enemy will be destroyed, death," the Son, the *Logos,* does these things, but by the paternal power. Therefore he makes all things to be spirit and spiritual. "And then also he himself will be subjected to God who subjects all things to him." For all opposition being destroyed, the active power reposes, and God will be in him according to "to be," according to repose, but in all others spiritually according to both his own power and substance. And this is: "That God may be all in all." For he is not all in each one, but "all in all." Therefore all things will endure, but with God existing in all, and for that reason God will be all things, because all will be full of God.

4. The Son Is Consubstantial with the Father Because He Is the "Power and Wisdom" of God

(40) Let us also speak of other names. "For I am not ashamed of the Gospel: the power and wisdom of God;"[288] Paul says this of Jesus Christ; for he is "the Gospel."[289] He says also concerning this: "Christ," therefore, is "both the wisdom and power of God."[290]

What then? "The wisdom and power of God," is that not God himself? For with God things are not as they are in bodies or in bodily things where the eye[291] is one thing, sight another, or as they are in fire, where fire is one thing, its light another. For both eye and fire have need of something other: the eye, of a light different from itself so that from it and through it vision can take place, and the fire has need of air so that light might come from it. But the power and wisdom of God are like vision: the power of vision has vision within it. This vision is externalized when the power of vision

---

288 A defective text showed only . . . *entiam; potentiam* was supplied in SC but the CSEL editor noted that power was already rendered through *virtutem* and therefore conjectured *sapientiam,* which I have accepted.

289 Rom 1.16.

290 1 Cor 1.24.

291 Once again we meet fourteen lines of philosophical fragments (Group II) assembled by Hadot in PV II 26. In his discussion of how the power of vision is distinct from and yet related to vision, Victorinus shows that the act proceeding entirely from the faculty is a model for consubstantiality. Cf. Plotinus, *Enn.* 3.6.2. Seeing is an immanent action.

is in action; then vision is begotten by the power of vision and is itself its only begotten, for nothing else is begotten by it. And vision encompasses the power of vision, not only within, when it is in potentiality, but above all, outside, when it is in action; so vision encompasses the power of vision. Vision is therefore *homoousion* (consubstantial) with the power of vision, and the whole is one: the power of vision is in repose, but vision is in movement; and by vision all things are made visible. Feelings are also present in vision, the power of vision remaining incapable of feeling and itself begetting vision without feeling. And the "power and wisdom of God" are God himself, and the whole is simple and one, of one same substance, together from all eternity and always from the Father, who himself is the begetter of his own existence. "Wisdom" and "power" are therefore actions; for he now designates action as power; indeed, Paul has joined together "wisdom" and "power." God is therefore the potentiality of these two things, and for that reason he is Father because they come from him. Indeed he begets them into action and impassibly, because power and action are *homoousia* (consubstantial), God and the "power and wisdom" of God. Since the latter are active, while remaining with God they care for whatever is external to him, always giving wisdom, always vivifying, not God but every creature made by God through their mediation. And if there is any passion, the passion is in the action.

In this way, whether the *Logos* is Jesus, or "light," or "reflection," or "form," or "image," or "power and wisdom," or "character," or "life," it will be clear that the *Logos* and God, the Father and the Son, the Spirit and Christ are *homoousion* (consubstantial).

5. The Son is Consubstantial with the Father Because He is Life

(41) Let us reintroduce the same argument, saying that Christ is life.[292] How Christ is *homoousion* (consubstantial) with God, John

---

292 Life is related to motion as substance is related to its definition. Cf. I 52,49. This whole development of the consubstantiality of Son with Father because the Son is life begins here and extends to the beginning of sect. 43. It represents for Victorinus an important point of contact between Scripture and philosophy.

says: "What was made in him was life;"[293] and again, "For as the Father has life in himself, even so has he given to the Son to have life in himself."[294] What is more simultaneous, what more identical? The Father has life in himself; the Son also has life in himself. What is it to have life in himself? It is to be life itself for himself, it is to receive life, not from another, but from himself and to give it to others.

Someone says that it is to be similar in substance, yet not to be *homoousion* (consubstantial). It was already stated that "similar in substance"[295] is neither said nor is it the case with substance; but, above all, if it is a case of resemblance in one same substance, the substance is called the same, not similar. For things are similar according to qualities, as, for example, fire and air are substances; according to substance they are identical—for both are *hulē* (matter); but, by their qualities, they are similar or dissimilar, for example, similar by motion, by power and other things. Likewise, both land and water are dissimilar by weight, density, or other such qualities; in these things this also happens: things which are similar are at the same time dissimilar by different qualities.[296] For that which is similar is not identical nor identically one, but identical in duality. There is also a unity in these things, not a substantial unity but a numerical unity.

Now we shall earnestly inquire about the substance which is in God and in the Son: is there selfsameness or identity, or is there in some way both selfsameness and identity? How therefore is there selfsameness with the Son going forth and accomplishing so many things in heaven and earth and finally taking on flesh? How is Jesus a Son, which signifies a birth? How also are there three substances, God, the *Logos,* the Holy Spirit? For it is not suitable to say, nor should it be said that there is one substance, that there are three persons. For if so, the selfsame substance both needed all things and suffered. Shall we, therefore, also be Patripassians? Far from that! Is there substantial identity, not individual identity? But if this is

---

293 Jn 1.3-4.

294 Jn 5.26.

295 There are nine more lines here of the Aristotelian philosophical fragments (Group IV) previously referred to in Hadot's collection, PV II 57.

296 Cf. *adv. Ar.* I 23,7-12.

so, either they are two from a preexisting substance, or from the
same substance, a substance identical in individuality is constituted
either by division or separation of a part. But neither by division nor
by diminishment was the Son born, but the Father is complete, both
always complete and always Father; the Son is complete and always
complete, and from eternity and unto eternity is he Son. How,
therefore, are they identical? For what is there of identity in two?
But the Father and Son are one, and the Father is Father, the Son is
Son, and the Father is not the same one as the Son nor is the Son
the same as the Father whose Son he is. Therefore, they are not one
if they are neither identical as individuals nor identical in substance.
It remains, therefore, that in some way there is both individuality
and identity in substance. For it is not permitted to say that there is
difference of substance between Father and Son.

In what way[297] there is selfsame substance we shall say: whether
we call them God and *Logos,* or God and the "power and wisdom"
of God or "to be" and "life" or "to be" and "to understand" or
knowledge, or "to be" and "life" and "to understand," or Father
and Son, or "light" and "reflection," or God and "character," or God
and "form and image," or substance and species (as it is there, not as
it is here),[298] or substance and movement, or power and action, or
silence and speech, it must be confessed that there is selfsameness of
substance. For if we call God "to be" and the Son "life," how do we
separate life from "to be" whether in the Father or in the Son?
Indeed the Father has life in himself and the Son also, except that
the Son received from the Father what he has. Therefore Father and
Son have originated from themselves, having from themselves the
power of life. Understand that I am using "having" as the Gospel
does: "And the Father indeed has life in himself." "He has" therefore not as someone has something other than himself, but that same
thing that he "has," he is, but we have used this word "has" in the
act of understanding. If therefore the "Father has life in himself,"[299] he is life and his substance is life. Likewise the Son, for he

---

297 The CSEL's substitution of *quomodo* (in what way) for *quoniam* (that)
     clarified the interrogative status of this opening sentence.
298 Cf. *adv. Ar.* I 40,32–34.
299 Jn 5.26.

says: "I am life."[300] This statement therefore signifies having life in himself. Therefore the Father is life, and the Son is life. All life as life[301] is movement, vivifying that which is able to be vivified; and for that reason the definition of the soul and of life is this: that which moves itself by itself; and that defines its "to be" and, so to speak, its substance. Much more therefore is this the case in respect to God and the *Logos*. What therefore shall we say? The Father is life and substance, and substance moving itself, and there is no other self-moving movement than life. Therefore both substance and life are identical. But because in movement the intellect distinguishes something other than movement and not perfectly other, namely "to live" itself insofar as it is other, by a kind of mixture of the other in each one, is a unity insofar as it is life and also movement. Again, insofar as it is movement and also life, this same reality is another unity. And for that reason it is the same substance. But whether they are the selfsame or identical, they are necessarily *homoousion* (consubstantial) and together in substance, since the two are together. Indeed there was never one without the other. These are therefore two unities. That, therefore, which is life and self-movement is the Father. But that which is movement and life through itself is the Son. For the cause of movement is life. The Father is then, and by predominance, original life, having hidden in him a movement which remains in repose, interior self-movement. But the Son is manifested movement, and that is why the Son, since he has proceeded from that which is interior movement, is existing as movement by predominance, because he is movement manifested. In this way the Son, also life, receives to-be-life from the Father who is life, born as principle from the preprinciple, as universal from the universal, as a whole from a whole, and therefore he says: "The living Father has sent me and I live on account of him."[302] If therefore the one who begets is in life, and if the Son as movement is the Son, but if he is life through movement, the Son is life, the Father giving him in movement both begetting and life; but the Father him-

---

300 Jn 14.6.
301 We here encounter eleven more lines of philosophical fragments (Group II) as cited in Hadot, PV II 32.
302 Jn 6.57.

self is life in itself. The Father and Son are therefore *homoousion* (consubstantial); they are always one; the Son is born from eternity; they are one within the other; separated without being able to be separated; for the Son is in the Father and the Father in the Son, and the Son is predominantly action, since the Son is life with action, but the Father insofar as he is "to be" is life, and insofar as he is to-be-life, he is action. Therefore the Father reposes in life and remains impassible; the Son acts and leads all things into manifestation. And God also acts interiorly, for action exists also in the Father but according to power, and in the Son action is according to action.

(43) It is necessary to recall the reasons for all the names that we have enumerated above: whether God and *Logos,* or light and reflection, or silence and speech, or others; in these names it is clearly evident that they are one and together and *homoousion* (consubstantial), and that there is an unbegotten begetting.[303]

6. Conclusion against the Homoeousians

a) Homoeousianism is traced back to Anomoeism

Where, therefore, is there any room for similarity?[304] For what reason do they say *homoiousion* (similar in substance)? It is always said—and this is the whole mystery—that there is one God, and Father and Son and Holy Spirit are one God. But how, if there is similarity, is there one God? But if there is *homoousion* (consubstantiality), necessarily there is one God. For if there is an appearance of otherness, it does not at once follow necessarily that there is duality. But if this otherness is similarity, it is necessarily a real otherness. And thus *homoiousion* (similarity in substance) necessarily requires otherness of substance. There are Arians, there are Lucianists, there are Eusebians, there are Illyrians but in adding, subtracting and changing, all are of diverse and heretical opinions.

---

303 Cf. *adv. Ar.* I 40,32–34; I 41,42–47.
304 Victorinus draws the only possible conclusion: since a "similarity in substance" presupposes otherness in substance, the Homoiousians should be equated with the Anomoeans; allusion is made here to Basil of Ancyra and his compromise formula "of similar substance."

b) If the Father and the Son are truth,
they are not similar but consubstantial

There is added this: if the Father and Son are *homoiousion* (similar in substance), how is it that the Savior says: "I am the truth"?[305] If what is said is true, since the Son is truth, the Father is inferior to him, being only similar to the truth and not the truth itself. What great blasphemy! But if God is truth and the Son is truth, as the Son himself says and truly says, God and the Son are *homoousion* (consubstantial). Therefore, there is not a double truth, but always one truth. And that which is similar in truth is situated very much outside and very much below truth, if by chance any similarity to truth may exist in this world where there is error and corruption and universal suffering. Therefore, to be truth itself is substance; for substance is not one thing, truth another; for that which is simple, that is truth: God is simple, the Son is simple; God is truth, the Son is truth; both God and the Son are one truth. For truth is in itself truth. Likewise if the Son is similar in truth, he leads his followers to that which is similar in truth. But if he is the truth, he leads them to the truth. But in fact he leads them to God and God is truth. Therefore he leads them to the truth. But it is impossible, when he is not the truth, to lead to the truth. Therefore, both Father and Son are truth, as it was also said: "The one whom the Father sends to me, that one comes to me."[306]

V. GENERAL CONCLUSION: THE BEGETTING OF THE SON IS A MOVEMENT WHICH INVOLVES NO CHANGE IN GOD

From the preceding statements it is not only concluded but demonstrated by clear evidence that movement in God is without change;[307] for it is not locomotion nor a begetting accompanied with suffering, or destruction or growth or diminishment, nor with any kind of change. For there above, moving is also self-moving; that which is "to be" is at once both itself and simple, and understood as unity, it is one, as it were, in power and action, always at least

---

305 Jn 14.6.
306 Jn 6.37.
307 A return to the conclusion of *ad Cand.* 30,16–17.

homoousion (consubstantial) in that which is "to be," but insofar as "to act" is from "to be," being Son and Father; but as was said, the Father is also in the Son and the Son is in the Father.[308]

VI. APPENDICES

1. Refutation of the Accusation of Patripassianism

(44) From this discussion shall we naturally fear that those of us saying these things are, as it were, Patripassians? This diabolical opinion is far from the truth. For the Patripassians reserve the name of God to the one whom we call the Father, granting existence solely to him and saying that he is the Creator of all things and that he has come not only into the world but also into the flesh, and that he does all the other acts which we say that the Son has done. For if we say that the Father is Father and the Son is Son, thereby saying a one and a one, and for that reason calling that which is one *homoousion* (consubstantial), not a single one but a one and a one, but saying that one is unable to suffer, the other has suffered, how then are we Patripassians? For God does not proceed outside himself nor is he manifested action; and in some way he is not in movement because interior movement, in some way, is not movement. But the *Logos* which consists in a power of movement is movement and action be predominance; he moves himself by his own power unto the creation of all existents. For as *Logos,* he is the cause of existents. But as cause,[309] he does not remain within himself while always remaining who he is as *Logos.* And according to this also he is unchangeable and immutable, but in existents he becomes different in accordance with the kinds of existents while remaining self-identical as universal *Logos* who is in the Father. Where then are the sufferings? Neither in the Father nor in the Son, but in the existents which because of their proper genus do not receive the total power of the universal *Logos.* Each of them exists, and the *Logos* distributes to each one what is proper to it insofar as they are angels, virtues, thrones, dominations, powers, souls, sensible things, finally flesh.

---

308 Cf. *adv. Ar.* I 39,4.
309 Neoplatonic notion of causality where the cause is immobile yet present in its effects. Plotinus, *Enn.* 4.8.6.

There is, therefore, suffering in these and according to the kind it is, but there is no suffering of the *Logos,* that is, of the Son. Therefore, according to the flesh the Savior has suffered, but according to the Spirit which he was before he was in the flesh, he is without suffering. Whence our teaching differs from that of the Patripassians. For to be Son is not a suffering, as was said, nor is it suffering to create something or to speak.[310] For by the divine power all things are done without suffering. And these acts are for the Son his predominant movement, both substantial and divine, not a suffering. Furthermore, the Patripassians were not concerned with this but with the cross, saying sacrilegiously that the Father was crucified, attributing sufferings to the impassible, and not understanding that there necessarily is something impassible, if there is another which suffers. But as for us, we say that the Son himself is incapable of suffering as *Logos;* but that he is capable of suffering insofar as "he was made flesh." But mercy, anger, joy, sadness, and other feelings of this kind are not passions up there, but are nature and substance. If, therefore, "the good odor" of the Spirit, since the Spirit through itself is excellent, leads "some into life, others into death," not by a change of its nature but because of the matter and the will of those receiving his action, likewise, even though its nature is immutable, the divinity is said to be affected or to suffer according to whether those receiving its action welcome it appropriately or otherwise: we express ourselves in this way because we judge divine things according to our senses. For in sensible things the animal insofar as it is animal, that is, the soul using a body, or indeed the ensouled body, is said to suffer in respect to sense; but strictly speaking there are no passions with regard to the soul considered alone. With much greater reason there are no passions for the Spirit, for the *Logos,* and for God.[311] For the divine nature is incapable of suffering.

---

310 Cf. *adv. Ar.* I 22,51–55.

311 Between this section and the middle of sect. 45 Victorinus completes his long demonstration of the Son's consubstantiality with the Father based on names for the Son found in the Profession of Faith (Antioch 341) which was attached to Basil of Ancyra' dossier of the Synod of Sirmium (358 summer); doctrines attributed to Arius are in this dossier.

2. Anathemas against All Heresies

(45) Let the Patripassians therefore depart, since we affirm both Father and Son, with the latter alone capable of suffering, through movement in matter.

Let the Arians depart, since we affirm a Son by nature, begotten "before all creation."

Let those also depart who say that Christ is *apo tou ontos* (from the Existent) because he would have been created by God who is the Existent God. For we affirm a Son by nature and say that he is from the Father and in the Father.

Let the disciples of Marcellus and of Photinus depart! For we affirm that the *Logos* himself was in the flesh and not that the *Logos* is different from the man in whom Christ was said to be, but that the *Logos* himself put on flesh. Those disciples affirm that there is a God, a *Logos,* a Spirit, and yet a fourth, the Son, that is, the man who is from Mary, the man whom the *Logos* assumed and directed as an instrument; they say also that a throne is prepared for this man. They have therefore forsaken the Trinity. But if there remains only the Trinity, this very man is also the *Logos,* the *Logos* whom above we have demonstrated as Son. "And the *Logos* was made flesh" does not signify that a corrupted *Logos* was changed into flesh, but that the *Logos* "through whom all things have been made" both made all things and "was made flesh," so that when he was in the flesh he might redeem the whole man by his passion and death[312] according to the passions of the body. For if the *Logos* was not the very man born of Mary, why is it said: "He emptied himself," and what does "taking the form of slave"[313] signify? And again what is signified by: "And the *Logos* was made flesh"?[314]

Let the disciples also of Basil and of the *homoiousioi* (similarity in substance) depart! For we affirm the *homoousion* (consubstantiality) both because of truth and because of the synod of Nicaea. For

---

312 From here until almost the end of sect. 47 Victorinus discusses the difference between salvation knowledge and theological knowledge. Salvation knowledge is of Christ crucified. He admits that Scripture is concerned with salvation, not with theology, but he is speaking of theology and salvation.

313 Phil 2.6-7.

314 Jn 1.14.

thus the Father and the Son are one, both of them, and they are both always and both together, since they are *homoousion* (consubstantial). But because they affirm *homoiousion* (similarity in substance), even if they profess that the Son has substance from the Father, they nevertheless affirm something different when they affirm that the Son is from God neither by begetting nor by creating, but by a conflict of these two, begetting and creating, just as as by the conflict between stone and iron there comes forth a flame. Affirming that, they are secretly Arians. First of all, they say that the Son of God is not Son by a begetting, but by creation, and that is the teaching of Arius. For that which springs forth and exists from conflict is a creation, and is "from nothing"—for flame comes neither from iron nor from stone, which is, above all, what the foolish Arius thinks. And if he was made from a shock, "there was a time when he was not."[315] And if the Son was made by a conflict of creation and begetting, creation and begetting preexisted the Son. But these things are after him. How therefore was there conflict between them? And this was the opinion of Arius. Then how is there this conflict: of what is there a conflict and in what is it produced? Would there be in God an abundance of wills in conflict? Would there be a conflict of passions or of differences or, above all, of contrary movements? And if this is so, the Father has suffered, he who is without suffering, and not from his substance did a Son appear for him! For if by a conflict of two things, whether of wills or of passions, neither a will nor a passion was produced, it is much more the case that neither is substance from the paternal substance, but it is a certain foreign substance which came forth from nothing. What impious blasphemy to think such things of the *Logos* who is "with" the Father!

3. The Remaining Exposition

(46) We have spoken of *homoousion* (consubstantiality) and we have spoken sufficiently, for this was our intention. But how, if the Son is *homoousion* (consubstantial) and is always with the Father, how does he proceed, descend, ascend, how is he sent, how does he do all that the Father wills? And how, since he is image of God, is he

---

315 Cf. *adv. Ar.* I 23,5-6; I 28,37.

seated at the right hand of God and what is this right hand, what is it to be seated; and what is meant by: "Through whom all things have been made," and how is "all things" to be understood, and what is meant by "Nothing was made without him"; and how does he himself also have a will and yet does all that he does by the will of the Father; and how has he, perfect and from a perfect Father, also taken, as though imperfect, a body and how does he now keep a body, although it is holy and spiritual and like the bodies of those men who will later be saints; and how being always begotten, always in self-movement, he is also self-begotten, truly by the power of the Father—for all these things the *homoousion* (consubstantiality) establishes—if anyone is worthy of understanding this, he will find all this also in this book.

4. *Confession of Faith*

That such is the faith, with the permission of God and Jesus Christ and the Holy Spirit, we shall affirm. Let no one say, understanding me in a blasphemous way, that it is my own teaching. Indeed, all that I say is said by Holy Scripture and comes from Holy Scripture. We shall affirm especially this, from which many heresies are born, the Gospel, the Apostle, the whole Old Testament speak only of God and of Jesus Christ, that is, of the incarnate *Logos*. For this one accomplished the mystery of our salvation, this one freed us, redeemed us; we believe in this one who is our Savior through the Cross and resurrection from the dead. Therefore Paul says: "For I willed to know nothing among you except Jesus Christ and him crucified."[316]

(47) We confess[317] therefore God, the all-powerful Father. We confess the only begotten Son, Jesus Christ, God from God, true light from true light, form of God, who has substance from the substance of God, Son by nature, Son by begetting, consubstantial together with the Father, that which the Greeks call *homoousion,* the "firstborn" before the foundation of the world and "firstborn

---

316 1 Cor 2.2.

317 This section is a profession of faith in consubstantiality using trinitarian and christological formulae. "True light of true light" will appear textually only at the Council of Rome in 368.

before all creation," that is, before coming into substance and before the regeneration, the reanimation, the revivification as "firstborn from the dead," *Logos* who is the universal *Logos* of all existents, but the *Logos* with God, the *Logos* who in latter times was incarnate, by the Cross conquering death and all sin, our Savior, Judge of all, always consubstantial with the Father and *homoousion* (of the same substance), power in act, both producing and making all things by the paternal power, producing both the substance of all existents and their revitalization, since he is eternal life and "the power and wisdom" of God, he himself being without change, without alteration insofar as he is *Logos* and that he is always *Logos* but experiencing without suffering, the passions involved in the creating of all things, and especially through action in matter; in like manner the source of water,[318] without alteration, without suffering, without movement, when it flows and becomes a river appears to take on the special kinds and qualities of the lands that it waters, while keeping its own power as water, and as the river waters the land without feeling any diminishment as to its "to be" as water, so Christ is that river of which the Prophet says: "It irrigates and waters the whole earth."[319] But Christ irrigates the whole universe, both visible and invisible; with the river of life he waters every substance among the existents. Yet insofar as he is life, he is Christ; insofar as he waters, he is the Holy Spirit; insofar as he is the power of vitality, he is Father and God, but the whole is one God. We confess, therefore, also the Holy Spirit having everything from God the Father, the *Logos,* that is, Jesus Christ, handing over everything to him which Christ receives from the Father.

And in this way we confess that these Three are together, in this way we confess that they are one and one God, *homoousion* (consubstantial), and always together, Father and Son and Holy Spirit, and that Jesus Christ is the Son of God by an ineffable power and inexpressible begetting, being *Logos* "with God," "image" and form" and "character" and "reflection" of the Father and the "power and wisdom"[320] of God, through which God appears and is

---

318 The river analogy is traditional; cf. Tertullian, *Adversus Praxean* 29 (PL 2.194C)

319 Gn 2.6.

320 Cf. *adv. Ar.* I 40,32–34.

made known, in the power of all things, both going forth and remaining permanent, producing all things through the action of the Son, that is, the *Logos,* Jesus Christ whom we confess always with word and with the whole heart as incarnate, crucified, rising from the dead, ascending into heaven, sitting at the right hand of the Father, coming as future judge both of the living and the dead, Father of every creature, and Savior. Amen. Grace and peace from God the Father and his son, Jesus Christ, our Lord, forever and ever to whomever in this way confesses these things.

AGAINST ARIUS

FIRST BOOK, PART B[1]

I. THAT THE TRINITY IS CONSUBSTANTIAL

Identity or Difference Among the Divine Names

(48) Spirit, *Logos, Nous,* Wisdom, Substance: are these terms identical in meaning, or are they different one from the other?[2] And if they are identical, is it because of something they have in common or because of everything. If they are identical by having something in common, which term is the primary one, which comes from another, and what is that which they have in common? If they are identical in everything, what is this and what is the difference among these terms, what they have in common? If they are different, one from another, are they absolutely different? Or, are they differ-

---

1 Hadot (TTT 839) considers this second trinitarian treatise to be Victorinus's masterpiece. Composed of Neoplatonic and Christian exegetical pieces, the treatise is unified by five key-words: *spiritus* (spirit), *logos, nous, sapientia* (wisdom), and *sanctus spiritus* (Holy Spirit). They tell the tale of original unity in substance, distinction and otherness in motion and action, with return to identity in self-knowledge. Intertwined is a masculine-feminine opposition. The question is raised as to whether these terms are identical or different. Are they identical to *substantia* (substance), identical to one another? This is, after all, the fundamental trinitarian problematic, that of the distinction between substance and hypostasis, that is, between substantial and personal names. For the Homoiousian, Father, Son and Spirit are personal names, and each was like the other in substance. But Victorinus proves that all three are Spirit, are *Logos,* etc. and that Spirit designates substance. Once again the notion of predominance, along with mutual implication, assists the solution. Although all are Spirit, *Logos, Nous,* etc., one and only one is Spirit, *Logos, Nous,* etc. predominantly. See above, Introd., sects. 53–55 for the role of the common names in Victorinus's theology.

2 In this and the following sect. we find again those philosophical fragments (Group II) assembled by Hadot, PV II 26–28. These help to bring out the possible modes of otherness and identity as well as negative theology.

ent, some being subjects, others, accidents, or different in some other way?

If, therefore, they are absolutely different, they are both *heterōnuma* (of a different name) and of a different substance. But there is no absolute difference of substance. Indeed the genus of existents is *on* (the existent), and the supreme genus consists in "to be." But since "to be" is said in an ambiguous way, *to on* (the existent) itself is also said ambiguously. For there is "truly to be." There is also mere "to be." If therefore *to on* (the existent) includes the truly *on* (existent) and the merely *on* (existent), but the truly *on* (existent) is genus of all truly *onta* (existents), and the merely *on* (existent) is genus of the merely *onta* (existents), all existents whether they are called thus *sunōnumōs* (by the same terms) or *homōnumōs* (by equivalent terms), are not absolutely different, one from another. Therefore by participation[3] in something common, all existents are related to one another. Indeed, to *tō onti* (the existent) the non-*on* (nonexistent) is opposed, as to a contrary by privation, without there being between them the least mutual participation; there is therefore no difference between them.

Therefore, existents, even when they are different and other, are nevertheless identical by having something in common and, through this mode of participation, they are at once identical and different; and that in two ways, either other in identity or identical in otherness. But if they are identical in otherness, they tend more towards otherness; but if they are other in identity, the identity is, above all, clearly evident. What corresponds to these two ways, this must be reviewed.

---

3 The analogy of being assures a communion of existents; this is an Aristotelian theory expressed in Platonic terms. The doctrine that substance has no contrary is found in Aristotle's *Categories* (3b23) and the doctrine that there is no absolute nonbeing is found in Plato's *Sophist* (258b). The link between contrariety and privation is Aristotelian; cf. *Metaphysics* 4.6 (101b18); 4.2 (1004b27); cf. Plato, *Timaeus* 36C. For Victorinus the predominance of identity over otherness corresponds to the *homoousios:* for Porphyry, the predominance of otherness over identity corresponds to the unity proper to the sensible world.

II. THE FIVE TERMS DEFINED IN THE LIGHT OF THE RELATIONS BETWEEN GOD AND THE *LOGOS*

1. Initial Thesis

(49) On the subject of God and the *Logos,* that is, of the Father and the Son, it has already been sufficiently said,[4] God allowing, that these Two are One. It has likewise been said of the *Logos,* that is, of the Son and the Holy Spirit, that in the One are the Two. If then the Two which are One and the Two which are in One are that One, since that One in whom are the two is with the One who are the Two and from eternity with him and they are always together identical one with the other, if then these Two are One, it is necessary therefore that these terms are identical. How so? Listen to my exposition.

2. Both One and Both in One

A. BOTH ONE[5]

a) The one who is not

Before all the truly existents was the One or the Monad, or the One in itself, One before "to be" came to it. For it is necessary to call and conceive as One that which has no appearance of otherness. It is solely One, the simple One, One by yielding to the need for naming.

It is the One before all existence, before all existentiality, and absolutely before all inferiors, before the *on* (Existent) itself; indeed this One is prior to the *on* (Existent); it is therefore before every entity, substance, subsistence, even before those things which are more powerful.

It is the One without existence, without substance, without knowledge—for it is above all that—infinite, invisible, wholly indis-

---

4 Cf. *adv. Ar.* I 13,23, and 28; I 30,59; I 30,15.
5 This deals with the first two hypotheses of Plato's *Parmenides,* namely, the One purely One, and the One Who Is. These assertions: the Father is One, the Son is the One who is One, or the Father is Nonbeing superior to Being, the Son is Being do not really harmonize with the main triad in the Victorine synthesis. We also note here the method of the reconciliation of opposites later found in Nicholas of Cusa. Cf. I 50,20; *ad Cand.* 14,1.

cernible for every other, both for those within it and those which are after it, even those which come from it; for it alone is distinguished and defined only by its own existence, not by act, so that its own constitution and self-knowledge are not something different from it; undivided in every way, without shape, without quality, though not deprived of quality, that is, not qualified by any lack of quality yet without color, without species, without form, lacking all forms, and yet not being that form itself by which all things are formed.

It is the first cause of all existents, both wholes and parts, the pre-principle of every principle, the preknowledge of all knowledge, the strength of all powers; swifter than movement itself, more stable than rest itself—for it is repose by an indescribable movement but it is superlative movement by ineffable repose—closer than any continuum, more profound than all the discontinuous, more finite than any body and greater than all greatness, purer than all incorporeal reality, more penetrable than all intelligence and body; of all realities the most powerful, it is the power of all powers; more universal than every genus, every species, it is the truly universal *on* (Existent), being itself the totality of the truly existents, greater than all totality, whether it be corporeal or incorporeal, more a part than any part, by an ineffable power purely existing as all the truly existents.

(50) This is God, this is the Father,[6] preexisting preintelligence and preexistence keeping himself and his own happiness in an immobile movement, and because of that, having no need of other beings; perfect above the perfect, Spirit having in unity a triple power, perfect and above the Spirit: for he does not breathe, but he is only Spirit in that which is his "to be," Spirit breathing upon himself[7] so that he may be Spirit, since the Spirit is inseparable from itself. It is itself for itself both the place and the inhabitant, dwelling within itself, alone in the alone, existing everywhere and nowhere; being one in its simplicity, it unites these three powers: universal

---

6 The teaching that the One is Father and "To Be" which is life and thought is found within Group II of the philosophical fragments cited by Hadot, PV II 28.

7 Under a Gospel vocabulary there is also at work the Stoic notion of *pneuma* with its "tonic" motion, outward and inward. Cf. Cicero, *De natura deorum* 2.7.19.

existence, universal life, and happiness, but all these realities are the One and the simple One, and by predominance in the power of "to be," that is, of existence, are present the powers of life and of happiness.[8] For the power which is the power of existence, by the fact that it is and that it exists is the power likewise of life and of happiness; it is, itself and through itself, idea and *logos* of itself, having both "to live" and "to act" in its own nonexisting existence, union without distinction of the Spirit with itself, divinity, substantiality, happiness, power of intelligence, vitality, excellence and absolutely all things universally, purely unbegotten, *Proon* (Pre-existent) unity of every union, itself by no means a union.

b) The one which is

Therefore with this One existing, the One leapt forth, the One who is One, one in substance, one in movement, for movement is also existence, since existence is also movement. This one is therefore essentially One but not as the Father is essentially in himself One, but as he who is essentially One according to power. For power already has, and to the highest degree, the "to be" that it will have when it will be in act, and, in truth, it does not have it, it is it; for power, through which act is actuated, is all things impassibly and truly under all modes, having itself no need of "to be" in order that it may be all things: indeed the power through which the act which is born of it acts is itself in act. This power is therefore unity.

B. BOTH IN ONE

a) The one which is life and Logos

(51) But this One whom we call the One who is One is life, life which is infinite movement,[9] creative of others, whether of the truly existents or of the existents, being the *Logos* of the "to be" of all existents, moving itself by itself, always in movement, having movement in itself, or rather it is itself movement; for thus the divine

---

8 Cf. Augustine, *City of God* 8.6 (FC 14.32–34).
9 This description of the act of the paternal power is found within philosophical fragments (Group II) assembled by Hadot, PV II 29.

Scripture says that God the Father gave to him this: that the "to-be-life" is within him.[10]

This is the Son, the *Logos* who is "with God," this one "through whom all things have been made,"[11] this is the Son, the total filiation of the total paternity, he who is always Son and from eternity, but Son by a movement moved by himself. For, advancing from its power, and, as it were, from an immobile preexistence, where it was not in movement insofar as it was a power, this movement nowhere in repose, awakening itself to act, hastening to produce all kinds of movement, truly a life which is infinite,[12] this movement in its vivifying action has, in some way, appeared outside. Necessarily therefore life has been born. But life is the Son, life is movement, life is substance which comes forth from vital preexistence for the establishment and the manifestation of all those universals which the Father is according to power so that preknowledge is made evident from the knowledge of the truly existents.

b) He is movement, therefore twofold, feminine and masculine: life and wisdom

Therefore this existence of all existents is life, and insofar as life is movement, it received a kind of feminine power, because it desired to vivify. But since, as has been shown, this movement, since it is one, is both life and wisdom,[13] life converted to wisdom and, what is more, to the paternal existence, better still, by a movement of return toward the paternal power, and having been fortified by that, life, returning to the Father, has been made male. For life is descent;

---

10 Jn 5.26.

11 Jn 1.1-3.

12 First mention of life as infinite: cf. Plotinus, *Enn.* 6.7.17. Life is feminine potentiality since it has the desire to vivify whereas conversion by contemplation is linked to masculinity. Life is descent; wisdom is ascent. The *Logos* has a feminine and masculine state; the mature Christ returns to the Father. The resurrection of Christians will also be passage from femininity to masculinity. Cf. Clement of Alexandria, *Stromata* 3.13.92: "The soul on high which was divine was feminized by desire and fell here below, into generation and corruption." By being androgynous the *Logos* can beget itself (I 64, 25-27). If life manifests itself as desire, then "to be" is "to will"; cf. Plato, *Phaedrus* 245C-E. Hadot asserts (PV I 272) that the feminine and masculine phases point to the Porphyrian exegesis of the "Chaldaean Oracles".

13 Cf. *adv. Ar.* I 13,37; I 32,50.

wisdom is ascent.[14] But it also is Spirit; the two are therefore Spirit; they are Two in One.

c) The virginal birth of Jesus: image of the eternal virginal birth of the Logos

And just as there was a necessity that life, existing as primal existence, should enter into the virginal power and by the masculine childbirth of the virgin be begotten as a man-Son of God—or in the first movement, I say first to be manifested, life was, first of all, as though alienated from the power of the Father and, in its natural desire to vivify, life, truly existing within, externalized itself by its own movement. When it once again turned towards itself, it returned toward the existence that it has in the Father, thus becoming male. And having come to the full completion of its all-powerful vigor, life became perfect Spirit, by turning above, that is, towards the interior, away from its tendency downward. The order to be realized also follows this model: as long as the Spirit was in the body, that is, in Jesus Christ, it was necessary for it to undergo a certain diminishment and be born of the Virgin and, as it were, because of this very diminishment, by the Fatherly power, that is, by its more divine and first existence, to arise, to be renewed, to return to the Father, that is, to the Fatherly existence and power.[15]

3. To Be and Life

a) God gives "to be" through life

(52) How this is so I now dare to say, so that by this exposition the many particularities of our position will be made clear. Let us propose our understanding in the following way. God is the potentiality of these three powers, existence, life, happiness, that is, of "to be," "to live," "to understand."[16] But in each one of these are the three, that is evident. And the "to be" is first, and this first "to be" insofar as it is "to be" is, by that very fact, "to live" and "to under-

---

14 A theological digression within the philosophical framework.

15 This passage recalls to Hadot (TTT 860) the famous passage from Amelius, cited by Eusebius, *Praeparatio evangelica* 11.19.1 in which Amelius compares St. John's prologue to the teaching of Heraclitus on the *Logos*.

16 This entire section contains more philosophical fragments (Group II) as collected by Hadot, PV II 31–32.

stand," without any union, but as simplicity at its simplest, and that is also evident, as was shown.[17] This also: that such "to be" is clearly God, as was shown,[18] a power capable of giving "to be" to all things, not from its own "to be" as part of the paternal "to be," and by creative power constituting for each one its own "to be," but this through the ministry of the *Logos,* that is, through life, which gives "to live" to all existents. And then there subsists something receiving "to be" insofar as this is to receive life.

b) Life is therefore simultaneously the Father's movement and self-movement

If therefore the "to be" of God, without giving any of its own "to be,"[19] gives "to be" to all things, but does this through the ministry of "life," but the very "to be life" is in the "to be" of God, they are one and identical: while the paternal "to be" dwells in repose, the "to be" of life, retaining its identity with the "to be" of God, is moved by its own power in dependence upon the paternal power. And since all power is natural desire, life willed to move itself, because in it there is awakened, without provoking passion, a natural movement which is accomplished in substance to attain that which is life. For a natural desire is not a passion. Therefore, insofar as it is the "to be" of God, in whom power is existence, the paternal reality, according to power, according to its very "to be," is also life. If therefore life moves itself, but movement is will, this movement, this will are paternal because life is paternal power. But if, according to its own "to be," life is movement, life has its own movement. But since movement goes from one point to another, in some way from the interior to the exterior, there is moved the power, the nature, the will for life, and this predominantly is its existence; that is why it is said to be the radiance, the procession, the manifestation[20] of

---

17 Cf. *adv. Ar.* I 50,14–18.

18 Cf. *adv. Ar.* I 50,1–14.

19 This is the first sketch of the doctrine of participation which is spelled out in Proclus, *The Elements of Theology,* ed. E. Dodds (Oxford 1933) 27–29. Life in "To Be" was Will confused with "To Be"; when the will is taken as an object, it wills to will itself and thus life is externalized, generated. Nature, as Aristotle taught, is tendency. Cf. *Physics* II, 1 (192b18).

20 These expressions certainly recall Wis 7.25, but Hadot (TTT 863) sees in

the Most High Spirit, life-giving creator for the universal totality of that which has the potentiality for "to be."

c) Life is therefore begotten

Therefore from life which is within—insofar as to be life is to be movement—is the offspring of the paternal "to be," life insofar as it is movement. But since movement as movement has advanced externally without being separated, however, from that which is within, so consciousness, receiving the original and universal power from the *Nous,* is according to movement both interior and exterior—for *Nous* is movement— and thus life, insofar as it is movement, became the Son, a manifested movement coming from the paternal movement which is hidden and which is existence according to primal power.

d) Life being at once interior and exterior, the Son is in the Father and the Father in the Son

Again, life as movement advancing from the paternal movement is at once interior and exterior. But in fact life is movement. Life is therefore both interior and exterior. Therefore God lives, life itself lives. Life is therefore both God and life. These two are therefore one, and in each one there is both the other and itself. Therefore in the Son is the Father and in the Father is the Son.

(53) Therefore the truth itself proclaims that these are *homoousia* (consubstantial), their otherness united through identity. And again, if the Father is life and the Son is life, since the Son as life is at once interior and exterior, insofar as he is movement God lives, the Son lives, but also outside all things live since the Son exists everywhere. And since the Father is in the Son, the Father also is everywhere. Likewise again, since the Father is in the Son, when you will see and know the Son, you will see and know the Father. "If anyone sees me, he also sees the Father."[21]

---

them the influence of expressions borrowed from the "Chaldaean Oracles". Cf. Hadot, "Fragments d'un commentaire de Porphyre sur le *Parmenides*" *Revue des études grecques,* 74 (1961) 410–38.
21 Jn 14.9.

e) Life, form of "to be," Son, revelation of the Father

Indeed for that reason it was said that the Son is "form" of the Father. But here the form is not understood as outside the substance, nor as with us, as an appearance added to substance; but this form is a certain subsisting substance in which there appears and is shown that which is hidden and veiled in another. But God is as something veiled. For "No one sees God."[22] Therefore the Son is the form in which God is seen. For if God is hidden existence, power, substance, movement, life, God is, as it were, without form. Therefore, if life is manifested and manifested through the power of movement, this life in its hidden movement is known, expressed, seen in the appearance, in the existence of movement. Now if the Father is "to be," the Son is life, since it is impossible to understand what "to be"[23] is—for this "to be" is hidden—and since life as life is also this "to be," therefore, "to be" is manifested in life. Life is therefore the form of "to be." But in fact "to be" is God the Father, but life is the Son. Therefore the Son, life of the Father, is the "form of God," in whom is contemplated the paternal power.

f) Faith in Christ, the incarnate Spirit gives life

It is necessary therefore to believe in the Son of God so that life may be in us, that life which is both true and eternal life. For if we shall have faith in Christ of Nazareth, who took flesh of Mary, we shall have faith in the Son of God who was the Spirit and has been made Spirit incarnate. How is this? Listen as I tell it.

III. THAT THE TRINITY IS CONSUBSTANTIAL

1. Identity and Difference among the Five Terms

a) They are identical

(54) But it is obligatory first to see how these terms differ and to whom they are to be attributed, to the Father or to the Son. I speak

---

22 Jn 1.18.
23 There is a discussion here of the unknowability of unformed *esse* ("to be"); cf. II 4,8–10; IV 19,10; *in Eph.* 2.6–8.

here of the Spirit, the *Logos,* the *Nous,* the Holy Spirit, Wisdom, Substance.

First of all, the Father and the Son are identical; the Son and the Holy Spirit are identical. Existence and life are therefore identical. Consequently, existence and happiness are identical. Again, "to be" and life are identical. And life and "to understand" are identical. Therefore, "to be" and "to understand" are identical. It was said concerning these points in the book which precedes this one and in other books that there are three in one and for that reason the three are identical:[24] *sunōnuma ara ta tria* (the three are then synonyms), according to the name through which each one of them obtains its own power. Indeed, "to be" is both life and knowledge. So also each one in relation to the other. They are therefore identical, identical and *sunōnuma* (synonyms). They are therefore begotten at the same time and they are consubstantial.

b) But they are different in manifesting themselves: others in identity

But does not some difference appear among these terms?[25] And especially on that account there is among them identity and not self-sameness. Indeed, certain realities are different when manifested,[26] both as they are and as they are known, from what they were in their hidden power. By existence within the same potentiality, they are together in power, and they are consubstantial, and to them alone it belongs to be one and identical; but to others truly from them, it belongs to be the same and other within identity.

2. The Five Terms as Proper Names and as Common Names

A. SPIRIT AND SUBSTANCE

a) As common names of the Three

(55) But it must now be examined what the other names placed

---

24 Cf. *ad Cand.* 31,12; *adv. Ar.* I 12,25; I 42,11–16.
25 Once again a certain predominance of one of the aspects of "to be" makes for the distinction of realities.
26 There is a use here of those philosophical fragments (Group II) which Hadot has collected in PV II 32.

first signify; I refer to Spirit, *Logos, Nous,* Holy Spirit, Wisdom, Substance. Spirit is the name for substance or for existence, because it truly signifies "to be," and one both uses it and understands it in the order of quiddity. If you wish to know what is God, the term Spirit designates his "to be." Therefore God and Spirit are terms which signify "to be." Again, what is life? That which is Spirit. Therefore, Spirit and life signify "to be." So also the Holy Spirit signifies "to be," through this very name, with a distinction from the first two named with the one term. This distinction, since it concerns substance, signifies "to be." From this it is now evident that, since each one of them is substance, each one of them signifies "to be." In these three, therefore, is Spirit, substance. They are, therefore, *homoousia* (consubstantial) since they are Spirit, an undivided Spirit, since it is certainly one in three.

b) As proper name of the Father

But in the natural order of power and action, since the paternal existence is one and having its own "to be," the three begetting themselves have been constituted in total power. Therefore, no existence preexists—for the Father is the begetter of his own substance, and for other existents he is the fountainhead. And given this existence, there is no division in each of these three between existence and power, insofar as this proper power is "to be," so that they constitute a total majesty, a total power, an absolute perfection, self-begetting, self-constituting, self-moving, self-moving eternally, consubstantial, simultaneously powerful, since the Father gives them both to be what they are and to be.

B. LOGOS

a) As common name of the Three

The Savior says: "All things that the Father has are mine and for that reason I said: he will receive of what is mine. For he will not speak from himself, but whatever he will hear, he will speak."[27] Therefore, if the Holy Spirit speaks, he speaks by the Son, and if the

---

27 Jn 16.15,13.

Son speaks, he speaks by the Father. These Three are therefore voice, *Logos,* and word, and for that reason these Three are one. But the Father truly speaks in silence, the Son speaks openly and by word, the Holy Spirit does not speak openly, but whatever he says, he says spiritually.

(56) These three are therefore true lights, or rather one true light, one *Logos,* one voice, one word, that is, one active power was in harmony with itself before making anything to be.

b) Digression on the soul

That the soul has a different substance is evident. For, created by the Spirit to triple power, it is neither purely a voice, nor a word, but as an *ēkhō* (echo), it listens so that it may speak, an impression of the voice rather than the voice. And this is the meaning of John: "The voice crying in the desert: prepare the way of the Lord."[28] For the soul in the desert,[29] that is, in the world cries out that it knows the Lord God and wishes to be purified to enjoy the Lord God. And the soul bears witness to God and was sent into the world to witness to the witness. For the "Witness of God" is Jesus Christ. Jesus Christ is therefore Son of God, John is son of the Lord. Indeed, John "was not the Light, but came to give witness to the Light."[30]

c) Logos, *as proper name of the Son*

The Son is therefore both word and voice, he is life, he is *Logos,* he is movement, he is *Nous,* he is wisdom, he is existence and first substance, he is the action of power, he is the first *on* (Existent), the true *on* (Existent) from whom, through whom, in whom are all *onta*[31] (existents); he is the mid-angle of the Trinity; he reveals the preexisting Father and sends forth the Holy Spirit for the sake of

---

28 Jn 1.23.

29 Cf. Jn 1.6–7. In the rest of this paragraph John the Baptist represents the soul sent into the sensible world to testify to the presence of the divine. This theme of the soul as God's prophet is found in Porphyry's works. Cf. Hadot, PV I 342, n.2.

30 Jn 1.18.

31 These next two paragraphs also contain philosophical fragments (Group II) as collected by Hadot, PV II 33.

perfection. For, as blessed Paul said: "The Gospel is the power and wisdom of God";[32] by "power" he is designating the Son, because "all is through him." For by the "Word" of "power" all things have been made, and by the "wisdom" of the Holy Spirit everything attains perfection.

d) Reciprocal unity and interiority of the Three

If, therefore, God is these realities, then the Three are simultaneously these realities, But since the two, God and the *Logos,* are one, all exist together in unity, coexisting in the Father as life, in which the Holy Spirit is present according to existence, since the Three were one and are always one. If, therefore, the Son, eternal life, is the luminous manifestation of preeternal life, yet life itself, is perfect and eternal life by knowledge—for life is perfect when it will have recognized[33] both who it is and from whom it comes, how it is from itself but by the will of the Father: for then, existing in itself, it would not be infinite, being by itself the savior and the saved—it is necessary to know and to say that the power of God is within it, that is, the Father is in the Son.

3. The Holy Spirit, "Mother" of Jesus

a) The incarnation of the Logos

Through itself, however, life was infinite,[34] and this is what: "And the *Logos* was made flesh"[35] signifies. For by infinite movement life descended towards inferiors and vivified corruption; for

---

32 Rom 1.16; 1 Cor 1.24.

33 The realization of one's own power arises through desire for insight. Because the condition for knowledge is otherness, in this instance self-knowledge becomes ecstasy or the externalization of life.

34 Beginning here and proceeding to the middle of sect. 58 there is an elaboration of what was affirmed in the previous note, namely, pure being renouncing itself in order to know being, and yet only becoming fully itself through this self-discovery, becoming the thought of its own being as self-consciousness. Hence, "self-generation" provides a new perspective on thought that is fruitful. In Christ's two births, eternal and temporal, the Holy Spirit is the mother of Christ. Cf. Plotinus, *Enn.* 6.7.39–40.

35 Jn 1.14; Lk 1.35.

that reason the universal *Logos* and power of life "was made flesh," as the angel said: "The Holy Spirit shall come upon you, and the power of the Most High shall overshadow you."[36] Jesus Christ is therefore born, according to the flesh, of Mary, and from the Holy Spirit, power of the Most High.

(57) Christ our Lord is therefore all things: flesh, Holy Spirit, power of the Most High, *Logos*. He accomplished the mystery, so that all life with flesh, filled with eternal light, may return, away from all corruption, into the heavens. Thus, he is not only flesh, not only Holy Spirit, not only Spirit, nor only *Logos*, but he is simultaneously all things, our Lord Jesus.

b) The Holy Spirit, i.e. the Nous, mother of the Logos in the eternal begetting

Therefore the Holy Spirit,[37] total happiness, in the first unbegotten begetting, which is and is called the only begetting, was his own Father, his own Son. For by the self-movement of the Spirit itself, that is, by the going forth of perfect life in movement, wishing to see itself, that is, its power: the Father, there is achieved its self-manifestation, which is and is called a begetting, and through this it exists externally. For all knowledge, insofar as it is knowledge, is outside of what it desires to know. I say: outside, as in the action of perceiving, as when it sees itself, which is to know or to see that preexisting and paternal power. Then in this moment, which is not to be conceived temporally, going forth, as it were, from that which was "to be," to perceive what it was, and because there all movement is substance, the otherness that is born returns quickly into identity. For it is not a luminous manifestation behind the back, but as eyes or faces mutually seeing each other by a reciprocal look, this same reality subsists in the one same way and perfect. But the eyes everywhere, as faces, are regarding each other and have no

---

36 Lk 1.35.

37 Within this discussion of the self-generation of *Nous* (Intelligence) linked to the action of Life's self-knowledge we find in sect. 57 and the first fourteen lines of sect. 58 a use of those philosophical fragments (Group II) cited by Hadot, PV II 33–34.

back, and only mystically was it said: "God is seen from behind."[38] Then, with no diminishment, the whole has remained always one, its internal unity brought to its highest power by the paternal power.

The Holy Spirit is then the first interior movement, which is the paternal thought, that is, his self-knowledge. Indeed, pre-knowledge[39] precedes knowledge. Therefore through this natural mode of knowledge understanding was externalized, the Son was born, became life, not that there had not been life, but because life at its height is life externalized; for life is in movement. This is the *Logos* who is called Jesus Christ, "through whom all things have been made," seed of all things so that they may exist, since he is life "without which" it is impossible that anything exists, whether among the existents or the nonexistents which are the accompaniment of existents. (58) But since we have said that the *Logos* and the Holy Spirit are one same movement,[40] the *Logos* as life, the Holy Spirit as knowledge and understanding, since we have said that life and knowledge are identical,[41] since we have said that understanding is put into movement in the first movement[42]—for such is the natural divine order: since it is a power, it was necessary that the understanding be put into movement to know itself—then, the Son who is the *Logos,* that is, life, was born by the paternal power begetting understanding, this *Logos* which is the "to be" of all existents, as their eternal source.

He who understood the Holy Spirit to be the mother[43] of Jesus was not therefore mistaken, both there above and here below; there above, as was said;[44] here below, in this way:

---

38 Ex 33.23.

39 The CSEL editors by conjecturing that *cognoscentiam* or knowledge is in the accusative rather than the nominative case, as in SC, with *praecognoscentia* (foreknowledge) in the nominative rather than the accusative case produce a more meaningful sentence.

40 Cf. *adv. Ar.* I 51,23–25; I 54,6.

41 Cf. *adv. Ar.* I 51,31; I 57,7–13,28.

42 Cf. *adv. Ar.* I 57,30–32; I 58, 5–11.

43 The vocabulary of Synesius who speaks of the Holy Spirit as feminine may come from the same source used by Victorinus, a Chaldaean source. Cf. I 16,23 and S. Boulgakov, *Le Paraclet* (Paris 1946).

44 Cf. *adv. Ar.* I 19,5 foll.

In the incarnation

It was necessary, for our liberation, that the universal divine, that is, the seed of all spirits which exist universally, that which is the first "to be," that is, the universal *Logos,* be made flesh by inferior matter and all corruption to destroy all corruption and sin. For the darkness and the ignorance of the soul, violated by material powers, had need of the help of eternal light so that the *Logos* of the soul and the *Logos* of the flesh after the destruction of corruption by the mystery of death, could thus raise up souls and bodies through the operation of the Holy Spirit to life again, to divine and life-giving understanding, uplifted by knowledge, faith and love.

Therefore, the angel replied to Mary and said to her: "The Holy Spirit shall come upon you and the power of the Most High shall overshadow you."[45] These two, the *Logos* and the Holy Spirit, in one sole movement "came" in order that Mary might conceive so that there might be constituted flesh from flesh, the temple and the dwelling of God: the Holy Spirit is, indeed, power in movement; for the principle of begetting is movement, but the "power of the Most High" is the *Logos:* for the *Logos,* Jesus, is the "power and wisdom of God." And of the *Logos,* that is, of the Son, he said: "He will overshadow you."[46] For human nature does not receive within it the divine in its perfection and according to all its splendor, as is clear; "And the *Logos* was made flesh" signifies this. But the statement: "He emptied himself"[47] signifies far better the overshadowing.

IV. CONCLUSION: CONSUBSTANTIALITY OF THE FATHER, OF THE SON, AND OF THE HOLY SPIRIT

a) Identity in substance, difference in act

(59) We hold therefore according to order, with the permission of God, that Father and Son are *homoousion* (what is consubstantial) and *homoousia* (consubstantial beings) according to identity in

---

45 Lk 1.35.
46 Cf. 1 Cor 1.24.
47 Phil 2.7.

substance. For the Spirit is one substance. The Spirit is "to be" it-self. But "to be" itself is both life and "to understand." These three are in each one, and for that reason there is one divinity, the totality is one, God is one, because the Father, the Son, and the Holy Spirit are one; with difference appearing only through power and action, because God in power and in a hidden movement moves all things and directs all things as in silence, whereas the *Logos,* Son which is also Holy Spirit, expresses himself through the Word to produce all things, according to life and according to understanding, serving as foundation for the "to be" of all things.

b) Logos, Nous, *wisdom and substance in Scripture*

From this it is evident that the *Logos* itself and the Holy Spirit and *Nous* and Wisdom are the same thing. Indeed, Paul also said by divine inspiration: "Who has known the *Nous* of the Lord?"[48] And again concerning him: "The power and wisdom of God."[49] Solomon also uses the word "wisdom " of him. And many names are referred to the Son. And Paul, writing to the Hebrews, also calls him substance: "Image of his substance;"[50] and he spoke likewise of the "consubstantial people." And Jeremiah: "Because the one who has stood in my substance and has seen my word";[51] and again: "If they had stood in my substance and had heard my words."[52] And the Gospel according to Matthew: "Give us this day our supersub-stantial bread."[53] In the parable Luke says: "The younger one said to the Father: give me the part of the 'substance' which belongs to me;"[54] and again: "There he wasted his substance."[55] For in descending here below, it did not keep its powers. These things are said of the soul, but I have cited this text against those who deny

---

48 Rom 11.34.
49 1 Cor 1.24.
50 Heb 1.3.
51 Jer 23.18.
52 Jer 23.22.
53 Mt 6.11.
54 Lk 15.12–13.
55 In the rest of this paragraph Victorinus wants to assert that Luke's text should be referred to the fall of the soul; cf. II 6 and Augustine, *Confessions* 1.18.28. The initial question as to whether the five key terms are identical or different is finally answered, but the philosophical material does not appear in this conclusion.

that the term *usia* (substance) is used in the Holy Scriptures. But it is added that God made the soul, that is, man "according to his image and likeness."[56]

V. THE *LOGOS* AND ITS TWO IMAGES: THE SOUL AND THE BODY

1. The sphere of the Logos

(60) What do these terms truly signify?[57] Listen, as I say. The highest *Nous* and perfect Wisdom, that is, the universal *Logos*—for in eternal movement they are identical—were circular movement, starting from the first *sēmeiō* (point), curving itself to the extreme periphery to turn towards this same *sēmeion* (point), while this point, cause of circular movement, remained inseparably turned toward itself; so that, going forth from the Father, advancing toward the Father, coexisting with the Father, the Son was in the Father and the Father in the Son: first substance, substance already in subsistence, spiritual substance, substance as *Nous*, substance begetting and creative, the preprinciple of all substance, of intelligible substance and of intellectual substance, of the substance of the soul as of material substance, and of all substance in matter.

If therefore the first movement is life, I say, and understanding—for the one and only perfect one is both—this movement is not only circular, but it is spherical; even more, it is a sphere and truly an absolutely perfect sphere. For if "to be" is both "to live" and "to understand," and if life is exactly "to be" and knowledge, both the

---

56 Gn 1.26.

57 From sect. 61 until the middle of sect. 64 we learn that man (spirit, soul, and body) is in the image of the Trinity inasmuch as the soul is "to be" and "to live" and "to know" and the body is bisexual in the image of the man–woman status of the *Logos*. In the intelligible world the soul pre-exists as image of the Image, that is, the Son of God. Cf. I 56,4–15 and 64,1–8 on the soul's origin; this is not unlike the description of the soul's descent in Macrobius, *In somnium Scipionis* 1.12. Midway between intelligibles and matter, the soul is free in its choice and, thanks to its *Nous* illuminated from on high, it can ascend. Because Porphyry held that the true self is in the intelligible world, he taught that self-knowledge is a conversion to one's original state with the Father. Cf. I 60,5–10; Porphyry, *In Platonis Parmenidem* 14.16–26.

extremes and the middle are in each. So also is it with knowledge. Therefore each one of them is three: they return upon themselves and all participate in one another, what is more, they are together without any discontinuity. This is the sphere, the first sphere, the perfect sphere, itself the only sphere. But, in truth, the others are spherical more through resemblance.

From this reasoning it necessarily follows that the *sēmeion* (point) is also the *grammē* (line) in potentiality, and the *sēmeion* (point) produces the *grammēn* (line): the point departs from itself without truly leaving itself; and always at the same time in repose and movement, ceaselessly returning upon itself in a circle, so that it is in all respects a sphere, since God is everywhere since he is indeed the *sēmeion* (point) from which comes forth all movement and towards which all movement returns through conversion. This is God, wholly *Logos,* wholly *Nous,* wholly Wisdom, all-powerful Substance and cause of substance, the one whom we fear, the one whom we adore, contemplating him only through the mind, the one who by his favor and will has raised us to himself, the Lord Jesus Christ, having mercy on us by the grace of his cross. *Amēn.*

2. The Soul in the Image of the Logos

A. THE SOUL, IMAGE OF THE IMAGE

(61) When the circular movement[58] begins (I say circular because this movement starting from a *sēmeiō* (point) returns to this same *sēmeion* (point), that is, from the Father to the Father in the manifestation of this movement and of the whole divinity and of the *Logos* and of the Son, there goes forth by the will of God an image, "according to the image and likeness of God,"[59] an image of the image, that is, of the Son. For the Son is image of the Father, as was shown.[60] But this is so because the Son is life.[61]

---

58 In the first half of sect. 60 we find Group II of the philosophical fragments collected by Hadot, PV II 35, where the sphere is spoken of as emanating from an original point.

59 Gn. 1.26.

60 Cf. *adv. Ar* I 19,5 ff.

61 The first half of this sect. 61 is made up of the philosophical fragments (Group II) which refer to the soul's fall and which represent for Victorinus a sort of commentary on Gen 1.26. Cf. Hadot, PV II, 35–36.

The soul has therefore been created as an image of life.[62] But the soul with its own *nous*, which is from the one which is *Nous*, is power of intellectual life. It is not *Nous*, but when it looks toward the *Nous*, it is as if it were *Nous*. For there, vision is union. But if it inclines downwards and turns from the *Nous*, it leads itself and its own *nous* below, it then becomes merely intellect, and is no longer both the intelligible and the intellect. But if it will thus persevere, it is the mother of things above the heavens, the light, not the true light, and yet with its own *nous* it is the light. If, indeed, it looks toward inferior things,[63] being petulant, it becomes a life-giving power, making live both the world and those things which are in the world, even the stone according to its proper mode as stone; it becomes this power, along with its *nous*. Truly, since the soul is a *logos* but not the *Logos*, since it is situated in the midst of Spirits and the intelligibles and *hulē* (matter), turning with its own *nous* toward both, it either becomes divine or becomes embodied for an understanding. Indeed, it is left to its own license, and deprived of true light, on account of the feeble light of its own *nous*, it is called back, since it certainly is only an *on* (existent). But if it is darkened, it is dragged down below. Indeed, the highest parts of *hulē* (matter), which are also the purest, having strength to be animated, give occasion to light, so that, if it wishes, it descends toward what is related to it. That is why it was said: "You discern also these things."

---

62 This is an important section for so-called image-theology to be used very fully by Augustine. Soul as an image or reflection of life is an intellectual triad ("to be," "to live," "to know") reflecting the divine sphere, but it produces its reflections in the sensible world; *adv. Ar.* I 64,1–7. The soul completed its manifestation by begetting souls. Cf. Plotinus, *Enn.* 3.7.11; Plato, *Timaeus* 37D (41D–42D), *Enn.* 6.2.22. Victorinus's notion of soul corresponds to Plotinus's intellectual triad, *Enn.* 5.1.8. Cf. P. Hadot, "L'Image de la Trinité dans l'âme chez Victorinus et chez saint Augustin," *Studia patristica* 6 (Berlin 1962) 411–24. Present here is the theme of the soul as not itself divine but a witness to the divine, a prophet; cf. I 56,8-15; Augustine, *Confessions* 7.9.13 and *City of God* 10.2 (FC 14.119-20).

63 From here through sect. 62 Victorinus treats of the fall of particular souls by their becoming absorbed in those things they have assumed, as body or as instrument; their attention to lower things distracts them from their true selves whereby they belong to the intelligible world, and in this way they cease to reflect or image the divine life. There is, however, a perfect reflection of the divine triad in the *all-soul* or universal soul. But through

B. LET US MAKE MAN

Someone says: if the soul is such as you describe, how was it said: "Let us make man according to our image and likeness"?[64]

(62) It must first be examined what man is, next, what image is, then the difference between "image" and "likeness," and then how man was created not "image" and "likeness" but "according to the image and likeness," and what is meant by "to our."

Indeed, man is ordinarily understood under a double aspect, as made up of body and soul.[65] Some think that man is made from a body and a triple soul; but others think that he is from a body and a soul having three powers; and again, some say that it is a question of a body, of a partial *nous*, of a soul and of the spirit which firms up the flabby body. Still others compose man of a body having the fourfold power of the four elements, of a twofold soul and of a twofold *nous*. This is my understanding.

For the body, as was demonstrated, was thus. For God "took dust and formed Adam," that is, he took already created earth, the best of earth and its flower; we have there the principles of body.

As for the twofold *nous* and the twofold soul, the Gospel according to Matthew and the Gospel according to Luke explain this. Indeed they express it thus: "It will be thus also at the coming of the Son of Man; then two men will be in the field; one will be taken, and one will be left; two women will be at the mill, one will be taken and one will be left."[66] Luke, however, added something about the twofold body: "That night there will be two in one bed, one will be

---

desire to vivify, particular or individual souls break out of the divine circle as purely vital and this is how life comes to the sensible world. Instead of turning towards their begetter, souls turn towards their begotten. Salvation, however, is still possible by reason of the feeble spark of intellect which can lead to thought, the way of conversion to their source. Cf. I 56,33; I 32,57.

64 Gn 1.26.

65 The discussion of the salvation of *nous,* soul, body ends towards the latter part of sect. 62 with the use once again of the philosophical fragments (Group II) cited by Hadot, PV II 36–37. This raises the problem of Origen's influence on Victorinus. Cf. J. Daniélou, "Bulletin d'histoire des origines Chrétiennes," *Recherches de science religieuse,* 52 (1964) 128. Cf. Hadot, MV 283.

66 Mt 24.39–41.

taken, the other left."[6][7] But there are others, similarly expressed. Therefore the "two in the field" are the two *logoi* or the two *nouses:* the heavenly *logos* and the other, material; the two women occupied in grinding are the two souls, the heavenly soul and the material soul. Therefore, the heavenly *nous* or *logos* and the heavenly soul will be taken. But the material *logos* and soul "will be left."

How that is, hear. It must be admitted that man is made up of soul and body: of a body, because made from already organized earth. The earth has, therefore, a material soul. And according to his animal body, "Adam was created" like other animals from water and earth to be "a living soul." But for Adam, this is not all. For God breathed upon his face. There, indeed, is the sensible power to which the *Nous* joins itself for the judgement of the senses. There is, therefore, another more divine soul with its own *nous.* For the sensible power is a material *nous* inherent and consubstantial with the material soul. If this is so, the heavenly *Logos,* that is, the *Nous* or divine mind, is within the divine soul. But divine soul is itself in the material mind, the material mind in the material soul, the material soul in the carnal body which, with all three, must be purified to receive the eternal light and eternal life: but this, faith in Christ accomplishes.

(63) Let us say therefore how such a soul has been created "according to the image of God" and "according to likeness," and whether man is only soul.[6][8] As Paul says, the "terrestial" man is one thing, the "animal" man another, the "spiritual" man is another, and these are all in one man, but he especially speaks frequently of the "interior man," for such is the soul. For he joins *Nous* and divine soul and calls this the heavenly man; the rest: the terrestial man.

C. TO OUR IMAGE AND LIKENESS

If this is so, our soul is "according to the image" of God and of the Lord Jesus Christ. If indeed Christ is life and *Logos,* he is image

---

67 Lk 17.34-39.
68 The first half of this sect. 63 in its discussion of the soul as an inferior triad imaging the higher triad makes use of philosophical fragments (Group II) as assembled by Hadot, PV II 37-38.

of God, image in which God the Father is seen, that is, in life one sees "to be." For this is the image, as was said.[69] And if Christ is life, but "to live" is the *Logos,* and if life itself is "to be," and "to be" is the Father, if again, life itself is "to understand," and this is the Holy Spirit, all these are three, in each one are the three, and the three are one and absolutely *homoousia* (consubstantial).

If then the soul as soul is at once "to be" of soul, "to live" and "to understand," if it is therefore three, the soul is as the image of the image of the Triad on High. For the soul as soul in its "to be," giving both life and knowledge, possessing these together, *homoousia* (consubstantial) in unity, before understanding and yet these three are individuated as in their own substances, without being separated by sectioning, by division, by overflow, by extension or reproduction, but they are always three, each one existing really in the other which really exists also, and this, substantially. Therefore the soul is "according to the image."

And just as the Father is "to be," while the Son is twofold, but twofold in movement and act, likewise the soul as soul is as the paternal power, while vivification and understanding are in movement. Therefore this: the "to be" of soul is "according to the image" of the Father and the Son, while its "to be" in such a way is "according to the likeness." The soul is therefore also *homoousion* (consubstantial) in its unity, and it is of similar substance in its triple power; it therefore begets itself, moves itself, is always in movement, as source and principle of movements in the world, as the Father and the Son are themselves creator and precause and preprinciple of the movement of the soul.

(64) Furthermore I speak darkly of a great mystery.[70] Just as the most divine unique Trinity has, through itself, produced, by shining forth, the soul in the intelligible world in its subsistence and proper substance, this soul that we properly call substance, so likewise the soul, a unique second trinity, has achieved manifestation in the sensible world, because this soul, while remaining on high, has begotten souls which come into this world. And therefore this is "according to the image and likeness."

---

69 Cf. *adv. Ar.* I 53,19–26.

70 In the beginning of this sect. 64 the same philosophical fragments (Group II) are utilized as in the beginning of sect. 63, namely, Hadot, PV II 38.

3. The body, image of the androgyny of the Logos

Let us see therefore if man is also "to the image and likeness of God" according to the flesh. Some say that he is this also according to the flesh, in foreknowledge of the fact that in the future Jesus would assume flesh. But I say: perhaps, if it is also said that the *Logos*, while he is *Logos* of the flesh, is indeed God and incorporeal and above every body: for he is power of all existents and God of all things, perhaps not without reason is man according to the image of the body of the *Logos*.

Indeed, if our body and our flesh are to rise, put on incorruptibility, and become "spiritual flesh," just as our Savior also was this in all respects, when he rose, ascended into heaven, and when he will return, if then "we will be changed" after the resurrection to receive a spiritual garment, nothing prevents man from having been created "according to the image" of that higher flesh of the *Logos*. Indeed, the prophet gives testimony to this, saying "And God made man according to the image of God."[71] If God made man according to the image, the Father made him "according to the image" of the Son. But if he also says this: "He made him male-female," and it was previously said: "He made man according to the image of God," it is evident that also according to the body and the flesh, extremely mystically, he made him according to the image of God, the *Logos* being himself both male and female, since he was for himself his own Son, in the first and the second birth, spiritually and carnally. Thanks be to God the Father and his Son our Lord Jesus Christ, from eternity and forever and ever. Amen.

---

71 Gn 1.27.

AGAINST ARIUS

SECOND BOOK

ABOUT THE *HOMOOUSIOS* IN GREEK AND IN LATIN[1]

I. THE ORTHODOX TEACHING AND ITS ADVERSARIES

1. The Orthodox Faith

E ALL CONFESS an all-powerful God; we alone for the moment confess Christ Jesus; yet soon all will confess him. We who have faith in Christ confess both God the Father and Christ the Son; our faith is in both because they are both together and individuals—as certainly as God is Father, so certainly is his Son Jesus Christ, so that our whole religion and whole hope is faith in Christ. But although we confess two individuals, nevertheless we affirm one God and that both are one God, because both the Father is in the Son and the Son is in the Father.

2. The Heresies

A. PATRIPASSIANISM

Some affirm that the Father alone is the unique God and that the Son is man; but let us omit this for the moment. Indeed, when we say that Jesus is Son, we confess that he was Son before he was born

1 This whole book is a discussion with the Homoeans, partisans of a mere likeness of Son to Father. The blasphemy of Sirmium, forbidding any mention of the term "substance" in trinitarian speculation was composed by Ursacius (c. 335–71) Bishop of Singidunum, now Belgrade, who with Valens bishop of Mursa, were the Arian leaders in the West and strong enemies of Athanasius whom they had previously opposed at the Council of Tyre in 335. This so-called blasphemy of Sirmium was intended to dis-

of Mary. For if the *Logos* "was in the principle," [2] and the *"Logos* was with God," and the *"Logos* himself was God," and if "he was in the principle," since it is he who afterwards was the *"Logos* made flesh,"[3] it is then the same thing to be *Logos* and to be Jesus. For if the *Logos* "was in the principle," the Son also was in the principle, that Son who, afterwards, was Jesus in the flesh, because of the mystery which he, by the command of the Father, accomplished. It must be confessed, therefore, that the Son was as early as the Principle.

B. ARIANISM WHICH DENIES THAT THE SON IS FROM THE SUBSTANCE OF THE FATHER

Do we say that he is from the substance of the Father or that he comes from outside the Father? But this must be investigated.

a) God has a substance

Do we not confess that God is? We do confess it. What then? This "to be" of God, do we speak of it as *anousion* or as *enousion,* that is, as without substance or as substance? As *anousion* (without substance), some say. I agree, but I ask: *anousion* (without substance) in what way? Is it that he is not absolutely substance or that he is above substance, that is, *huperousion* (hypersubstance)? Who then would say that God is without substance while confessing that he is? For his "to be" is his substance, but not that substance known to us; but he himself, because he is "To Be" itself, is not from substance but is substance itself, the parent of all substances, giving himself "to be" from himself, first substance, universal substance, substance before substance. On account of this, therefore, because he is *huperousios* (hypersubstance), some have called him *anousios* (with-

---

guise their Anomoeanism, the doctrine that the Son was totally unlike the Father. These Latin adversaries argued that *ousia* (substance) and *homoousion* (consubstantiality) were not found in Scripture and were untranslatable into Latin. This is a tightly argued theological polemic in defense of the meaning of the Latin translation of *homoousion* as *substantia,* and hence the word *consubstantialis* (consubstantial).

2 Jn 1.1–2.
3 Jn 1.14.

out substance), not that he is without substance, since he truly is. Let us adore God, therefore, and affirm that he is, that is, that he is *enousion* (substance), who has created all things, heaven and earth, world, spirit, angels, souls, animals, and man "according to the image and likeness"[4] of the image of those on high.

b) The Son is from the substance of the Father

What then? Since God is *enousios* (substance), he is certainly called Father; thus we confess him to be also Father of the only begotten Son; this is the faith of all. But does not the word by its ambiguity mislead the understanding? "Indeed I have begotten you," God also said of men. If, therefore, "I have begotten" both signifies "I have created" as creature and "I have naturally begotten from my own substance," what makes it pertain more to the only begotten Son? What makes it pertain to the one who is Son? What makes it pertain to him who is the one and only Son? What makes it pertain to him in whom the Father is? What makes it pertain to him who is in the Father? What makes it pertain to him who is the *Logos,* who "was in the principle," and "was with God," and "is God," and "through whom all things have been made," and "without whom nothing has been made"?[5] But what does this signify: that Christ is the only begotten? For if God is the Father of all things through creation, in what way is he the Father of the only begotten if not by another way than he is Father of creatures, begetting from substance, not from nothing. But there was no other substance before all things than the substance of the Father. Therefore, Christ is from the substance of the Father.

C. ARIANISM WHICH ASSIGNS A BEGINNING TO THE SON

(2) Judge now! We confess also that Christ is. Let us ask in the same way this question: his "to be," is it *enousion* (a substance) or *anousion* (without substance)? It was already said above: that which has "to be" cannot be *anousion* (without substance). What then? This "to be," whence is it, *ek tou anousiou* (from the without sub-

---

4 Cf. Gn 1.26.
5 Cf. *adv. Ar.* II 1,25–32.

stance) or *ek tou enousiou* (from the substance), that is, from "to be" or from "non-to-be"? God, as they say, is "to be"; Christ also is "to be" but nevertheless he has begun. This is true. But this "to be" which began, began from that which was to have already been in some way; like all divine things or what issues from them, they are always and have always been potentiality.[6] Their procession, however, is action, a manifestation through movement, a kind of birth. What part of God is born, since God is unbegotten? Is it believable, or is it permitted to say that Christ has been made or born from nothing, he whom we call Son of God,[7] he who is the "Lord of glory,"[8] and the other names which we said above[9] and in other books.[10] This is, however, what the most recent heresy affirms.

D. MARCELLUS AND PHOTINUS

And this heresy[11] is similar to the one which says, either that Christ began from Mary or that the *Logos* did not himself become flesh but that he assumed man so that the *Logos* himself might direct him. The latter theory belonged to Marcellus, the former to Photinus.

E. HOMOEOUSIANS AND HOMOEANS

We shall, therefore, expel all those who have these opinions or similar ones about Christ. We speak to those who affirm that Christ is Son of God, and a born Son certainly, since they confess an "only begotten Son," above all, "begotten," not made. This is the minimum. They add: "Son from the Father, God from God, true light

---

6 A brief refutation of the Homoiousians. There is no becoming in God, only a manifestation or action of what was hidden within the potentiality-power of God. There is some use here of philosophical fragments (Group III) as cited by Hadot, PV II 53.

7 Jn 1.3.

8 1 Cor. 2.8.

9 Cf. *adv. Ar.* II 1,43–47.

10 Cf. *ad Cand.* 2,10–14; *adv. Ar.* I 3,5–22; 40, 32–35; 41, 42–50; 43, 1–4; 47, 38–39.

from true light," and above all, the following: "Spirit from Spirit, and the Son in the Father, and the Father in the Son." When they confess that, it is without conviction, by reason of fear rather than of truth. Some refuse to mention substance here; others mention it but wish to call it similar, not identical.

It should first of all be considered by the latter what the prophet Isaiah said: "There was no God before me and after me there will be no God like unto me."[12] If Christ is Son, Christ is certainly after God. But after God there is nothing like unto him. Christ is therefore not like unto God; or if he is not after God, certainly he is with God; for in no way can he be before God; therefore he is *homoousion* (consubstantial). And David expressed it thus: "No one is like unto you."[13]

Next—what we have many times taught—substance as substance, especially if it is a homogeneous substance which is realized in two or more individuals, is said to be identical substance, not similar.[14] Thus the soul is substance: even if there are many souls, as souls they have one and the same substance, not that this substance precedes them and preexists them, but that this substance coexists always with them; so also is this the case with other things. With greater reason is this the case in God, since he is the origin of substance; with him, by a certain divine origin, the Son, having received substance from the Father, with him and in him·the Son always is, as different and identical, of the same substance, not that the substance of the Father diminishes nor that the substance of the Son is received from an outside source, but by a consubstantial and perfect unity, the Son is God and "power" of God who has always been and always existed. This is God and the *Logos,* God and his form, Father and Son, God and Jesus Christ, God and his "power and wisdom";[15] therefore, *homoousion* (consubstantial).

---

11 This passage alludes to the profession of faith, Sirmium 351, an Arian formula and Basil of Ancyra's letter which tried to moderate extreme Arianism; note that doctrines attributed to Photimus correspond to those of Sirmium, 351. Cf. Hilary, *De synodis* 38 (PL 10.509–12).
12 Is 43.10.
13 Ps 34(35).10.
14 Cf. *adv. Ar.* I 23,7–40; 25,5–7; 30,6–10; 41,9–19.
15 1 Cor 1.24.

3. Brief Explanation of the Word homoousion (consubstantial)

This word *homoousion* (that which is consubstantial) is used as *homoeideis* (that which is specifically the same) when there are things in the same species simultaneously existing; likewise, when there are *homoēlikes* (contemporaries), of the same era, of the same age. Here, in fact, *homoousion* signifies consubstantial, that which is cosubstantiated, without composition or separation, but always together with regard to the powers of being and distinguished by actions.

II. DEFENSE OF *OUSIA* (SUBSTANCE) AND OF *HOMOOUSION* (CONSUBSTANTIAL)

1. Objections of Adversaries

(3) Here some questions[16] arise: first, in the Holy Scriptures no mention is made of substance and, above all, *homoousion* (consubstantial) is not read there; then, if the *homoousion* is the case, whenever the Son suffered, the Father suffered; third, if the *homoousion* is the case, the Father is not greater, the Son inferior, and there is no longer a difference between the one who sends and the one who is sent. These and other questions of this kind are asked.

2. The Substance of God and of Christ: res (reality) and nomen (name)

A. *RES* (THE REALITY): GOD AND CHRIST HAVE ONE SUBSTANCE

First, let us consider this with regard to substance: is there no substance in God or in Christ, or is it that the term substance is not read in Scripture?

If there is no substance, as we said above, shall we so understand this in the sense that he is wholly without substance or in the sense

---

16 Victorinus, throughout most of this book, grapples with the conciliar decisions using arguments from the common fund and explaining distinction in the Trinity by the predominance of one aspect of "to be" in each case.

that he is wholly above substance?[17] We are not allowed to say that God is not; for, that which is God, that which is Spirit, that which is light, that is substance. For why do we also add "true light"?[18] Do we truly understand substance in divine things and thus in God as we understand bodies in material things and the soul in incorporeal things? For this is substance up there: to be above substance. All confess that God is, since he is the power of substance, and above substance for that reason, and, by that, himself substance. Indeed, it belongs to the power of being that it can be. Certainly God is all-powerful, and he is himself all that of which he is the origin or cause, by power and in a certain way; whence it was said by Paul: "So that God may be all in all."[19] Therefore he is also *on* (existent), both existing and substance, although he is above all that, because he is Father of all; he is, therefore, all things by power. Therefore, one should not fear to affirm substance of God, because when the terms are lacking to speak properly of the first or the highest realities, it is not inappropriate for us to use for our understanding of these intelligibles words that are known to us, so that in this case we rightly call substance that which is the "to be" of God.

In the same way let us understand also that Christ both is substance and that he is substance from his Father since he is himself also light from light, God from God, Spirit, *Logos* "through whom all has been made," and since he is *Logos* in such a way that he has willed to come in his own substance to the mystery of the flesh; for this reason it was said by the Apostle: "And not according to Christ, because in him dwells the total fullness of the divinity corporeally,"[20] that is, *ousiōdōs* (substantially). For God is power and the *Logos* is action, but each one is in the other. For that which can be is power, and that which is, can be. Therefore, power itself is action, and action itself is action by power. Therefore, both the Father acts and the Son acts; and the Father is on that account Father, because power begets action and, on that account, the Son is action because action comes from power. Therefore, both the Father

---

17 Cf. *adv. Ar.* II 1,26–27.
18 Cf. *adv. Ar.* I 47,3; II 2,24.
19 1 Cor 15.28.
20 Col 2.8–9.

is in the Son and the Son in the Father, but both are in each individual, and that is why they are one; they are, however, two because that by which[21] each is greater, manifests it as different; the Father is more power; the Son, more act; the Son is therefore different because he is more act; for he is more action because action is external.

If this is so, both the Father is substance and the Son is substance, and they are one substance, and substance from the Father, and substance together, and always and from eternity together Father and Son are the same substance and together substance, that is, *homoousion* (consubstantial).

B. THE NAME IN SCRIPTURE

1. Res *(reality) and* Nomen *(name)*

Or is the term substance not read in the Divine Scriptures? First, he who denies this confesses the reality but searches Scripture for authority. But how is it not unjust not to admit the reality when you prove it by reason because the ancients omitted the word perhaps by some chance or motive? In truth, what do they deny being read in Scripture? Substance? Or the use of the word substance for God or Christ? Or is it the word *homoousion* (consubstantial) itself?

2. Substance Is Used in Scripture of God and of Christ

The word substance is used in Scripture of God and of Christ. Of God we read in the prophet Jeremiah: "Who has stood in the substance of the Lord and has seen his Word? Who has lent his ear and heard?" Likewise, a little later: "And if they had stood in my substance, they would have heard my words."[22] Likewise the word substance is read in the prophet David: "And my substance is in the lower parts of the earth."[23] We read of Christ in Paul to the

---

21 The CSEL text change of *quod* (which) to *quo* (by which) strengthens the whole concept of distinction by the predominance of one aspect of "To Be."

22 Jer 23.18; 23.22.

23 Ps 138(139).15.

Hebrews: "He who is the character of his substance."[24] There are yet other examples, but indeed I think that this suffices.

3. If, in its Scriptural uses, Substantia (Substance) translates Hupostasis (subsistence), what relation is there between Hupostasis and Ousia (Substance)?

a) Hupostasis and ousia

(4) But then with the Greeks there is used the word *hupostasis* (subsistence), not *ousia* (substance). Let us see what is the difference.

The Greeks call *onta* (existents) those which are eternal as well as those which are in the world and terrestial. Among the eternal, therefore, God is the omnipotent cause of all, both source and origin of all existents, that is, *tōn ontōn pantōn*. What then? Do we give "to be" to God, or do we give "to be" to all things but not give it to God? Certainly reason requires that God is the first "to be."[25] Because, indeed, "to be" can be understood while not clearly knowing what it is, at the moment it becomes comprehensible, it is called *on* (existent), that is, a certain form coming into knowledge; this "to be" becomes such a "to be" is now called *on* (existent) or *huparxis* (subsistent). Every *huparxis* has "to be." "To be" is not necessarily *kai huparxis* (also subsistent) or *on* (existent) except potentially, not manifestly so that it is called *on* (existent). For *on* (the existent) is "to be" but determined by a certain form. Because pure "to be" is conceived as pure only at the very moment when it is conceived as having henceforth received a form—for the form begets knowledge— this clearly proclaims that it is one thing to be a form and another thing to be formed. But that which is formed is "to be," the form is that which makes known the "to be." Therefore, "to be" we give to

---

24 Heb 1.3.
25 Victorinus shows in this passage which extends into a good part of sect. 6 that "substance" stands for "being" which is present in Scripture; the hypostasis is not the undefined notion of substance but "to be" with form *(esse cum forma)*. God is primary "To Be" *(primum esse)* whereas his Son is the Form, revealing the Father, Pure "To Be" *(Esse)* since it is predominantly "to be" is predominantly substance; formed "To Be" since it is predominant determination is predominantly hypostasis. Victorinus reserves *subsistentia* (subsistence) to designate the determinations of the divine substance or the divine being, that is, Father and Son.

God, but "form"[26] to Christ because through the Son the Father is known, that is, through the form the "to be" is known; and of this it was said: "Whoever has seen me, has seen the Father also."[27] Therefore, God is also *huparxis* (subsistent), and Christ is *huparxis* (subsistent). For *huparxis* (subsistent) is "to be" with form. And because they are always together, the form is "to be" and "to be" itself is form, whence it follows that the Father is in the Son and the Son in the Father. For there is "to be" also in the Father, which is power, which is prior to that which is the form. "To be" is likewise again also in the Son, but he has this, which is his own "to be" from the Father so that for him this is "to be form." Each one, therefore, is in the other, and both are one. Therefore, God is *on* (existent), the Son is *on* (existent), for *to on* (the existent) is this: to be with form.

Indeed, all that which is *on* (existent) is to be with form. This *on* (existent) is also called existence and substance and subsistence: for that which is *on* (existent) exists and subsists and is a subject. But that which is "to be" without anything joined to it is that which is simple, that which is one. Therefore, "to be" more manifested is subsistence and existence, and is called substance. If then subsistence is said of God, with greater reason substance is said, and above all, this word because it signifies: subject, and original subject, which is appropriate for God; but not subject as a substance in the world, but as a subject more noble, more primordial, and which is true "to be" inasmuch as he is source of the totality of things, because God gives to existents the "to be" proper to each one.

Therefore the "to be" having a form and the "to be" which is first and alone are called beings *homōnumōs* (by homonymy). Indeed, since that which is primary "to be" is pure, this is predominantly substance. But again since the form is also "to be", it is also substance, but this is called *hupostasis* (hypostasis). Indeed, "to be" which already has a form is subsistence; but "to be" which has a form is God, because God is also Father; likewise the Son, since he is *Logos* and Son. Therefore, subsistence is more properly said of these two than is substance, since that which is original "to be" with a form is called subsistence. But this is also called substance. And that

---

26 Cf. Phil 2.6.
27 Jn 14.9.

is why it was said: "From one substance there are three sub-sistences," so that that itself which is "to be" subsists in a triple manner: God himself, and Christ, that is, *Logos* and Holy Spirit.

Therefore the word *hupostasis* (hypostasis) is rightly applied to God, rightly to the *Logos*, that is, to Father and Son.

b) Hupostasis *(Hupostasis) and* ousia *(substance) in Scripture*

But the Latins translate this word as "substance" because we have said that "to be" can, of course, also be called substance, but "to be" which has a form, even more so. Since these things are so, *hupostasis* (hypostasis) is read in Scripture, but this is *ousia* (sub-stance), as we have proven.

(5) Let us now see whether there, where we read the word, *hupostasis* (hypostasis) signifies something other than *ousian* (sub-stance). For many think riches and fortunes to be signified by this word, namely, *hupostasei* (hypostasis).

But he said: "If they had stood in the *hupostasei* (hypostasis) of the Lord, they would have seen his Word."[28] What do we under-stand here *hupostasis* (hypostasis) of the Lord to be except that it is God? But God is Spirit, light, omnipotent power and such things of this kind. This one who "stands" also knows: but he who knows does not go astray; therefore, he "stands." But, knowing God, he knows and "sees" the *Logos,* Son of God. Therefore it is evident that this is the *hupostasis* (hypostasis) of God, which, when it is known, the Word also is known: for they are together, and this is *homoousion* (consubstantiality). This he reiterates again: "Because if they had stood in my *hupostasei* (hypostasis), they would have also heard my Word." Above he used "to see," here he used "to hear"; the one and the other signify "to know." For one who "stands" in the substance of the thing, knows a thing, that is, in the first source of the thing, so as to know all that is proper to it.

What then? When elsewhere in David or in the Gospel there is used and read *hupostasis* (hypostasis), is anything other than *ousia* (substance) understood? "My *hupostasis* (hypostasis), says David,— it is a question of God—"My *hupostasis* (hypostasis) is in the lower

---

28 Jer 23.18.

regions of the earth."[29] For he says: let no one believe himself hidden, because I am everywhere, I and all that I am and "my substance," even "in the lower regions of the earth." For God or the Spirit of God which is the substance of God is everywhere.

(6) I now also wish to see this in the Gospel through a parable used as an example. For he said: "A father of a family divided his *hupostasin* (hypostasis) between his two sons."[30] Here certainly we understand fortune and patrimony. But if it is necessary to refer this parable to God, *hupostasis* (hypostasis) will be here also understood as total power and virtue. One son who deserted God "consumed" this [hypostasis]. Indeed, he who "separated"[31] himself from God has not the Spirit of God, nor the light, nor Christ: this one consumed within him the substance of God. For this is the *hupostasis* (hypostasis) of God, as we have said. Whether we now call this riches or patrimony makes no difference. For it was thus said by the Apostle Paul: "O the depth of the riches of the wisdom and of the knowledge of God."[32] If then the "riches of God"[33] are "wisdom and knowledge," and if "wisdom and knowledge" are "the power of God," itself, but the "power of God" is Christ, but Christ is *Logos,* and *Logos* indeed is Son, if the Son is himself in the Father, therefore this Son is the riches of the Father, he himself is his *hupostasis* (hypostasis). Henceforth it matters not at all whether we understand *hupostasis* (hypostasis) as riches or as *ousia* (substance), provided that there is signified by that God himself.

Therefore we read in Scripture in reference to God either *hupostasis* (hypostasis) or *ousia* (substance). But this is also understood of Christ.

---

29 Ps 138(139).15.
30 Cf. Lk 15.12.
31 Cf. Lk 15.12–13.
32 Rom 11.33.
33 Cf. 1 Cor 1.24.

3. *The* homoousion *(consubstantial):* res *(reality) and* nomen *(name)*

A. THE *RES* (REALITY): THE FATHER IS IN THE SON, THE SON IN THE FATHER[34]

It was said: "I am in the Father and the Father is in me."[35] This is, indeed, repeated for this reason, because the Son could be in the Father without the Father being also in the Son, but it is repeated so that we may understand that the fullness of the two and the self-sameness of each is in each one. But if it is the same *hupostasis* (hypostasis), they are, therefore, *homoousion* (consubstantial). But it is the same; for Christ is "God, from God, light from light." They are, therefore, *homoousion* (consubstantial). And if Christ is that from eternity and always, they are necessarily together; therefore, they are truly *homoousion* (consubstantial).

B. THE *NOMEN* (NAME): IT IS DEDUCED FROM SCRIPTURE

(7) But indeed this word itself, *homoousion* (consubstantial) is not read in Scripture. But all truths which we affirm are found there. I speak to you, because you already confess of God either that he is light or that he is Spirit; therefore you say: "God from God, Spirit from invisible Spirit, and true light from true light," all of which are the *hupostaseis* (hypostases) of God. When indeed you affirm that Christ is "God from God, light from light," and such names, where have you so read them in Scripture?[36] Or is it permitted to you to speak thus, whence the *homoousion* (consubstantial) is better proved, while it is not permitted to us to say *homoousion* (consubstantial)? Indeed, if for this reason you say "light from light"

---

34 This passage is the longest anti-homoean discussion available. Latin theologians like Phoebadius and Gregory of Elvira (d. after 392) were strong opponents of Arianism; cf. especially II 7,1–21. Jn 14.11 is considered by Victorinus to be the best scriptural expression of the *homoousios.* He shows that the word "substance" if not literally in Scripture is certainly deduced from the Scripture. Note also that in II 9,1 there is a literal echo of the formula of the Sirmium creed, May 22, 359, and of formulas used at Rimini. Cf. Victorinus, *De hom. rec.* 3,2; hence this Book II is later than the Dated Creed of May 22, 359.

35 Jn 14.10.

because God is also called light and Christ is called light, and likewise also the Father is called God and Christ is called God, this certainly is evident; but indeed, "God from God" is not read in Scripture, nor is "light from light." But it was legitimate to draw these expressions from Scripture. Therefore it is legitimate to compose from Scripture terms not read there. You deny that *homoousion* (consubstantial) is read in Scripture. But if similar terms or those derived in a similar way are read in Scripture, we ought to have an equal right to this derivative.

Light is the *ousia* (substance) of God. This light is life, and this life is knowledge. That God is this, that Christ is this has been sufficiently shown: "The Father lives and I live."[37] "The Father has life in himself and he has given to the Son also to have life in himself."[38] "All things that the Father has, he has given to me."[39] By these testimonies and others we often prove that the same things are in the Father and in the Son, and that this is always and from eternity; and on that account this was called *homoousion* (consubstantial).

(8) But what is the origin of this term? Listen to the Gospel, listen to the apostle Paul, listen to the prayer of oblation. Since God is life, and eternal life, we Christians, that is, we who believe in Christ, are taught in the Gospel how we ought to pray to God the Father; in this prayer we ask for many things, then we ask for "bread";[40] this bread is life; for it was said: "For this is the bread which descends from heaven";[41] this life, both of Christ and of God, that is, eternal life, by what name does he call it? *Epiousion arton* (supersubstantial bread): bread from the same substance, that is, consubstantial life coming from the life of God. For whence would we be sons of God except by participation of eternal life which Christ gave to us, bringing it to us from the Father? This, therefore, is our petition: *Dos hēmin epiousion arton* (Give us our

---

36 Cf. *adv. Ar.* I 47,3; II 2,24.
37 Jn 6.57–59.
38 Jn 5.26.
39 Jn 16.15.
40 Cf. Mt 6.11.
41 Jn 6.58.

supersubstantial bread),[42] that is, life from the same substance. Indeed, if what we receive is the body of Christ, and if Christ is life, we ask for *epiousion arton* (supersubstantial bread). For the divinity dwells in Christ corporeally. The Greek Gospel, therefore, has *epiousion*[43] (supersubstantial), a word derived from substance and clearly referring to the substance of God. This term, either because they had not understood it or because they could not render it in their own language, the Latins have not been able to express and they used only *cotidianum* (daily), not also *epiousion* (supersubstantial). Therefore this term is also read in Scripture, and substance is used in reference to God; the term can be said in Greek, and even if it is not translated into Latin, it is nevertheless said in Greek because it is understood.

We then who believe in Christ, because we hope from him eternal life, because he is himself life, as long as we follow him and are with him and around him, we are around eternal life and we are called *laos periousios,* that is, a people close to his substance.[44] That is why the holy Apostle expressed himself thus in Greek in the Epistle to Titus: "*hina lutrōsētai hēmas apo pasēs anomias kai katharisē en heautō laon periousion zēlōtēn kalōn ergōn* ("that he might redeem us from all iniquity and might cleanse to himself a people around his substance [*periousion*], a pursuer of good works"). Since the Latin translator did not understand *periousion* (around his substance): *okhlon peri ousian tou Khristou onta*[45] (a group being around the substance of Christ), that is, around the life which Christ both has and gives,[46] he translated it as a numerous people. But what does it profit for salvation that a people be numerous? This, however, that it is *periousios,* that is, associated closely with the substance of Christ, is the greatest cause and, as it were, necessity for its salvation.

---

42 Cf. Mt 6.11; Victorinus quotes in Greek the words that are essential to his argument, *dos hēmin epiousion arton.*

43 Cf. Mt 6.11.

44 Ti 2.14.

45 Ti 2.14; Victorinus quotes Titus in a Greek text which reflects that found in most modern editions of the New Testament.

46 Victorinus adduces an exegetical comment on Ti 2.14 which he quotes in Greek.

Thus the prayer of oblation, understood in that way, is addressed to God: *sōson periousion laon zēlōtēn kalōn ergōn* (save a people around your substance, a pursuer of good works).[47]

Therefore, all these words, derived from *ousia* that is, substance, are used in Scripture. Thus, therefore, there was composed *homoousion* (consubstantial), to refer to God and Christ; and this term is not inconsistent with reason. It contains *ousian,* that is, substance, as do the terms mentioned above, and it is derived in the same way. And this term condemns all heretics. It was necessary, therefore, that it be used by the Fathers. It must therefore be expressed and always used.

C. REPLIES TO THE HOMOEANS' ATTACKS AGAINST *HOMOOUSION* (CONSUBSTANTIAL)

a) Is this a term that is not understood?

(9) But, they say, since this term is not understood, and gives scandal, it is necessary to remove it from the profession of faith and from preaching or certainly to translate it into Latin.

It is not understood, they tell us. In that case it is untranslatable into Latin. It is not understood? Why then do you fear it? For they who attack something, fear it. But if you fear it, you are heretics: having been excluded by this term, you desire to steal back into the Church. For if you refuse *ousian* (substance) in God, you wish to suppress *homoousion* (consubstantiality) for the same reason, because *ousian* (substance) is thereby affirmed. Therefore, you understand it and you fear it. But if Basil also says *homoiousion* (similar in substance), this term is also against you, and that is why you also reject it, because, briefly, you deny *ousian* (substance) in God. If then you reject *homoousion* (consubstantial) because you understand it, and if Basil himself also understands, he who wishes to say *homoiousian* (similar in substance)—we shall speak of this later—it is not the case that *homoousion* (consubstantial) is a term that is not understood.

---

47 On this little "fragment of the fourth-century Roman liturgy" see K. Gamber, "Ein kleines Fragment aus der Liturgie des 4. Jahrhunderts," *Revue Bénédictine* 77 (1967) 148–55.

b) Should it be translated into Latin?

Let it be translated into Latin, they say. Because it is difficult to translate it, for that reason you ask it. And if it is translated, will you rally to it? A great miracle! A word makes you heretics, or rather, the sound of the word, because it is said in Greek. Then, if I shall translate it into Latin, since the Church includes the Greeks and since the whole of Scripture, the Old as well as the New Testament, has been put into writing, both Greek and Latin, if we do not use the word in Greek, what shall we answer when the Greeks ask us about this? We must necessarily say *homoousion* (consubstantial); therefore, we must use it. What then? In the Scriptures are there not many names, either Greek or Hebrew, which are either translated or not translated? For example, *"Hēlei, hēlei, lama zaphthanei"*;[48] like-wise, Golgotha and Emmanuel; likewise, "If anyone does not love our God Jesus Christ, let him be *anathema, maran atha,*"[49] and many others of the same kind, either translated and nevertheless used; or not translated and used as they are, for example, *anathema* which is translated neither into Greek nor into Latin and has been used and is still used everyday; likewise, alleluia and amen, which are said in an immutable way in all languages. It is therefore legitimate to use *homoousion* (consubstantial) in the same way.

c) Should it be suppressed?

Certainly whenever a word should be suppressed, it is because it is obscure or contradictory or says too little or too much, or because it is useless. This word is not obscure. For we have also explained what it signifies; and you, because you understand it, fear it; and Basil, because he understands it, changes it. But it is not contradictory. For we already confess terms which refer to substance—for substance is God, Spirit, light which are said of God the Father and Christ—then this word *homoousion* (consubstantial), since it is referred to substance, cannot be contradictory. But is too little or too much expressed by this term? It must then be corrected rather than suppressed. Now, indeed, is it superfluous? But how? Because

---

48 Mt 27.46; Victorinus's Greek differs from what is found in modern
    editions of the New Testament, *Hēlei, hēlei, lama sabakhthanei.*
49 1 Cor 16.22.

it was already said. And where was it said? Or because it is useless?
Is it useless because it excludes heretics, especially Arians? This term
which has been used by our Fathers as a wall and rampart? But it
was used only recently. That is because only recently the poisonous
pack of heretics has been let loose. And yet it was established in
conformity with the ancient faith—for it had also been taught
previously—established then by many bishops (three hundred and
fifteen) of the world, in the city of Nicaea, who afterwards, sending
to all the churches across the entire world the profession of faith
that they had defined, kept thousands of bishops both in those days
and in succeeding years in one same faith. Moreover, this term was
approved by the emperor, the father of our emperor.

d) How can it be translated into Latin?

(10) But we wish that it be translated into Latin. Nor will this
be refused to you. You who deny substance in God, although you
have been vanquished by Basil, and you, Basil, who confess a substance in God, the one and the other, by your own words confess
the *homoousion* (consubstantial).[50] Indeed, you say "God" and the
same God you call "light," the same God you call "Spirit."[51]
Whoever says these terms speaks of the substance of God. For whoever says "Father," or "all-powerful," or "good," or "infinite," and
such terms, is not speaking of substance but of quality. Likewise,
you call the Son *"Logos,"* "light," "Spirit," and these terms signify
substance. Again, when you say "God from God, true light from
true light," you destroy the argument of Basil who feared lest there

---

50 Concerning this section and into sect. 11, Hadot asserts (TTT 920) that
consubstantialis is unknown in the Latin controversies prior to Candidus
the Arian (cf. *Cand.* I 7,1) and Victorinus. It should be noted, however, in
my opinion that this word is found in the *Enneads* of Plotinus, *Enn.*
14.4.28 and 4.7.10. For Victorinus this word "consubstantial" signifies
the same reality existing in many. The word "substance" is usually used
with reference to the Father; therefore the Son and the Spirit are of the
same substance. Victorinus argues that expressions like God from God and
Light from Light express the communication of substance, therefore a consubstantiality. This points up the difference between substantial and accidental names; this is directed against the Anomoeans who made qualitative
differences to be substantial differences and concluded to unlikeness of
substance; cf. Augustine, *De trinitate* 5.3.4 (FC 45.177).
51 Cf. *adv. Ar.* II 2,22–26.

be a higher substance from which the two come. For if one says "God from God, light from light," then the substance of the Father is the substance of the Son because God the Father himself is the very substance from which the substance of the Son comes, *Logos,* light, Spirit. Indeed, when one says "Son," likewise "Savior," likewise "Jesus," Christ is spoken of according to quality not according to substance. So with the remaining names, they are attributed to the Father or to the Son. Therefore, you confess substance. But certainly you believe Basil, who confesses the same names on the subject of God and of Christ: "light," "God," "Spirit," *"Logos"* and confesses substance.

But indeed among these terms *homoousion* (consubstantial) is not found. That is so, if you do not understand "same substance" in *homoousiō* (consubstantial). But if, however, when this word is formed, the same in two or in many is signified: *hōs homoeides,* that which is of the same species, and *homoēlix,* that which is of the same age, and *homōnumon,* that which is of the same name, and *homonoia,* that which is of the same heart, of the same *ennoia* (mind), it follows, therefore, that that which is consubstantial is of the same substance. But if *homo* is understood as *homou, homoousion* will be translated into Latin as *simul consubstantiale* (together consubstantial), which is not from some other but from the power of God from all eternity. And indeed, if the *Logos* "was in the principle and the *Logos* was with God," since the principle has nothing prior to it—if it had something prior it would cease to be principle— God is from eternity and the *Logos* is from eternity: both, therefore, are together and always together, nor is there a moment when one is without the other, nor is there a moment when the Son is a part of nothingness. Hence, Arius is refuted, he who declared: *ēn hote ouk ēn* (there was a time when he was not). And he had also this formula: *ex ouk ontōn* (from the nonexistent) is the Son, that is, from nothing.[52] *Homoousion* (consubstantial) signifies being substance simultaneously. Against each sacrilege struggles the meaning of this term which is called *homoousion* (consubstantial). Or if, indeed, it is so, that *homoousion* (consubstantial) is "of the same substance,"

---

52 Victorinus quotes both expressions in Greek, cf. *adv. Ar.* I 23,5–6.

like *homoeides* (identity), as we taught above,[53] then there is refuted the quoted formula: "Christ is from nothing." If, indeed, God and *Logos* are the same substance, God and *Logos* not only are not from nothing, but are not even from a similar substance. If indeed *homoousion* (consubstantial) is understood to be derived from being substance together, that is, cosubstantiated, God and the *Logos* are together and from eternity, always together are the Father and Son.

(11) From this there is refuted the formula: "There was a time when he was not."[54] If this is so, by this one word, that is, by *homoousiō* (consubstantial) is destroyed all the poison of the Arian doctrine. O learned bishops! O holy bishops, confirming the faith by the Spirit. O word of God, word truly of God, because God and the *Logos* are shown by it to be together from eternity and always the same substance. Therefore, *homoousion* (consubstantial) was translated into Latin; whence it must also necessarily be used and explained under its Greek form.

D. STATEMENT OF THE FORMULA:
"GOD IN GOD, LIGHT IN LIGHT"

But let us now also add something: that through your confession and through the Scriptural text the Latin translation of *homoousion* (consubstantial) is confirmed. The Scriptural text says: the Father is in the Son and the Son in the Father. And lest that not suffice for faith, our Lord Jesus Christ himself says: "I am in the Father and the Father is in me."[55] What therefore? These names, are they inherent, one in the other? Or is it not that their virtues or substances or wisdoms and powers are inherent? The Father insofar as he is Father cannot be in the Son; likewise, the Son as Son cannot be in the Father, but that which is for each one the power of substance is in the other; from this it results that to be one in the other is equivalent to being one, although subsisting[56] as individuals, they

---

53 Cf. *adv. Ar.* II 10,24.
54 Cf. *adv. Ar.* I 23,5–6.
55 Jn 14.10.
56 The word "subsistence" means the appropriation of the act of "to be." Séjourné thinks that Victorinus is the inventor of the word "subsistent" as

are nevertheless one, because there is conceived and named the same thing in each one. Therefore, the Father is in the Son and the Son in in the Father, but in this way.

If this is so, let us consider now the other terms. You say, and you say rightly: "Jesus Christ, our Lord, God from God, light from light."[57] It is almost the same and likewise logical to say this also— let us therefore say and truly say—"God in God, light in light." Certainly this formula is not converted, because only one word is repeated there. For Father and Son are two names, and therefore can be converted, so that it can be said that the Father is in the Son and the Son in the Father. But, indeed, since one term is expressed in the two members: "God in God," it is also expressed in the same way when it is said of the other. The same reasoning also holds when one says: "light in light." Therefore, by the necessity of one term being used, the formula is pronounced only once, but because of the two, Father and Son, it is twice that it is understood and heard. Let us say therefore: "Jesus Son of God, God from God, light from light." Let us also say this: "God in God, light in light." If indeed, as we all confess, both the Son is in the Father, and the Father in the Son—but the Father is both God and light, yet so that the Son is these things, from the Father—it follows necessarily and it is true to say, both that "God is in God," and "light is in light." Or is this difficult to accept? But necessarily it must be admitted both that this is so and that things are that way.

(12) What if these formulas also are Scriptural, and, of these two formulas, one is used with such clearness, that one knows it has not been invented by me but has already been authorized by Sacred Scripture. David who sings hymns, in the book of Psalms, which is called the key of all the mysteries, in the thirty-fifth Psalm chants a psalm to God, sings praise to God in this way: "For in you is the source of life; in your light we shall see the light."[58] Do we think that that is addressed to God, or to Christ, or to both? Because to both, it is rightly addressed: for in the Father is the Son and in the Son is the Father. But if it is addressed to God the Father, it will be

---

constituting a person, thereby distinguishing it from others (DTC 15.2914). Hadot believes the word had been used before.
57 Cf. *adv. Ar.* II 2,22–26.
58 Ps 35(36).10.

this: "If they had stood in my substance, they would have also seen my Word."[59] But if it is addressed to the Son, it will be this: "Whoever has seen me, has seen the Father also."[60] Therefore, "in your light we shall see the light."[61] "Light in light" is therefore scriptural; therefore also "God in God." For it should not be doubted that this follows, since that which is expressed in the same way is approved both by reason and Scripture. That this may be true, it is sufficient now to say this; Isaiah expresses it thus: "The Egyptian has worked for you and merchants of Ethiopia and Saba, men of the highest stature, will walk before you and be your servants; they will follow you from behind, chained by handcuffs, and they will venerate you and beseech you, because God is in you and there is no God outside of you."[62]

III. FINAL PROFESSION

If this is so, let us summarize everything; then *homoousion* (consubstantial) will be clarified, as understood in Greek and translated into Latin.

We believe in God the Father almighty and in his Son the only begotten Jesus Christ our Lord, God from God, light from light, God in God, light in light, consubstantial, together substantial. And so all the rest which is connected with the profession of faith and with the faith.

It has been clarified and explained: the *homoousion* (consubstantial) in its full sense is at once: of the same substance, in the same substance, and always together. If one wishes, one can keep to this Latin translation. But if one prefers to keep the one Greek word which contains both meanings with the maximum of meaning and the minimum of length, let one persevere in using it in speaking of God and of Our Lord! But, in truth, may *homoousion* (consubstantial) be more and more maintained, written, affirmed, explained, announced in all the Churches. For this is the faith of Nicaea, this is the faith of the Apostles, this is the Catholic faith. In this way the

---

59 Jer 23.18.
60 Jn 14.9.
61 Ps 35(36).10.
62 Is 45.14.

Arians, in this way all heretics are vanquished. Peace with those who think this way, from God the Father and from Jesus Christ our Lord. Amen.

AGAINST ARIUS

THIRD BOOK

CONCERNING *HOMOOUSIOS*[1] (CONSUBSTANTIAL)

I. SUMMARY OF THE PRECEDING BOOKS

1. The Soul, Image of the Logos, *the* Logos, *Image of God*

 HE *LOGOS* OR THE DIVINE *NOUS* uses as a center and as a body the celestial soul: this, indeed, uses the sensible *nous* or *logos*; the latter resides in the sensible soul so that it itself is in the sensible body and, for that reason, in every kind of body. But everything which is from the divine reality is related to them not as part of them but as an image[2] —that

---

1 In this book Victorinus teaches that the Church's almost exclusive reference to Father and Son testifies, not to the nondivinity of the Spirit, but to the consubstantiality of Holy Spirit and Son. He responds to the Pneumatomachi (Fourth-Century heretics who denied the full Godhead of the Holy Spirit) when he shows that the Father–Son dyad is really a Father–Son–Spirit triad. Cf. 7,5–8; 18,18–25. He discusses the identity and the difference between the Son and the Holy Spirit. Thus his Trinity is a double dyad: Father–Son and Son–Spirit. The dyad is "to be"-movement *(esse-motus)* and life-knowledge *(vita-scientia)*. Hence the *esse-vivere-intelligere* schema remains fundamental, with *vivere* and *intelligere* as *motus* in relation to *esse*. Cf. III,4 and 5; book III is summarized in IV, 16, 1–18,44. Victorinus pursues his usual method of combing the Scriptures for texts relating to the Holy Spirit; cf. III 10–16.

2 The opening chapter and the first paragraph of its sequel present a summary of *adv. Ar.* IB and II. This is the image theme and includes the consubstantiality formulas of God from God *(Deum de deo)* and Light from Light *(Lumen de lumine)*. The Son is described as the Father's self-identity; cf. II 2,7–11 and 3,34–41; I 53,9–26; II 4,19-22.The Son as Image makes it possible for man to have the only positive knowledge of God open to him; insofar as man can identify himself with the conversion of the *Logos*, the return to the interior through the Spirit, man can know God and become saved. Cf. Porphyry, *Sententiae* 25 (Mommert, 11.5). On the soul as image see above, Introd., sect. 69.

has been proven also and established in the other books[3] —since certainly in the divine realities themselves, the *Logos* is the Image of God. So, therefore, is it with the others. Therefore, it is the same with all of the divine realities. Indeed, just as the *Logos* is the Image of God, so also is the soul an image of the *Logos*. And all other things of this kind which are there are images. But in sensible nature there are not images, nay rather it is necessary to speak of appearances and simulations.

2. The Image of the Light is Consubstantial with the Light

For the progression of things is such that the radiance of the light is the image of the light. It follows that there is one same substance in the supreme and eternal things, because the image of the light is light. For just as from the Spirit comes only Spirit, and from the true only the true, and from God only God, so also from substance comes only substance. For "Spirit" and "true" and "God" designate substance. But everything which has its own "to be" is substance. But this "to be" of which we speak must be understood in one way with respect to that which is "to be," in another way with respect to that which is "to be in a certain mode"; inasmuch as the former is that of substance, the latter that of quality. But this distinction is found here in sensible things and in the world. But in divine and eternal things these two are one. For all that which is there is simple, and God is that very same which is light, which is the sovereign good, which is existence, which is life, which is knowledge. And on this topic we have also spoken in other books.[4] Therefore, there, all is substantially simple, without composition, one as to number, not numerically one but one prior to number, that is, before numerical unity, that is, absolutely simple, alone, without any appearance of otherness.

Consequently, that which is born of it, the image, is not by divi-

---

Death to sin and to the body is a conversion (Rom 6.10 and Porphyry, *Sententiae* 9 (Mommert, 2.14).

The first two sentences of the book form the philosophical fragment as set out in Group II by Hadot, PV II, 37.

3 Cf. *adv. Ar.* I 19,24–28 and I 20, 32.

4 Cf. *ad Cand.* 19,5–10; *adv. Av.* I 4,13; 19,31–49; 20,10; 20,41.

sion nor by emanation, but by radiance[5]; not by extension but by appearance, not so much duplicating the power as activating the power. For where is action except in power and whence does it come except from power? And when or where is power except with action and in action? Power and action are not then different in each other, and they are never similar because they are always identical.

3. The Logos, Light of Light, Consubstantial Revelation of the Father

And because by radiance light is revealed, or by action power is revealed, for this reason: "Whoever has seen me, has seen the Father."[6] And because no one sees the power itself alone: "No one has ever seen God."[7] And since power is life in repose and knowledge in repose, but life and knowledge are actions, if someone were to see God he must die, because the life and knowledge of God remain in themselves and are not in act, but every act is exterior: indeed, for us to live is to live externally; to see God is therefore a death. "No one," says the Scripture, "has ever seen God and lived."[8] Indeed, like is seen by like. External life therefore must be forgotten, knowledge must be forgotten, if we wish to see God, and this for us is death.

(2) But since this life and knowledge are the Logos which is Christ, through Christ we also are the Logos. "All is through him."[9] The Logos is, therefore, both life and knowledge. Why? Because all that, life and knowledge, is movement and addition. We therefore, if we are in Christ, see God through Christ, that is, through the true life, that is, through the true Image. And through an image which, because it is true, is therefore of the same substance, because the power is also in the action. There we see God, therefore, and hence this: "Whoever has seen me, has seen God." Because indeed action comes from power, for that reason the Son comes from the Father,

---

5 There is evidence here of the philosophical fragments (Group III) cited by Hadot, PV II 53.
6 Jn 14.9.
7 Jn 1.18.
8 Ex 33.20.
9 Jn 1.3;1 Cor 8.6.

and from the Spirit, the *Logos*.[10] And because from the Spirit comes the Spirit, for that reason from God comes God; therefore, from substance comes an identical substance, as we have taught above.[11]

II. THE FATHER AND THE SON: THE TWO

1. Consubstantiality of the Father and the Son as First "to be" and First Movement

God is power, that is to say, that he is the first universal "to be"[12] of existence; with him, that is, in him, he has life and knowledge, or rather, that which is "to be" is life and knowledge, by a movement that is interior and turned toward itself. There is, therefore, movement in God and from this also action. That is why it was said: "Amen, amen I say to you, the Son can do nothing of himself, if he does not see the Father do it. For whatever he does, this same thing the Son also does."[13] Similarly therefore the Father also both accomplishes and acts, but interiorly. Consequently, since he needs nothing external, he is always full, always total, always happy.[14]

In fact, since life and knowledge are movement—for all life vivifies and all that which is vivified is necessarily external; likewise, intelligence: because it knows it is exterior and what it knows is in the interior, and life having been drawn outside, the intelligence also knows either by shining or by illuminating—consequently from God

---

10 See above, Introd., sect 19 for Victorinus's teaching on progression in the Trinity.

11 Cf. *adv. Ar.* III 1,6–18.

12 In an extended passage ending with the first paragraph of sect. 4, we are given the Victorine theogony. "To be" *(esse)* here corresponds to "Existence" *(existenia)* in I 30,21ff. Cf. I 57,7–58. There is an inconsistency here inasmuch as *esse* is equated with potentiality when it is often used to indicate act or action begetting potentiality–power; *adv. Ar.* IV 15,4 and 18,45–46 and 23,6. The dyadic opposition between being and action reveals itself as triadic insofar as action is twofold, both life and thought. Cf. I 32,36–37.

13 Jn 5.19.

14 This and the two paragraphs following contain the philosophical fragments (group II) given by Hadot, PV II 23–24.

and from one same substance come substance and life and knowledge, and the same movement, when it is interior within itself, is
the same thing as substance which, thence when it looks and turns
to the exterior, that is, to work and act, is then a begetting, is then a
birth. And this birth, because the movement is unique, is the only
begotten Son. But this unique movement is either that life or that
knowledge of which we have spoken.

Indeed, it is necessary that life is movement. For all life vivifies.
Whence, life is movement which, if it is existing in itself and is converted toward itself, is for itself substance; but if it looks outside, it
is called movement by predominance; for movement in the interior
is repose: either repose in movement or movement in repose. Indeed,
it is necessary that from these two, I say from movement and from
repose, God is both Father and substance itself because, by a quasi-
community and a certain form, he is the source of the two, while
being himself simple and one, and always one and alone, and, as we
said above, total.[15]

This movement when it is taken and understood as movement in
repose, is God, is the Father himself, always and from eternity
Father, because movement is always from substance[16] and in substance or rather, is substance itself. This same movement, when it
looks to the exterior—to look to the exterior is to be movement or
motion which is precisely to will to see oneself, to think of and to
know oneself; but the one who sees himself exists as double, and
there is known the seeing and that which is seen, the one who sees
being himself the one seen, because he sees himself, this turning
toward the exterior is, therefore, being begotten or being toward the
exterior in order to know what one is—therefore, if this movement is
toward the exterior, it is begotten, and if begotten, this is the Son,
the only begotten, because he is alone, he who is total act and total
movement, universal and unique. But movement is identical with
substance. Therefore, both Father and Son are one and the same
substance. They are, therefore, consubstantial, that is *homoousion*.

---

15 Cf. *adv. Ar.* III 2,21.
16 In this discussion of substance and its action as life and thought, use is
   made of the philosophical fragments (Group II) collected by Hadot,
   PV II 34.

2. The Movement is All

(3) The Son is therefore all things as the Father is all things. But because substance is, by its power, prior to act and to movement—I said prior, however, with respect to power and cause because substance is cause of movement for all movement is in substance—therefore it follows necessarily that the begetter is the Father, and necessarily likewise, all that the Father has, the Son also has. "All," he says, "which the Father has, he has given to me";[17] and likewise: "The Father, inasmuch as he has life from himself, so has he given to the Son to have life from himself."[18] Therefore, like the Father, so the Son is life and life from himself. Indeed, this is the very life which is power of living for himself and for others, without receiving it elsewhere. Life is, therefore, movement, original movement, unique movement, self-movement, only begotten movement. This is the *Logos*. Truly this is the life through which all things live. And because it is life, it is he "through whom all things have been made,"[19] and "for whom" all things have been made, because all things after being purified return to eternal life; and all things have been made in him because "these things which have been made are in him life." For there is nothing which is such that its own "to be" is not from that life which is "to be." Therefore, all things have been made in Christ, because Christ is *Logos*.

But life also never began,[20] because it is always from itself and for itself, so that it never ceases and is always infinite: it extends across all things and in all things, from divine and supercelestial things to heavenly things and all the heavens, to ethereal things, airy, moist, earthly, to all things originating from the earth, and finally to

---

17 Jn 16.15.
18 Jn 5.26.
19 Jn 1.3; cf. Col. 1.16.
20 In this paragraph it is seen that life is eternal because soul is a self-moving principle (Plato, *Phaedrus* 245E). Cf. also IV 6,38 and 9,18 as well as I 23,54. Texts which refer to the omnipresence of life, that is, matter as animate, are I 26,26–43; I 51,10–15; IV 10,45–11,38. This is a Platonic and Stoic doctrine also as can be seen in Synesius, *Hymn* 1.316ff. [See Synesius, *Hymni et opuscula,* ed. N. Tersaghi 2 vols. (Rome, 1939–44) 2.175.] Hadot (TTT 935) emphasizes the Chaldaean sources of this doctrine of Synesius; cf. W. Theiler, op. cit., 27–31. For the philosophical fragment involved, cf. Hadot, PV II 33.

all other things. Therefore, our body and our flesh itself have something vital, and all matter has been animated so that the world may be; whence, living beings came forth by the command of God.

In the flesh itself, therefore, life is present, that is, the *Logos* of life[21]; it follows that Christ is present, wherefore the "*Logos* has been made flesh." It is not astonishing then that the *Logos* has taken flesh mysteriously to come to the aid of the flesh and of man. But when he took flesh, he took the universal *logos* of flesh. Now for that reason he has triumphed, in the flesh, over the powers of all flesh, and for that reason he has come to the aid of all flesh, as was said in Isaiah: "All flesh will see you as the salvation of God,"[22] and in the book of the Psalms: "All flesh will come to you."[23] Likewise he also took the universal *logos* of the soul. For it is clear that he also had a soul, since the same Savior said: "My soul is sorrowful even unto death."[24] And likewise in the Psalm: "you will not abandon my soul in hell."[25] Moreover, that he had taken the universal *logos* of the soul is clear from these words in Ezechiel: "All souls are mine, as the soul of the Father, so also the soul of the Son."[26] Likewise he is revealed as universal *Logos* of soul by the fact that he is angry, for example, when he curses the fig tree, and when he says: "Amen I say unto you, it will be more tolerable for the people of Sodom and Gomorrah in the day of judgment than for you."[27] So also in many passages. Likewise also he desires when he says: "Fa-

---

21 The Stoic doctrine of the *Logos's* omnipresence in the world was seen as a certain intellectual preparation for the acceptance of the Incarnation. Christ assumed the whole man—body and soul as well as the *Logos* or idea of man. Hadot (TTT 939) sees in this discussion a preoccupation with Apollinarianism, the first great Christological heresy, and the teaching named after its leader Appolinaris (ca.310–ca.390) that in Christ there is no human spirit, the spirit being replaced by the Divine *Logos*. In discussing Christ's soul, Victorinus follows the Platonic schema of the tripartite soul which was rational, irascible, concupiscible. Because Christ is *Logos*, in assuming a body and soul he assumes mankind, becoming a second Adam, a New Man to whom all men are related. This cosmic role of Christ recalls Irenaeus.
22 Lk 3.6; cf. Is 40.5.
23 Ps 64(65).3.
24 Mt 26.38.
25 Ps 15(16).10.
26 Ez 18.4.
27 Mt 10.15.

ther, if it is possible, may this cup be taken away from me."[28] There
also he reasons: "But rather let your will be done."[29] There are
these texts and many others by which it is shown that he is the universal *logos* of the soul. Therefore the whole man has been taken,
both taken and liberated. For in him were all universals, universal
flesh, universal soul; and these universals have been raised upon the
cross and purified by the Savior God, the *Logos,* the universal of all
universals—for all things have been made through him—he who is
Jesus Christ, our God and Savior and Lord. Amen.

(4) Therefore the *Logos* who is like the seed and the power of
the existing of those things which are and of those things which can
be or which could have been, the *Logos* who is the "wisdom" and
the "power"[30] of all substances, the *Logos* which reaches from God
to all acts, this *Logos* is God through the power of the Father and
one sole God with the Father, by the very act by which he constitutes himself as Son.

III. FATHER, SON AND HOLY SPIRIT: THE THREE

1. To Be, To Live, To Understand

Indeed, since these three are living and intelligent existences, we
must consider that these three, "to be," "to live," "to understand"[31] are three so that they are always one and contained in
"to be" but in that "to be," I say, which on high is "to be." In this

---

28 Mt 26.39.

29 *Ibid.*

30 For the two words cf. 1 Cor 1.24.

31 A long development extending through the first paragraph of ch. 17
supplies a precise discussion of the mutual implication of *esse, vivere,
intelligere* which distinguishes Victorinus's understanding of this triad
from that of Plotinus, *Enn.* 6.6.15. It also distinguishes it from that of
Proclus, *Elements of Theology*, 252–54. The remote sources for the
implications of life can be found in Plato, *Phaedo* 105C ff, Aristotle,
De anima II 4(415b13), Plato, *Sophist* 250A, 254D; Plotinus, *Enn.* 2.8.8.
Cf. also Jn 17.3. In this section substance corresponds to "to be" *(esse),*
and subsistence corresponds to "to be" determined *(esse cum forma).*
Note that individuation is once again by predominance of one aspect of
"to be." Cf. Plotinus *Enn.* 6.2.8. The hypostases correspond to the necessary and inseparable distinctions introduced by thought into the unity
of being.

"to be," therefore, is this "to live," this "to understand," all, as to substance, subsisting as one. For "to live" itself is "to be."[32] For in God it is not such as it is in us, where that which lives is one thing, and the life which makes it live is another thing. Indeed, if we suppose and admit that life itself is and exists, and that that which is its own power is identical with its "to be," it will become clear that we must take as one sole and same thing "to be" and "to live." This reasoning has the same force when applied to knowledge, the knowledge of God, of course. Therefore, this "to understand" in itself is the same as its own "to be," and this "to be" which is "to understand"; this "to understand" in itself is knowledge. Therefore, "to be" is "to be" of life and "to be" of knowledge, that is, it is itself life and knowledge. Then, that which is life and that which is knowledge are one sole and same "to be." Because if these, as individuals and two by two, are one, it follows that "to live" itself is the same as "to understand." For if "to be" is "to live," if "to be" is the same as "to understand," it follows that "to live" and "to understand" are one, since they have one sole "to be." To that is added that "to be" itself is nothing other than "to live." For that which does not live loses "to be" itself, so that as long as each thing exists, just so long does it have its own "to live"; whence, the "to be" dies with life. But we, when we speak of eternal things, we understand differently the "to live." namely, in the sense of knowing that one lives. But to know is to understand. Therefore, to know is to understand, and to know that you live is to live. Therefore, to understand, this will be "to live."

If this is so, if to live and to understand are one, and since "to be" which is to live and to understand is one, these three are one in substance, three in subsistence. For since they have their own power and signification and they also are as they are named, necessarily they are both three and nevertheless one, since the three constitute together each unity that each one is singly. This is expressed by the

---

32 In these philosophical fragments (group II) extending through sect. 5 (Hadot, PV II 24–26) we are led to reason to consubstantiality. The mutual implication of "to be" and life and thought is made explicit. If life and thought are implied in "to be" that is finite, then "to live" is identical with "to think." Therefore, the three are one, and each one is the three. This is compared to the three aspects of the act of vision.

Greeks in this way: *ek mias ousias treis einai tas hupostaseis*[33] (there are three hypostases from one substance). Since this is the case, "to be" is as the foundation for the rest. For "to live" and "to understand" are, as it were, secondary and later in relation to it; they either seem to be inherent in "to be," according to what might be called their primitive state, or they appear, in some way, to go out from "to be" while preserving in their own "to be" that first "to be" which is their source. For there is never being without living and understanding, never living and understanding without being; this is what has already been proved.

(5) For the understanding of this reality, here is an example.[34] Let us take sight or vision in itself, in its own power and nature, existing potentially; this is its "to be", having the capacity to exercise vision which will be its "to live"; likewise, having the power for seeing, which is to recognize what is seen, which is its understanding. These things, if they remain in potentiality, are said to be nothing other than "to be"; they remain, as it were, in repose turned upon themselves; they do not exercise any other act than that of "to be," being purely only vision or sight; and for that reason they must be considered only as "to be." But from the moment when this vision will begin to exercise the act of seeing, the vision, then, by a kind of going out of itself—I say "by a kind"; in fact, it neither proceeds nor departs from itself, but by the tension and exercise of its own power, which is for it to live, vision will begin to perceive all things which are found before it or before which it goes—since its own work of seeing is fulfilled, vision is henceforth the life of vision, life which, by the actuation of the visual movement, shows well that vision lives when it is only the act of seeing, pure visual sensation, without distinguishing or judging what it sees. We think of it this way when we consider vision alone without understanding. But since in fact this seeing, which for vision is "to live," is not truly seeing unless it grasps and understands what it sees, this seeing is at the same time also a "judging what one sees." Thus in seeing is included discernment. If one sees, however one sees, one cannot not also dis-

33 Victorinus repeats in Greek a principle that was first stated in Latin at *adv. Av.* II 4,51.

34 In this section consciousness is self-consciousness. In this way knowledge is linked with conversion; to know is to turn within, towards oneself.

cern what one sees. Therefore, as we have said, in the act of seeing is
contained the act of discernment, and in the act of vision is the act
of "seeing." Therefore there is no composition between them; what
is more, they are simple; by their very "to be," vision, seeing, and
discernment are only one. In this way also in the discerning is present the seeing, and in the seeing is present the "to be" of vision, and,
to tell the truth, there is no inherence, but by its very act of being
vision, vision is to see and to discern. Thus, all are in each one, or
each one is all or all are one.

2. God, the Son and the Holy Spirit are in the Relation of "To Be," "To Live," "To Understand"

A. ELEVATION TOWARDS THE CONTEMPLATION OF GOD

(6) Arise and look up, O my spirit, and acknowledge the power
by which you have been breathed into me by God. To understand
God is difficult but not a hopeless effort.[35] For he has willed that
we should know him and therefore by his divine work he has created
the world, so that we should discern him through all these things.
Certainly it is the *Logos,* who is his Son, his "image" and his
"form,"[36] who has opened to us a way of understanding, from himself to the Father. Therefore, in what nature, in what genus, in what
force or power do we place God so that we understand him and conceive him? Or by what semblance of understanding do we touch him
or rise to him? And since we say that he is unintelligible, by this we
are in some way judging that he is intelligible. Certainly, by the
breath of God, we have a soul, and from that there is a part in us
which is supreme in us. Therefore, we touch him by that point
where we are from him and dependent on him. Certainly, after
the coming of the Savior, since in the Savior we see God himself,
since by him we are taught and instructed, since we have received
from him the Holy Spirit, master of understanding, what else will
such a master of understanding give us except to know, to understand, to confess God? Our ancestors also asked what God is or who

---

35 Sect. 6 opens with an enumeration of man's ways of knowing God. Cf.
Plotinus, *Enn.* 5.1.11 for the circle metaphor. The argument here is that,
since it is through Christ that we know God, without consubstantiality
there could be no knowledge of God.

36 For "image," "form" cf. Col 1.15, Phil 2.6.

he is. And this is the answer given them by the one who is "always
in the bosom of the Father".[37] "You see me and you seek my
Father? I have been with you a long time. Whoever has seen me, has
seen the Father. I am in the Father and the Father is in me."[38]

B. THEOLOGICAL EXPOSITION

a) Initial thesis

Therefore, what do we say that God is? Of course, Spirit, and
Spirit of life. For it has been said: "The Father is life."[39] And like-
wise: "Christ is Spirit."[40] And he himself has said again of himself:
"I am the life";[41] and: "As the Father has life from himself, so he
has given the Son also to have life from himself."[42] In the same way
the Spirit is the Holy Spirit; certainly, he himself is also life. For
Christ received all things from the Father and Scripture says: "I gave
all things to him."[43] And similarly: "All that he has is mine."
Therefore, he has life and he has "to be" life from himself. Why so?
Because where life is, there is "to be" life from itself. And if this is
so, there is also the "to know" that one is life, and to know which
"to be" is "to live" and which "to be" is that which is life.
Therefore, all are joined together and all are one, and one substance
and truly *homoousia* (consubstantial) either together which is
homou or one and the same substance.

b) Development

The Father and the Son, "To Be" and Movement

(7) "To Be" is therefore the Father. For this "To Be" is principle
for the others and prior to the appearance of those which follow.
This is God, he who is God with the two others; this is one God
because that which is "to live" and "to understand" is the same as

---

37 Cf. Jn 1.18.
38 Cf. Jn 14.9–10.
39 Cf. Jn 6.57.
40 Cf. 2 Cor 3.17.
41 Jn 14.6
42 Jn 5.26.
43 Cf. Jn 16.15.

that which is "to be," and for these two, that which is "to live" and "to understand" comes forth from that which is "to be". Let no one then separate the Holy Spirit and, by a blasphemous sacrilege, suspect that he is an I know not what; for he also comes from the Father, because he also is the Son who is from the Father—for they are after that which is "to be." For "to be" is existence or subsistence or indeed if, by a certain fear on account of these too well known names, one goes higher and uses the following expressions: existentiality or substantiality or essentiality, which correspond to *huparktotēta* (superabundance), *ousiotēta* (substantiality) *ontotēta* (existentiality). With all these terms I speak of that "to be", remaining in itself, self-moved, giving strength by his own power whereby all things are given life and empowered. This "to be" is the divine perfection and perfect in all ways, full, absolute, above all perfections. This is God, above the *Nous,* above truth, omnipotent power, and for that reason not a form.

But the *Nous,* and truth are form,[44] but not an inseparable form as inherent in another; no, it is an identical substance or image or form inseparably linked to the power of God the Father to reveal him. Therefore, the one that we have called the first "To Be," who is God, is also called silence, repose, immobility. If this is so, the progression of the power—which certainly is not progression but manifestation,[45] or if it is progression, it is one not leaving that from which it proceeds, but is progress with continuity, rather therefore a manifestation; for there is nothing outside from which the progression could be made; indeed, God is everywhere and God is all things; therefore, the progress of power is manifested as action. If God is silence, this action is called Word; if God is immobility, this action is called movement; if God is essence,[46] this action is life, because, as we have taught,[47] in that which is "to be," there is also "to live," in the silence the Word which keeps silent, and in that

---

44 In the next eight lines use is again made of those philosophical fragments from the second group cited by Hadot, PV II 29.
45 In the description of the Divine Begetting as a manifestation of the Godhead once again the philosophical fragments (Group II) are utilized; Hadot, PV II 53.
46 Essence *(essentia)* translates substance and reappears in IV 6,5, but is never used elsewhere.
47 Cf. *adv. Ar.* III 4.9–28.

which is repose or immobility, there is present either a hidden movement or a hidden action. And so necessarily also movement or action
is born from immobility, or the Word is born from silence, or life is
born from essence. Therefore, these things, essence, silence, immobility, are the Father, that is, God the Father. But, in truth, life,
Word, movement or action are the Son and the only Son because
life, word, movement or action are nothing other than one thing,
and all these things are by predominance movement or action;
indeed, all these things are in act; life and word exercise their power
by movement and are efficacious by movement.

But as for the universal movement which is the original movement, it arises from itself.[48] For what is movement if it is not movement from itself for itself? For if it is moved by another, there is
something other than movement, because it is moved by another.
And if that which moves—I know not what—is not movement, it
cannot move; for it will not have the wherewithal to move. In the
contrary case, movement is born from movement. Movement is then
born from itself, but that is to say: "The Father has given to him
that he may be life from himself for himself."[49] (8) Therefore
movement is also unique movement, self-movement and, since it was
hidden in the Father and was manifested from there, it is movement
from the Father, and because this movement comes from movement,
for this reason it is self-movement and unique movement, whence
the only Son.

This is the *Logos* who is universal and present in all things,
"through whom all things have been made." This is the life for all
things, because "all those things which have been made live."[50] This
is also Jesus Christ because he has saved all things for life. There is
therefore one sole movement and one unique Son, because there is
also only a unique life, only one life which is eternal life. Therefore
the Son is *homoousios* (consubstantial) with the Father. Indeed, the
Father is life and the Son is life, which is *ousia* (substance). Likewise the Father is movement and the Son is movement which also

48 The Platonic notion of self-moved motion (*Phaedrus* 245C-E) was opposed
     by Neoplatonists to the Aristotelian notion of the unmoved mover; cf.
     Macrobius, *In somnium Scipionis* 2.14–16.
49 Jn 5.26.
50 Cf. Jn 1.3–4.

is this *ousia* (substance). For there on high there is not anything which is an accident. Therefore, the Father also is word—although his is a silent word, he nevertheless is word—and the Son is word; and this also is *ousia* (substance). For all that which is or acts and works is *ousia* (substance). And where there is most *ousia* (substance), there is the word. For it is not like a word here which merely sounds in the air but rather it is like an efficacious word here. There is one only Son therefore, because one sole movement. One only life, because there is one sole life: eternal life. For that is not life which some day must die. But never will life die if it knows itself.[51] But it will not be able to know itself without knowing God, God who is life, who is true life and the source of life. If this is so, then by knowing God it will know all things, because all things come from God, because God is in all things, because God is all things. This John proclaims: "This is eternal life, that they may know thee the only true God, and him whom thou hast sent, Jesus Christ."[52]

The Son and the Holy Spirit, living and knowing in one sole movement

Life is knowledge. But whether it is life, whether it is knowledge, there is one movement, and the same movement produces life and through life, knowledge and through knowledge, life. But this movement is *Logos* and this *Logos* is Son. He is, therefore, only Son insofar as he is Son. But insofar as he is *Logos,* he is twofold. For he is life, he is knowledge, in both directions having been efficacious for the salvation of souls, by the mystery of the Cross and thus by life, because we had to be freed from death, and by the mystery of knowledge also, by the Holy Spirit, because he was given as teacher and "taught" all things and gave "testimony" to Christ. This is knowledge producing life, and from that comes the knowledge of God, which is for us to become true life, and this is giving "testimony" to Christ. Thus Christ, that is, the *Logos* is the Son of God and the Son is life, and, because it is the same movement, the Son is also equally knowledge. But the Son exists as Jesus by the act by

---

51 On self-knowledge as the way to God, cf. Proclus, *Elements of Theology,* 203.
52 Jn 17.3.

which he makes himself knowledge, so that there are two existences:[53] that of Christ, that of the Holy Spirit, in one movement
which is Son.

And thus Jesus is also from the Father: "I have come forth from
the mouth of the Most High."[54] And the Holy Spirit is also from
the Father, because one movement produces each existence. And
because "all that the Father has he has given"[55] to the Son, for that
reason the Son also, who is movement, gave all to the Holy Spirit.
For all that he has, "he has from me,"[56] he says. Indeed, because
the Holy Spirit himself is also movement, whatever he has is from
movement. For the Son did not give it to him, but he said: "he has
it from me." For originally movement is life, and life itself is
knowledge and awareness. Therefore, whatever has awareness, has it
from life. Such is the supreme trinity, such is the supreme unity:
"All things that the Father has are mine; that is why I have said
that he will receive of what is mine and will declare it to you."[57]

Conclusion

(9) This will then make it clear enough that "to be" which is the
Father, that life which is the Son, that knowledge which is the Holy
Spirit, are one sole substance,[58] while being three subsistences,
because, coming from "to be" which is substance, and being itself
substance, as we have taught, movement is effective as a twofold
power, that both[59] of vitality and of wisdom and understanding so

---

53 Existence, cf. *adv. Av.* IV 33,32. Beginning with II 4,31 this word is used
   to designate the hypostases because both words designate the *esse-cum-
   forma,* the determination of the substance in common.
54 Sir 24.3.
55 Cf. Jn 16.15.
56 *Ibid.*
57 Cf. Jn 16.15.
58 In this first paragraph substance is shown to be common to Father, Son
   and Spirit who are distinguished according to act or movement. Although
   Victorinus's argument has made use of philosophical formulae, he returns
   here to a theological framework and has recourse to Scripture. He concentrates on showing that the three hypostases are both *Logos* and Spirit,
   but that these common names become proper to the second and third
   hypostases by applying the principle of predominance previously explained.
59 The "both" *(et)* is a CSEL addition.

that evidently in each one[60] are the three. Therefore, the Holy Spirit is knowledge and wisdom.

C. SCRIPTURAL EXPOSITION

1. The Three are in Each One

a) The three are knowledge and life[61]

The Holy Scriptures prove that this is so. "Who has known the mind of God except the Spirit alone?"[62] The Spirit himself will give testimony to our spirit."[63] Who can be a witness without knowledge? And I mean knowledge itself because it is wisdom that teaches us that we are the sons of God.[64] Likewise: "Who, moreover, searches hearts, who knows thoughts? The Spirit."[65] This likewise shows how both are joined with respect to knowledge: "I speak the truth in Christ."[66] Where there is truth, there is knowledge. Because Christ is truth, for that reason he is also knowledge, which is the Holy Spirit. And likewise: "I do not lie, my conscience giving testimony to me in the Holy Spirit."[67] For what else is conscience other than "science with another"? Now this means our knowledge with the Spirit. Therefore, the Spirit is knowledge, and Christ is knowledge, because he is truth. Therefore both Christ and the Spirit are knowledge.

But indeed Christ is life. What if the Holy Spirit is life? For, as we have said, there is one movement, and life is the same as knowledge.[68] What does he, indeed, say, this man taught by Christ, that is, by God—taught, I mean, by knowledge, which is one and the same thing whether it is from Christ or from the Holy Spirit—what then does Paul say when he wishes to declare that both are the same

---

60 Cf. *adv. Ar.* III 2,43,52–53.
61 In these opening paragraphs Christ is reality, the Holy Spirit is knowledge of the reality; therefore, both are Truth. The Spirit witnesses to Christ.
62 Cf. 1 Cor 2.11–16; Rom 11.34.
63 Rom 8.16.
64 Cf. Rom 8.16.
65 Rom 8.27.
66 Rom 9.1.
67 Rom 9.1.
68 Cf. *adv. Ar.* III 8,25–27.

reality? "Truly the prudence of the Spirit is life."[69] For error, imprudence, and ignorance are impassioned, self-rebellious, self-contradictory. And because of this, "prudence of the flesh," which is imprudence, is death because it does not know God. Therefore, "prudence of the Spirit is life and peace."[70]

(10) Since these are already united and are one, let us now show that God himself is both knowledge and life, although these come from him. For Paul says: "O the depth of the riches of the wisdom and of the knowledge of God!"[71] And it is likewise said thus: "The manifold wisdom of God."[72] From this cause Christ is also called the "Mystery of God;"[73] from this cause also Christ is called Wisdom. Hence also this: "So that you may be able to comprehend with all the saints what is the breadth and length and height and depth, to know also the love of Christ which surpasses knowledge."[74] Thus God is also knowledge, and knowledge frees us; but through Christ nevertheless, because he is the "knowledge" and the "door"[75] and the "life"[76] and the *Logos* of all things, "through whom all things have been made."[77] Therefore, we ought both to "know" these things and also to have "love" for Christ.[78]

These texts and many others suffice to show clearly that God, Christ and the Holy Spirit are knowledge. That they are also life is proved by one text, sufficient for me; for in other books we have proved it more abundantly:[79] "For just as the Father has life in himself, so has he given to the Son also to have life in himself."[80]

---

69 Rom 8.6.
70 Cf. Rom 8.6.
71 Rom 11.33.
72 Eph 3.10.
73 Cf. Eph 3.9; cf. I Cor 1.24.
74 Eph 3.18–19.
75 In emphasizing that Christ is divine, the very door to God, Victorinus reveals here the persistent influence of the *homoiousion* document which came out of the reunion at Sirmium (summer 358).
76 Cf. Rom 11.33; Jn 10.7; Jn 14.6.
77 Cf. Jn 1.3.
78 Cf. Eph 3.19.
79 Cf. *adv. Ar.* I 5,12–13; I 5,16,25; I 6,12 ff; I 15,2–3; I 41,1 ff; I 41,51; I 5 3,2; II 7,16; II 8,2 ff.
80 Jn 5,26.

Likewise, he says: "As the living Father has sent me, so also I live on account of the Father."[81]

b) The three are Logos

Therefore, these three are individuals such that all these three are what each individual is. For all, therefore, there is one substance. The Father, therefore, the Son, the Holy Spirit, God, *Logos,* the *Paraklētos* (Paraclete) are one because they are the power of substance, vitality, happiness,[82] silence—but silence conversing with themselves—word, word from word.

What also is the will of the Father except the silent Word, and the Word conversing with himself? Then in this way, since the Father is word and the Son is word, that is, a signifying and efficacious word, then, I say, if both Father and Son are Word, they are one substance.

Next: "Just," Scripture says, "is my judgment, because I seek to do not my own will, but the will of him who sent me."[83] Therefore, one will, consequently one substance, because the will itself is also substance.

Moreover, that the word itself is life is shown as follows: "You do not will to come to me to have life."[84]

Then—and in this consists the whole mystery that I am exposing— "All that has been given to me by the Father I have with me."[85] Because, in fact, movement is the same as "to be," and "to be" is movement, and because, according to a certain way of seeing, "to be" is prior to that which is moved by it, but prior *kata to aition,* that is, as cause. For this reason the Father has given also movement to the Son, movement which has also "to be." Therefore, movement is "to be." The *Logos* who is movement has then also "to be." But "to be" is life and knowledge. The Son therefore has all things because he has the "to be" of the Father.

Therefore, "the Son fulfills the will of the Father."[86] But what is the will except that, since the Father is life, his life is movement?

---

81 Jn 6.57.
82 This triad appears here for the last time; it is replaced definitively by *esse-vivere-intelligere.*
83 Jn 5.30.
84 Jn 5.40.
85 Jn 6.37.

This will is to make other things live. This, therefore, is also the will of the *Logos,* that is, of Christ. "What is," he says, "the will of the Father who sent me? It is that I should lose nothing of what he has given me, but that I should raise it up on the last day. For this is the will of my Father who sent me, that whoever beholds the Son and believes in him shall have everlasting life, and shall rise up on the last day."[87] To see Christ is to know God, the Son of God, life and God of life, and this is to have received the Holy Spirit.

That the word is life is proved thus: "After whom shall we go? You have the word of eternal life, and we have come to believe and to know that thou art the Christ, the Son of God."[88] This is the whole mystery: Christ, the Son of God, Christ the Word, and the Word itself, the Word of eternal life. Therefore this Word is the same as life, and he who hears and believes this Word knows God and therefore also has the Holy Spirit. (11) Here the full faith has been proclaimed, indeed by the disciples.

Likewise he says to the Jews: "If you knew me, you would know my Father. You know neither me nor my Father."[89] And rightly so. For, although the Son is both in the Father and the Father in the Son, existence or substance in life and life in substance, nevertheless since substance is invisible, it is apprehended only in life. But Christ is predominantly life, although he is substance. Therefore the Father is known in the Son. Whence: "Because you do not know me, neither do you know my Father. If you knew me you would also know my Father."[90] It is by "me" that you "would know" that that which is, exists, because I am also knowledge, which is the Holy Spirit.

Likewise he said to them, because he is word and the Father is also word, and they are therefore one substance: "He who sent me is true, and the things I have heard from him I say."[91] The Father speaks to the Son, the Son to the world, because the Father does all things through the Son, and the Son does all things by the power of

---

86 Jn 6.38.
87 Jn 6.39–40.
88 Jn 6.68–69.
89 Jn 8.19.
90 Jn 8.19.
91 Jn 8.26.

the word of the Father, that is, the Word speaking with himself does all things by the Word speaking openly. But the Word speaking with himself is God with the Son, because Father and Son are one God.[92] He himself says, in addition: "Amen, amen I say to you, if anyone keep my word, he will not see death."[93] And again: 'For I know the Father, and I keep his word."[94] They are both word, but as I have explained it.[95]

c) Digression on the taking of the soul
by the Logos at the time of the incarnation

About the true greatness and quality of the *Logos* we read in John: "For this reason the Father loves me, because I lay down my life that I may take it up again. No one takes it from me, but I lay it down myself. I have the power to lay it down, and I have the power to take it up again."[96]

It is clear enough that Christ has never been called soul, no more than God is called soul. Indeed, the Father is called God, is called Spirit; likewise, the Son is called *Logos,* is called Spirit, and without doubt God, indeed since both are one God. Therefore these realities, the *Logos,* the *Pneuma* are above the soul by their own superior substance; the substance of the soul is far different and inferior to them, since it is breathed in by God and begotten and is alone properly called substance, because it depends on the forms which are in it and proper to it, and in the same manner as matter *(hule).*

(12) To this is added that God is life, that Christ is life, and each of the two has life from himself, but so that, by the Father's gift, Christ has life from himself. Therefore life is superior to the soul. For *zōē* and *zōotēs,* that is, life and vitality, are prior to the soul.

---

92 In the state of interiority, of repose in God, there is dialogue between the Father and the *Logos*; in the begetting of the Son there is dialogue of the Son with the world. Cf. 12,30-31.

93 Jn 8.51.

94 Jn 8.55.

95 Cf. *adv. Ar.* III 11,13-18.

96 Jn 10.17-18. From here until almost the end of sect. 12 Victorinus raises the philosophic question of an incorporeal entity's mode of presence in the corporeal world. Christ's soul is assumed by the *Logos* but is not identical to him. The human soul is only an image of the Image. God and the *Logos* are life: the soul receives life, and so the soul is *similar* in substance to God.

Therefore, these realities there are *homoousia* (consubstantial), namely, God and the *Logos,* the Father and the Son, for, certainly, as the former is Spirit, the latter is Spirit, and as the latter is life, the former is also life; likewise, word and word, etc. The Spirit, therefore, has the "power of taking, of leaving and taking up again the soul."[97] Indeed, this is life, and life which is life from itself has the "power of taking, of leaving" that which, by its own power, by participation in it, it causes to live.

Indeed, the soul has been made according to the image of the Image of God: "Let us make man according to our image and likeness."[98] Therefore the soul is inferior; in addition, it originated or was created by God and the *Logos*, never God himself or the *Logos,* but a certain *logos,* not the *Logos* who is Son, not the general and universal seed, origin, source of all those things "which through him were made." As for the *logos* of this soul, I remember that I already spoke of its mode and nature,[99] and I shall return to it in the proper place.[100]

Therefore the universal *Logos,* because he is Spirit and life, not soul, has "the power from himself to leave soul," and again to take soul. Therefore, God and the *Logos,* either because they are life, or because they are Spirit, live and live always because they live from themselves. These are, therefore, *homoousia* (consubstantial). The soul, in fact, is *homoiousios* (similar).

When the soul[101] is taken by divine beings—that is, by the *Logos;* for it was not taken by God, for the *Logos* is movement, the soul is also movement, and movement which is self-movement, hence the soul is "image" and "likeness" of the *Logos;* therefore when the soul is taken by divine beings, this taking adds nothing to life, since it is through life, that is, through the power of living that the soul possesses its own life. Therefore, when the Spirit takes soul, it pro-

---

97 Jn 10.17–18.
98 Gn 1.26.
99 Cf. *adv. Ar.* III 3,34 ff.
100 Cf. *hymm.* II 9.
101 The soul is transformed because its action becomes that of the *Logos;* all that the soul had it received from the *Logos.* As an incarnate soul, the *Logos* can act in a sensible way. At death Christ's human soul remains linked to the *Logos;* the present operation of the *Logos* in the world becomes that of the Holy Spirit.

jects, so to speak, its power towards inferiors and towards actions, while it fills the world and worldly things. Therefore the Spirit, and especially the *Logos,* the Spirit who is life, has in its power both the taking and the leaving of soul.

But when the Spirit takes soul, it is born, so to speak, in the world, and its power enters into dialogue with the world. When, in fact, it leaves the soul, it withdraws from the world and does not act in the world in a bodily mode, nor does it yet act spiritually. This is what we call his death, and then he is said to be in hell, not certainly without the soul. Hence he prays that God "may not abandon his soul in hell."[102] Therefore because he must return to the world and to his action, he leads with him his soul from hell. Therefore he retakes, as it were, his soul, that is, he retakes it for the sake of action in the world. And because only the full and total *Logos,* that is, he who is Spirit and soul and body, can exercise an activity in the world, it was necessary then that he be newly sanctified, since he had newly assumed all that. He went, therefore, to the Spirit and he returned sanctified, conversed with the apostles, then sent the Holy Spirit. Who therefore is the Holy Spirit? It is the *Logos.* For there is one movement. And for that reason it was said: "And if I go and prepare a place for you, I shall come again."[103] For who came after the departure of Christ except the Holy Spirit, the Paraclete?

2. The Three are One

a) God and the Logos are one as "to be" and life

(13) That it is as I say, that the Father and the Son are one, and likewise that Jesus and the Holy Spirit are one, this is what John has expressed in a continuous passage.

For he begins with the *Logos:* "I am," he says, "the way, the truth, and the life. No one comes to the Father except through me."[104] For who comes to "to be" and to the true "to be" which is the Father, except through life? For life, which is true life, because it is eternal, this is truly "to be." For in nothing is life changed, in nothing is it corrupted, for change and corruption are kinds of

---

102 Ps 15(16).10.
103 Jn 14.3.
104 Jn 14.6.

death. True "to be" is life. "God lives,"[105] he tells us. Therefore, God is to-be-life. "And I," he tells us, "I live." Whoever comes to Christ, comes to life, and so through life to God himself. Therefore, God and the *Logos* are joined together. And hence this was said: "He who has known me has known also the Father."[106] And: "He who saw me saw also the Father."[107] And hence also this: "You do not believe that I am in the Father and the Father is in me."[108] Hence also this mystically: 'And if you ask anything in my name, I will do it." What is to ask in the name of Christ? It is to ask to become an eternal soul, to see the light of God, to come to see him, to have eternal life, not riches nor children nor honors, nothing worldly, but to ask for all that which is spiritual, all that through which we may be joined to Christ and united to God. Indeed, this is: "So that the Father may be glorified in the Son";[109] that is, in eternal life, which "I shall give to those who ask it."[110]

b) Jesus and the Holy Spirit are one as life and knowledge

Identity between Jesus and the Holy Spirit

(14) What is added next treats very fully of the Holy Spirit, what he is, whence comes what he is: "If indeed you love me," he says, "keep my commandments. And I shall ask the Father and he will give you another Paraclete, to dwell with you forever."[111]

What is the Paraclete? Someone near the Father who defends and upholds all faithful and believing men. Who is this? Is it the Holy Spirit alone? Or is he also identical with Christ? Indeed, Christ himself said: "God will give you another Paraclete."[112] Insofar as he said "another," he spoke of one other than himself. Insofar as he said "Paraclete," he expressed the likeness of their work and the identity of their action in some manner. Therefore, he is also Spirit

---

105 Cf. Jn 6.57.
106 Cf. Jn 14.7.
107 Jn 14.9.
108 Jn 14.10.
109 Jn 14.12.
110 Jn 14.13.
111 Jn 14.15–16.
112 In Victorinus's works "Paraclete" means the Son and the Holy Spirit interceding for men with the Father.

Paraclete, and the Holy Spirit is another Paraclete, and he is sent by the Father. The Holy Spirit is therefore Jesus.

For the Spirit is movement. Whence also the Spirit is movement as Spirit: "For he breathes where he wills."[113] And now he says: "The Spirit of truth."[114] And so his proper name is Holy Spirit. Christ also is Spirit. God is Spirit also. All, therefore, are Spirit. But God is Spirit substantially. For movement is interior to him, insofar as he is substance, or rather the very substance is movement, but movement remaining within himself, as we have already often said and as we shall repeat for the sake of remembering.[115] But in fact, Jesus and the Holy Spirit are movement, movement which is truly in movement, therefore a movement acting externally; but Jesus is manifested Spirit, since he is in the flesh; the Holy Spirit is Jesus hidden, since he is Jesus infusing knowledge, no longer Jesus performing miracles or speaking in parables.

That the Spirit is Jesus himself, Jesus himself teaches thus: "I will not leave you orphans, I will come to you."[116]

That he is himself hidden in the Holy Spirit, he teaches thus: "The world will see me no longer; but you, you will see me, because I live and you will live."[117] But he also attributed this to the Holy Spirit: "So that in you may be the Spirit of truth for eternity."[118] And he said of himself: "I am the truth."[119] Then he added: "Whom the world cannot see."[120] And of himself he said: "Henceforth the world will see me no longer."[121] Then he added, "Because it neither sees him[122] nor knows him." But also no one knew Christ: "He came unto his own, and the world did not recognize him."[123] He added: "You will know him, because he dwells in you

---

113 Jn 3.8.
114 Cf. Jn 14.17.
115 Cf. *adv. Ar.* III 2,43,52–53.
116 Jn 14.18.
117 Jn 14.19.
118 Jn 14.16.
119 Jn 14.6.
120 Jn 14.17.
121 Jn 14.19.
122 Jn 14.17.
123 Jn 1.11.

and he is in you."[124] And of himself he spoke thus: "You will see me."[125]

And since Christ is life, concerning himself he added: "Since I live and you will live."[126] And because the Holy Spirit is knowl-edge—but the world itself is deprived of both life and knowledge—for this reason he added: "Since he dwells with you and is in you."[127] But whence is it that the Holy Spirit is in them or already dwells there if he is still to come? Is it not that already he has begun to be in them through Christ? Therefore, they are joined and come from one reality, which is movement.

That is shown still more clearly by what follows. For he says: "These things I have spoken to you while yet dwelling with you. But the Paraclete, the Holy Spirit, whom the Father will send in my name, he will teach you all things that I say."[128]

"I," he says, "I dwell in you."[129] For life has been given, and now Christ does not depart from them. They are therefore animated also with a spiritual movement: this is the dwelling of Christ in them: and these are the souls in which the Spirit dwells and from which he never withdraws himself.

(15) Nevertheless it was said: "Now I shall go to the Father."[130] What this means can be easily understood if one understands it is said of the mystery, the mystery of the flesh. For, spiritually, since he is both in the Father and the Father is in him, where or why will he go? But it pertains to the very mystery according to which the Spirit came to Christ, under the form of a dove, according to which now the Spirit will be sent by the Father, and he will be sent while Christ is going to the Father and asking that the Spirit be sent. Indeed, life was recalled from death, and life, not life itself, because that is the *Logos*—for this does not know death, rather, this itself kills death—but life such as it is with men, this life of Christ then, risen from the dead, this very life which he certainly assumed simul-taneously with the body and that he reassumed in leaving hell.

---

124 Jn 14.17.
125 Jn 14.19.
126 Jn 14.19.
127 Jn 14.17.
128 Jn 14.25–26.
129 Cf. Jn 14.25.
130 Jn 14.28.

Therefore, for the sake of sanctifying this life he had to go to the Father, but with his body and soul, that is, to penetrate by his power and his existence in that which in himself was the Father. In this way therefore he went to the Father.[131] Finally, the duration of this absence is not fixed. But it was said that on the night which followed the sabbath, he appeared to Mary, was unwilling "to be touched,"[132] before going to the Father. Mary[133] announced it to the disciples; the same night he came to them, showing hands and side, now not forbidding them to touch him. Then Thomas felt him, touched him, Christ himself urging this, because Thomas was disbelieving, and this signifies that Christ was already sanctified. How brief, therefore, was this lapse of time! But on account of the mystery it was said: "I shall go to the Father."[134] For since he is in the Father and the Father is in him, where will he go?

With regard to the same mystery therefore: "The one that the Father sends you,"[135] because the Father sends when Christ sends. Next, he says this: "The Father sends in my name," that is, in my place, or "in my name," since Christ is Spirit, and the Holy Spirit himself is Spirit, or "in my name," because the Holy Spirit himself will give testimony of Christ. For this was said: "He will give testimony of me."[136] Who is this? "The one I send you from the Father."[137]

They are, therefore, all linked together: I send, I send from the Father, I send the Spirit of truth. Therefore, the one who is found in the midst of you, the *Logos,* that is, Jesus, he himself sends. Indeed, the original and universal movement, which is vital movement and which is life, sends forth the movement of understanding which, as I

---

131 In this passage which extends to the early part of sect. 17 we hear of Christ ascending in body and soul to the Father to make contact with the principle of sanctification (the Spirit). The Holy Spirit's proper action in the world is to testify to Christ; cf. Jn 16.8–10. Christ saves but the Holy Spirit gives consciousness of salvation. Pentecost is a consciousness-raising, a baptism not of water but of knowledge. Cf. Victorinus, *in Eph.* I 21–23 (1252C). Note the formula of Antioch (341) in *adv. Ar.* III 15.56.
132 Cf. Jn 20.17.
133 On this and the following sentence, cf. Jn 20.18–29.
134 Jn 14.28.
135 Cf. Jn 14.26.
136 Jn 15.26.
137 Jn 15.26.

have taught,[138] comes from life and is life itself. For to know what one is, this is to live, this is to be. But this "to be," what is it other than to be from the substance of God, which is to be Spirit? Whence we are made spiritual, having received the Spirit from Christ, and thus eternal life. This trinity was therefore called Spirit. For it was said: "God is Spirit."[139] Likewise, it was said by Paul in the second epistle to the Corinthians: "But the Lord is Spirit. But where the Spirit of the Lord is, there is liberty."[140] Certainly this was said of Christ. In fact, the Holy Spirit himself is called holy because he sanctifies the saints, that is, he makes them holy. And certainly he himself is the Spirit of God; for he is called: "prudence," "wisdom," and "knowledge" of all things.[141]

Their difference: the proper act of the Holy Spirit, to give testimony of Christ

This is indeed what he adds concerning him: "He convinces the world of sin, of justice, and of judgment."

"Of sin, since they do not believe in me,"[142] that is, they do not believe, either that Christ is life, or indeed that Christ is Son of God, sent from God to remit sins.

"Of justice, because I go to the Father."[143] For, having endured so many sufferings in the mystery, he goes to the Father because he has kept faith with the Father's commands, since he said when he wished otherwise: "Your will be done."[144] Likewise, because he was leaving his disciples, leaving them in the sense that he would not be seen as before, it was justice, because of his actions, to go to the Father, not only that he should go to the Father, but that he should be henceforth with him. For on that account it is said: "He sits at the right hand of the Father."[145]

"Of judgment, finally, because the Prince of this world is already

138 Cf. *adv. Ar.* III 8,25-37.
139 Jn 4.24.
140 2 Cor 3.17.
141 Is 11.2-3.
142 Jn 16.8-9.
143 Jn 16.10.
144 Mt 26.39.
145 Cf. Rom 8.34; Heb 1.3.

judged."[146] For by the mystery of the cross all the powers opposed to Christ have been conquered by this same Christ.

"This is," he says, "what the Holy Spirit will teach you."[147] What interpretation is chosen? Does the Paraclete complete the mystery of our salvation while Christ departs leaving it incomplete? Or is this because Christ and the Holy Spirit are the same reality, or because Christ sends him, or because the Spirit "has everything"[148] belonging to Christ, has all those things which are accomplished through Christ?

(16) And nevertheless let us see what the Spirit will do: whether he will give knowledge of the deeds of Christ and, by making this knowledge understood, have the power of witness or rather, of judgment, whether for penitence or for punishment.

"Of sin," he says, "because they have not believed in me."[149] Therefore, so that the world may henceforth know its punishment.

"Of justice, moreover, because I go to the Father."[150] This can also designate the sin of injustice which they who crucified him committed because he called himself the Son of God. And now he goes to the Father. This will be the same with all men if they believe in God, if they accomplish God's commandments; they also will go to the Father. For they are justified. Indeed, "Abraham believed and that was credited to him as justice."[151]

Next, "in judgement," he says, "because the Prince of the world has been judged."[152]

This, as one sees, does not pertain to salvation, which was already completed by Christ, but pertains to the knowledge of things accomplished by Christ. For the Father is silence, speaking interiorly; Christ is the voice, the Paraclete, utterance of the voice. Therefore, the Holy Spirit in this action is another Paraclete, a cooperator in the mystery of salvation, just as Christ is a cooperator in the true spirit of sanctification, because he is God. If, therefore, in this way also Christ is identical with the Holy Spirit, but God is Christ in the

---

146 Jn 16.11.
147 Cf. Jn 16.13.
148 Cf. Jn 16.14.
149 Jn 16.9.
150 Jn 16.10.
151 Cf. Rom 4.22.
152 Jn 16.11.

mystery of eternal life, God is the Holy Spirit in the action of sanctification.

But God sanctifies, as it was said: "Sanctify them in truth."[153] The Son says this to the Father. Therefore, the Father sanctifies. Likewise Christ sanctifies, as it was said: "And for them do I sanctify myself, that they may be sanctified in truth."[154] Likewise the Holy Spirit sanctifies. For to baptize also pertains to sanctification. Therefore it was said in the Acts of the Apostles: "John baptized with water. But you, you will be baptized by the Holy Spirit,"[155] because he pours himself out on them to bring them knowledge. For they have been already sanctified by baptism, under the invocation of God, of Christ and of the Holy Spirit. And indeed this was thus expressed: "Sanctify them in truth."[156] And the truth is Christ; the Paraclete is also the Spirit of truth. Therefore, everyone who is baptized and says that he believes and receives faith, receives the Spirit of truth, that is, the Holy Spirit, and is made holier by the Holy Spirit. And for that reason it was said in the Acts of the Apostles: "But you shall receive power when the Holy Spirit comes upon you,"[157] not for sanctification but for knowledge, and for those things which Christ promised, in the Gospel, concerning the Holy Spirit, that is, concerning the Paraclete.

First, that he would give testimony of Christ. For he says as follows: "You shall receive power when the Holy Spirit comes upon you, and you shall be witnesses to me in Jerusalem."[158] But Luke also speaks of it; in truth, the Spirit had not yet been sent, but nevertheless he already speaks of testimony.[159] Yet in all his letters what else does Paul do except give testimony of Christ? And after the departure of Christ, Paul alone saw Christ, and he appeared to him alone. Therefore the Spirit was present through Christ, and Christ through the Holy Spirit. Likewise John and Peter give testimony: "What we have heard, what we have seen, and what we have

---

153 Jn 17.17.
154 Jn 17.19.
155 Acts 1.5.
156 Jn 17.17.
157 Acts 1.8.
158 Acts 1.8.
159 Cf. Lk 24.48.

touched."[160] And in the Acts of the Apostles, they also, and Luke who wrote of these events, say of David: "Since he was a prophet, and knowing that God had sworn to him with an oath that of the fruit of his loins one should sit upon his throne, he, foreseeing it, spoke of the resurrection of Christ; because neither was he abandoned in hell nor did his flesh undergo decay. Therefore this Jesus God has raised up, and we are all witnesses to it."[161] When do they say that? "When a great noise came from heaven and there came a wind of great force, which filled the whole house and they were filled with the Holy Spirit, and began to speak in diverse tongues."[162]

Next the apostles witness concerning "the sin of the world, that it had not believed in Christ."[163] Thus in the Acts: "As you yourselves know, the one whom, by the settled purpose and foreknowledge of God, you have delivered by wicked hands, and you have nailed to the Cross and put to death, this is the one that God has raised up."[164]

Likewise, in the Acts of the Apostles, Peter recalls that "David did not ascend into heaven, but that he spoke thus: the Lord says to my Lord: 'sit at my right hand.' "[165] Paul also said this: "He who rose again is at the right hand of God."[166] Therefore they taught that after the resurrection "he went to the Father."[167] He immediately added: "who also intercedes with the Father." Therefore if Christ also intercedes, he is also the Paraclete. Likewise in the Acts there is testimony that he went to the Father: "He was lifted up before their eyes, and a cloud took him out of their sight. And while they were gazing up to heaven," and so forth.[168]

(17) Three things have already been said concerning testimony in regard to Christ: concerning sin, concerning justice.[169] Now we

---

160 1 Jn 1.1.
161 Acts 2.30–32.
162 Acts 2.2–4.
163 Jn 16.9.
164 Acts 2.22–24.
165 Acts 2.34.
166 Rom 8.34.
167 Cf. Jn 16.10; Rom 8.34.
168 Acts 1.9.
169 Cf. Jn 16.9–10.

speak of judgment. Thus through the Holy Spirit, Paul spoke to the Romans: "The God of peace will speedily crush Satan under your feet."[170] Likewise he says to the Ephesians: "Ascending on high, he led captivity away as a captive."[171] Likewise in the Apocalypse, Jesus himself said: "And I possess the keys of death and of hell."[172] Likewise we read there: "And there was a battle in heaven, Michael and his angels battled with the dragon."[173] And the whole passage shows that the "devil has been judged."[174]

IV. CONCLUSION: BOTH ONE AND BOTH IN ONE

1. The Father and the Son

Since it has therefore been proved that these three powers, both by their common and their proper acts, and by the identity of their substance, constitute the unity of divinity, it is not illogical to reduce them to two: to the Son and to the Father. Indeed, since the Father himself is in some way twofold as existence and action, that is, substance and movement, but interior movement, and *autogonos* (self-begotten) movement, movement by the very fact that it is substance, it follows necessarily that the Son, since he is movement and *autogonos*[175] (self-begotten) movement, is the same substance as the Father. For these among themselves are identical; without any conjoining they are one and without multiplicity they are simple, different only by their own act of existing—but by strength and power, since never is there one without the other, they are identically one; they are different only by their acts, since, while the act which is exterior advances even to the experiencing of suffering, the other act remains always interior and eternal, being original and sub-

---

170 Rom 16.20.
171 Eph 4.8.
172 Rv 1.3.
173 Rv 12.7.
174 Jn 16.11.
175 This reference again to the Son's self-generation is meant to show at this point that the Father and Son are one, and since the Holy Spirit is in the Son, it is right to speak mostly of Father and Son when thinking of the Trinity, as indeed the Scripture does.

stantial, and for that reason always being Father so that, for the same reason, the other is always Son.

Paul in all his letters says: "Grace and peace to you from God our Father and from our Lord Jesus Christ."[176] Likewise: "Not by men, nor through a man, but through Jesus Christ, and through God the Father."[177] Likewise in the Gospel: "I and the Father are one."[178] "I am in the Father and the Father is in me."[179]

(18) We also, with piety, always use the names of Father and Son,[180] and rightly so, according to the reasoning expressed above.[181]

Indeed, the Son is movement, as we taught above, and movement itself is life and also knowledge or wisdom.[182] Certainly it is Paul who has expressed with the greatest force what we want to make understood: "I give thanks to my God always for you, in Christ Jesus, because in everything you have been enriched in him, in all word and in all knowledge."[183] We have said that the Word is Christ, that is, life, knowledge, Holy Spirit. Therefore, they are one. For "In Christ," he says, "you are enriched."[184]

2. The Trinity

Since this is so, if God and Christ are one, while Christ and the Spirit are one, one can rightly say that the three are one in power and substance. Nevertheless the first two are one yet differ insofar as the Father is actual existence, that is, substantiality, while the Son is existential act. But the two remaining ones are two in such a way that Christ and the Holy Spirit are two in one, that is, in movement, and thus they are two as a unity is two. But the first two are as a

---

176 Rom 1.7; 1 Cor 1.3; 2 Cor 1.2; Gal 1.3; Eph 1.2; Phil 1.2; Col 1.2; 2 Thes 1.2; Phlm 3; cf 1 Tm 1.2; 2 Tm 1.2; Ti 1.4.
177 Gal 1.1.
178 Jn 10.30.
179 Jn 14.10.
180 Cf. *adv. Ar.* III 17,12–24.
181 Cf. *adv. Ar.* III 8,37–42;
182 Victorinus ends the long discussion of the two dyads by showing that they imply the consubstantiality of Father, Son, and Holy Spirit who are distinguished by their acts.
183 1 Cor 1.4–5.
184 Cf. 1. Cor 1.5.

two which is one. Thus, since there are two in one and two which are one, the Trinity is one.

3. Appendix: the Holy Spirit

Indeed, what should I say about the Holy Spirit,[185] whom I have treated fully,[186] what many things should I recall? From him Christ in the flesh is conceived; from him Christ in the flesh is sanctified in baptism; he himself is in Christ in the flesh; he is given to the apostles by Christ in the flesh, so that they may baptize in the name of God, of Christ, and of the Holy Spirit; he is the one whom Christ in the flesh promised would come; with a certain difference of acting, the same one is both Christ and the Holy Spirit, and because Spirit, on that account also God, because Christ insofar as he is Spirit is therefore God. That is why the Father and the Son and the Spirit are not only one reality, but also one God.

---

185 In this appendix on the Holy Spirit Victorinus emphasizes the Holy Spirit's role in the very life of Christ.
186 Cf. *adv. Ar.* III 14,1–17.

AGAINST ARIUS

FOURTH BOOK[1]

I. THE SON, CONSUBSTANTIAL FORM OF THE FATHER, AS LIFE IS FORM OF "TO LIVE"

1. The Father is "to live," the Son life, and Each is in the Other

A. IDENTITY AND DIFFERENCE BETWEEN THE "TO LIVE" AND LIFE

a) Initial exposition

E LIVES AND LIFE,[2] are they one thing, or the same thing, or are they different things? One? But why two terms? The same thing? But how so, since it is one thing to be actually, another thing to be actuality. Are they therefore different? But how would they be different, since in that which lives there is life, and in that which is life, it is necessarily the case that it lives? Indeed, that which lives does not lack life, since then there would be life that does not live. Therefore they are

---

1 In Book IV the concentration is on the dyad rather than on the triad, but the dyad is Christ and the Holy Spirit. It conjoins act *(actus)* and form *(forma)*, the *actus* of book IV now explicitly identified with the interior movement *(motus intus)* of book III. The Father and Son are reciprocally implied here not as "to be" *(esse)* and movement *(motus)* but as act and form, with the Son's preexistence as interior form *(forma intus)*. The model for the Son's begetting is the generation of knowledge as self-consciousness. The "form" has two states: life and knowledge. Book IV concentrates on the consubstantial form of God; its Scriptural bases are Jn 5.16 and 6.57, and Phil 2.5–7. Note that in this book *esse-vivere-intelligere* equals *actus* whereas *existentia-vita-intelligentia* equals *forma*. The *esse* or "To Be" which is the Father is best expressed by *vivere* or "To Live," but the latter's form is *vita* or life.

2 In this section Victorinus questions whether "He lives" and "Life" are the same or other. He then shows that otherness in identity is grounded

different in one another, and consequently, in one another, whatever they are, they are two; and if, in some way, they are two, they are not, however, two purely and simply, since indeed they are one in the other and that is the case in both of them. Are they therefore the same thing? But the same thing in two is other[3] than itself. This identity therefore, is both the same and other in anyone of these. But, if there is an identity, and each of the two is identical to itself, both are identical and one.[4] Indeed, each one being what the other is, neither of the two is double. Therefore, if each of the two, by the very same thing that he is, is also the other, each one of the two will be one in himself. But, since each one of the two is one in himself, it is the same one in the other. But, since it is the same one, both are truly one. For they do not differ from each other, neither by the power of being, nor by time; perhaps by cause, in that one is prior to the other.

b) Development

In their state of identity, "to live" and life are consubstantial

(2) That this may more easily be judged, we shall reconsider the above in a better way.[5] "To live" and life are such that what "to live" consists in is life, and what life consists in is "to live": not that one is duplicated in the other, or that one is with the other—for that would be a union: for from this, even if the connection were inseparable, there is only a union, not a unity—now in fact they are such that in the very act that is "to live," is "to-be-life," and in the same way, "to-be-life" is "to live." For we speak of these two: of "to

---

in an original unity. This passage represents a new development which attempts to learn the relationship between the First One and the Intelligible Triad; it may be seen as an attempt to reconcile Plotinus and the "Chaldaean Oracles." It was believed that these Oracles were the divine revelation of certain gods although they reached the world through one "Julian the Theurgist," who lived under Marcus Aurelius. They represent the last important sacred book of pagan antiquity and a major influence upon Neoplatonism from Porphyry to Psellus. Cf. Lewy's work on the "Chaldaean Oracles," cited earlier, and E. Dodds, "New Light on the 'Chaldaean Oracles' " *The Harvard Theological Review* 54 (1961) 263-73.

3 The CSEL reading has not been followed here (*alteris* for *alter is*).

4 Reading with CSEL *et* for *est*.

5 In this chapter there is again evidence of the philosophical fragments (Group II) gathered by Hadot, PV II 39-40.

live" and life, not of that which, passively receiving life, possesses
also "to live," although, this is both a third thing and receives the
"to live" only in the measure that it possesses life as something other
from another; but we speak of "to live" and life as two which are
one.

From this it is evident what is the greatness of the power which is
revealed in what is proper to self-existents, in their own substances,
since, their substance remaining one and identical, they maintain
their own "to be," without undergoing any change. For the proper
"to be" of life is to be self-moving. But to be self-moving is to live.
Therefore, "to live" and "to-be-life" are "to be." They are therefore
one and the same substance. Indeed, for each one, substance consists
in its own "to be." Indeed, in celestial and eternal things, that is, in
the intelligibles and the intellects, there is neither accident, nor
quality, nor duality or admixture; but all are living substances and
intelligent, pure, simple, in the manner of unity; by the very fact
that they are, they both live and understand, and reciprocally, by
the very fact that they live and understand, they also are. "He lives"
and life are therefore one substance.

In the state of the otherness, "to live" is the cause of life[6]

(3) But since the concept has so developed and the exposition so
proceeded that, as we have said, in the "to live" is life, and insofar as
life is, it is life, in the measure that it lives, it is necessary now to
seek, and to seek attentively, whether this natural and mutual implication represents only the unique and pure simplicity of one existence or indeed whether it really forms two existences.

If there is no difference between "to live" and life, if it suffices

---

6 In ch. 3, use is made of philosophical fragments from Group III collected
by Hadot, PV II 40–41. Here at the end of Ch. 3 Victorinus dwells upon
the original unity of the three hypostases which is the basis for their
reciprocal action. He emphasizes that there is no distinction in the intelligible world between being and substantial quality. Note that "to live"
(vivere) in God is before life *(vita),* but in all others *vita* is before *vivere*
(cf. III 4,12). In the absolute unity there is no priority of one over the
other. The God of whom Scripture speaks is indeed the living God,
but, philosophically speaking, "to live" must beget life. Life, thus begotten,
is the Son of whom Scripture speaks. This witnesses to the priority of the
concrete but also to the necessity of the universal form or idea of life.

to posit the "to be" of life to have "to live" inherent in it, we shall justly and rightly say their "to be" which joins them to existence is one and not two.

But if, first of all, "to live" is other than life, if there is, besides, between them this difference, that at one time life is cause of "to live," and at another time "to live" is the cause that there is life, then they are two, but redoubled one in the other and thus absolutely united in themselves. It matters indeed that they are double, under the relationship of the Power and of his own divine *Logos,* double in such a way that the one who is produced by the other has the same nature and power as the one from which he proceeds.

But there is between them a certain difference, although it is small, their redoubling is not without reason. Indeed, action is not the same as to act, nor power and act, nor, to speak more truly, cause and effect. For that is origin, this, what was begotten. Whence, since these two, "he lives" and life are "to act," and act although they are within each other and are together, nevertheless it is necessary to consider them as different from the point of view of power and nature, so that one is cause of the other, and the other is its effect.

But to my knowledge and according to my well-established opinion, since in the primordial and original source of the first divinity, "to live" is first, life is second—for so reason will teach and truth itself will confirm—it follows that "to live" is the cause of life and that life is the effect of "to live"; nevertheless "to live" itself is also life. For these things are together and always together, which will be called *homoousion* (consubstantial). Other is the relationship of life with the living of second and of third rank or of a rank still later, for which it is cause and principle, so that actually life is the same thing and is at the same time as "to live." But the "to live" of second rank receives, from life, that it is with life. That first and original "to live" at the same time equally life is cause of life and origin and principle of the living. I well know that all this can seem obscure—not so much the repetition of things themselves as that of words, namely, that these two are joined by such mutual implication that where there is "to live," there is life, and where there is life, there is "to live"; whence, when any one whatsoever is posited, it will seem useless to repeat the other.

B. THE FATHER IS "TO LIVE," THE SON IS LIFE

a) God lives and is life because he is Spirit

(4) Listen, reader, listen to that which will surprise you: all these difficult things, so involved, so obscure, we shall explain in a simple reasoned treatise concerning God and divine realities.

Certainly we all confess God as omnipotent God, God above all things, God before all things, God from whom are all things. When we confess God, we also confess without doubt that he is. What do we believe, what do we think that he is? "God is Spirit,"[7] he says; God is light and true light. What do we believe that this is that is called "Spirit"? We are compelled, are we not, to think of Spirit as an existing, living, intelligent substance? Some[8] think that when it is a question of realities on high, and especially about God, the word "substance" is unsuitable as if the term were low and alien and applicable to later realities. But why is this term to be avoided by us since, for each one, his own being is being substance. And in the book of Jeremiah God speaking, says as follows: "But if you were standing in my substance, you would be seeing my Word."[9] So also there, not much later, and in many other texts this term is used. The Spirit is therefore substance, that is his "to be."

Let us assemble therefore what was said in the Gospel according to John: "God is Spirit, and those who adore him must adore him in spirit and in truth."[10] "God," he says, "is Spirit," that is the "to be" of God. Therefore the Spirit is the substance of God. This same substance is that which is living, not so that it is one thing to be substance, another to be living, but so that the living itself is the substance itself. If indeed it was said by the same John: "It is the Spirit who vivifies,"[11] truly he vivifies who lives and who is the power of life. Therefore the Spirit lives, God lives. Therefore the Spirit is also life, as John likewise says: "The Spirit is life."[12] Therefore God,

---

7 Jn 4.24.
8 Those who think the word "substance" unsuitable for God are the Homoeans. The bishops at Rimini had written to Constantius that it was an unworthy name for God *(ut indignum nomen deo)*. Cf. I 30,36–59.
9 Jer 23.18.
10 Jn 4.24.
11 Jn 6.63.
12 Cf. Jn 6.63.

since he is Spirit, both lives and is life. Paul also says to the Romans: "There is therefore now no condemnation for those who are in Christ Jesus, who do not walk according to the flesh. For the law of the Spirit of the life in Christ Jesus has delivered you from the law of sin and of death."[13] "The Spirit of life," he says. Indeed, these three are Spirit: God, Jesus, Holy Spirit.

(5) But I think that it has been proven concerning God that he is also Spirit, but a Spirit that both lives and makes live, and that he is life substantially, so that all these things are understood as one simple substance, so that to be Spirit is "to live" and "to-be-life."

b) "To live" which is God begets life

But this "to live"[14] is not our "to live"; it is not the "to live" of animals, nor of elements, nor of creatures made from elements; it is not that of the world, that of all the things in the world, that of the angels, demons, nor even of those which in the world some call the gods of the world; no, I say, the "to live" of soul, the "to live" of each soul, or the "to live" of the universal and soul-source, is not the "to live" in God, is not God; no, the "to live" of God is not that of the angels on high, nor of the thrones on high, nor of the glories nor of others existing in eternity whether among the intellects or the intelligibles. But this "to live" of God is the "to live" from which all those things, according to their mode of existence, receive life and live, he somehow advancing and breathing on them in the measure that they are capable of receiving the power of his living strength; and he, he is from himself, for himself, through himself, in himself, alone, simple and pure, without a principle of existing; but from him there flows or proceeds or is born the principle through which would be created the "to live" of the others.

Indeed, "to live" begets life. For by natural power the agent is prior to action. For the agent begets action and, as it were, from this action receives its name, while it itself gives to action its reality.

This doctrine, at the same time that it is right, is also in true accord with reason. Certainly God, to whom for his omnipotence

---

13 Rom 8.1–2.
14 In sect. 5 we find the philosophical fragments (Group III) where God as primordial "To Live" is the cause of life, the first form. Hadot, PV II 41.

and original transcendence the name of God belongs, God, God, I say, first—if in the works of God one can speak of a first; but the understanding proper to the human mind[15] must, in order to exercise itself, to grasp things, things which exist simultaneously or which are produced simultaneously, attribute origin to the one and a going forth from the origin to the other and, as it were, a kind of time; God, I say, begot the existences and universal substances of the universals. Plato calls these "ideas,"[16] the original forms of all the forms in existents; this kind, for example, is: *ontotēs* (existentiality), *zōotēs* (vitality), *nootēs* (intellectuality); and likewise *tautotēs* (similarity), *heterotēs* (differentiality), and others of this kind. Therefore the genera of all genera are poured forth abundantly by God as well as the universally original potentialities of all potentialities.

Therefore, *ontotēs,* that is, the quality of existing or quality of that which is an essence, or *zōotēs,* that is, vitality, that is, the first universal power of life, that is, the first life, and the source of all living, likewise *nootēs,* the force, the strength, the power or the substance or nature of understanding, these three, then, should be considered, each one singularly, as being the three simultaneously, but in such a way, that they are said to be and are named in accordance with that which predominates in each one. For there is none of these three which is not the three. For this "to be" is "to be" if it lives, that is, if it is in life. But indeed as for the "to live" itself: that is not "to live" which has no understanding that it lives. They are therefore a mingling,[17] as it were, and in reality they are simple with a simplicity which is triple. For whatever by its very "to be" is also other than itself must never be defined as double but always as one.

---

15 It is reason which introduces difference into a unity and time into eternity, Plato, *Timaeus*; Plotinus, *Enn.* 3,5,9; 4.8.4.

16 Hadot comments (TTT 987) that this begetting of Ideas by God is found in the "Chaldaean Oracles" (cf. W. Kroll, *De oraculis Chaldaicis,* 23) which describe the flowing from God of the river of ideas; cf. Proclus, *In Platonis Parmenidem commentaria,* ed. V. Cousin (Paris 1864) 800.

17 Since "to live" *(vivere)* was formerly (III 7,3) identified as manifestation of "to be" *(esse)* with the Son, the present identification of the Father with "to live" requires that "to live" be without form and incomprehensible. Therefore he defines this "to live" as the interior movement *(motus intus)* which defined "to be" *(esse)* in III 2,12–54. This accents the dynamis of "to be" *(esse)* which lives, being motion turned inward.

Truly we have spoken abundantly of this, also in other places.[18]

(6) Therefore, because God is "to live," the supreme, the first, the source, the originally original "to live," he has begotten these three; that is, by his own act of living[19] he brought them forth so that they might be. Therefore by this action they came forth, and this offspring, this begetting is such that from the agent is born the act, from the "to be" is born the quality of that which is an essence or the essence, from the living is born vitality or life, from understanding is born *nootēs* (intellectuality), there is born the universal understanding of universal ideas.

Therefore "to live" is prior to life, although in "to live" is life; but "to live" is in some way the parent of life, and life is in some way the fruit, the begotten, since it is begotten by the living. God is, therefore, "to live," that first "to live," living from its very self, before the "to live" of all things, and before the "to live" of life itself. For he is acting and always acting, with no principle he is acting, not by action is he acting, lest this action, for example, might be the appearance of a principle; but he acts so that the action of the agent has either been begotten or has appeared or has flowed out; certainly this "to act" consists in "to live."

c) Therefore the Father is "to live," the Son is life

Therefore, God is "to live" and the original "to live," but life is as the begotten. Therefore the Father is "to live," the Son is life.[20] For "That which has been made in him is life."[21] And the Son himself also says: "I am the way, I am the truth, I am the life."[22] This life is that which is born from the fact that the Father lives. And here is this: "For I came forth from the Father."[23] Likewise, he

---

18 Cf. *adv. Ar.* III 4,6–46; I 50,10–15; IV 21,26–31.

19 How can a determined form be generated from undetermined act? The determined form is preformed in the act. Is this the Porphyrian–Victorine conclusion? Neither in Plato nor in the Oracles is this said; cf. Plato, *Parmenides, Timaeus* (39E); H. Lewy, *Chaldaean Oracles,* 110. The argument here takes shape through the use of the philosophical fragments (Group III) cited by Hadot, PV II 42.

20 As "to live" begets life, so God begets the Son. This touches upon the problem of the origin of the first genera. Cf. IV 25,26–31 and 24, 34–39.

21 Jn 1.3–4.

22 Jn 14.6.

23 Jn 16.27.

speaks thus of himself: "Let him who thirsts come to me and drink. He who believes in me, as the Scripture said, from within him there shall flow rivers of living water."[24] This is also why he answers the Samaritan woman thus: "If you did know the gift of God, and who it is who says to you 'Give me to drink,' you perhaps would have asked of him, and he would have given you living water."[25] Likewise later: "Whoever drinks of this water will thirst again." The water of Samaria denotes the soul in its earthly sojourn. "But whoever drinks of the water that I will give him shall never thirst; but the water that I will give him shall become in him a fountain of water, springing up unto life everlasting."[26]

By these and innumerable other examples of this kind it becomes sufficiently clear that Christ, the Son of God, is life and eternal life, indeed he who, like the Father, is also Spirit. "For that which is born of the Spirit is Spirit."[27] "But the Spirit breathes,"[28] and from himself he breathes. But to breathe is to live. But that which breathes from itself lives from itself. That which lives from itself, lives from eternity and for eternity. For never does that one abandon itself which is for itself the cause that it should be that which exists.

Therefore, since the Father is "to live," as we taught above,[29] since "to live" is to be life, likewise since life is begotten by "to live," that which is "to live" is necessarily life. For life also lives, by the very fact that it is life and life from itself; indeed, it has from itself "to live," having it, nevertheless, from that first "to live" which is "to live" originally, which is the Father, in whom is found, and from whom comes forth that life which itself contains "to live," and "to live" from himself; that this life is the Son Jesus Christ we prove, we understand and confess.

(7) All these things which have been said by me, let us see them signified by the very words of the Savior in the Gospel according to John: "The living Father has sent me and I live on account of the

---

24 Jn 7.37–38.
25 Jn 4.10.
26 Jn 4.13–14.
27 Jn 3.6.
28 Jn 3.8.
29 Cf. *adv. Ar.* IV 6,18.

Father."[30] But lest anyone should not believe that Christ in the flesh said this, he immediately added: "This is the bread which has descended from heaven."[31] Next, that he is life and eternal life he so testifies, so teaches: "Unless you will take the body of man as the bread of life and will drink his blood, you will not have life in you. He, however, who will eat his flesh and drink his blood has eternal life."[32] All, therefore, that Christ is, is eternal life, whether Spirit or soul or flesh. For of all these he is *Logos*. But the *Logos* is original life. Therefore, also, those things that he assumed are life. Consequently, they will also merit eternal life in us through the Spirit whom Christ gives to us, since these things are also made spiritual. But lest anyone believe that Christ said that only of the carnal Christ, and not of his total self which is Spirit, soul, and flesh; what does he add? "What then if you should see the Son of Man ascending?"[33] Who is the Son of Man? Spirit, soul, flesh. For he had these things when he ascended, and he ascended with them. What therefore does he add so that he may be known as Spirit? "Where he first was," that is, where he was "Spirit and life,"[34] which the Father is, which God is.

d) Father and Son, "to live" and life, are consubstantial

It follows that they are *homoousia*, that is, they are consubstantial; at no moment are they existents outside each other; they are originally original, one and the same substance, of equal force, of the same power, majesty, strength; in no way is one prior to the other except that one is cause of the other, and in that they are different, but it is a difference in identity. Indeed, because they are the same, they are one God; because they are truly other, therefore they are first and second; and because one is cause of the other, for this reason, the one who is cause is the Father, and the one who comes forth from the other is the Son. But in substance there is between them no difference, not temporal distinction, nor predominant char-

---

30 Jn 6.57.
31 Jn 6.50.
32 Jn 6.53-54.
33 Jn 6.62.
34 Jn 6.62-63.

acteristic, but one movement, one will, and if at times there is an appearance of difference of will, nevertheless, it is always identical.

2. The Son is Consubstantial Form of the Father As Life is Form of "To Live"

A. ANNOUNCEMENT OF A PLAN CONCERNING THE CONSUBSTANTIAL

(8) That this is so, let us first of all teach by Holy Scripture. Next, as order requires, as the necessity of things demands, let us consider why, of these two in whom is present one and the same substance, why one possesses the power proper to the sender, the other, that which is proper to the sent, one possesses the power of the one who orders, the other, that of a servant, why, again, one is endowed with a movement of acting free from passions while the other, through the infinite acts in the creating of infinite ages and what they contain, has undergone even unto death innumerable passions.

B. THE SON IS THE LIFE AND THE FORM OF THE FATHER

1. Initial Exposition

The First lives; he lives from himself, he lives eternally, and this is God. This "he lives," as I have taught,[35] has the force of existence or of substance and has within itself both the nature of life and of understanding; in his own "to be" there is the "to live" of which we spoke, and the "to understand," and this is God. Therefore, the "to be" of God is cause and Father of existence. And since in his own "to be" he possesses life, and in that it belongs to him to know who he is, he is also source of universal life and of understanding.

For of these three which are in God by simple existence, or which are God, it is "to be" that God is by predominance, because it is through himself that he has "to live" and "to-be-life," or "to know"

---

35 Cf. *adv. Ar.* IV 2,24; 4,20–24; 5,3.

and to be knowledge, as we have taught above and in many places,[36] so that the two remaining ones, I speak of life and of understanding, we take as begotten from "to be," having their own "to be" from the first "to be," and receiving by the movement of existing proper to each one, one the power and the name of life, the other, understanding. For in all three are the three, but they receive their own name according to a certain order which is born from the movement itself; it is not that they are triple, each one in their three individualities, but they actuate, through their own movement, what they are said to be. Indeed, "to be" is the first movement[37] which is called movement in repose, likewise interior movement; for since it acts so that it exists, it is rightly called both movement in repose and interior movement. This movement, we say that it is "he lives" and "to live."

Now in fact, since from this "he lives" and from this "to live" a form is formed, constituted in some way and begotten as having the form of "he lives" and "to live," this form is called life, is called Son. For just as any form whatsoever, whether it is situated there where is the form of which we speak, or elsewhere, leads us to the knowledge of the one of which it is the form, thus life makes us understand what is "to live." For "to live" is act, and it is a course which is in act at every moment; that is why it was said: "No one has ever seen God."[38] For who may see "to live" which is God without the life which, to indicate the traits which determine this "to live" condenses and realizes itself under a certain form so that it might be the form of living? Therefore, the form of "to live" is life, through which or in which, the one who is "he lives" and "to live" is seen, understood, and recognized.

This is what clearly signifies this word of the Savior: "Whoever has seen me, has also seen the Father."[39] Indeed, the Son of God is the form of God, that is, life which is the form of living. For it was said by Paul to the Philippians: "Who although he was in the form of

---

36 Cf. *adv. Ar.* IV 5,1–4; 5,42–44; 6,1–7; I 50,10–15; III 2,12–16; III 7,1–5.
37 A slight use is made here of the philosophical fragments (Group II) collected by Hadot, PV II 24 and 25.
38 Jn 1.18.
39 Jn 14.9.

God, did not think it robbery to be equal to God."[40] Likewise to
the Colossians: "He who is the image of the invisible God."[41] Therefore, Jesus Christ is both the image and the form of God. But we
have said that in the form one sees that of which it is form; and, in
the same way, through the image also, one sees the one of which it is
the image, above all if the one whose image it is, is invisible, as it was
said here: "Image of the invisible God";[42] and in the same way it
was said in the Gospel according to John: "No one has at any time
seen God, except the only begotten Son who went forth from his
bosom."[43] And likewise the following was said to Moses: "You will
not see my face. For who has seen my face and has lived?"[44]
Nevertheless, he promised to let himself be seen from the rear, that
is, the back and the rest of the body with the exception of the
face.[45]

2. Development

a) Summary of the teaching concerning "to live" and life

(9) How many mysteries there are here, how many kinds of questions, how many signs to declare that God and Jesus Christ are substance, and that they are both one substance, and that they are both
together one substance, and that substance is from the Father to the
Son. All these points and others of this kind, can in no way be explained, understood and demonstrated unless the spiritual interpretation drawn forth by clear concepts is understood.

Let this proposition, therefore, be for us settled: that God is
Spirit, and he is the Spirit from whom both the Son is Spirit and the
Holy Spirit is Spirit. For "That which is born of Spirit is Spirit."[46]
But the "Spirit vivifies."[47] Whatever vivifies certainly itself lives.
And that which lives, because it is Spirit, lives from itself. And that
which lives from itself is the same as "he lives." And because that

---

40 Phil 2.6.
41 Col 1.15.
42 *Ibid.*
43 Jn 1.18.
44 Ex 33.20.
45 Cf. Ex 33.23.
46 Jn 3.6.
47 Jn 6.63.

which lives from itself, being "he lives" himself has no subject different from himself to which one could attribute the term "to live" —indeed, he does not receive "to live" but he himself lives, being "he lives" or "to live"—because "he lives," "to live" is act in itself, it results that "he lives" insofar as he lives from himself, has never had a beginning. For he has not relied on another so that he will never abandon himself nor be abandoned. From eternity, therefore, and for eternity he lives, original and universal substance of all "to live," not that there is, as it were, substance and afterwards living substance, but that very same thing which is living, that same thing is substance. Indeed, since the living, the "he lives," the "to live," is understood as "to be" and "to be" in a certain way, one cannot not say that that which is for itself its own "to be" is substance. This, by all Sacred Scripture and by the voices of the things themselves, is called Spirit.

(10) But the Spirit breathes and breathes from himself, and God is Spirit. In fact, "he breathes" is "he lives." Therefore, he lives from himself and always, the Spirit who is God. He lives, I say, and in the act of living and by that very act, since he lives, he exercises life. From the living God, therefore, is born life, and from God, living from eternity for eternity, is born eternal life. And because "he lives" himself is substance, that which comes forth from "he lives," itself, is substance on a par with, identical, equal and simultaneous, because "he lives" is himself life, and life itself is present in "living" so that there may be life. The Spirit is, therefore, "to live" and life is Spirit. They are mutually implied, in each one is also the other, not as a duplication or addition but by the simplicity of existing from itself and in itself, as though each were the duplicate of the other and yet never other than itself. Indeed, "to live" is found with life, and life again is found in that which is "to live."

But "to live," as we have taught,[48] is God; life is Christ; and because "to live" is in some way the begetter of life—indeed, through this act that is "to live," life, as a kind of fruit, is begotten—"to live" is the Father, life is the Son. Certainly these, because one comes from the other, are because of that, two; for what reason indeed would they be two unless one comes from the other? And always

---

48 Cf. *adv. Ar.* IV 6,17–18.

that which is from the other is Son, and that from which the other comes is Father. But now, they are not so other as to be different and separated, but only as one coming from the other, as the producer and the produced, the begetter and the begotten; but by the unity of substance both are one, since both "to live" is life and life itself is "to live." Hence Father and Son are one God. And because existence possesses naturally only one circular movement—for as life is present as in "to live" and likewise "to live" is present in life, there is then only one circular movement—it follows that since in life there is also present "to live," for that reason the only begotten Son is consubstantial with the Father, the Son himself being also unique as the Father is unique. That is why there is one and the same substance, and they are together and always together; this is indeed the *homoousion* (consubstantial), *homou ousian ekhon* (having substance together), having equal strength and power of existing, the same natural substance, with no temporal priority, which we call consubstantial, "to live" being prior to life only as causing it, so that that one is and is called the begetter and Father, and this one is and is called the begotten and Son. Therefore, since they are in one another, and although the Father since he is Father is not the Son, and again the Son since he is Son of the one of whom he is the Son, is not the Father, nevertheless by the force of things, through the equality of their substance, "to live" being life, life being "to live," with good reason the divine voice of the Savior has declared: "I am both in the Father and the Father is in me." Thus also this is said: "I and the Father are one."[49]

b) God as supreme "to live," that is, as pure act

Truly, since, by the force of things and the course of nature[50] itself, all things would be nothing if they did not live, and deprived

---

49 Jn 14.10.

50 The philosophical fragments (Group III) cited by Hadot, PV II 42–43 extend through the first paragraph break in ch. 11. They tell of life emanating from the *Logos* and extending even to matter (Plotinus, *Enn.* 4.7.9) so that all things which exist are living. For the hierarchy of existents in the Chaldaean Oracles, cf. W. Kroll, *De oraculis Chaldaicis,* 31. As to the Neoplatonic exegesis of Virgil's line: *Novies, styx interfusa coercet,* with the nine spheres, and the soul as the river of life, cf. Hadot, PV I 402–6; MV 226.

of vital movement, they would be thought to have neither material mass nor any appearance or form of existence—for the nature of the disorderly flux and reflux, a force that is deceptive and without consistency, is incapable of "to be"; nor does it receive form so that it is said to be something. (11) Consequently, deprived of being something, the flux does not even keep its own "to be" so that we may not say, with good reason, that it is in any way; but when any form whatsoever seizes it,[51] stops its movement, in its totality and in all its parts, gives it any form at all, this thereby embodies it and closes it so that we also believe it to be something. [We believe this] because by vital movement it is confined by well-defined limits which separate it from the infinite, and is presented most clearly to the senses. Therefore force and vital power cause existing material things to appear to be. [This force and vital power] flowing from that *Logos* who is life, whom we call the Son, as it makes its way and moves through archangels, angels, thrones, glories and the rest that are above the world—first in incorporeal things and those *aüla* (without matter) clean and purer by their natural substance—imparts its light in a greater communication of itself. Coming by degrees, the force arrives soon at the soul and at the soul-source of the soul. And because the soul is the image of the *Logos*, this kind of relationship gives a more rapid rhythm to the wave of the descent. And since the soul hastens toward the beings it must animate, the élan of the vital force toward the beings that it must animate becomes itself more impetuous. Hence, immersed in matter,[52] having become prisoner of the elements of the world and finally of carnal ties, mingling in corruption and death, it lends then an appearance of life to the dregs of matter.

---

51 This whole description of the formation of matter, making it sensible, is like that of 8,36–40 where form also appeared as limiting the infinity of motion and making it known. Form makes a thing living and knowable.

52 From here until the early part of sect. 13 Victorinus discusses the fact that although life is descent, it does not really descend. The desire to vivify becomes a passion and soul is led into matter. Three themes are reunited here; forms and hierarchy and myth. Form regulates disordered movement. For Porphyry the disordered movement of which Plato speaks in the *Timaeus* is not found in matter itself but in body, already composed of matter and form. Cf. Hadot, PV II 379 and 401. Also used here are philosophical fragments (III) cited by Hadot, PV II 43–45. Cf. Jn 6.57; 8.26.

Then all things live, terrestial, humid, aerial, fiery, etherial, celestial things. They live not by the first *Logos*, nor even with the light of perfectly pure life, but with a vital light troubled by contact with matter. The supercelestial realities also live, those removed from matter and from bodily ties living more fully, such as purified souls, thrones, and glories, likewise angels, and spirits themselves, some having life within their substances as from another while others are life itself. But Jesus Christ and the Holy Spirit (for soon we shall teach about the latter)[53] are life and simultaneously God and nevertheless from God; they are life but universal life. They live, they live from themselves, not having the act of "to live" from another, but so that their very "to be" is "to live," "to-be-life," "to be knowledge," by the gift of the Father, that is, the originally existing "to live."

Therefore since all these things that we have enumerated are living, and there is nothing among eternal or mundane or material things whose nature it is to live, it must be confessed that there is a force, a power by which all things are vivified, by which, as from a source of life, they are raised into vital spirits so that they are living, they have "to be" by participation.

(12) Who is this one and whence is he, who breathes a vital breath upon everlasting and mortal beings, by whom all things thrive, by whom they subsist, by whom they receive their proper acts, and from whom the begotten and those about to beget come forth? God, without doubt, God, the object of the veneration of our mind, Father who makes to live and divine power of life. This God, we shall call him the power of life, as we did elsewhere,[54] or supreme and original life, universally universal life, and the origin, cause, head and source of all the living, principle of existents, Father of substances, he who, through the "to be" that he is himself, gives "to be" to all others, dispensing, according to the proper force and power of those who receive it, the power and substance of "to live." What then is he or in what category? He is the living one, the true living one insofar as he allows us to speak of him. He lives both from eternity and he lives for eternity, having from himself this "he lives"

---

53 Cf. *adv. Ar.* IV 16,1–18,44.
54 Cf. *adv. Ar.* I 31,9; I 50,13; I 52,3–4.

itself which, for him, is his substance. Indeed, there is no necessity nor even possibility of adding action to him as an accident, lest at any given moment he be inferior to himself; but he is always perfect, full and total; in his "to be" is present his "to be" in such a mode.

The other things which are after God are both powers and actions; powers are the things considered already as "being" by their own force, so that they seem to be and to have all that which their existence, by the mature procession of acts, will bring them to have in their operation; but things are called acts when in realizing their natural development, they beget and make appear externally what they are potentially. Thus the seed is already trunk and foliage in potentiality; so also is man or woman in potentiality the outpouring of passionate desire. But these things are distinguished only in the world and the sublunary region. Indeed, on high, in the aether and in the heavens, all beings are acts and live in act, but begotten and already become what they must be: For, from their origin, destined to their own functions, they carry on their own acts by the sympathy of nature which holds them together. (13) If those things which are in the world are acts, how much more are acts and actions those things which are among the eternal realities and are supercelestial, those which have begotten these worldly things! Likewise also the soul and the angels which were souls and the angels higher than souls.

For the soul also moves itself with an *autogonō* (self-begotten) movement, that is, with its own movement, born from itself and for itself; and it is said to be *autokinētos* (self-moved), and for that reason *aeikinētos* (always moved). Therefore it is always in movement because it is always "to act" and "to be *energeian* (energy) itself so that this very movement is its substance. For it was said: "Let us make man according to our image and likeness."[55] The soul has, therefore, *autogonon kinēsin,* that is, a movement born from itself, as it is with God, as it is with Christ, but because it is not that Spirit which is prior to it, it is therefore a different substance and created, not existing from itself, but created so that it has movement from itself; certainly, the soul is one thing, life another.

---

55 Gn 1.26.

c) Christ as life, that is, as form of "to be"

Indeed, life is a habit of living, and it is a kind of form or state begotten by living, containing in itself "to live" itself and that "to be" which is life, so that both are one substance. For they are not truly one in the other, but they are one redoubled in its own simplicity, one, in itself because it is from itself, and one which is from itself because the first simplicity has a certain act within itself. For repose begets nothing; but movement and the exercise of acting forms for itself from itself that which it is or rather that it is of a certain mode. For "to live" is "to be"; but to be life is a certain mode[56] of being, that is, the form of the living produced by the very one for which it is form. But the producer, "to live," never having a beginning—for that which lives from itself has no beginning since it lives always—it follows that life also has no beginning. Indeed as long as the producer has no beginning, that which is produced has not a beginning. As both are together, they are also consubstantial.

But "to live" is God, life is Christ, and in "to live" is life, and in life is "to live." In this way certainly one is in the other because produced and producer are one in the other: for as the producer is in the product, so also the product is in the producer, especially if these always are. Therefore the Father is in the Son and the Son in the Father. And indeed, the producer is producer of a product, and the product, product of a producer. Therefore one is their substance, not one in two or two in one but because, in the very substance in which is God, in this same substance is the Son, that is, in the following way: as God lives, so the Son lives also; in whatever kind of substance the Father is, the Son is in such a substance.

d) An objection: Does one not thus introduce two unbegotten?

(14) But, they say, if the Father lives, the Son also lives, and for that reason both are the same such substance, but this substance is "he lives," and since each one of the two is "he lives," each of the two is without beginning, each is eternal.

But this conclusion is excluded by the sacred words of the evangelist, since the Son himself, Our Lord Jesus Christ tells us: "The

---

56 CSEL reading, *modus* has been accepted in place of *motus*.

Father lives." This is the source without beginning. But from where else could the principle come? "And I," he says, "I live on account of the Father."[57] If therefore he lives "on account of the Father," he has received his "to live" from the Father, and if he has received it, he is begotten by the unbegotten; and if "he lives" is in each one a determined existence and a power of substance, with this "he lives" that they possess under the mode of unity, Father and Son possess equally one and the same substance, but the Son receives it from the Father. "Indeed that which is born of the Spirit is Spirit." Therefore from such substance of the Father comes such substance of the Son.

And the better to show that it is his substance, a substance one and identical which is given to the Son by the Father, it has been said that this substance is "he lives" and life.[58] Therefore the same substance belongs to God and from God to Christ the Son, the evangelist saying this: "For as God has life from himself, so also he gave to the Son to have life from himself."[59]

Therefore, Christ is *homoousios* (consubstantial) with God, that is, of the same substance, namely, of the first, original, universal substance, from which all existents also live, having a life *epakton* (acquired), that is, received from without, not begotten from itself; they live, not that their "to live" is that proper to God and to the Son, but because all other existents participate in life in the exact measure that Christ bestows it upon them. Truly in God "to live," as the original "to live," is the producer of life, being for both, one and the same source of their existence, without any one of the two being prior to the other, as to time or power, at least in the order of substance. Whence, if we take this *homoousion* (consubstantial) in the sense of "same substance," no doubt they are of the same substance; for the one who lives is already also life, that is, God, and the one who is life, himself lives, this is Christ, and both have life from themselves, just as it was said: "As the Father has life from himself, so also he gave to the Son to have life from himself."[60]   But if we understand *honoousion* (consubstantial) as *homou ousian einai* (to

---

57 Cf. Jn 6.57.
58 Cf. *adv. Ar.* IV 2,23–24.
59 Jn 5.26.
60 *Ibid.*

be together one and the same substance), *homoousion* (consubstantial) is shown still more easily and more clearly: that which I have said to be the Father or the Son, "to live," indeed and life, are so together and always together that in the "to live" is life and, reciprocally, life is "to live."

e) A comparison: the present and eternity[61]

(15) And indeed let us take an example: although what I am saying is more the reality, not an example.

We have said that God is nothing other than "to live," but the original "to live,"[62] the one whence comes all the "to live" of all the others; he is action itself, existing in acting, in this movement having his own "to be," which is having either existence or substance, although truly not having it but existing itself as that which is originally and universally "to live." But that which is produced from this act and is in some way its form is life.

Indeed as the *aiōn* (aeon) is produced by the always present act of all things, so it is by living and by the act of living which is always present that life is produced, and as we express it, vitality, which is somehow the form of life, is begotten according to its own power and substance.

But our "to live" also consists in an always present time; indeed, we do not live the past nor do we live the future, but always are in the present; for the present is the only time; and it alone, because it is the only time, is said to be the image *tou aiōnos* (of the aeon), that is, of eternity. For just as the *aiōn* (aeon) has all things always present and has them always, we also, through present time, have all that we can have; therefore this time of ours is image *tou aiōnos* (of the aeon), because our present is not always present to the same things and because it is not always identical to itself.

Therefore, by living there is produced life, and by existing together with "to live," it is formed. But the formation is manifestation; but the manifestation arose, indeed, from hiddenness, and this arising from hiddenness is birth, the birth of one who, before coming

---

61 In most of this section Victorinus treats of eternity as total presence and of life as an image of eternity. Use is made of the philosophical fragments listed by Hadot, PV II 45.

62 Cf. *adv. Ar.* IV 3,32; 5,13–19; 6,1–7.

forth, already existed. Hence also, life is in living before it is life; nevertheless, life is after living because life is from living, and life is always and from eternity, because life is in "he lives," in the "he lives" from eternity. Therefore, since God is "he lives," since Christ is life, since life is born to its own existence from "he lives," it follows necessarily that "he lives" is the Father, that life is the Son so that, as we have taught above,[63] life is in "he lives," and in life is present also "he lives." Therefore, the Son is *homoousios* (consubstantial) with the Father, as we have taught above with examples.

3. The Son and the Holy Spirit

a) "To live" and "to understand," unique movement of "to be"

(16) Now this follows: an effort to explain what the Holy Spirit is in relation to these two.

These things have been both said and proven about God: God is "to be"; he is Spirit, which is "to live"; likewise he is light, which is "to be understanding and knowledge"; indeed, light allows nothing to be hidden, nothing to be obscure; it exposes, it enlightens, it illumines. It is therefore God. This very same reality which is God is "to be," first and original "to be," giving "to be" to all existents according to the capacity of those which receive it, as we have previously taught; this "to be" is "to live," this "to be" is "to understand," that is, that which is "to be" is Spirit, it is the light. Indeed, these things, in unity and simplicity, yea, more, being themselves one and simple, are "to be." This "to be" we rightly call either existence or substance.

But since the first of these is "to be," and since the two others, "to live" and "to understand" are known to be movements, since every movement is born from repose—but "to be" is repose; from "to be" is born movement, and consequently, action; but the movement of this first "to be" is "to live" and "to understand"; both indeed are one movement and one unique movement, appearing as two powers with a double function—they are one and the same substance. For movement is for them substance; indeed, for them it is not one thing to be, another thing to move oneself. So likewise it is

---

63 Cf. *adv. Ar.* IV 14,1–35.

not one thing "to live," another, "to understand," at least as far as substance goes. And indeed it is proper to the living to understand and to the understanding, to live: one sole movement circulates across their acts but so that the act and the operation of living is permanent while the act of understanding is intermittent.

Therefore, although Christ is life, although the Holy Spirit is knowledge and understanding, nevertheless all that the Holy Spirit possesses he has received from Christ, and Christ from the Father; that is, from "to be" has come forth life and "to live," has come forth knowledge and "to understand."

There is nothing astonishing here, since that first "to be"[64] is such that, since it is "to be," it is also "to move itself." (17) Although it is called repose, it moves itself, but it moves itself with an interior movement, whence it lives for itself and understands itself. Therefore from the interior movement, there is born the exterior movement, the movement outside; from "to be" which is interior, there is also born "to be" which is exterior, from interior "to live," exterior "to live," from interior understanding to exterior understanding, through self-moving life and knowledge. For they are movement, "to be" coexisting as identical with them, so that this trinity is both interior and exterior; interior, when God is one and alone, exterior, when he is Jesus Christ, interior and exterior, while both are one God.

And from that it follows that, since God is *homoousion* (consubstantial) with Christ, necessarily also Christ is *homoousion* with the Holy Spirit, and through that, that is, through Christ, is consubstantial with God.

b) The Holy Spirit comes from the Father, because he is in Christ

And he indeed has come forth from God. For if all movement which is exterior comes forth from the movement of God which is interior, then, he also, comes from God. And indeed knowledge and understanding are the existence, the strength, and the power of all consciousness; and precisely that itself is also movement for the same reason for which movement is also substance. Necessarily

---

64 In this sentence Hadot sees reference to the philosophical fragments (Group II) cited in PV II 24.

therefore, the Holy Spirit is in Christ, or indeed is Christ himself; and through Christ he has all things, because, from the life that is Christ there appears understanding.

c) Difference between Christ and the Holy Spirit

And because of that also the Holy Spirit is other than Christ. For this was said: "He has all things from me."[65] "He has," and "from me," that makes two. Therefore they are other. But because they are movement, the Holy Spirit is himself movement, as Christ is movement.

And because Christ is the true life, and gives true "life to those who believe in him,"[66] that is, "eternal" life, and because he is present with the Father for those who believe in him, that is, who believe that he is the Son of God, and who believe that through faith we are, for that reason, "reconciled" with God through Christ.[67]

But because the memory of himself and of God is obscured in human souls, there is need of the Holy Spirit. If knowledge and understanding "what is the breadth, and length and height and depth"[68] is added to strengthen love and faith in Christ, through the Holy Spirit who is knowledge, man "will be saved."[69] For the Holy Spirit fully gives "testimony" of Christ and "teaches"[70] all things and is the interior force of Christ, giving knowledge and advancing us to salvation; whence, he is another Paraclete.[71]

Indeed, to men dead through sins, life first had to be given so that they might be raised up to God through faith: it was already to live with the life of God that brought Christ into the flesh, so that he might come to help even the flesh. That is why, to men strengthened through faith,[72] through Christ the Son of God, it was necessary, it seemed, to give also the knowledge of Christ and in like manner of God, and also of the world, "to judge it."[73] When they will have

---

65 Cf. Jn 16.14–15.
66 Cf. Jn 3.15.
67 Cf. Rom 5.10.
68 Cf. Eph 3.16–18.
69 Cf. Mk 16.16.
70 Cf. Jn 14.26; 15.26.
71 Cf. Jn 14.15; 14.16.
72 Faith looks towards knowledge; *ad Cand.* 20,3 and *adv. Ar.* I 2,6–40.
73 Cf. Jn 16.8.

understood these things, men would be more easily freed[74] by their knowledge of themselves and of divine things to attain the light of God because of their contempt for worldly and earthly things and by the desire which knowledge of divine things excites. (18) Knowledge, therefore, came later, that is, after faith began to work. Indeed, after the departure of Christ who, by his miracles and teachings, had sown faith, faith in the fact that he is Son of God and gives true life to those who believe in him, all was completed by the Spirit; and faith in Christ by knowledge, with Christ himself always present. For he said this: "For he will not speak on his own authority, but whatever he will hear he will speak, and the things that are to come he will declare to you. He will honor me, because he will receive of what is mine."[75]

Therefore, from life comes understanding, and life itself comes from living, that is, from the Father comes the Son, and from the Son, the Holy Spirit. For he added this: "All things that the Father has are mine";[76] "I said that all that the Father has is mine, because all the Father has is the Son's, "to be," "to live," "to understand." These same realities the Holy Spirit possesses. All are therefore *homoousia* (consubstantial).

d) Identity between Christ and the Holy Spirit

Nevertheless they are identical. To show that he is always present, this is said in the Gospel according to Matthew: "Going now, teach all nations, baptizing them in the name of the Father and of the Son, and of the Holy Spirit, teaching them to observe all that I have commanded you; and behold I am with you all days, even unto the consummation of the world."[77] From this it is shown that the Holy Spirit is somehow identical to Jesus, although they are different through the proper movement of their action, because the former teaches the understanding, the latter gives life. Indeed by the same

---

74 The mystery's purpose is the liberation of souls; cf. Victorinus, *in Eph.* 1.4 (1238 C); Augustine, *City of God* 10.32 (FC 14.179–86). Is this liberation through knowledge? Cf. I 48,20; *in Eph.* 1,4 (1240 C-D). Is there a gnostic aspect of salvation here or does knowledge merely mature one's faith?

75 Jn 16.13–14.

76 Jn 16.15.

77 Mt 28.19–20.

unique and first movement it happens that the one who lives, lives truly, understands and understands truly, and the one who understands truly lives truly.

And so that it may appear clearly that Jesus and the Holy Spirit are identical, let us pay attention to this. The Holy Spirit is, is he not, teaching, understanding, and wisdom itself; but wisdom is attributed also to Christ and to God, and Christ is called by that name, because it is "Gospel" that Christ is the Son of God[78], because Gospel is defined: "Power and wisdom of God," as Paul says to the Romans. Likewise Solomon: "All Wisdom comes from God and has always been with him, before all time."[79] Behold *homoousion* (consubstantial) is evident since wisdom is given by God and from God to Christ and to the Holy Spirit. And since it was said that wisdom "has always been with God" it is evident that *homoousion* (consubstantial) also signifies: together with the Father. Next, since it was said: "Before all time,"[80] we see that Christ does not begin then when he is in the flesh. Likewise: "First of all things wisdom was brought forth."[81] If Christ is "firstborn,"[82] Christ is "wisdom." That which follows next designates the Holy Spirit: "And the understanding of prudence is from everlasting."[83] If the Holy Spirit is "prudence" and understanding and knowledge and teaching, he is without doubt Christ, since Christ himself is "from everlasting," that is, from eternity, and the "firstborn,[84]" and, what is more, the only begotten.

These texts and others that I have commented upon in numerous other books[85] well prove that not only are God and Christ *homoousion* (consubstantial), but also the Holy Spirit.

---

78 Cf. Rom 1.16; 1 Cor 1.24.
79 Sir 1.1.
80 *Ibid.*
81 Sir 1.4.
82 Cf. Col 1.15.
83 Cf. Sir 1.4.
84 Cf. Col 1.15.
85 Cf. *adv. Ar.* I 12,1–3; I 18,55; III 9,1–8.

II. THE MODE OF PROCESSION OF THE SON, CONSUBSTANTIAL FORM OF THE FATHER

1. Summary of the First Part

Let us admit or accept therefore that God is the first, original "to live" which is true and original "to be." For that which does not live is not. We have shown that this "to live" by its very operation produces and begets life.[86] Indeed, in that which is life, knowledge and understanding are present. Therefore, God lives, and in living God is life, and since he is life, he is understanding, but as one and simple he is these three, and they are in him so that the three are nothing other in him than "to be," which he is by predominance. God is original existence, living necessarily and knowing himself. Hence, indeed, he knows all things because he knows himself. This is the cause of all existences and for that reason is all things. Therefore life and understanding, understood according to "to be," remain always in the interior to exercise one sole act, which is "to live," but "to live", for God, is "to be." Therefore this total "to be" is the one and omnipotent God.

2. Position of the Problem: What Relation is there Between the Interior Form of God and his Exterior Form?

A. FIRST STATEMENT

What therefore? If it acts upon itself in the interior, or rather if life and understanding act upon themselves,[87] how could they, as it were, appear exteriorly? And what is exterior or interior?

---

86 Cf. *adv. Ar.* IV 6,8ff.; IV 10,1-19; IV 15,1-8.

87 From here until the middle of sect. 19 there is continuous use of philosophical fragments (Group III) in which "to be" is explained as indetermination with "being" as intelligible determination. Cf. PV II 46. In its own way this is an exegesis of Phil 2.5 studied fully in 29,39-33,25. This was a text greatly used by the Homoiousians; for the latter also Jn 5.25 meant that the Son was like the Father. It was Gore (DCB 4.1135) who recognized in Victorinus a likeness to Synesius who defined the Son as Form of the Father.

B. SPECIFICATION OF THE TERMS OF THE PROBLEM

a) God has an interior form and an exterior form

Philosophers and teachers of the Law have asked two questions[88] about the *on* (existent) and the *Logos:* what they are, and where they are. What are they? We must explain their substance or existence. Where are they? Are they in God or outside, in all others, or in each one and everywhere? (19) Certainly we have discussed these things exhaustively and completely in other books.[89] But now we shall speak of them summarily and briefly.

Before the *on* (existent) and before the *Logos,* there is that force and that power of being that is designated by the word "to be," in Greek *to einai.* This very "to be" must be taken under two modes, one that is universal and originally original, and from it comes the "to be" for all others; and according to another mode, all others have "to be," this is the "to be" of all those which come after God, genera or species or other things of this kind.

But the first "to be"[90] is so unparticipated[91] that it cannot even be called one or alone, but rather, by preeminence, before the one, before the alone, beyond simplicity, preexistence rather than existence, universal of all universals, infinite, unlimited—at least for all others, but not for itself—and therefore without form; it is understood by a certain intuition and is perceived, known and believed by

---

88 The debate here, as Hadot rightly notes (TTT 1019) is between the tradition of Numenius and that of Plotinus, that is, the tradition which admits life and knowledge in the bosom of the Primary Principle and the tradition which denies all life and knowledge to the One. Cf. Plotinus, *Enn.* 6.7.17.

89 Cf. *ad Cand.* 14–18, 21–23; *adv. Ar.* I 52-53.

90 For Hadot this is the capital passage for an adequate understanding of the Victorine Neoplatonism. He sees here the influence of certain post-Plotinian tendencies, referring once again to that anonymous commentary on the *Parmenides* dated probably from the second half of the fourth century (Palimpseste de Turin, XII, folio 93, lines 29–35); W. Kroll, "Ein neuplatonischer Parmenidescommentar," 615. Cf. Hadot, TTT 1019.

91 We find there the second use of the notion of unparticipated as absolutely transcendent, incommensurable. "To Be" *(Esse)* taken absolutely has no conceptual content; it is infinite. According to Hadot, this is the first time in the history of thought that a negative theology is applied to "to be"; cf. PV I 408.

a preunderstanding rather than understanding. This is what we have called "to live" or "he lives," the infinite "to live," superior to the "to live" of all universals, "to be" in itself, "to live" in itself, not to be something or to live[92] something. Whence, it is not *on* (existent). For the *on* (existent) is something determined, intelligible, knowable. Therefore, if it is not *on* (existent), neither is it *Logos.*

For the *Logos*[93] is both defined and defining; for it is either reason or the power of existence itself, or indeed those realities that our understanding receives in it in order to know the proper "to be" of each one; it does not know unless it notices and grasps what are the things which give to each one its substance. And this *Logos* is the universal power of things, "through whom all has been made,"[94] containing in itself under a universal mode the substances of all things, and providing for the existence of each one of them that which belongs to each and is proper to it. Therefore, since it provides for each thing that which belongs to it and is proper to it, it defines and it delimits. This the *on* (existent) also does. For by imposing a limit to the infinite, in substances, it gives a form to the substance of each thing so that each thing thus obtains its own existence, and eliminating the infinity of substance, it submits the thing to the grasp of the understanding. Then, as the power of things, in view of begetting and accomplishing existences, it is the *Logos.* But, insofar as it defines and encloses, providing to each one its own form, it is the *on* (existent), since, henceforth, there will have been realized effectively a determined form of "to be."

(20) Since this is so, let us see whether the "to be" of that first has a *Logos.*[95] If we have said that it is infinite, and if we now add that it is without measure and that it is indistinct, it follows that we do not understand, that we do not grasp the realities which constitute its "to be."[96] Therefore, it has no *Logos.* But since it is impos-

---

92 Cf. *adv. Ar.* IV 8,9; IV 12,13–15; IV 18,45–46.
93 This seems to be the Stoic notion of *logos* transposed into Middle Platonism. Cf. I 5,1–9.
94 Cf. Jn 1.3.
95 Chs. 20–26 are formed from an extended series of philosophical fragments (III) that, with two short breaks occupy Hadot, PV II 47–54. They refer to the self-hidden knowledge or Form in God self-manifested without change in God.
96 Cf. *adv. Ar.* IV 19,17.

sible that, if it is in any way, this Existent which is infinite should be without its *Logos*,[97] it therefore has its *Logos*, without doubt, but latent and hidden, so that to be *Logos* itself is to be in "to be," or rather, the *Logos* itself is nothing other than very "to be." This "to be" is what I have called the first "to live," the universally universal "to live."[98] And although "to live" itself, as we have taught,[99] is also life and understanding—realities at once defined and defining: for these are powers of the *Logos;* and indeed life is something defined and formed; as for understanding it is at the same time defining—nevertheless because life and understanding are interior and turned toward themselves, they are totally *agnôsta, adiakrita,*[100] unknown and undiscerned. Likewise also, God who is "to be," that is, "to live, is unknown and undiscerned and his form, that is, the understanding of life, is unknown and undiscerned; for life and understanding are nothing other than "to be," which is "to live." Since this "to live" is infinite, its form also is infinite, dwelling in it, and being nothing other than "to be." But when the form began to be exterior, then the manifest form is image of God, revealing God through itself; and the *Logos,* no longer in God, that is, the *Logos pros ton theon,* is life and understanding, now *on* (existent), because it is sure knowledge and existence which are grasped in concept and notion.

b) Is there identity between the interior form and the exterior form?

But how did these things appear exteriorly? Has the form itself, which is interior, been projected exteriorly? Or has it gone forth by its own movement? But since this interior form is indistinct and infinite, how, in that which is exterior, is it known? Or is this latter different from the former? But if different, it is therefore not born from the former, through projection or by its own movement. And if it is different, it is not equal, nor identical, and absolutely not

---

97 In this sentence Victorinus says that the Logos must be eternal and that true life is awareness of life. Cf. Plotinus, *Enn.* 6.7.17.

98 Cf. *adv. Ar.* IV 6,10; IV 15,6–8; IV 18,45–46.

99 Cf. *adv. Ar.* IV 18,47–59.

100 The phrase *id est* is omitted in CSEL. Here until the conclusion there is a review of the Arian controversy and of Victorinus's response that the begetting is a self-begetting.

homoousios (consubstantial). And next, whence has this form appeared? (21) From another than God? Then, there are two principles? Or, from nothing? But there is no nothing in the kingdom of the God *tōn ontōn* (of the existents). Next, if it came forth by the power or will of God this power or will of God is not nothing. Indeed, if God is omnipotent, his omnipotence is both the cause of all things and the very existence of all things.

Do we dare then to formulate the only remaining hypothesis? This form has arisen from itself. And how so, since it was in the Father?[101] Was the Father unaware or did he order it? If by the Father's order, he did not then come through himself? Or he was unaware? Is there something then which can be done not by the power of God? Or then, is there something which is done without him, whereas of the *Logos* who is called his form, the following was said: "Through whom all things have been made, and without him nothing was made"[102]? What is this? What solution is there for confusions of such magnitude? What solution if it be not the Truth, or, as it really is, the Holy Spirit of Truth? Let the listener only attend to what he inspired in us! We shall explain by means of the simplicity of one thing: it will be suitable to take what will be said without any consideration of time, from eternity, without beginning in time, but in such a way that the begetter and the begotten are both one principle.

3. Solution of the Problem: the Form is Exteriorized by Knowing Itself as Known

Teaching of Reason

A. INITIAL THEOREM: IMMUTABILITY OF THE DIVINE BEGETTINGS

First of all, among the eternal, divine realities and the absolutely first, dwelling quietly and in that existence where they are, with no change of themselves through movement, they begot[103] first, God,

---

101 Phil 2.5.

102 Jn 1.3.

103 In this section on the teaching of reason, Hadot considers that Victorinus is at his best philosophically and theologically. To explain the mode of

next the *Logos* or *Nous,* or whatever is different or one and the other, as Spirit, as "to live" or life, as understanding or knowledge. Only the soul is moved in begetting. All these things we teach as follows.

B. GOD AND HIS FORM

a) God as "to be," "to live," "to understand"

God is *tri-dunamos* (tri-powered), that is, one having three powers, "to be," "to live," "to understand," so that in each one power there are three powers, and anyone of the three is three powers, receiving its name by the power wherein it predominates, as I have taught above and in many places.[104] For nothing must be called "to be" unless it understands. Triple therefore in each individual, their individuality and triple also their unity in trinity. But these three in their progress, as we shall show, (22) have shared with all existents, in act, in potentiality or could have been—existence, life, understanding, which they give to them according to the proper

the Son's begetting, thought is primarily identified with the divine "to be" by the act of knowing; then, taking itself, thought, for object as thought of thought, it gives itself its own hypostasis without losing its unity with the act of "to be" in which it is grounded. Neoplatonism has always seen the divine begettings as self-begettings, but only Victorinus teaches an identity between the begetter and the self-begotten. His success hinges on the identity of the form which emerges from "To Be" with "to be." This is God and knowledge of God. This teaching is made possible by the logical distinction, introduced by Numenius, between knowledge which knows and knowledge which knows itself, a distinction rejected by Plotinus in *Enn.* 2.9.1. Hadot (TTT 1027) states that Porphyry enabled Victorinus to make a rapprochement between the two doctrines of Numenius and Plotinus. The ultimate source of this doctrine is *Timaeus* (42E) and Porphyry, *Sententiae* 24 (Cf. Hadot, TTT 1029). Plotinus considers the mode of begetting among divinities in *Enn.* 5.2.1 which is literally cited in Victorinus's Book IV 22,8–9. Hadot thinks that Victorinus did not take this quotation directly from Plotinus but from a Neoplatonic source [Porphyry?] who extracted from *Enn.* 5.2.1. a definition of God and of the mode of begetting proper to God; or the source uses the beginning of two treatises of Plotinus, *Enn.* 5.2.1.– *adv. Ar.* IV 22,8–9; and 3.4.1–*adv. Ar.* IV 21,19–25. For another opinion, one advanced prior to Hadot's, see Henry, *Plotin et l'Occident,* 49–54. W. Theiler (*Die chaldäischen Orakel,* 18, n. 4) thought that this Plotinian sentence was in Porphyry's commentary on the *Enneads,* translated perhaps by Victorinus.

104 Cf. *adv. Ar.* IV 5,36–41; I 54,9–10; II 3,39–44.

capacity of things and of substances and according to the communication of themselves they wish to bestow. For there are in all things
an appropriate "to be," "to live," "to understand," "to feel," so
that these are the shadow or the image of three highest of all.

b) Unum omnia: *the omniexistent and his omniexistence*

Therefore God, although he is, as is affirmed by all, the one and
the only one, some, however, have said that God[105] is the one that
is all, and not the one; for he is principle of all things," therefore
"not all but all in a transcendent mode."[106] But this is the reason
for this: first, indeed, that God is one and alone, because these three
do not result from composition, but since being each one what they
are, they are also, by that fact, the two others, we believe, so that
they are necessarily one and only one, with no kind of otherness, of
this we have often spoken.[107] Indeed, as for what was said: "one
that is all and not one, for the principle of all,"[108] does not this expression evidently and clearly designate God the Father "of all
things" and their principle," who "since he is not one" is, rather,
"all things," because he is cause and "principle" of all things, and he
is in all things. Since such is the case, God will be the all-existent, the
all-living, the all-seeing and all-understanding one.

And since we have said[109] that act produces power—for the first
realities have a mode of being such that all divine things are energies,
that is, acts and operations—it follows necessarily that from the
principle which is God there is born the original source of all the
universally universal powers. For this progress of realities is such
that, since all is from God, both powers and acts, have come forth
from God who, himself, must be considered as above powers and

---

105 In these two small sections Victorinus uses the only literal Plotinian text
he cites to show that we conceive God by starting from existents, life,
knowledge of existents; he then uses it to show that the Form of God is
transcendent. God is beyond all and therefore unknowable when the
Form of God is identified with the "to be" of God. As Hadot points out,
Plotinus makes the "One" the subject of the sentence whereas Victorinus
makes "God" the subject of the same sentence; Hadot, PV I, 418–19.

106 Plotinus, *Enn.* 5.2.1.

107 Cf. *adv. Ar.* IV 1,15–16; IV 5,45–47; IV 21,26–29.

108 Cf. *adv. Ar.* IV 22,8–9.

109 Cf. *adv. Ar.* IV 15,7–13.

acts. (23) But since we have said that God is a certain act which is "to live," but the "to live" above all "to live," "to live" from eternity to eternity, a notion simultaneously comprising "to be" and "to understand"[110]—and this "simultaneously" must be taken in such a way that there is not a shadow of composition—it follows necessarily that by the act of living, as I have taught, there is produced that form that we call the universal power, formed through each of the acts that we have enumerated: omniexistence through the omniexistent, omnivitality through the omniliving, omnivision through omniseeing, with each aspect of the power as known and determined.[111]

c) Nec unum nec omnia

The preexistent and his preexistence, the preknowing and his preknowledge

But since he is called all-in-one or "one that is all" or since he is called "one that is all" or "neither one, nor all,"[112] it follows that he is infinite, that he is unknown, indiscernible, unknowable, and that he is what is porperly called *aoristia,* that is, infinity and indetermination. Indeed, although he is the "to be"[113] of all things, the "to live" of all things, the "to understand" of all things, and he is that, while being one, and one without the least appearance of otherness, how does it happen that he is called "not one"? Because he is "principle of all things," therefore of the one himself. From this we are obliged henceforth necessarily also to put forward these statements about him: that his "to be," "to live," "to understand" is incomprehensible, and not only that his "to be," "to live," "to understand" is incomprehensible, but that this "to be," "to live," "to understand" seems not to exist, because it is above everything. That is why it is said that he is *anuparktos, anousios, anous, azōn,* without

---

110 Cf. *adv. Ar.* IV 15,4.9.
111 Cf. *adv. Ar.* IV 15,8.11; IV 22,21.
112 Cf. *adv. Ar.* IV 22,8–9.
113 Hadot remarks in reference to these two sentences (TTT 1032–33) that similar reasoning is present in the anonymous commentary on the *Parmenides:* "He himself is neither one nor many but supersubstantial by relation to the existents which come from him; so that he is not only beyond the many but even beyond the concept of himself, for from him the One and the Monad come forth."

existence, without substance, without understanding, without life, certainly, not by *sterēsin* (privation), but through transcendence. For all things which words designate are after him; that is why he is not *on* (existent), but rather *Proon* (Preexistent). In the same way the realities produced in him are preexistence, the preliving, and preknowing. But all these things have been understood and named from secondary phenomena.

d) The interior form of God, as knowledge identical to its object and turned towards itself

For after knowledge had appeared, preknowledge was both understood and named;[114] in the same way, for preexistence and previtality; certainly, they existed but they were not yet recognized, not yet named. Therefore also unknowable is all that which is God. But since then the knowable is both found and spoken of when there is knowledge—for they are relative terms and they contain each other and mutually beget or perish, one with the other—this was not yet knowable because there was no knowledge, not that the know-

---

114 This long section beginning here and proceeding to the first third of ch. 28 brings forward the whole question of knowledge in God. As will clearly appear in 27,1 to 28,22 there is first of all the act of "to be," absolutely pure and unknowable and yet in it knowledge is identical with it; by making itself knowledge identical with "to be," it knows itself at once as being and as knowledge. Its act of self-begetting consists in being at once God and itself. This radically differentiates this doctrine from the Plotinian doctrine of intelligence which if it indeed admits a self-begetting of the intelligence, never admits that the intelligence is the One, even in a state of conversion towards self, save perhaps in the treatise at 3.9.1 in some lines apparently strongly influenced by Numenius and which Plotinus will explicitly reject in *Enn.* 2.9.1. For example, "The Intelligible Object is the Intellectual Principle itself in repose, unity, immobility," and, "we cannot conceive a duality in the Intellectual Principle, one phase in some vague calm, another all astir." Interior knowledge passes from an unbegotten state to a begotten state. It is like Aristotle's reasoning in *Metaphysics* 12.9 (1074 b21–40). God in thinking can think only himself. Victorinus adds the nuance: because for him to know is to be, and to know himself is to be himself. For Victorinus, it is because God is knowledge that his knowing is the thought of thought. Knowing includes the "to be" and the "to live." The knowing of God is in this state of interiority knowing and being, but being by predominance; cf. Plotinus, *Enn.* 6.2.8. God will be known by his form insofar as this form is begotten; this begotten form is the Son, the image of God.

ledge given as knowable did not exist, but because there was certainly that which could be knowable but was not yet knowable. Then he becomes knowable in potentiality and is recognized as such, when it is understood that he is also able to be understanding. In this way therefore in God there was a knowable in potentiality and therefore he was knowable because there was also a knowledge in potentiality and therefore a knowledge.

(24) What therefore results from these statements? Since if these things were born afterwards, they were in God, and if they were in God, because God is one, these also are one, and that which God is and these are one, because God is these things. Likewise, therefore, the knowable and knowledge are identical but so that that which is knowable is knowledge. Indeed since these three are one power—for "to be" is nothing other than "to live" and since "to live" itself is "to understand" and to be understood—all the power of each one of them is contained in "to know" or to be knowledge. But there cannot be knowledge unless there is a knowable. But in those first realities where "to be" is "to live" and "to understand," there cannot be a knowable unless there is knowledge itself, not yet manifested, but possessing itself interiorly, dwelling in repose, immobile and turned towards self, giving itself to itself as knowable. Indeed since knowledge itself remains hidden, since it is in itself, without even returning into self as coming from the exterior, but since it is plunged originally in that in which its "to be" remains immobile, its form is so that it can be knowable. But when knowledge has been awakened and has somehow gone out to envelop itself within its own gaze, it will make itself knowledge by knowing itself; then it becomes the knowable, because knowledge becomes in act its own knowable.

Therefore, if it is permitted to say this, I say that in this way there is this First, this one, this unique, this God, Spirit, breathing, light, illuminating, existent, omniexistent, existence, omniexistence, living, omniliving, life, vitality, omnivitality, understanding and knowing, omniunderstanding, omniknowing, omniintelligence, omniknowledge, omnipotent, perfect in every way, illimited, immense, at least for others, but for itself limited and measured, above everything and because of that, none of the things and rather that from which all things come, therefore one and only one, "principle of all things indeed," being therefore not "one that is all" remaining in itself and yet not in itself, lest the hearer understand this as two terms, but being himself the dwelling or the permanence, repose, reposed, reposing rather, because repose is begotten by reposing, as we have taught above;[115] that is why it is said also that he was in some way seated at the center *tōn pantōn ontōn,* that is, of all existents, and from there, with his universal eye, that is, by the light of his substance, by which he is "to be" or "to live" or "to understand" he sees the radii of existents under an immutable aspect because he is repose, and from the center there is one sole look directed simultaneously upon all things. This is God.

C. THE MODE OF BEGETTING OF THE SON, I.E. THE MODE OF GOING FORTH OF THE FORM FROM GOD

a) Movement and repose in God

But how is God Father and who is the Son? Or, how is he Son and later, how is the Son, Jesus?

To be "principle of all things" is to be prior to all things. "To be principle of all things" is not so much to be in repose as to be repose itself. For all things which have been begotten or created have been begotten or created through movement. But movement itself, insofar as it is movement, is repose before moving itself.

For the generation of contraries comes from their contraries in such a way that, if one contrary comes to birth, that from which this contrary is born must perish; for example, from life comes death and from death, life; likewise, from "to be", non-to-be, and from non-to-be, "to be"; and similarly, from repose, movement, and from movement, repose. (25) But let us sharpen our attention and by a bold understanding of things see the force and the height of what is proposed. A careful examination will show that there is a certain existence even in things which appear to perish. Indeed, since life is a thing to which "to be" is present and from which death is born, death also has "to be," if life is born from death. Likewise, if from "to be" there is produced non-to-be, necessarily there will be also non-to-be itself, if from that is born "to be." Likewise, if there is repose from movement, it is necessary that repose exists, if move-

---

115 Cf. *adv. Ar.* IV 5,20–22; IV 6,1–7; 12–17.

ment is born from repose. What then? Should it not be believed that by the birth of contraries, their contraries either die or no longer exist? It seems so, but it is the opposite. Indeed, both contraries remain and do not perish because of their eternal, substantial quality. How this is so, I shall say. May God assist me so that the explanation may be easily given.

"To be" among eternal realities is "to be" which is "to live," which is "to understand"; we have also said this often and have proved it.[116] But on high "to be" is such that on high there are living and understanding substances. Let us admit that these substances provide three things according to the mode of the existents and by participation of themselves keep all things active both among the intelligibles and among the intellects—these alone are simple, divine, eternal; they are present indeed in things of this world and in material things, but they have for their support carnal beings, changing and mortal. Here then, if there is death, it is death of bodies, and if one pays closer attention, one will see that there is not even death of bodies, I mean, insofar as they are matter, but there is only a dissolution of these bodies by a kind of destruction as to the appearance which is fleetingly realized in them. Therefore, only the appearance of body is dissolved when it is resolved into elements; but the latter remain and they are that from which life will arise. Indeed, since in the world there is also matter, it exists always in well-determined elements, and since the images of the three on high, here also, that is, in the world, also manifest themselves, what can death do, since these three, even in their images, are eternal? I call images the powers flowing through all things in the course of the passage of the soul. Therefore, since these are eternal, since the elements in matter are also eternal, if death dissolves only the aggregates, nothing totally perishes. It is then rightly said that death is produced from life since through the vital force itself of every composed body is produced its decomposition into determined elements, and when these same elements are assembled anew, restoration is accomplished out of death, in view of a new composition. In this way we must

---

116 Cf. *adv. Ar.* III 4,9–10; III 4,25–32; IV 2,18–23; IV 8,10–14; IV 16,6–10; IV 24,10–11.

understand "to be" in the world, and in this way also, repose and movement.

But among divine realities, because there is nothing corporeal, there is no death, but there is also life of another kind, because that is the original and true life. And on account of that, progression there is not a generation, or if "generation" is acceptable, it is rather appearance and manifestation. Likewise these divine realities are "to be" and non-to-be according to another mode, and movement and repose also according to another mode.

b) God, "to be," "to live," "to understand," and his form, existence, life and knowledge, in their state of identity

Indeed God lives. But he is "to be" and "to understand," and these three which are one, produce three powers, existence, life and knowledge, (26) but because these three are one—I have explained how they are one:[117] they are one so that anyone among them is the three and these three are one, but in God these three are "to be," in the Son, "to live," in the Holy Spirit, "to understand"—it follows, therefore, that "to be," "to live," "to understand," in God are "to be," but existence, life, knowledge, in God are form, for they come forth from the interior and hidden act of the one who is "to be," "to live," "to understand." For these three are in the interior and hidden, and rather, God is above "to be," above "to live," above "to understand"; that is why he is called *anousios* (without substance) or *anuparktos* (without existence) and likewise *azōn* (without life) and *anous* (without understanding); by a certain pre-knowledge it is discovered that he is these three, and known rather through his own form, but one inherent and consubstantial with him; and this is what is meant by: the Son is in the Father.

But since this is so, the Son is the same as the Father. For that reason the Son is also God, because the form is that, because it is nothing other than the one of whom it is the form. Indeed, since God is "to be," "to live," "to understand," but his form is existence, life, knowledge, please know that I say this while holding that God is beyond these. If this is so, the form is identical to substance. For in the same way that "to be," "to live," "to understand" signify the

---

117 Cf. *adv. Ar.* I 54,8 ff.; III 4,35–38; III 9,6–7; III 10,1.

existence or having of these, so, although there are two *logoi,* one
through which each thing is, the other through which each thing has
its mode of "to be," nevertheless, since in God the mode of "to be"
and "to be" are identical as to their power, it necessarily results that
there is in God only one *Logos,* the form having the same power as
the substance. Therefore, if the form of this substance has the same
power and is the same as substance itself—for it is substantial form—
the Son will be the same as the Father, or there is neither Father nor
Son before the going forth externally, but only one itself.

c) The going forth of the form: understanding externalizes itself in understanding itself as understanding

The interior understanding which understands itself as "to be"

(27) Since this is the case, since God has at once "to understand"
and knowledge,[118] knowledge in him is therefore identical to life
and to "to be." But since there is a greater intensity of acting in "to
understand" than in "to be" and "to live," and since this "to be" is
to understand what it is, necessarily, if God is "to understand" or
knowledge, when God understands, he knows himself. And when he
knows himself, not as an object different from the subject, it follows
that this knowledge is self-knowledge. Because this is a fact, this
knowledge makes itself to be, it comes forth into existence, its own
"to be" is constituted, and in the same way, by the act of understanding there also exists its "to live." Since all these are born from
themselves or, rather, are existing from themselves, the unbegotten
God exists from the unbegotten. And since these unbegotten are
one, the One God is one and simple. And this knowledge is as an
interior knowledge which, without any movement, understands itself indeed, since, in understanding, it exists, and in existing, it
understands, and this is God, and certainly this knowledge is from
eternity and to eternity.

The understanding which understands itself as knowledge

(28) But since we call the Son of God the image of God—and the

---

118 The philosophical fragments (III) forming the first part of this chapter
are those given in Hadot, PV II 54.

form[119] has been begotten, so that from that which is "to be," "to live," "to understand" are begotten existence, life, knowledge; indeed, there is in these a certain form through which, as through an image, there is known what is "to be," "to live," "to understand"— it follows necessarily that God is known through the form. For himself in himself "no one has ever seen."[120] Therefore, the form of God, when understood to be in God, is God himself. But when God understands himself, he understands himself through the form. But it is necessary that the form itself also understand. For it is an understanding and living existence, since it understands nothing other than those things which are God; and this I have already often taught.[121] But when knowledge itself understands that it is knowledge—for it necessarily follows that knowledge also understands itself—going out, as it were, from itself, it has understood itself and made itself exterior, that is, outside, by self-understanding, that is, by its own movement. That is why it is exterior knowledge.

And this is the Son, this is the *Logos*, the born Son, because he is other than God, yet from God, that is, from the one who is existing and living knowledge, who is God and who is interior, knowledge which by understanding itself brought itself outside and existed, existing as image of the Father, in whom it was and in whom it is always, and being begotten through the interior knowledge which is "to be" and "to exist," and because of that, this is the image of the image.

Consubstantial relation between interior knowledge and the knowledge of knowledge

(29) There are therefore two intelligences,[122] one existing interiorly, because it is proper for it "to be," the second existing because it is proper for it "to be by understanding." This exterior one, this

---

119 The first part of this chapter is made up of the philosophical fragments (III) assembled by Hadot, PV II 55. They express God's interior thought manifesting itself as exterior form and we note that the Son is sometimes defined as life, sometimes as knowledge; cf. IV 6,18.

120 Jn 1.18.

121 Cf. *adv. Ar.* IV 26,6; IV 26,11.24.

122 In these first two paragraphs the philosophical fragments employed (Group III) touch on the two kinds of knowledge; self-knowing and the knowing of knowing; cf. Hadot, PV II 55.

is the Son. Since this knowledge which is knowledge by understanding itself, has understood God, it has evidently understood the knowledge which remains interior—this is God—and thus, understanding "true to be," "true to live," "true to understand," it has gone forth also as "true to be," "true to live," "true to understand." And indeed, whoever understands the one, both has the one and is the one, according to the knowledge of the one that he has in himself.

So therefore the Son,[123] that is, the knowledge begotten by self-understanding, knew God and all those realities which as unbegotten are God himself, and by understanding signifies: by seeking the *plērōma* and by understanding the *plērōma*.

That is why the Son is identical with the Father. And indeed, since the Father is the *plērōma*, he necessarily has his infinite *khōrēma* (receptacle), granted that it is limited for itself, where it contains and encloses its *plērōma*. In the same way the Son, by receiving and seeking—for to be a *khōrēma* (receptacle) is to receive— but understanding all that the Father is, has gone forth as *plērōma*, having been begotten as "all from all." And because knowledge understands knowledge, since knowledge is true light, this understanding knowledge is "light from light," and because both are knowledge, this is "true light from true light."[124] And likewise since the interior knowledge is God, this knowledge which is knowledge by self-understanding is "God from God."

D. CONSUBSTANTIALITY OF THE FATHER AND THE SON

They are therefore *homoousion* (consubstantial) in all things, in "to be," and "to live," and "to understand"; likewise, insofar as both are *khōrēma* (receptacle) and *plērōma;* likewise, in sofar as they are image and image; for it was said: "According to our image";[125] and insofar as "light" and "light"; and insofar as "true light" and "true light"; and insofar as "Spirit" and "Spirit"; and insofar as movement

---

123 In these three sentences Victorinus discusses the notion of Pleroma found in Paul's Epistle to the Ephesians, the mystery of the diffusion of the Spirit in souls and the destiny of souls. Cf. Victorinus, *in Eph.* 21–23 (1250 C); *hymn.* I.

124 Cf. *adv. Ar.* II 2,22–26.

125 Gn 1.26.

and movement, but the Father is movement in repose, that is, interior movement and nothing other than movement, not movement in movement; but the Son is movement in movement; both are, nevertheless, movement; likewise, both are action and operation; both are life and both having life from themselves; will and the same will; virtue, wisdom, word;[126] God and God; living God and living God; eternal and eternal; invisible and invisible; for it was said by Matthew: "No one has known the Son except the Father, nor the Father, except the Son."[127] They are both together; for this is what *homoousion* (consubstantial) signifies, beyond the same *ousian* (substance).

Teaching of Scripture: Identity Between the Form of God, the Son of God, the Logos and Jesus Christ

A. THE FORM IS THE SON OF GOD[128]

All this can be understood in this full text: "All that the Father has, he has given to me, and all that the Father has, I also have."[129] "All," he says. If "all," the Son is *homoousios* (consubstantial) with the Father.

They are therefore identical; and if identical, equal; and if equal, Paul rightly said of the Son, of Jesus Christ: "Who, although he was in the form of God, did not consider it robbery to be equal to God."[130] (30) Many divine and magnificent mysteries are contained here.

First, that Christ is the "form of God,"[131] in whom one sees that he "has all that God has." For this is the "form" which is also called "image,"[132] as it was said of him "who is the image"[133] of God.

---

126 Cf. 1 Cor 1.24; Jn 1.1.
127 Mt 11.27.
128 In this development running through the first paragraph of sect. 33 there is a commentary on Phil 2.6. If there is no distinction between God and his form, then God the Father became incarnate. But Phil 2.6 shows that the Son is both in the "form of God" and distinct from the Father, recognizing his equality and renouncing it.
129 Cf. Mt 11.27; Jn 16.15.
130 There is much use in this and the two following paragraphs of Phil 2.6.
131 Cf. Mt 11.27; Jn 16.15.
132 Cf. Col 1.15.
133 Gn 1.26; Col 1.15.

Therefore, God also has his image, and the Son is the "image" of
God. And indeed, if it was said: "No one has ever seen my face,"[134]
and it was said: "You will see me from behind," there is without
doubt a face for God, there is through the Son an image of God, or
rather the Son is also the "image of God," as was said: "Who was
in the form of God." Whence it was rightly said: "Let us make
man according to our image and likeness."[135]

Therefore the Son is, and if he is, he is different. For Father is
not the same as Son, Son is not the same as Father; yet through
those realities that I treated above, they are identical; identical, that
is, having the same realities, but each one through his own existence.
That is why they are both the same and different. And indeed since
it was said here: "Although he was in the form of God," it certainly
must be understood that the "form" is different, "God" is different.
But you will see that there is place for the misrepresentation that the
"form of God" is in God himself a form in such a way that there is
one indistinguishable substance. What? How shall we understand the
rest of the text: "He did not consider it robbery to be equal to
God"? Only someone possessing his own existence believes himself
or speaks of himself as equal to another. What truly is this: "He
emptied himself, taking the form of a slave." We have learned of
Christ that he died. Have we also learned that of God? But no one
ever said that. Next, when it is said of the Father; "He who has
raised his Son from the dead,"[136] is it not clear enough that the
Father is one reality, the Son another? That he who raises is one
reality, that he who is raised is another? Therefore, as to the "form
of God," the "form" is one thing, "God" is another.

And certainly God also has a form, but the Son of God is the
manifested form, while the form of God is a hidden form. Such is
the case for all the rest: existence, life, knowledge, insofar as they
are God's, they are hidden within, but insofar as they are the Son's,
they are manifested; so for the rest: *khōrēma* (receptacle) and
plērōma, "image," "true light," "truth," "Spirit," "movement,"
"action," "operation," "life," and life from himself, "will,"

134 Ex 33.20,23.
135 Gn 1.26.
136 Rom 8.11.

"power," "wisdom," "word,"[137] "God," "living God," and all the other names. But these latter realities are, as it were, external and manifested, while the former realities are within the Father and included in the very existence or rather they are that same reality which is existence, whereas in the Son they are in the act, acting in the open.

Finally, "all these things the Son has,"[138] but by the gift of the Father; which he has expressed very strongly in this: since "the Son has life from himself,"[139] he says, but added: "The Father has given him to have life from himself." He is therefore the true image and he has an identical existence in all things, but by the gift of the Father. Therefore, Father and Son are *homoousion* (consubstantial), but by the gift of the Father.

Indeed, from what we have called the Father: "to be," "to live," "to understand," there is begotten existence as life and knowledge.[140] And this is the form of God, this is the Son. But since the Son is in the Father, there is one whole, God acting within, working within, relating with himself, enjoying himself, being in himself the source and the fullness of all. (31) But since, as we have demonstrated, knowledge necessarily in virtue of its own power in turning inward upon itself has understood itself, thus becoming in a way twofold—interior and exterior so to speak—the Son has been begotten from the existence of the Father. For existence is knowledge which is also life.[141] Therefore, God is manifest and exists from God. And since in anyone of the three are the three joined together, "to be," "to live," "to understand," when knowledge has begotten knowledge, the Son has been begotten, and "The Son has all that the Father has,"[142] and he has it from the Father.

B. THE SON IS *LOGOS*

Likewise, since these Three are those through whom all things are created—for all existents receive their own "to be," their own "to

---

137 Cf. 1 Cor 1.24.
138 Cf. Jn 16.15; Mt 11. 27.
139 Jn 5.26.
140 Cf. *adv. Ar.* IV 26,4–7; IV 28,2–3.
141 Cf. *adv. Ar.* IV 28,11–22; IV 29,3–12.
142 Cf. Mt 11.27; Jn 16.15.

live," their own "to understand"—the Son, since he is all these, indeed, as image of the Father, and is action in action, that is, so that he communicates them to others, according to the nature of the existents, it follows necessarily that he is for all and for the ensemble of the whole, the *Logos,* that is, the strength and the power through which "to be" comes forth so that there may be existents, the *Logos* "through whom" God has made and makes "all things," and "without whom nothing was made."[143] Some call this "active movement, active word, creative reason,"[144] Since nevertheless, although he acts through the Father, there is in him the Fatherly power, he acts of himself. That is why he uses many expressions such that, although what he does is his own, nevertheless he refers all that he does to the Father, as: "The Father has sent me," and "I do not my will, but that of the Father."[145] And a thousand others of this kind. Let us consider, however, this passage where we shall find him as though acting through himself as from his own spontaneity: "He did not consider being equal to God a robbery."[146] And likewise: "He emptied himself, taking the form of a servant." he who had the form of a master. All this characterizes one acting by his own will. But it may be held that he is acting although the Father is also acting in him, as in these statements: "I give life for eternity,"[147] and "I am the door, I am the life, I am the truth";[148] likewise: "For just as the Father raises the dead and vivifies them, so also the Son vivifies those whom he wills."[149]

This true, this manifold and in all respects the truest knowledge establishes both that the Son is in the Father and that the Father is in the Son, and yet as different as they are, the two are nevertheless one. But since the Father is one reality, the Son another, indeed, since the Father is the source of the Son, the Son is like a river[150] that flows from the source—but in the source the water remains and

---

143 Jn 1.3.
144 These are the names of the Stoic *logos*; cf. Seneca, *Epistulae* 65.12.
145 Jn 6.38.
146 Phil 2.6–7.
147 Jn 10.28.
148 Jn 10.7; Jn 14.6.
149 Jn 5.21.
150 This descent of the river of the *Logos* was described in 11,7–20. It is reminiscent of the emergence of the river of ideas from the paternal

is in repose, pure, unpolluted, without appearance of springing forth, invisibly replenishing its fullness; likewise as a river, with more apparent movement, flowing through various places, is altered and changed in some way by the nature of the terrain through which it cuts the course, so the Son himself, while dwelling always pure, impassible and unsullied, in his own water and substance which is that of the Father, yet because of the difference in the regions and places he traverses, above the skies, in the skies, under the skies, sometimes frothes in breaking upon the rocks which are like certain kinds of souls opposing him, sometimes peacefully floating, flowing among the plains—it follows therefore that the Son is passible not in his substance but in his action and operation. For when he was accomplishing the mystery of his coming, he already endured passion: "so that he emptied himself," in order that he might take the character of "a servant."[151] So also with the rest of the mystery, in all these things there is act and there is operation, although in the first act[152] of his existence also, as we have taught in many books, he came forth by a passion of withdrawal from the Father;[153] whence there followed darkness, that is, matter,[154] which was not created. But this we shall treat more fully elsewhere.

(32) Now what has been established, what has been proven? God is Father, the Son is God; they are *homoousion* (consubstantial); and yet the Father exists in his own substance, and the Son, although in this same substance of the Father, is so as producing an act existing for himself so that he experiences passions in the act. The Son never is, never was, never will be separated from his Father for eternity; by his own action, he is at once, since such is the nature of acting, both with his Father and in his Father and outside his Father; that is why it is said that he is at once within and without when he acts, because

---

source found in the "Chaldaean Oracles" (W. Kroll, *De oraculis Chaldaicis*, 23–24); for example, the ideas dash themselves upon the bodies of the world as upon rocks.

151 Cf. Phil 2.7.

152 Cf. *adv. Ar.* I 51,32.

153 Not only in his salvific act but in his substantial act the Son in some way is distinguished from the Father. The opposite was said in I 22,51–55 and will be said in IV 32,4–5.

154 Matter results from the passive infinity provoked by life's vivifying motion. It has its necessary place as the ultimate of the series.

the act is given to him by the Father, since the Father himself is acting; we say that he himself acts and yet the Father does all through him; he is the *Logos,* the *Logos* of all things, of the universally universal, as of genera, of species, of individuals, the *Logos* which, since he is the *Logos* of all things, he is *Logos* of the incorporeal and *Logos* of corporeal things, so that they might exist according to the strength of their capacity to be.

C. THE INCARNATION; THE FORM, WHICH IS THE *LOGOS* AND THE SON, IS JESUS CHRIST

That is why also by the arrangement of the mystery, in most recent times, the *Logos,* because he is *Logos* of all existents, after the Holy Spirit had overshadowed the Virgin Mary, was incarnate, this one whom we have shown above[155] to be Son, so that he might be in the body in the same way that the Holy Spirit is in us, not wholly—for as God he is everywhere—but according to a part of himself. For in all divine things the part is always the same as the whole; as in the soul in bodies, as virtue and learning in minds, or the sun and its light in eyes.

But that the *Logos* himself, as we have shown,[156] the very same one who is the Son, was in the body is affirmed by all the Gospels, by every apostle, by all the prophets. When they foretold that Christ would come, they foretold that he would come in the flesh, since they say that already before being in the flesh, he was seen, having appeared, for example, to Abraham, to Jacob; and when he himself was in the flesh, he said: "Abraham has seen my day and rejoiced."[157] And the Apostle in that sacred passage full of mysteries, declares especially that the Son of God existed before flesh and that he afterwards took flesh: "Have this mind in you which was also in Christ Jesus, who though he was in the form of God,"[158] Certainly this was before he was in the flesh. Therefore he indeed existed before being in the flesh. What were his quality and his grandeur? The "form," he says, "of God."[159] What is this? The "form" is

---

155 Cf. *adv. Ar.* IV 31,12–14.
156 Cf. *adv. Ar.* IV 31, 12–14; IV 32,16.
157 Jn 8.56.
158 Phil 2.5–6.
159 Phil 2.6.

identical to the Father. What is the "form"? That in which the
Father is contemplated. "Whoever has seen me, has seen also the
Father."[160] Certainly, this was not insofar as he was visible, but insofar as he is himself, God, divine substance, *Logos,* life; this, therefore, he was before taking flesh. For what does Paul add? "He did
not think it robbery that he was equal to God."[161] Therefore, he is
thinking about himself and about God. He brings it about that he is
not equal to God. Therefore, he was equal. What next does he add?
"But he emptied himself." What "did he empty" or whence, if he
was not? He adds to this: "And he took also the form of a servant;
he was made to the likeness of men and was found as a man in exterior aspect; he humbled himself, being made obedient even unto
death, but the death of the cross."[162] What then in every part of
this text does not declare that Jesus Christ is Son of God? For it was
said thus: "God sent his Son,"[163] and, having been sent, he did all
things by the choice of his power and of his will, so that he did not
will to be "equal," so that "he emptied himself," so that "he took
the form of a servant." There existed therefore the one who was
"the form of God." He existed, therefore, the one who "emptied
himself." But this is Jesus himself who "took the image of a servant"
and "was found as man," who "was obedient even unto death"—
and that Jesus Christ might be more fully designated—even "unto
the death of the cross."[164]

(33) These things for men who are also believers have been sufficiently proven: the Son existed before being in the flesh; and it is
the same Son who was in the flesh, the one "begotten before all
ages,"[165] the one who "ascended into heaven and descended from
it,"[166] the one who is "for us the bread from heaven,"[167] who in
the flesh said: "Father, give back to me my glory that I had with
you,"[168] certainly above the heavens and before being in the flesh,

---

160 Jn 14.9.
161 Phil 2.6.
162 Phil 2.7–8.
163 Gal 4.4.
164 Cf. Phil 2.6–7.
165 Sir 1.1.
166 Cf. Jn 3.13.
167 Jn 6.32.
168 Jn 17.5.

the one who is the *Logos*, the *Logos* who "was in the principle,"[169] the *Logos* who "was with God," the *Logos* who is God, the *Logos* "through whom all things have been made and without whom was made nothing,"[170] the *Logos* who "enlightens man coming into this world,"[171] the *Logos* who "was made flesh,"[172] You have heard that the *Logos* was "in the principle," you have heard that the *Logos* himself "was made flesh,"[173] hear then that this is the Son of God himself and that he is begotten from the Father, so that there is, as we said above,[174] a begetting. The evangelist says: "No one has ever seen God, except the only begotten Son who is in the bosom of the Father";[175] but we will express better by the word core (*gremio*) what the Greeks call *en kolpō*, that is, in the bosom. But this word or the other signifies both that the Son was begotten, that is, that he is exterior, and yet that he is with the Father, since it was said: "The one who is in the bosom of the Father."[176] By means of all the Scriptures, the diligent and faithful seeker will understand that these things are so.

As to the Holy Spirit, we have already set forth in many books that he is Jesus Christ himself but in another mode, Jesus Christ hidden, interior, dialoguing with souls, teaching these things and giving these insights; he has been begotten by the Father through the mediation of Christ and in Christ since Christ is the only begotten Son.[177] We have explained this in many books and it is quite clear that we have proved it by many examples.

III. CONCLUSION: THE CONSUBSTANTIAL TRINITY[178]

In this way and by this understanding, just as God the Father is *homoousion* (consubstantial) with the Son and the Son, because he

---

169 Jn 1.1.
170 Jn 1.3.
171 Jn 1.9.
172 Jn 1.14.
173 Cf Jn 1.1; 1.14.
174 Cf. *adv. Ar.* IV 28,1–29.23.
175 Jn 1.18.
176 Cf. Jn 1.18.
177 Cf. *adv. Ar.* III 8,25 ff.; III 14,1–17; IV 16,1–18,44.
178 In these final three paragraphs Victorinus states that the Holy Spirit is

himself is life, is consubstantial with the Father, but because Christ is knowledge, Christ and the Holy Spirit must be understood as *homoousion* (consubstantial). That is why, if the Son is joined to the Father and understood as identical with the Holy Spirit—identity of the same kind as that of the Son with the Father and yet such that, although the Father and Son are one, yet the Father exists as Father, the Son also as Son, each one through his own existence, but both have one and the same substance, so Christ and the Holy Spirit, although both are one, yet exist each one through his own existence, Christ through his, the Holy Spirit through his existence, but both are one substance—it results from this that all, that is, the whole Trinity, in one same way, the Father united with the Son, and the Son united with the Holy Spirit, and, for that reason, the Father united with the Holy Spirit through Christ, and, indeed, existing as individuals, the whole Trinity is one; and there exists this *homoousios* (consubstantial), since there is, for them all, together and from eternity, one and the same substance.

This is our salvation, this is our liberation, this is the plentiful salvation of the whole man: to believe thus in God the Father almighty, thus in Jesus Christ the Son, thus in the Holy Spirit. Amen.

---

in Christ as Christ is in the Father. This double dyad has been explained throughout Book III. Here, faithful to the vocabulary he has respected throughout Book IV, Victorinus distinguishes common substance *(substantia)* from proper existence *(existentia)* [in *ad Cand.* 31.8, from action *(actio)*, in *adv. Ar.* III 9.3, from subsistences *(subsistentiae)*], this existence being "to be" accompanied by a determination, that is, having at once more concrete content and intelligible content than the substance which is pure "to be." Cf. II 4,23 ff. Christ is the "mean" in the motion of procession; the Holy Spirit is the "mean" in the motion of return, conversion. The book fittingly ends with the translation of the *homoousion* according to its two aspects: all at once *(simul)* and the same *(eadem)*; cf. II 11,5–6.

THE NECESSITY OF ACCEPTING THE *HOMOOUSION*[1]

I. ORTHODOX DOGMA AND THE
HOMOOUSION (CONSUBSTANTIAL)

AM ASTONISHED that despite the unity in our understanding,[2] we continue our contest. We all think rightly, and yet we are not united. I shall express, therefore, the whole mystery, the words, the opinions, the ideas of all, in a brief statement, so that we can expel Arius.

The Greeks, those called Hellenes or pagans profess a great number of gods, the Jews or Hebrews only one God. As for us, since truth and grace have come with the fulfilment of time, against the pagans we profess only one God, and against the Jews, a Father and a Son. Thus in speaking of these two, Father and Son, but holding fast to one God, we reject each of these religions because of that aspect by which they are mutually opposed. And indeed the pagans by gross error have called both the elements and their own nourishment, gods. The Jews because of error deny the Christ of flesh whom they otherwise confess. Our dogma because it has taught truth and corrected error must therefore be approved.

This dogma will be more easily understood if the force of the word *homoousion* (consubstantial) used by the ancients is well understood. And I wish no one to be misled when I apply this word only to the Father and the Son; for the Holy Spirit is also both from

---

1 The plan of this treatise is like that of *adv. Ar.* II. It is a rather straightforward summary of his previous teaching. Victorinus asserts that orthodox trinitarian doctrine opposes the errors of paganism and of Judaism, and that the word *homoousion* is the best expression of orthodox dogma. Séjourné (DTC 15.2909) sees many of these arguments borrowed from Phoebadius of Agen, *Liber contra Arianos,* published in 358 against the second formula of Sirmium 357.

2 Although this book does summarize the four books *Against Arius,* it responds to a new situation: the efforts of reunification in the west 362–63. See above, Introd., sects. 83–5.

the Father and in the Son. However, this manner of reasoning will especially prevail against Arians and heretics.

II. DEFENSE OF *OUSIA* (SUBSTANCE) AND OF *HOMOOUSION* (CONSUBSTANTIAL)

1. Substantia

A. THE REALITY: GOD AND CHRIST HAVE ONE SUBSTANCE.

Do we confess that God is? That is so. Do we confess that Christ is? Yes. I speak of "to be" in this way: God is, Christ is. But what is this "to be"? It is to be light, to be Spirit, to be God, to be *Logos*. Therefore, we confess these, no one denies these.

B. THE NAME: *SUBSTANTIA* IS IN SCRIPTURE

The Greeks call "to be" *ousian* (substance) or *hupostasin*[3] (hypostasis); we call it in Latin by one term: substance; and a few Greeks use *ousian* (substance) and rarely; all use *hupostasin* (hypostasis). Certainly one differs from the other, but for the moment let us omit this.

The divine Scripture has often used *hupostasin* (hypostasis) in Greek, substance in Latin. And it has said of the substance of God in the prophet Jeremiah: "That if they had stood in the substance of the Lord they would have seen my word."[4] But what is it: "to stand in the substance"? To know the substance of God, which is "true light," which is infinite Spirit.[5] If they had known that, they would have known the *Logos* of the Lord, that is, "they would have seen the word"[6] of the Lord. And shortly after, the same Jeremiah uses the same words.

David says: "And my substance is in the lower regions of the

---

3 In Scripture "hypostasis" is used more than "substance."
4 Jer 23.18.
5 Cf. *adv. Ar.* I 47,3; II 2,24.
6 Cf. Jer 23.18.

earth."[7] He speaks also of God and says "substance." And it is clear what this is.

The Apostle says to the Hebrews: "He who is the character of his substance."[8] He said that Christ is the character of the substance of God. There are many other examples. But what is the point of all this? To show that the word substance is in Scripture and is used of the substance of God.

2. Homoousion

A. THE REALITY

THE NOTION CAN BE DEDUCED FROM: *DEUM DE DEO*

But the substance of God is light, spirit, God. Likewise the substance of Christ is *Logos,* light, Christ. Hence we all truly say that Christ is "true light from true light," "God from God." It is therefore rightly said that Christ is of the same substance, that is, *homoousion* (consubstantial). You therefore confess *homoousion* (consubstantial), when you say: "Light from light, God from God."[9] Why do you oppose it?

B. THE NAME: TWO MEANINGS OF THE WORD

Besides, the Greek *homo* is such that when joined to a word it at one time signifies "of the same reality" and at another time signifies "together with the reality." The reality here is, for example, the species, which in Greek is called *eidos.* If this *homo* and *eidos* are joined together it signifies also: "of the same species," just as *homōnymon* signifies "of the same name." Therefore when *homo* is joined to *ousian,* it becomes *homoousion,* that is, "of the same *ousia,*" that is, substance. From this is condemned Arius who said that Christ comes "from nothing".[10]

Likewise we have said that *homo* also signifies *homou,* and joined

---

7 Ps 138(139).15.
8 Heb 1.3.
9 Cf. *adv. Ar.* I 47,3; II 2,22–26.
10 Cf. *adv. Ar.* I 23,5–6; I 28,37.

to any reality that it says nothing other than to be together with the reality, for example, *homoēlikēs* or contemporaneous, and *homotrophous* from *homou* and *traphentas* which means nourished together. Therefore, *homoousion* is simultaneously substantial or consubstantial. Observe that we also have the terms in Latin. Since this is the case, from this also there is condemned Arius who said: "There was a time when he was not." And indeed if we say: "Always Father, always Son," and if the *Logos* was "in the *principle,*" and the *Logos* was "with God,"[11] since the principle is without beginning and without time, God always was, the *Logos* always was, always the Father, always the Son. If this is so, there is excluded, as I said, this formula: "There was a time when he was not." Observe then that in both its meanings *homoousion* (consubstantial) stands opposed to the entire heresy of Arius.

III. REPLY TO THE OBJECTIONS OF ADVERSARIES

A. DOES THE NOTION OF THE BEGETTING OF GOD IMPLY SOMETHING MATERIAL?

(3) If all these things are true, accept *homoousion* (consubstantial). For if you refuse it, you cannot hide that you are a new Arius. But as is clear from your conciliar acts you certainly confess that Christ is "God from God, light from light,"[12] but also that he is made, and thus born not from the substance of God but from nothing. And you state that this was heard from others through arguments rather than coming from your own declarations. And, indeed, what arguments? O God, O Christ, help us! "If Christ is born of God, then God is divided or diminished." These are the indignities or others like them which you so often offer, as though God were corporeal, as though he were matter. For such things can have division or diminishment.

But we have already said many things on this subject:[13] how in divine things, in the incorporeal and above all in the soul, in the

---

11 Cf. Jn 1.1.
12 Cf. *de hom. rec.* 2,17–18.
13 This paragraph borrows philosophical fragments (Group III) which assert the immobile begetting of God; cf. Hadot, PV II 48.

Spirit, in the mind, and still more in God there can be movement or generation.[14] Indeed, things absolutely perfect can be neither increased nor decreased, above all in substance. For since these things are *autogona* (self-begotten) and *autodunama* (self-powered), whatever they produce is of their own nature, and on high begetting is not begetting by change, nor is there any passion on high, not even any appearance of passion—I speak of God, of the Spirit.

And besides, why do you constrain us with these reasonings of yours to avow that Christ was born from nothing? Will your blasphemy be lessened because you think these very things? Or why is your profession not open, if you think the same? But do you not see that you say contradictory things? For you say: "God from God, light from light." Is this from nothing when you name the source? Therefore, Christ is from God, he is not, therefore, from nothing, he is from light, not from nothing. For "from God" signifies from God's substance. Indeed, "by God" signifies something different. Indeed, all is by God, but Christ alone is from God. Truly, Christ himself is *Logos* or the *Logos* is Christ.

(4) Finally, search out what the *Logos* is and you will find that the *Logos* cannot be from nothing.

B. IS THE MODE OF BEGETTING UNKNOWABLE?

But they mislead you, they, I say, who not understanding the manner of begetting say: "Who can declare the birth of the Lord"?[15] First, "who" or still more "no one"[16] do indeed seem to signify men. But the Holy Spirit can declare and explain this manner of begetting. That is why we ourselves with the permission of God the Father and of Jesus Christ our Lord have set it forth.[17] Certainly it is not a hopeless enterprise, but we have described it as by a miracle.

Next, supposing that the manner of begetting is unknown, we speak of substance when we say that the Father and Son are *homo-*

---

14 Cf. *ad Cand.* 30,1–26; *adv. Ar.* I 4,1–18; I 43,34–43; I 57,19–30; III 2,12–54; IV 21,19–25.
15 Is 53.8.
16 Cf. Is 53.8.
17 Cf. *adv. Ar.* IV 28,1–29,23; I 57,7–58,14.

ousion (consubstantial). But how God is Father and how the *Logos* is Son is known with difficulty. But for the moment this is not, it seems to me, in question. For we must confess that the Son is from the substance of the Father and then seek how he is Son, which is truly difficult and has been treated by us elsewhere.[18]

IV. CONCLUSION: PROPOSAL OF THE FORMULA: *DEUM IN DEO, LUMEN IN LUMINE*

Then, for a moment, certainly with regard to *homoousion* (consubstantial), and to satisfy you (for we desire peace with all men), we know how to translate it: *homoousion* signifies primarily consubstantial, or simultaneously substantial.[19] Secondly, if we say: "God from God, light from light" (but the Father is light, and likewise the Son is light), since we affirm also that in the Father is the Son and the Father is in the Son, we affirm also "God in God, light in light," because we rightly say: "God from God, light from light," and this will be the true and full *homoousion* (consubstantial). Do you hesitate? What if this also is in Scripture? To contradict it is blasphemy. David in the thirty-fifth psalm: "For he is the fountain of life, and in your light we shall see the light."[20] Confess now this formula and the *homoousion* (consubstantial)!

Similarly, this objection can be offered also against anyone who affirms a similar substance. For we affirm the same and cosubstance. Certainly it was said in Isaiah: "There is no God before you; and after you, there is no God like unto you."[21] And David: "What God will be similar to you?"[22] These texts are against those who affirm a similar substance, but there are besides many other points that I have developed more fully and more abundantly in refuting the treatises that they themselves have published.[23] For we shall not

---

18 Cf. *de hom. rec.* 4,7.
19 I have adopted the new conjecture in CSEL; "primarily" *(primum)* is omitted between *vel* and *simul* which takes the second phrase explanatory of the first. A longer explanation of this can be found in *De hom. rec.* 2,20–39.
20 Ps 35(36).10.
21 Is 43.10.
22 Ps 34(35).10.
23 This is an allusion to Basil of Ancyra's letter; cf. Hadot, MV 263–71. This

speak of those who affirm a dissimilar substance[24] nor of those who take for Patripassians those who develop the ideas that we are setting forth. All those, indeed, and other heretics have been easily refuted in a larger treatise.[25]

O God the Father and God the Lord Jesus Christ, be with us, so that in thy people there shall be *homonoia* (concord) through the *homoousion* (consubstantial). Amen.

---

is directed against the Homoiousians; cf. *adv. Ar.* II 2,20–49. Victorinus therefore affirms that this treatise IA has been written in answer to the homoiousian libels; cf. I 28,8–32,15.

24 This is the only time Victorinus mentions the Anomoeans, those extreme Fourth-Century Arians who taught that the Son was totally unlike the Father. They were condemned not only by the orthodox party but also by the Homoiousians.

25 Cf. *adv. Ar.* IA.

HYMNS

FIRST HYMN[1]

RUE LIGHT, ASSIST US,   O God the Father
all powerful!
Light of light, assist us, mystery and power of God![2]
Holy Spirit, assist us, the bond between Father
and Son!
In repose[3] you are Father, in your procession,[4] Son,
And binding[5] all in One, you are the Holy Spirit.

O God, you are the First One,[6] the One come forth from itself,
the One before the One.[7]

---

1 The general structure of this hymn is close to that of *adv. Ar.* Book III, where the divine triad is shown to be constituted of two dyads: the One (Father-Son) and the One-Many (Son-Spirit). The hymn is Christocentric. It is not impossible that the hymns were composed before the theological treatises; cf. Hadot, MV 259, n.24 and 280.

2 Cf. Rom 1.16; 1 Cor 1.24; Eph 3.9.

3 W. Theiler, *Die chaldäischen Orakel,* p. 15, n. 3 compares the present passage with Synesius, *Hymn* 9.63.

4 This is one of Victorinus's constant themes, namely, the opposition between the Father as repose or hidden motion and the Son as externalized motion; cf. *ad Cand.* 21,5; *adv. Ar.* I 4,15; I 34, 9–12; I 42,2–11; III 2,33; IV 8,26–27.

5 Victorinus emphasizes here the binding or sanctifying role of the Holy Spirit. He is the *copula* as the movement of knowledge or return to the Father, linking Son to Father, and all others as well. Yet the Son is the "mean" between Father and Holy Spirit because the Son communicates to the Holy Spirit what he receives from the Father.

6 For Victorinus the three Ones, deriving from the Neo-pythagorean tradition, represent the Father, the Son and the World since the second dyad comprises the Son and the Holy Spirit. On this tradition of the three ones, cf. E. Dodds, "The *Parmenides* of Plato and the Origin of the Neoplatonic 'One' " *Classical Quarterly* 22 (1928) 136–9.

7 This expression, according to *adv. Ar.* III 1,28 and IV 19,11 can signify either that the Father is prior to the second One or that he is prior to all determination, even that of "one." The first sense corresponds to a well-established Neo-pythagorean tradition; cf. A. Festugière, 23 ff. The second is witnessed to by the anonymous commentary on the *Parmenides,* Kroll,

You precede all plurality, known even though limitless.
In you no plurality, for no plurality even proceeds from you.
This plurality, indeed, the One born of you begets rather
                than possesses.
Without measure is the Father then, but the Son is both measured
                and measureless.
You yourself, O Father, are One, and One is the Son whom
                you beget.

One also what your Son begets: the One whether Multiple or Whole,
For he is the seed of the *ontos* (existence) for all things.
But you are the interior power of this seed;
In this seed, from this seed are born all things which the
                "Power of God" produces;
Towards this seed return[8] again all those things it has begotten.

Christ therefore does all things, he who is the whole
                "Power of God."[9]
For Christ as movement[10] in repose is none other than
                the God Supreme.
But when he is movement in movement, Christ is the
                "Wisdom and Power" of God
In no way distant from the substance, for movement is
                very substance.
And because this movement is in God and is very God,
It is called "God from God," born, however, because it is movement
—For every movement is born—and since God and the movement
Of God are one, God and the movement of God are one same God.
Yet the movement of God is also movement itself.
But as movement of God, this movement has God within it, and
Again, God has movement in himself since this movement is

"Ein neuplatonischer Parmenidescommentar," 603 and this text is cited in
adv. Ar. IV 23,17–18.

8 The return of all things to God is a concern of Victorinus and this return to
the original seed is achieved through spiritualization, the proper work of
the Holy Spirit.

9 After stressing the identity of movement and substance, Victorinus asserts
that the Father's movement is Christ.

10 1 Cor 1.24.

movement of God.

Thus in the Son is the Father and in the Father, the Son himself.

There are therefore two singulars[11] since they are always within
each other,

For both therefore, one is the power, one is the substance;

But by the gift of the Father the Son is this unique substance.

Indeed "to be" is prior; to move is later,

Not that any time is there, but among divine things the order
is power.[12]

For "to be" precedes self-movement, prior not in time but in reality.

This "to be" in God the learned call substance.[13]

Here, however, movement has arisen; for substance
begets movement,

And can the begetting of substance be other than substance?

Therefore movement is from the Father. The Son then is the same
substance as the Father.

This is he whom the Greeks have called *Logos,* God himself
within the Father,

Destined to be the cause of the birth and appearance of all things.

For "without him," "nothing" has been created, "through him"[14]
all was created.

If Christ is this *Logos,* if this *Logos* is life,

The *Logos* is begotten from the Father. For he is the
"living God."[15]

So, God being substance and God being life by his substance,
in which,

Since the begotten Son is also life, the *Logos* and God
are one substance.

---

11 Victorinus uses *singuli* (singulars) to refer to hypostases; cf. *adv. Ar.* I
49,5; 63,21; II 3,40; III 4,37; 9,7; 10,19; IV 10,14; 21,27; 33,39; *hymn.*
I 77.

12 "Power" has a very special meaning here for Victorinus. It means the
characteristic and therefore predominating power according to the doctrine
of Victorinus for whom the "proper name" of each "singular" in the
Trinity is drawn from the predominant power.

13 This is directed against the Homoeans who refused to use "substance" in
reference to God.

14 Cf. Jn 1.1–3.

15 Cf. Jn 6.57.

Hence never separated and yet always distinct,
The one sent is equal to the one who sends and yet
abides as source,
While the one sent, the Son, runs always as a river,[16]
sowing life.
Hence both are one substance, God the source, Son, the river.

But because in divine things the substance is the same as life,
Life itself is wisdom itself, just as "to be" precedes
Simple and primary "to live" within it,
So "understanding and wise" is present whenever "to live" precedes,
Not that one of them really precedes the other or is totally other.
But so that by the progression of acts there are thrice a
triple singularity.

Christ[17] is therefore the universal act: act when he proceeds as Son;
He is act as life by which all things proceed and are created.
The same Christ becomes teacher and master, likewise the
perfecting Spirit,
Leading all to their end, infusing laws[18] of wisdom in souls sown
through the ages.
But since Christ is wisdom,[19] likewise Christ as Son proceeding
from the Father
Reveals the Father, and the Spirit reveals Christ.
Hence Christ has all from the Father,[20] hence the Spirit has all
from Christ.

---

16 The metaphor of the source and the river helps to show the identity and
distinction of the Son, river of life, from the Father, source of life, cf. *adv.
Ar.* I 47,20 and IV 31,35. Notice the passage here from the dyad to the
triad; just as substance is simultaneously life, so life, is simultaneously
knowledge. In the unit of one movement are present both Christ and the
Holy Spirit; the three are in each one, and the Trinity is therefore an
ennead (nine).

17 The Christocentric character of the hymn is strong here; Christ is "act"
hidden in the Father, "act" manifested in himself, and "act" once again
hidden in the Holy Spirit.

18 There are two notions here derived from Plato's *Timaeus*, namely, the
sowing of souls in time, and the receiving of the laws of wisdom.

19 On Christ as "wisdom" a name he shares with the Holy Spirit, cf. *adv. Ar.*
I 2,19–42; III 10,5; IV 18,37; *hymn.* III 196-8.

20 Cf. Jn 16.15.

Thus Christ is mediation between the Father and his other Self,
The Spirit, filling the role of Father in giving "to be" to all,
And for all things, this "to be" is "life" and this is
     "what was made"[21] in Christ.
And because he unites and saves all and reveals the true God,
The Holy Spirit is uniting those who follow Christ, who are reborn
    in Christ.

Christ is therefore all, hence Christ is mystery.[22]
Through him, all things, in him, all things, for him, all things![23]
He himself is the Whole whose depth is the Father,
By his procession, he is length and width of the Father.
Hence Christ appearing in time to teach[24] the depth and, indeed,
     the mystery.[25]
And Christ hiding within, teaching interiorly, is the Holy Spirit.

All therefore are one in the Spirit, all one in Light.[26]
Hence for each the substance is real,[27] for the Three it is one,
Proceeding from the Father to the Son, returning to the Father
    in the Spirit,
For the Three exist as singulars, and the three singulars
    are in each.
This is the Blessed Trinity, this blessed unity.

---

21 Cf. Jn 1.3–4.

22 Cf. Eph 3.9.

23 The Son is the whole economy; in the role of Father, he gives being, he is himself the life of all beings, and as Holy Spirit he unites all things.

24 I have accepted the CSEL reading of *ad* instead of *id* and *docendum* instead of *doctum* which alters the tense to a clearer meaning. A certain corruption of the text had been recognized by Hadot, TTT 1070.

25 A certain pan-Christism is striking here: Father and Holy Spirit are defined in relation to Christ. The Son's depth is the Father; the Father's width and length are the Son; cf. Eph 3.10.

26 Cf. Eph 3.18.

27 This is the precise formula of orthodoxy, namely, the real *existence* of each hypostasis and the *unity* of substance.

SECOND HYMN[1]

HAVE MERCY LORD! Have mercy Christ!
    Have mercy Lord
    For I have believed in thee,
    Have mercy Lord
    Because through thy mercy I have known thee.

Have mercy Lord! Have mercy Christ!
    Thou art the *Logos* of my spirit!
    Thou art the *Logos* of my soul!
    Thou art the *Logos* of my flesh!

Have mercy Lord! Have mercy Christ!
    God lives,[2]
    And God lives forever,
    And because before him was nothing, God lives from himself.[3]

Have mercy Lord! Have mercy Christ!
    Christ lives,
    And because God gave begetting to him, Christ lives
            from himself,[4]
    Because he lives from himself, Christ lives always.

---

1 The first invocation is addressed to the three divine persons in the liturgical manner of *Kyrie eleison,* and should, therefore, be studied in any documentary history of this prayer. Just as the first hymn was linked to Book III, this second hymn is close to Book IV, and there are many parallels between this hymn and the hymns of Synesius. In his work, PV I 463–68, Hadot names Prophyry as their common source. In his fine monograph Hadot speaks of this hymn as a poem (MV 281) composed immediately after Victorinus's conversion and baptism as his personal prayer. Cf. *hymn.* II 38.

2 The tone becomes didactic after the invocation as happened also in *hymn.* I. If *hymn.* I 7–16 described the three Ones (Father, Son, and World), *hymn.* II describes the three lives: the Father who lives through himself eternally, the Son who lives through himself eternally by the Father's gift, finally the living soul in the image of the first two. This doctrine has issued from the encounter between Jn 5.26 and the Platonic theory (*Phaedrus* 246C) concerning the self-moving character of the soul; cf. *adv. Ar.* I 27, 26; I 63 and IV 13,5.

3 Cf. Jn 5.26.

4 Cf. Jn 5.26.

Have mercy Lord! Have mercy Christ!
>   Because God lives and God lives forever,
>   Hence life was born eternal,
>   But eternal life is Christ the Son of God.

Have mercy Lord! Have mercy Christ!
>   But if the Father lives from himself,
>   And by the Father's begetting, the Son lives from himself
>   As consubstantial with the Father, the Son lives forever.

Have mercy Lord! Have mercy Christ!
>   O God, Thou hast given me a soul;
>   But the soul is image of life because the soul lives.
>   Let my soul also live eternally.[5]

Have mercy Lord! Have mercy Christ!
>   If to your likeness God the Father
>   And to the image[6] of the Son I was made man[7]
>   Created for time, may I live because the Son knew me.

Have mercy Lord! Have mercy Christ!
>   I have loved the world[8] because you made the world;[9]

---

5 The hymnal prayer based on the soul's essential reality in the image and likeness of eternal life begs the realization of this essence, i.e. life eternal.

6 In all the texts which treat of Gn 1.26 and here, "according to the image" *(ad imaginem)* is interpreted as the soul's relation to the image of God who is the Son or Life. "According to the likeness" *(ad similitudinem)* is related to the order of quality, of moral perfection and not of substance; Cf. *adv. Ar.* I 20,52; I 63,28; *adv. Ar.* I 62–64. "In the likeness of the Father" is therefore a new formula for Victorinus, perhaps inspired by Mt 5.48: "Be ye perfect as your heavenly Father."

7 Cf. Gn 1.26.

8 Note the autobiographical character: the soul's destiny is a drama in three acts: preexistence, fall, return; cf. Augustine, *Confessions* 10.27.38.

9 "World" in this stanza has a Johannine overtone; cf. Jn 15.19; 17.14; 1 Jn 2.15; it is at once the visible world and the evil in the world. Cf. R. Brown, J. Fitzmyer, R. Murphy (eds.), *The Jerome Biblical Commentary* 2 (Englewood Cliffs 1968) 830–31. The soul, seeing in the world the work of God, the reflection of divine beauty, is drawn toward the world. But it falls prisoner there because the world contains a principle hostile to God and to those who are of God. When the soul receives the Spirit, it turns from the world to return to God. Cf. Victorinus, *in Eph.* 1.7 (1243 C).

I am detained in the world while the world hates
          thy creatures.
Now I hate the world, for I have now experienced the Spirit.

Have mercy Lord! Have mercy Christ!
          Help your fallen ones, Lord, help your penitents,
          Because by thy divine and holy judgment
          That I have sinned is mystery.

Have mercy Lord! Have mercy Christ!
          I know, O Lord, thy command,
          I know that my return[10] is written in my soul.
          I hasten, if thou commandest, to return, our Savior God.

Have mercy Lord! Have mercy Christ!
          Long do I fight back,[11] long do I resist my enemy,
          But I still have the flesh[12] in which there was victory over
               the devil,
          Which gave you great triumph,[13] and us the bulwark of faith.

Have mercy Lord! Have mercy Christ!
          Deep in my heart is the wish to depart from world and earth,
          But without thy support, too feeble are my wings[14] to

---

10 Victorinus speaks here of the soul's return because of its vocation for union with God, following a kind of law of the heart. Cf. Victorinus, *in Gal.* 4 (1178 C) and 4.26 (1186 B); Heb 4.11; Kroll, *De oraculis Chaldaicis,* 52; *see* Hadot, TTT 1074; Victorinus, *ad Cand.* 1,7; Augustine, *Soliloquies* 1.1.2 and 1.1.5.

11 This description of the soul's struggle with its body seems inspired by Rom 7.14–25. The Pauline and Neoplatonic spiritual experiences come together here; cf. Victorinus, *in Eph.* 1.4 (1240 A). Do these ideas derive from Porphyry's *De regressu animae?* The soul's powerlessness calls for a savior, and the Christian mystery of salvation is this paradox; it is in the flesh itself, the spirit's enemy, that the flesh is conquered. Cf. Col 2.15; *adv. Ar.* I 39,22; III 3,31; *in Gal.* 6.14 (1196 D) and 1.11 (1151 B).

12 Cf. Rom 7.14–25.

13 Cf. Col 2.15.

14 Victorinus connects the Pauline inefficacy of the soul to renounce sensible things with the loss of wings in Plato's *Phaedrus* 246C.

fulfil my wish,[15]
Give me the wings of faith[16] that I may fly to God on high.

Have mercy Lord! Have mercy Christ!
Now I seek the gates[17] which the Holy Spirit opens,
Witnessing to Christ[18]
And teaching what the world is.

Have mercy Lord! Have mercy Christ!
You who represent God the Father from whom
you are begotten,
Give me the keys of heaven[19] and subdue the devil in me,
That I may rest in the abode of light, saved by thy grace.

---

15 Cf. Rom 7.18.
16 Just as the soul without wings cannot ascend, so, only with grace does the inefficacious desire become the living hope of salvation.
17 Christian sentiment here borrows its expression from the Neoplatonic description of the soul's ascent. The soul's way is the Milky Way, proceeding from the door of man (Cancer) to the door of the gods (Capricorn). Such is the description given by Macrobius, *In somnium Scipionis* 1.12, following Porphyry, *De antro nympharum* 28. The same images—door, key, throne of light—are in Synesius's *hymn* I. Victorinus has the Holy Spirit open the doors and Christ give the keys of heaven. The opening of the gates of heaven by the Spirit is entirely spiritual, that is the Holy Spirit reveals the vanity of the world and the divine character of Christ to the soul.
18 Cf. Jn 15.26; Jn 16.8.
19 Cf. Mt 16.19, and the keys of the kingdom.

THIRD HYMN[1]

GOD,
Lord,[2]
Holy Spirit,

> O Blessed Trinity.

Father,
Son,
Paraclete,

> O Blessed Trinity.

Giver,[3]
Minister,
Distributor,

> O Blessed Trinity.

Spirit of works,
Spirit of services,
Spirit of graces,

> O Blessed Trinity.

One principle
And one with the other
And always one with the other

> O Blessed Trinity.

---

1 There are two parts to this hymn: (1) an enumeration of the names and the
salvific functions of the Father, Son and Holy Spirit (1–108); (2) a more
systematic exposition of the relationships among the three based principal-
ly upon the substance, form, notion triad (140–71; 172–91; 192–220; 221–
51). The hymn ends with three stanzas devoted to the redemptive role of
Christ (252–69) and four stanzas of the final prayer (270–85). This hymn
presupposes knowledge of the dossier of Basil of Ancyra. Each aspect of
the above triad is at once proper and common, designating at once One of
the Three and each of the Three (whence the enneadic formula: 248–50).
The Holy Spirit's role is strongly marked. To the Son's cosmological and
vivifying function this hymn opposes the repairing or restoring action of
the Holy Spirit who leads creation back to the Father by reforming it. This
hymn seems to be contemporaneous with *adv. Ar.* III and IV.
2 Cf. 1 Cor 12.3–6.
3 Cf. 1 Cor 12.3–6.

God, because Father of substance and himself substance,
The Son and Spirit are substance,
But three times one same substance
                    O Blessed Trinity.

Perfect Father,
Perfect Son[4] of a perfect Father,
Perfect Holy Spirit of a perfect Son,
                    O Blessed Trinity.

Source,
River,
Overflow,

                    O Blessed Trinity.

In the Three,
A threefold action,
But only one,

                    O Blessed Trinity.

Existence,
Life,
Knowledge,

                    O Blessed Trinity.

Charity,[5]
Grace,
Communication,

                    O Blessed Trinity.

God is charity,
Christ is grace,
Holy Spirit is communication,
                    O Blessed Trinity.

---

4 Cf. the profession of faith at Antioch (341).
5 Cf. 2 Cor 13.13.

If there is charity,[6] there is grace,
If charity and grace, there is communication,
All therefore in each and One in Three
            O Blessed Trinity.

Hence the apostle Paul, divinely inspired, says:
            "The grace of our Lord Jesus Christ
And the charity of God
And the communication of the Holy Spirit be with you."
            O Blessed Trinity.

Unbegotten,
Only Begotten,
Begotten from the Begotten,
            O Blessed Trinity.

Begetter,
Begotten,
Begetting anew,[7]
            O Blessed Trinity.

True light,
True light from light,
True illumination,
            O Blessed Trinity.

Repose,
Progression,
Return,
            O Blessed Trinity.

Invisibly invisible,[8]

---

6 2 Cor 13.13.

7 The notion of a procession of the Holy Spirit distinct from the begetting of the Son is completely foreign to Victorinus. There is only one begetting, a unique motion with a two-fold function: Christ and the Holy Spirit; cf. *adv. Ar.* III 8,29.

8 The Holy Spirit no longer acts in the visible world but within souls to

Invisibly visible,
Visibly invisible,
        O Blessed Trinity.

All power,
All action,
All knowledge,
        O Blessed Trinity.

Impassibly impassible,
Passibly impassible,
Impassibly passible,
        O Blessed Trinity.

Seed,
Tree,
Fruit,
        O Blessed Trinity.

All from one,[9]
All through one,
All in one,
        O Blessed Trinity.

One, one simple, one and only, only one and always;
One, a second one, one from one, at once one and all;
One, uniting all, the working power of one,
So that all may become one,
        O Blessed Trinity.

Unbegotten from eternity,
Begotten from eternity,
Begotten so that all might be eternal,
        O Blessed Trinity.

---

whom he reveals the Son; he is Jesus hidden in souls; cf. *adv. Ar.* I 12,13–32.

9 We find echoed here Rom 11.36 and perhaps the profession of faith from the Synod of Antioch (341).

You command creation,
You create,
You recreate the created,
> O Blessed Trinity.

You, Father, are substance for all,[10]
You, Son, life,
You, Holy Spirit, salvation,[11]
> O Blessed Trinity.

Substance is life itself
Life itself is salvation[12] because it is eternal,
Therefore the Father is both Son and Holy Spirit,
> O Blessed Trinity.

You give "to be" to all,
Thou, Son, givest form,
Thou, Spirit, reform.[13]
> O Blessed Trinity.

Thou, God, art Father of the infinite and finite,
> O Blessed Trinity.

Thou, O Son, because thou art life, art infinite,
Because thou callest back life from the dead, thou art finite,
Thou also art Father of the infinite and finite,
> O Blessed Trinity.

---

10 For about 150 lines we have rather close reasoning. The two triads chiefly studied by Victorinus here are substance–life–salvation (109–34) and substance–form–notion (135–251), and again the enneadic framework is stressed.

11 "Salvation" here signifies a self-limitation of life by knowledge.

12 This stanza specifies the meaning of "salvation," that is, life is salvation because it is eternal, made thus by knowledge.

13 The identification of the Holy Spirit's proper gift of knowledge with "reformation" points to a source common to Victorinus and Augustine; cf. *De vera religione* 55.113.

Thou, also, Holy Spirit, art finite because thou art salvation,
And because thou retainest through the finite what is infinite.
Thou art Father of both the infinite and finite,
           O Blessed Trinity.

If then there is thrice the Fatherly unity,
And from you, O God, comes all paternity,[14]
One is God and all paternity,
           O Blessed Trinity.

You, O God, procreated[15] the *Logos,* thus God became Father,
And because the *Logos* himself was procreated by you, because you
              are in him, the *Logos* became God,
These two you joined as one by the Holy Spirit; therefore the simple
              and one became one in three, Spirit, *Logos,* God,
           O Blessed Trinity.

First *On* (Existent),
Second *On* (existent),
Third *On* (Existent),
Three, one and simple *On* (Existent),
           O Blessed Trinity.

The All-*On* (Existent) is substance,
The *On* (Existent) is formed substance,
Formed substance is known either to itself only, or to others or to
              itself and others,
           O Blessed Trinity.

God you are substance,
Son, you are form,
Spirit, you are knowledge,
           O Blessed Trinity.

---

14 Cf. Eph 3.15.
15 The word "create" is not used technically by Victorinus in opposition to
    "beget."

The First *On* (Existent),
O God, you are the true *On* (Existent),
Therefore, O God, you are the entire and total substance.
                    O Blessed Trinity.

The Second *On* (the Existent), the entire form is Christ,
But universal substance when universal is form;
Therefore since substance is form, Christ is also God,
                    O Blessed Trinity.

The Third *On* (Existent) is Holy Spirit; and Holy Spirit is
                    manifestation of all existence;[16]
But manifestation never manifests unless it is known; but to know
                    in divine things is the same as to possess, for
                    that knowledge is substance itself.
Therefore the Holy Spirit possesses God, possesses Christ whom
                    he manifests;
                    O Blessed Trinity.

O God, you are limitless, infinite, invisible, but to some limitless,
                    infinite, and to others invisible, to thyself limited,
                    finite, visible;
Hence, then, you also have form; therefore you are identical with
                    Logos because *Logos* is form;[17]
And because to you form is knowledge, but knowledge is
                    Holy Spirit, therefore you are God and *Logos*
                    and Holy Spirit.
                    O Blessed Trinity.

You, O Son, are visible for you are the universal form of things, for
                    when you give life to all, from life there
                    comes form;

---

16 If "existence" has a technical meaning here, the completed existence is
"substance"; cf. *adv. Ar.* I 30,21-26; existence becomes substance when it
is externalized in life and internalized in knowledge. But existence can here
also be an equivalent for "substance."

17 We find here the same affirmation of the form, of a *Logos,* of a knowledge
identified with being as in *adv. Ar.* IV 19-24.

But form is always in substance and all form is knowledge;
Therefore in substance you are God, in form, *Logos,* in
        knowledge, Holy Spirit;
        O Blessed Trinity.

You also O Holy Spirit are knowledge;
But all knowledge is knowledge of form and substance; therefore
        you know God and have the form of God;
Hence you are God and Son, O Holy Spirit;
        O Blessed Trinity.

O God you are "to be";
O Christ, you are "to be Spirit";
O Paraclete, your "to be" is to reveal what Spirit is;[18]
        O Blessed Trinity

Hence the Father sent Christ,
Christ sent the Paraclete,
That Christ might appear by the Paraclete,
That the Father might appear by Christ,
        O Blessed Trinity.

O God, you are substance[19] secret and hidden;
O God, you are form secret and hidden;
O God, you are knowledge secret and hidden;
Therefore, the *Proon* (Preexistent) of the *onta* (Existents),
        you are, O God
        O Blessed Trinity.

O *Logos,* you are the already public and manifest substance;
        and because public and manifest,[20] you are form,

---

18 This is based on the fact that to be spirit is to reveal oneself. As revelation, the Spirit is therefore the completion of the divine substance.
19 Although the same triad is here: substance–form–notion, there is now an insistence upon the opposition of the hidden and the revealed. The preexistent is the Existent yet hidden. Moreover, the form of the substance must itself be substance; cf. *adv. Ar.* I 53, 11–13.
20 Cf. Jn 1.18.

and because form of the Father, for yourself,
                    you are substance;
Therefore the Father is in you because the Father is substance;
                    but you are of identical substance,[21] for there
                    is not any other substance;
If therefore the *Logos* is manifest form, and form is substance
                    itself, if the manifest form and the manifest
                    substance are knowledge, you are also, O *Logos*,
                    both God and Holy Spirit;
                    O Blessed Trinity.

All knowledge is knowing; all knowing is substance, and knowing
                    itself is form;
You are therefore O Holy Spirit revealed form and
                    manifest substance;
But you are saving and rebegetting substance, not abiding or
                    begetting substance;
                    O Blessed Trinity.

One substance therefore is God, *Logos* and Spirit, dwelling in
                    three and existing thrice in all three;[22]
But this is both form and knowledge;
So every simple singularity is tripled;
                    O Blessed Trinity.

You, O God are unknown, you, O God, are incomprehensible;
But of the unknown and incomprehensible, there is a sort of form
                    without form;
Hence you are called *Proon* (Preexistent) rather than *On* (Existent),
                    more lack and repose, hence the form of knowledge
                    is that of inactive knowledge;
                    O Blessed Trinity.

---

21 This is directed against the Arians for whom the Son originates from
nothing.
22 Each of the three must be the Three to be total existent; their reality
requires their reciprocal implication, and so each must be simultaneously
substance, form, and notion. The Holy Spirit's salvific role as bond of the
universe (cf. *Hymn.* I,6) presupposes his role in trinitarian life; he reunites

You, O *Logos,* being form, are the form of the Father;

> hence image of the Father; and since you are form
> of the Father, form is for you substance itself, and
> because form, the substance is the same; hence
> the Father is in you and you are in the Father;

And because you are form, you are knowledge; therefore,

> substance is known to you, hence the Father is
> known to you, since you are in his bosom, born
> from him;

Therefore, you are also true *On* (Existent), *ek tou ontos to on,*

> (coming from the Existent); but the total *On*
> (existent) is in the Three.
> O Blessed Trinity.

You, Holy Spirit, are a bond;[23] but a bond is whatever unites two;

In order to unite all, you first unite the two;

You, the third, are the embrace of the two: embrace identified with

> the one, since you make the two one.
> O Blessed Trinity.

The three are therefore one,

And three times over,

Thrice are the three one,

> O Blessed Trinity.

Hence the supreme Father sends[24] the *Logos;* as sent, he creates and

> serves all,

Taking a body unto himself for our salvation, as well as

> the holy cross,

Returning to the Father as victor, he sent another self to save us.

> O Blessed Trinity.

---

form to substance, he is their substantial bond.

23 The Holy Spirit is the copula or bond because he unites by being the two and himself. Cf. *adv. Ar.* I 50,20; IV 2,6.

24 The economy of the Incarnation reproduces the trinitarian economy, that is, the Father sends the *Logos* and he sends the Holy Spirit; cf. 196-99. Thus the mission of the Holy Spirit is linked to the return of Christ to the Father; cf. *adv. Ar.* III 14. On the descent and reascent of Christ, cf. *in Eph.* 4.10 (1247 B-C).

Always Christ is with God, according to substance; for he is life
        forever;
But since life is action, and action begins in order to act, for this was
        Christ born;
From eternity Christ acts as God; therefore, from eternity Christ
        was born as God;[25]
        O Blessed Trinity.

He who ascends to heaven[26] is Christ;
He who comes down from heaven is the same Christ;
Therefore Christ is not from man,[27] but for man;
        O Blessed Trinity.

This is our God;
This is one God;
This is the one and only God;
        O Blessed Trinity.

To him we all pray,
The one whom we implore,
The one who is Father, Son and Holy Spirit,
        O Blessed Trinity.

Give pardon to sins,
Bestow eternal life,
Grant peace and glory,[28]
        O Blessed Trinity.

---

25 The problematic of the Incarnation raises the question of the preexistence
of Christ. And the question's answer is that Christ is life and therefore
action; hence he is simultaneously begotten (having an origin) and eternal
inasmuch as he is the action of God who always acts. Cf. *hymn.* II 15–22.
26 Cf. Jn 3.13; Eph 4.9.
27 The expression "from man" was attributed to the Photinians, *adv. Ar.* I
21,34. Against this Victorinus maintains that "man" is not for Christ a
point of origin, but a point of outcome. For this Victorinus bases himself
upon Eph 4:10 where the One who ascends to heaven is the same as the
One who descends from it.
28 The final prayer has a triple character; we can relate life to the Son, peace
and glory to the Holy Spirit.

Free us,
Save us,
Justify us,

       O Blessed Trinity.

INDICES

INDEX OF PROPER NAMES

INDEX OF GREEK WORDS

INDEX OF GREEK PHRASES

INDEX OF HOLY SCRIPTURE

(Books of the Old Testament)

(Books of the New Testament)

THE FATHERS OF THE CHURCH SERIES

(A series of approximately 100 volumes when completed)

> *translated by L. Schopp*
The Magnitude of the Soul
> *translated by J. McMahon*
On Music
> *translated by R. Taliaferro*
The Advantage of Believing
> *translated by L. Meagher*
On Faith in Things Unseen
> *translated by R. Deferrari, M–F. McDonald*

OCLC 856032

Volume 5:   SAINT AUGUSTINE   (1948)
The Happy Life
> *translated by L. Schopp*
Answer to Skeptics *(Contra Academicos)*
> *translated by D. Kavanagh*
Divine Providence and the Problem of Evil
> *translated by R. Russell*
The Soliloquies
> *translated by T. Gilligan*

OCLC 728405

Volume 6:   WRITINGS OF SAINT JUSTIN MARTYR   (1948)
The First Apology
The Second Apology
The Dialogue with Trypho
Exhortation to the Greeks
Discourse to the Greeks
The Monarchy or Rule of God
> *translated by T. Falls*

OCLC 807077

Volume 7:   NICETA OF REMESIANA   (1949)
Writings of Niceta of Remesiana
> *translated by G. Walsh*
Prosper of Aquitaine: Grace and Free Will
> *translated by J. O'Donnell*
Writings of Sulpicius Severus
> *translated by B. Peebles*
Vincent of Lerins: The Commonitories
> *translated by R. Morris*

OCLC 807068

Volume 8:   SAINT AUGUSTINE   (1950)

361

Letters (83–130)
translated by W. Parsons

OCLC 807061

Volume 19:   **EUSEBIUS PAMPHILI**   (1953)
Ecclesiastical History (books 1–5)
translated by R. Deferrari

OCLC 708651

Volume 20:   **SAINT AUGUSTINE**   (1953)
Letters (131–164)
translated by W. Parsons

OCLC 807061

Volume 21:   **SAINT AUGUSTINE**   (1953)
Confessions
translated by V. Bourke

OCLC 2210845

Volume 22:   **FUNERAL ORATIONS**   (1953)
Saint Gregory Nazianzen: Four Funeral Orations
translated by L. McCauley
Saint Ambrose: On the Death of His Brother Satyrus I & II
translated by J. Sullivan, M. McGuire
Saint Ambrose: Consolation on the Death of Emperor
Valentinian
Funeral Oration on the Death of Emperor Theodosius
translated by R. Deferrari

OCLC 806797

Volume 23:   **CLEMENT OF ALEXANDRIA**   (1954)
Christ the Educator
translated by S. Wood

OCLC 2200024

Volume 24:   **SAINT AUGUSTINE**   (1954)
The City of God (books 17-22)
translated by G. Walsh, D. Honan

OCLC 807084

Volume 25:   **SAINT HILARY OF POITIERS**   (1954)
The Trinity
translated by S. McKenna

OCLC 806781

Volume 26:   **SAINT AMBROSE**   (1954)

Letters (1—91)
translated by M. Beyenka

Letters (204–270)
translated by W. Parsons

Volume 33:　　　SAINT JOHN CHRYSOSTOM　　　(1957)
Commentary on St. John The Apostle and Evangelist
Homilies (1–47)
translated by T. Goggin

Volume 34:　　　SAINT LEO THE GREAT　　　(1957)
Letters
translated by E. Hunt

Volume 35:　　　SAINT AUGUSTINE　　　(1957)
Against Julian
translated by M. Schumacher

Volume 36:　　　SAINT CYPRIAN　　　(1958)
To Donatus
The Lapsed
The Unity of the Church
The Lord's Prayer
To Demetrian
Mortality
Works and Almsgiving
Jealousy and Envy
Exhortation to Martyrdom to Fortunatus
That Idols Are Not Gods
translated by R. Deferrari
The Dress of Virgins
translated by A. Keenan
The Good of Patience
translated by G. Conway

Volume 37:　　　SAINT JOHN OF DAMASCUS　　　(1958)
The Fount of Knowledge
On Heresies
The Orthodox Faith (4 books)
translated by F. Chase, Jr.

366

The Sacrament of the Incarnation of Our Lord
The Sacraments
    translated by R. Deferrari

OCLC 2316634

Volume 45:   SAINT AUGUSTINE   (1963)
The Trinity
    translated by S. McKenna

OCLC 784847

Volume 46:   SAINT BASIL   (1963)
Exegetic Homilies
    translated by A–C. Way

OCLC 806743

Volume 47:   SAINT CAESARIUS OF ARLES II   (1963)
Sermons (81–186)
    translated by M. M. Mueller

OCLC 2494636

Volume 48:   THE HOMILIES OF SAINT JEROME   (1964)
Homilies 1–59
    translated by L. Ewald

OCLC 412009

Volume 49:   LACTANTIUS   (1964)
The Divine Institutes
    translated by M–F. McDonald

OCLC 711211

Volume 50:   PAULUS OROSIUS   (1964)
The Seven Books of History Against the Pagans
    translated by R. Deferrari

OCLC 711212

Volume 51:   SAINT CYPRIAN   (1964)
Letters (1–81)
    translated by R. Donna

OCLC 806738

Volume 52:   THE POEMS OF PRUDENTIUS   (1965)
The Divinity of Christ
The Origin of Sin
The Spiritual Combat
Against Symmachus (two books)
Scenes from Sacred History Or Twofold Nourishment
    translated by C. Eagan

Volume 59: **SAINT AUGUSTINE** (1968)
    The Teacher
    The Free Choice of the Will
    Grace and Free Will
        translated by R. Russell

OCLC 712674

Volume 60: **SAINT AUGUSTINE** (1968)
    The Retractations
        translated by I. Bogan

OCLC 712676

Volume 61: THE WORKS OF SAINT CYRIL OF JERUSALEM I (1969)
    Procatechesis
        translated by A. Stephenson
    Lenten Lectures 1–12 (Catecheses)
        translated by L. McCauley

OCLC 21885

Volume 62: **IBERIAN FATHERS I** (1969)
    Writings of Martin of Braga
        Sayings of the Egyptian Fathers
        Driving Away Vanity
        Exhortation to Humility
        Anger
        Reforming the Rustics
        Rules For An Honest Life
        Triple Immersion
        Easter
    Paschasius of Dumium
        Questions and Answers of the Greek Fathers
    Writings of Leander of Seville
        The Training of Nuns and the Contempt of the World
        Sermon on the Triumph of the Church for the Conversion of the Goths
        translated by C. Barlow

OCLC 718095

Volume 63: **IBERIAN FATHERS II** (1969)
    Braulio of Saragossa
        Letters of Braulio
        Life of St. Emilian
        List of the Books of Isidore of Seville
    Writings of Fructuosus of Braga

Rule for the Monastery of Compludo
General Rule for Monasteries
Pact
Monastic Agreement
translated by C. Barlow

OCLC 718095

Volume 64:   THE WORKS OF SAINT CYRIL   (1970)
                     OF JERUSALEM II
Lenten Lectures (Catcheses) 13—18
translated by L. McCauley
The Mystagogical Lectures
Sermon on the Paralytic
Letter to Constantius
translated by A. Stephenson

OCLC 21885

Volume 65   SAINT AMBROSE   (1972)
Seven Exegetical Works
     Isaac or the Soul
     Death as a Good
     Jacob and the Happy Life
     Joseph
     The Patriarchs
     Flight from the World
     The Prayer of Job and David
translated by M. McHugh

OCLC 314148

Volume 66:   SAINT CAESARIUS OF ARLES III   (1973)
Sermons 187—238
translated by M. M. Mueller

OCLC 1035149; 2494636

Volume 67:   NOVATIAN   (1974)
The Trinity
The Spectacles
Jewish Foods
In Praise of Purity
Letters
translated by R. DeSimone

OCLC 662181